Elderly people in modern society

SOCIAL POLICY IN MODERN BRITAIN

General Editor: Jo Campling

ELDERLY PEOPLE IN MODERN SOCIETY

Anthea Tinker

LONGMAN
London and New York

Longman Group UK Limited
Longman House, Burnt Mill,
Harlow, Essex CM20 2JE, England
and Associated Companies throughout the world

*Published in the United States of America
by Longman Publishing, New York*

© Longman Group UK Limited 1981, 1984, 1992

First published 1981
Second Edition 1984
Third Edition 1992

British Library Cataloguing-in-Publication Data

A catalogue record for this book is available from the British Library

Library of Congress Cataloging in Publication Data
Tinker, Anthea.
  Elderly people in modern society / Anthea Tinker. – 3rd ed.
    p.   cm. – (Social policy in modern Britain)
  Rev. ed. of: The elderly in modern society. 2nd ed. 1984
  Includes bibliographical references and index.
  ISBN 0–582–06189–X
  1. Old age assistance – Great Britain.   2. Aged – Services for –
Great Britain.   I. Tinker, Anthea.   Elderly in modern society.
II. Title.   III. Series.
HV1481.G52T5   1992
362.6'0941 – dc20   91–41742
                                                              CIP

CONTENTS

PART FOUR.   DOCUMENTS

To the beloved memory of my grandparents

EDITOR'S PREFACE

This series, written by practising teachers in universities and polytechnics, is produced for students who are required to study social policy and administration, either as social science undergraduates or on the various professional courses. The books provide studies focusing on essential topics in social policy and include new areas of discussion and research, to give students the opportunity to explore ideas and act as a basis of seminar work and further study. Each book combines an analysis of the selected theme, a critical narrative of the main developments and an assessment putting the topic into perspective as defined in the title. The supporting documents and comprehensive bibliography are an important aspect of the series. A number in square brackets, preceded by 'doc', e.g. [doc 6, 8] refers the reader to the corresponding items in the section of documents which follows the main text.

In *Elderly People in Modern Society*, Anthea Tinker has brought together for the first time the literature and research evidence from many sources about this important group of people. Viewing the topic in the widest perspective, it provides basic information on the development of the services together with a more theoretical approach, redefining concepts like community care in relation to elderly people and their needs, and identifying likely issues for the future. It will be invaluable for students and indeed professionals in a variety of disciplines.

Jo Campling

AUTHOR'S PREFACE TO THE FIRST EDITION

Many people, academic, professional and the elderly themselves, have influenced my thinking on this subject. I have quoted some of them and express my gratitude to them for allowing me to do so.

I am particularly grateful to the following. To Mrs Joan Clegg, formerly Senior Lecturer in Social Policy at the City University, who encouraged my early research. The material for this book was collected while I was at the City University, and I am grateful to everyone there for their help. To the staff and students of the University of London, Department of Extra-Mural Studies (particularly the Social Work Course) with whom I discussed many of these ideas. To Mrs Carole Austin and Mrs Jenny Wren who typed the script. But most of all, to my husband, Eric, for his practical help without which this book would not have been written.

I alone, of course, am responsible for the views expressed, which do not necessarily reflect those of the Department of the Environment, and for any errors.

Anthea Tinker
January 1980

AUTHOR'S PREFACE TO THE SECOND EDITION

Since writing this book a number of events have taken place. These include change in legislation, a Government White Paper, *Growing Older*, and the World Assembly on Ageing. At the same time much of the research which was in progress when I wrote this book has been completed.

In this new edition I update some of the original material and add a new chapter discussing some of the important new developments in policy and practice which have occurred in the last three and a half years.

I renew my thanks to my husband and again say that my views are not necessarily those of the Department of the Environment.

Anthea Tinker
July 1983

AUTHOR'S PREFACE TO THE THIRD EDITION

Eleven years ago I wrote the first edition of this book and updated it in 1983. Since then there have been many important developments in the field of ageing. Foremost among these has been the growth of interest in gerontology, the study of ageing. This theme is taken up in this new edition. At the same time popular interest in elderly people has grown and reasons for this are explored.

In Great Britain the decade was marked by what became known as the Thatcher years. Social policies changed direction in many ways but in others remained remarkably similar to those of the 1970s. The period was also marked by a growing awareness of what happens outside this country.

In this new edition I update the original material and include the important new developments in policy, research and practice. But I have deliberately left in references to early studies because it is salutary to realise that many findings, for example about community care, are depressingly similar to those of the 1950s. It is also not without significance that I have changed the title of the book from *The Elderly in Modern Society* in *Elderly People in Modern Society*.

It is hoped that this book will not only be of general interest but also will be helpful to students and others who wish to follow up particular topics in essays, dissertations and theses. This is why many references are given in the text.

My thanks go to my husband for his support in writing this book, to colleagues in the Age Concern Institute of Gerontology, King's College, London and Age Concern England, and to students who shared their knowledge, and to Liz Moor who typed the final drafts with such speed and accuracy.

Anthea Tinker
June 1991

LIST OF ABBREVIATIONS

ACE	Age Concern England
ACIOG	Age Concern Institute of Gerontology
AIDS	Acquired Immune Deficiency Syndrome
BASW	British Association of Social Workers
BMA	British Medical Association
CAB	Citizens Advice Bureau
CIPFA	Chartered Institute of Public Finance and Accountancy
COI	Central Office of Information
CSO	Central Statistical Office
CPA	Centre for Policy on Ageing
DHA	District Health Authority
DOE	Department of the Environment
DOH	Department of Health
DHSS	Department of Health and Social Security
DTI	Department of Trade and Industry
EC	European Community
EOC	Equal Opportunities Commission
FES	*Family Expenditure Survey*
FREE	Forum on the Rights of Elderly People to Education
GB	Great Britain
GHS	*General Household Survey* (a continuous annual survey in GB)
GP	General Practitioner
HAS	Health Advisory Service
HIP	Housing Investment Programme
HMSO	Her Majesty's Stationery Office
MHLG	Ministry of Housing and Local Government
MOH	Ministry of Health
MORI	Market and Opinion Research International

MPNI	Ministry of Pensions and National Insurance
NAB	National Assistance Board
NAHA	National Association of Health Authorities
NAO	National Audit Office
NCC	National Consumer Council
NCSS	National Council of Social Service
NCCOP	National Corporation for the Care of Old People
NFHA	National Federation of Housing Associations
NHS	National Health Service
NIITPC	National Housing and Town Planning Council
NHBC	National House Building Council
NISW	National Institute of Social Work
NOPWC	National Old People's Welfare Council
OT	Occupational Therapy
OECD	Organisation for Economic Co-operation and Development
OPCS	Office of Population, Censuses and Surveys
QALY	Quality Adjusted Life Year
RAWP	Resource Allocation Working Party
RICA	Research Institute for Consumer Affairs
SBC	Supplementary Benefits Commission
SCPR	Social and Community Planning Research
Sec. of St.	Secretary(ies) of State
SERPS	State Earnings Related Pension Scheme
SSI	Social Services Inspectorate
STICERD	Suntory-Toyota International Centre for Economics and Related Disciplines, London School of Economics
UK	United Kingdom
UN	United Nations
WO	Welsh Office

ACKNOWLEDGEMENTS

We are indebted to the following for permission to reproduce copyright material:

Blackwell Publishers for extracts from Finch J, *Family Obligations and Social Change* (Polity Press, 1989); Centre for Policy on Ageing for extracts from Norman A, *Rights and Risk* (National Corporation for the Care of Old People, 1980). The revised edition of *Rights and Risk* published in 1988 by the Centre for Policy on Ageing; the Controller of Her Majesty's Stationery Office for extracts from DHSS, *Helping Mentally Handicapped People in Hospital* (1978) and MHLG, *Housing Standards and Costs – Circular 82/69*; the Controller of Her Majesty's Stationery Office/Office of Population Censuses and Surveys for extracts from Green H, *Informal Careers* (1988); Age Concern, England for figure 8.1; The Central Statistical Office for tables 2.1, 2.2, 2.3, 2.4, figure 5.1 and document 4; Her Majesty's Stationery Office for table 7.1, 7.2, 8.2, 8.3, 11.1, document 20, document 21, document 30, document 33; The Institute of Fiscal Studies for figures 3.1 and 3.2; and The Office of Population, Censuses and Surveys for tables 2.1, 2.2., 2.3, 2.4, 6.1, 6.2, 6.3, 6.4, 6.5, 7.3, 8.1, figure 6.1, document 10, document 14, document 35 and document 36; *Social Work Today* for documents 2 and 29

Part one
THE BACKGROUND

Chapter one
INTRODUCTION

This book is intended for students of social policy and administration (now usually referred to by the generic term social policy), gerontology and for all who are concerned about elderly people. Social science students, social workers, town planners, the medical and allied professions, together with those working for voluntary bodies such as the Citizens Advice Bureau (CAB), all share an interest in this relatively new subject.

Social policy is a hybrid subject which owes its origins to the other social sciences. Because it is a synthesis – an interdisciplinary way of studying certain social institutions, problems and processes in society – it can draw on the theory of other disciplines, such as economics, politics and sociology. It has the advantage of looking at a subject from many perspectives. The problem lies always in deciding in what depth to consider each aspect. In this book, for example, decisions had continually to be made about how far to explore such issues as the social implications of the family, the medical aspects of health, the architectural aspects of design and the political theories of decision-making. But to bring together these aspects, even though not always in great depth, and to relate them is the function and the fascination of social policy.

This book also reflects the current state of social policy in another way. The study of the subject has gone on in parallel with the growth of the Welfare State, through the expansion and extension of the statutory and voluntary social services. Probably as a result of this, social policy has tended to concentrate on two major facets: a study of social pathology; and an evaluation of provision by the statutory and voluntary services. Until recently policy makers and researchers have paid much less attention to alternative systems of providing care. However, not only does the market (e.g. private health care insurance) have a considerable role to play, but the involvement of family and neighbourly help has, in the past, been largely ignored. In the last 20 years more attention has been given to examining the wider aspects of the supply of social services. Researchers have looked beyond the conventional suppliers of services (statutory and voluntary bodies) to the more ill-defined area of what is provided by family, friends and neighbours.

Like social policy, gerontology – the study of ageing – is a relatively new academic discipline. It is less developed in this country than in the United States, but is now beginning to expand. This is partly because there are now more older people in the population than in the middle of the century. Among other reasons are the interest of the commercial sector in the growing number of elderly people with substantial assets, the involvement of old people themselves and media interest (Tinker, 1990a). Professionals are increasingly finding that older people form one of the main client groups. Within gerontology geriatric medicine is well established but has tended to concentrate, as does most medical practice, on the problems which older people have. Research in both the clinical and biological aspects of ageing is more advanced than social gerontology. The latter is described as 'the study of the ways in which social and cultural factors enter into the ageing process' (Hendricks and Hendricks, 1986, p. 15). Although social gerontology has been slower to develop, sociologists, demographers, psychologists, geographers and other social scientists are now displaying more interest and undertaking research.

Elderly people are particularly interesting to study. Not only are they one of the largest of what are labelled 'special groups', but they are also the group to which in due course most people will belong. Unlike deviant groups such as offenders, elderly people represent a cross-section of ordinary people whose sole common denominator is their age. Because they are such a large group and because most people will in time reach old age, it is a matter of self-interest to consider their role in, and contribution to, society as well as their problems and needs.

This book attempts to present some of the evidence about elderly people in society, neither assuming that they necessarily have the same characteristics as younger age groups, nor assuming that they present no problems. There are widely contrasting images of this group. Senior citizen, or silly old woman? Consumers of large amounts of social services, or the proud minority who prefer to suffer cold or poverty and not ask for help? A golden age, or one which is 'sans everything'? This book is intended to bring together existing evidence about elderly people and how they live. It is not written from a particular political or other stance and its aim is to give the facts and summarise both research and the views of others. For those who have extended essays or a thesis to prepare it gives ample references and points to other sources of information.

The outline of the book is as follows. Part one provides background material. First a picture is presented of elderly people giving basic data about who they are. This brings out some of the reasons why they represent one of the most important challenges to social policy. Alongside this demographic background there is a discussion about how society sees ageing. Then follows a review of the literature which shows that what has been written falls into a number of different categories.

Part two seeks to outline the major general developments in policy, first with a broad brush and then in detail for individual services, with a concentration on statutory provision. This is followed by evidence about informal networks of care.

In Part three an assessment is made of elderly people in society. First there is a discussion about the contribution of elderly people both to their own welfare and to that of others. Then there is an examination of some of the general problems. These include different views of need, variations in services, the evaluation of services and the meaning of community care. Finally, the topic is considered in perspective and similarities and differences with other groups discussed.

Part four comprises the documents which relate to the text.

Chapter two
A PROFILE OF ELDERLY PEOPLE

INTRODUCTION

One of the concerns of social policy is with particular groups. It is important, therefore, that they should be defined with some accuracy. Levels of disability can be measured. Offenders can be categorised by type of crime and by kind of sentence. Ethnic minorities can be divided into groups by country of birth, country of parents' birth and by the colour of their skin.

In contrast, elderly people are the whole of a generation who have reached a certain age. *Our Future Selves* is the apt title of one book (Roberts, 1970). They are not a deviant group or one small special section of the population. They are ordinary people who happen to have reached a particular age. This cannot be emphasised too much, particularly to professionals who are, as a result of their training and experience at work, concerned primarily with the abnormal.

PROBLEMS OF DEFINITION

The most commonly accepted definition of elderly people in social policy is those over retirement age, i.e. 60 for a woman and 65 for a man in the United Kingdom (UK), because this is the age at which people are eligible for a pension. However, 65 is also used sometimes for both sexes and the move towards equal opportunities may lead to this becoming more usual practice (see also Ch. 5).

The lack of a generally agreed definition creates difficulties for those who wish to compare research data. What is particularly interesting is the distinction which is increasingly being made in medical and social studies between the young and the old elderly. For example, Hodkinson confirms that it is elderly people over the age of 75 with whom the geriatrician is mostly concerned (Hodkinson, 1975). Two studies which came out in 1978, *The Elderly at Home* (Hunt, 1978) and *Beyond Three Score and Ten* (Abrams, 1978) made comparisons between elderly people under the age of 75 and those above that age. It is significant that 80 and over replaces 75 and over as a category in *Social Trends 20* and *21* (Central Statistical Office (CSO), 1990 and 1991). Interest is also now being focused on the over 90s (e.g. Bury and Holme, 1991) and on centenarians (e.g. *Population Trends*, Winter, 1984; pp. 12–13).

The 'third age' has also become a focus of increasing attention. Peter Laslett traces the origin of this interest to the founding of the Universities of the Third Age in France in the 1970s (Laslett, 1989). In his book, *A Fresh Map of Life*, Laslett describes the life course as: 'First comes an era of dependence, socialisation, immaturity and education; second an era of independence, maturity and responsibility, of earning and saving; third an era of personal fulfilment; and fourth an era of final dependence' (Laslett, 1989, p. 4).

If elderly people are such a varied group, why are they then labelled as one group? One main reason is that retirement marks a watershed. Becoming 65 usually means the end of employment and the beginning of entitlement to a pension. In pre-industrial society and for the self-employed, the definition may be less satisfactory. People may go on working for as long as they are physically capable and, if they continue in their job, their status remains that of a worker. But for most people now retirement brings an end to that particular role.

THE FOLLY OF GENERALISING

Few people would attribute the same characteristics to a 30-year old as they would to a 60 year old. Why then should the 60s and 90s be classed together as one group? It is very easy to assume that all old people want this or feel that. It might be more realistic to generalise if people were divided according to how old they appeared in behaviour, attitudes and thought. 'As old as you feel' is one approach, and if to act old is to be set in one's ways, to lack flexibility of thought and to look generally old-fashioned, then there are many people in their 20s and 30s who would qualify.

Social class, family support, physical and mental disability, religion and work patterns vary among elderly people as much as they do among the rest of the population. A growing number of writers are pointing to the wide differences between various groups of older people such as between men and women and between the

7

white population and ethnic minorities (e.g. Phillipson and Walker, 1986; Victor, 1987; Fennell *et al.*, 1988). It is therefore only reasonable to expect that the demands of this group on society, their expectations of it and their contributions to it will be as varied as those of the rest of the population.

David Hobman, the former Director of Age Concern England (ACE), once rightly rounded on a speaker at a conference who described this group rather patronisingly as 'old dears'. He pointed out that some might well have been the exact opposite of 'old dears'. There is a tendency for *all* age groups to generalise on occasion about other age groups, e.g. 'immature young', 'wet behind the ears', 'middle-aged fixed in their ways', etc. It seems unlikely that someone who is awkward and finds difficulty in making friends in early life will suddenly become the life and soul of the bingo sessions on reaching the magic age of retirement. And why the association between bingo and old age? Just as some teenagers enjoy chess while others opt for pop music, so the leisure pursuits of elderly people are likely to be just as varied.

HOW SOCIETY SEES AGEING

It is difficult to make comparisons with attitudes in past years since so little is known except what is recorded in fiction. Was there a time when old people in this country were looked on as founts of all knowledge and repositories of great wisdom? Even if there was, there are several reasons why this should not be so now. Children were much less likely to have had a grandparent alive in the last century and so the latter had scarcity value. Older people were also likely to have had comparatively greater skills and knowledge, since these changed little from generation to generation. Today the rapid increase in knowledge and changes in technology make it difficult for one generation to keep up with the next. This is especially so in specialist subjects.

Shakespeare painted a depressing picture of old age in *As You Like It* and one commentator on social policy took the final two words of one speech 'Sans Everything' as the title of her book (Robb, 1967). The physical changes that come with age are varied and do not necessarily develop at the same time in each old person. It is useful to have some understanding of these physical and mental changes, and to know what is normal and what is abnormal. Keddie, a consultant psychiatrist, argues that: 'Positive thinking is needed here. Unfortunately many of the public still feel that little can be done for an elderly man or woman who is ill – it is assumed that the old person's condition is simply due to his age. In fact, most old people are suffering from a treatable disease of one sort or another' (Keddie, 1978, p. 64). Hodkinson, a geriatrician, has taken a similar view (Hodkinson, 1975, p. 19). Freer, writing about health and health care of elderly people, claims that much discussion is inappropriately negative, pessimistic and too often couched in crisis terms (Freer, 1988, p. 13).

In what way then does society view this ageing process, and what bearing has this on social policy? There is little doubt that in a society that seems geared to youth there is great emphasis on remaining young. Advice on appearance, particularly hair and skin, is not confined to women. And when people are old the terms used to describe them, such as members of 'evergreen' clubs, seem to deny the process of ageing. This may be reinforced by the nostalgia of some elderly people for their youth.

Growing importance is being attached to the effect of images of ageing and steps are being suggested to counteract poor images. Featherstone and Hepworth, who have written extensively on images and ageing, comment:

Human society is a process and it is dangerous to assume that attitudes towards elderly people and images of old age which currently exist enjoyed the same currency in the past or necessarily will do so in the future. Hence for all the talk about our youth dominated society we should be aware that while the qualities associated with youthfulness have been valued in history, this valuation must be related to the balance of power between the generations, which undergoes periodic fluctuations (Featherstone and Hepworth, 1990, p. 274).

Note also the jealousy of some elderly people for what they see as the delights and privileges of the young.

Will more attention now be focused on elderly people since their numbers have increased so rapidly? A distinguished social scientist claimed in 1975 that although the fortunes of teenagers had been the focus of discussion and research since the 1960s, elderly people were about to come into their own (Abrams, 1975) [doc 1]. Yet society does not always find it easy to come to terms with this group. As Hobman has noted, there are a great many myths about ageing [doc 2]. Comfort has argued that ageism – discrimination against the old on the grounds of their being old – is part of the prejudice against elderly people [doc 3]. Its impact on employment policies is explored in Chapter 5.

The sociological concept of disengagement must also be noted. This is the theory that the individual, recognising the inevitability of death, starts a process of advance adjustment to it. But this view is now strongly challenged as neither necessarily happening, nor being desirable. Older people themselves are recording their anger at being put into a ghetto at 60 or 65. For example, one wrote about the experiences of her generation under the title of *The Alienated* (Elder, 1977). Other authors, recording the views of old people, entitled their book *I Don't Feel Old: the experience of later life* (Thompson *et al.*, 1990). In the 1980s and 1990s many newspapers and journals published articles giving a more positive picture of the accomplishments of older people.

It is important to raise these questions about how society sees ageing because it has implications for social policy. The assumptions that 'the elderly' are a social problem or even burden, that they have similar aspirations and that they all need certain services are all questionable.

NUMBERS

When considering the provision of social services it is important to try to get as accurate an estimate as possible of how many recipients there will be. As with any kind of crystal gazing, the future is not always easy to predict. Some elements, however, are relatively certain. If, for example, there are 4 million young people aged 16–18 about to leave school and go on to higher education or work, it is probable that in 10 years' time something like that number will be needing services appropriate to people in their late 20s. But forecasting further ahead on these figures assumes no major alteration in circumstances. War can wipe out almost a complete generation. Illnesses, such as AIDS, or an increase in unhealthy habits such as smoking or drug-taking can cause premature death or turn a healthy person into one who is physically disabled. On the other hand, medical advances, such as the early diagnosis of illnesses or cures for what seemed terminal illnesses, can prolong life.

One striking feature has been the increase in the numbers of elderly people since the beginning of the century. While the total population in the United Kingdom has grown, it has been at a much slower rate than that which has occurred among elderly people [doc 4]. Table 2.1 summarises this growth. From this table it can be seen that projections show that both the total population and that of people of pensionable age will increase. The projected rise in

Table 2.1. Population figures United Kingdom 1901–2025

	Total population *(millions)*	*Percentage* *increase p.a.*	*Elderly** *(millions)*	*Percentage* *increase p.a.*
1901[1]†	38.2	–	2.4	–
1951[1]	50.5	32.0	6.9	188
1981[1]	56.3	11.0	10.0	45
1989[2]	57.2	1.5	10.5	5
1991[3]	57.6	0.5	10.5	NIL
2001[3]	59.2	2.5	10.7	2
2011[3]	60.0	1.0	11.7	9
2025[3]	61.0	1.5	13.6	16

* Males over 65, females over 60.
† UK as then constituted.
[1] Estimated figures derived from CSO, *Social Trends* (No. 13), 1983, Table 1.2, p.12.
[2] Estimated figures derived from OPCS, *Population Trends* 62, Winter, 1990, p.43.
[3] Projected figures from OPCS, *Population Projections 1989–2059* (1989 based) (OPCS, Series PP2, No. 17, HMSO, 1991).

numbers of the latter is less than a quarter of a million until 2001. Figure 2.1 shows the picture for the UK. Fluctuating numbers are largely due to changes in the birth rate. The low birth rate during World War I, the post-war bulge, the trough of births in 1940–2, the post World War II bulge, the baby boom of the 1960s and the 'baby bust' of the 1970s, all affect numbers of elderly people in subsequent years [doc 5]. These changes in the birth rate are one of the reasons why demographic forecasting has proved to be fraught with problems.

REGIONAL AND LOCAL VARIATIONS

It has already been stated that generalisations about elderly people are dangerous. It is equally unwise to assume that overall figures, such as the percentage of elderly people in the population, will be the same for every part of the country. There are considerable regional variations.

The national average percentage of people above retirement age was estimated to be 18 per cent in 1989. In some areas, such as the South West, it was 21 per cent, while in others, such as Greater London, it was 17 per cent. The reasons for these differences are various. An above-average number of elderly people can be the result of people finding an attractive area to which to retire. Younger

Figure 2.1   Projected size of the elderly population

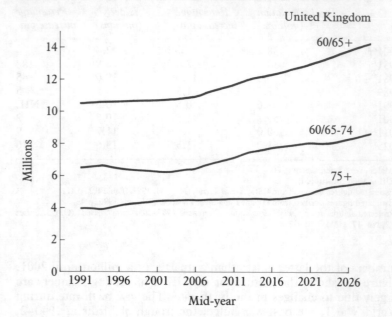

Based on Government Actuary's 1989 projections.
Source: Gerontology Data Service at Age Concern Institute of Gerontology, King's College London.

people may have moved out from an inner city area into the suburbs, leaving a disproportionate number of old people. Or there can be a bulge of people reaching retirement age at the same time, as a consequence of a large group of younger people having in the past moved at the same time to new work or a new town. The area which suddenly became full of young families becomes in due time largely one of elderly people, especially if little housing becomes available for their children when they get married. Within an area too, there may be pockets where large numbers of old people live, perhaps because of the nature or affordability of the housing, or the lack of facilities for families.

Those concerned with social policy have to take these variations into account. At a national level allowance is made for the number of elderly people when deciding on the level of grants to local authorities. Similarly, extra help is sometimes given to those pro-

Table 2.2. The very old as a percentage of elderly people in the United Kingdom 1901–2025

	All elderly people* (millions)	Elderly people* under 75 (millions)	The very old – 75 and over (millions)	Percentage of all elderly people who are very old
1901[1]†	2.4	1.9	0.5	21
1951[1]	6.9	5.1	1.8	26
1981[1]	10.0	6.8	3.2	32
1989[2]	10.5	6.5	3.9	37
1991[3]	10.5	6.5	4.0	38
2001[3]	10.7	6.3	4.4	41
2011[3]	11.7	7.1	4.5	38
2025[3]	13.6	8.2	5.4	40

* Males over 65, females over 60.
† UK as then constituted.
[1] Figures derived from CSO, *Social Trends* (No. 13), 1983, Table 1.2, p.12.
[2] Estimated figures derived from OPCS, *Population Trends*, 62, Winter, 1990, p.43.
[3] Projected figures from OPCS, *Population Projections 1989–2059* (1989 based) (OPCS, Series PP2, No. 17, HMSO, 1991).

Due to rounding not all details add to totals.

fessionals who care for elderly people – for example higher capitation fees for doctors with elderly patients. Locally, all those who plan services – social workers, planners, housing managers and other professionals, need not only a demographic profile of their area but also projections which will enable them to forecast future trends in demand.

THE VERY OLD

It has already been seen that the total number of elderly people will not rise appreciably in the near future. What is most significant now is the decline in the number of young elderly and the rise in the number of old elderly. Table 2.2 demonstrates that a drop of about 200,000 in numbers of the under 75s and a rise of about 400,000 of the over 75s is projected by the beginning of the next century. The percentage of elderly people who are over 75 has risen from 21 per cent in 1901 to 38 per cent in 1991. It then rises to 41 per cent in 2001 and fluctuates after that (Table 2.2). Looking at the over 80s in the UK there were estimated to be 0.7 million in 1951 and 2.2

million in 1991. Numbers are projected to increase to 2.9 million in 2025 (Central Statistical Office (CSO), 1991, p. 24 and [doc 4]).

As already discussed, part of the reason for this increase in the numbers and proportions of very elderly people is the bulge in the birth rate in previous years. But there is another process involved – this is a rise in the expectation of life. Expectation of life at birth in 1901 for a male was 48 years and for a female 51.6 years. In 1951 this had risen to 66.2 and 71.2 years respectively (CSO, 1983, p. 91). In 1989 it was 72.8 years for a male and 78.4 for a female (CSO, 1991, p. 114).

The significance of the growing number of very old people is that this group makes the highest demands on health and social services [doc 6]. Disability rises rapidly with age, as the recent Office of Population and Censuses (OPCS) survey showed (Martin *et al.*, 1988). Those who are over 75 years make greater demands than those between 65 and 75, and those over 85 years make even heavier demands. In the 1981 Census one-fifth of all women aged 85 and over were in a residential institution. However, one should beware of generalisations. A study of the over 90s concluded that the depiction of very old age as constituting major levels of dependence needs to be qualified (Bury and Holme, 1991).

PROPORTIONS OF ELDERLY PEOPLE IN THE POPULATION AND DEPENDENCY RATES

Elderly people have formed an increasingly large section of the population since the beginning of the century, but the percentage is projected to remain at 18 per cent until 2011 when it becomes 19 per cent (Table 2.3).

In relation to the social services, which have to be paid for largely by people of working age, the percentage of the population which is dependent is significant. Two groups are usually regarded as dependents, children under school-leaving age and elderly people over the age of retirement. The latter are not considered to be of working age, although some do work. It is also assumed that all those of working age do work, and if at any time any large number are unemployed (and therefore dependent), this could upset calculations.

Interestingly dependency rates, that is the number of dependents related to those of working age, have altered little throughout this century (Table 2.4). The reason there has been so little change during a period of rapidly increasing numbers of elderly people is

Table 2.3. Elderly people* as a percentage of the population of the United Kingdom 1901–2025

	Total population (millions)	Elderly people* (millions)	Elderly people as percentage of total
1901[1]†	38.2	2.4	6
1951[1]	50.5	6.9	14
1981[1]	56.3	10.0	18
1989[2]	57.2	10.5	18
1991[3]	57.6	10.5	18
2001[3]	59.2	10.7	18
2011[3]	60.0	11.7	19
2025[3]	61.0	13.6	22

* Males over 65, females over 60.
† UK as then constituted.
[1] Estimated figures derived from CSO, *Social Trends*, 1983 (No. 13), Table 1.2, p.12.
[2] Figures derived from OPCS, *Population Trends*, 62, Winter, 1990, p.43.
[3] Projected figures from OPCS, *Population Projections 1989–2059* (1989 based) (OPCS, Series PP2, No. 17, HMSO, 1991).

Table 2.4. Percentage of the population who are 'dependents' 1901–2025 United Kingdom

	Total population (millions)	Elderly* people (millions)	Children under 16 (millions)	Percentage* who are 'dependent'
1901[1]†	38.2	2.4	13.2	41
1951[1]	50.5	6.9	12	37
1981[1]	56.3	10.0	12.6	40
1989[2]	57.2	10.5	11.5	38
1991[3]	57.6	10.5	11.7	39
2001[3]	59.2	10.7	12.6	39
2011[3]	60.0	11.7	12.0	40
2025[3]	61.0	13.6	12.0	42

* Children under 16 (15 for 1901–51), males over 65 and females over 60.
† UK as then constituted.
[1] Estimated figures derived from CSO, *Social Trends* (No. 13), 1983, Table 1.2, p.12.
[2] Estimated figures derived from OPCS, *Population Trends*, 62, Winter, 1990, p.43.
[3] Projected figures from OPCS, *Population Projections 1989–2059* (1989 based) (OPCS, Series PP2, No. 17, HMSO, 1991).

Figure 2.2   Projected dependency rates[1] 1991–2029

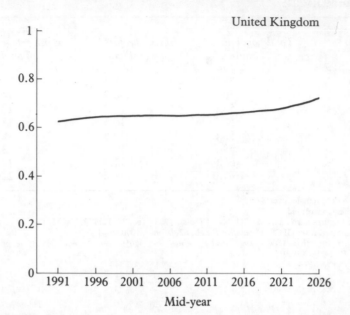

[1] The dependency ratio is the under 16s and elderly people of pensionable age (i.e. men at 65 and women at 60) and over as a porportion of the working population. Based on Government Actuary's 1989 projections.
Source: Gerontology Data Service at Age Concern Institute of Gerontology, King's College London.

that there has been a simultaneous decline in the birth rate. In a review of the 1980s OPCS points out that the total fertility rate has stayed at or about 1.8 since 1981, remaining below the level for long-term replacement of the population (OPCS, *Population Trends 62*, 1990, p. 1). This has been the case for over 15 years.

Not until the second decade of the next century does the ratio of dependents increase much above today's level (Fig. 2.2). In *Fewer Babies, Longer Lives* it is suggested that the annual entry of young people to the labour force has been declining throughout the 1980s, but that the fall during the next four years from 1989 will be particularly steep (Ermisch, 1990). Ermisch states that, whilst the number of entrants will rise after 1993, and continue to increase during the first decade of the next century, the influx of young workers will remain at a much lower level than during 1975–85. As the number of workers per pensioner decreases there will be pressure on pension provision (Ch. 13) and on numbers available to care. Some suggest that the effects of the so-called 'demographic time bomb', the sharp fall in numbers of young people joining the labour market, have been exaggerated (National Economic Development Office, 1989). It is suggested that although the decline in the number of young people entering the labour market will accelerate in the early 1990s, the population of working age will remain roughly stable, before rising slowly from the mid 1990s to the end of the century, and that there is potential for growth in the labour force.

THE BALANCE OF THE SEXES

In general there tend to be more women than men among elderly people, especially among the very elderly, because women, on average, live longer. Whether this will continue is a matter for debate because no one knows why women do live longer. If it is because they have in the past tended to drink less, smoke less and been subject to less stress, then the position could well soon be reversed. There is already evidence that women are drinking and smoking more and becoming more involved in stressful occupations (Department of Health and Social Security (DHSS), 1976c, pp. 38–9). More women are also becoming drivers with the subsequent dangers of death and accidents. Another factor that can alter the balance is if large numbers of either sex emigrate or are killed.

In the foreseeable future women are expected to continue to outnumber men heavily in the upper age groups in the UK:

in 1989 there were 3.0 million men and 3.9 million women aged 65–79 and 0.6 million men and 1.4 million women aged over 80.

It is projected that:

in 2025 there will be 3.9 million men and 4.6 million women aged 65–79 and 1.1 million men and 1.8 million women aged over 80, (CSO, 1991, p. 24).

Part of the reason for the excess of females is the greater improvement in female mortality, but it is also due to the remaining effects of male mortality during World War I and the high levels of male emigration before then.

The significance of these figures is that women are more likely to be physically disabled and to suffer from ailments such as arthritis. The 1988 *General Household Survey* (*GHS*) showed that elderly women over the age of 75 are greater users of health services than men of the same age (Grundy, 1991a). The 1985 *GHS* also found that elderly women were twice as likely as men to live alone (OPCS, 1989).

WITH WHOM ELDERLY PEOPLE LIVE

A striking feature of recent years has been the growing proportion of elderly people living alone. In 1961, 7 per cent of households in Great Britain (GB) were made up of one person over pensionable age, while in 1989 this had risen to 16 per cent (CSO, 1991, p. 37). What is particularly significant is the link between growing older and living alone. The *GHS* in 1988 showed that in Great Britain in 1988 50 per cent of the over 75s (29 per cent of men and 61 per cent of women) lived alone. The figures for those aged 65–74 were 27 per cent (17 per cent for men and 36 per cent for women) (OPCS, 1990, p. 16).

The trend towards smaller households seems likely to continue. In Great Britain one-person households are projected to increase from 5.3 million in 1987 to 7.1 million in 2001 (CSO, 1989, p. 37). But for people of pensionable age the predicted rise is only from 3.7 million in 1987 to 3.9 million in 2001. So people over retirement age are expected to form a declining proportion of one-person households, from 62 per cent in 1987 to 55 per cent in 2001 (CSO, 1989, p. 37).

In 1985 in Great Britain, one-third (36 per cent) of people aged 65 and over lived alone, 45 per cent with their spouse alone, 7 per cent with their spouse and others, 3 per cent with siblings, 7 per cent with a son or daughter and 2 per cent with others (OPCS, 1989, p. 186). In the case of married couples this was nearly always with their child or children. Overall co-residence rates between adult children and their elderly parents or parents-in-law are low in England and Wales, but vary considerably with socio-demographic characteristics (Grundy, 1991a and b).

The number of elderly people living alone could be hailed as an advance in that they are not being forced to live either with relatives or in residential care. There is indeed a good deal of evidence that this is what they want. But there are implications for services. For example, an old person living alone may find it difficult to summon help in an emergency.

MARITAL STATUS

Widows comprise one of the largest groups of elderly people. In 1988 in Great Britain 79 per cent of all those widowed were women (OPCS, 1990, p. 24; see also Gibson, 1990). Nearly two-thirds (65 per cent) of women aged 75 or over were widowed, whereas a similar proportion (62 per cent) of men in this age group were still married. This reflects the fact that on average women live longer than men and also tend to marry men older than themselves.

INTERNATIONAL COMPARISONS

One of the most remarkable demographic contrasts in the world today is the variation in the proportion of elderly people aged over 65 (Clarke, 1987, p. 23). The main contrast is between the more developed countries where elderly people are on average 12 per cent of the population and the less developed countries where they average only 4 per cent. One of the reasons for a rise in the percentage of elderly people is a drop in the number of young people due to a decline in the birth rate, as has happened in developed countries.

CONCLUSION

Numbers of elderly people have quadrupled since the beginning of the century. While in 1901 in the UK people over pensionable age represented 6 per cent of the population, in 1991 this figure had grown to 18 per cent. Future projections suggest that there will be little rise in numbers or proportions of people of pensionable age until the beginning of the next century. There is, therefore, a period of stability for ten years. But numbers of the very elderly will increase (Table 2.2) while the under 75s will decline. These changes reflect past variations in the size of birth cohorts and also actual and anticipated declines in mortality. By 2025 numbers of people of pensionable age, both the under and over 75s, in the United Kingdom, will have risen by 3 million compared with 1991 and the proportion will rise from 18 per cent to 22 per cent. Elderly women outnumber elderly men in all age groups.

There are still some unanswered questions about elderly people. What, for example, will be the position of elderly people from ethnic minorities? The percentage of the total population aged over 65 from the New Commonwealth and Pakistan was just under 1 per cent (*cf.* 1.5 per cent Irish-born) in Great Britain in 1986–8. Figures for 1986–8 show that most of the ethnic minority groups have markedly different age structures from the white population; for example, 21 per cent of the white population was aged 60 or over, compared with only 7 per cent of the West Indian/Guyanese population, which was the highest proportion among ethnic minority groups (CSO, 1991, p. 25). There is also danger in generalising over groups from ethnic minorities. For example, Indian, Pakistani and Bangladeshi populations are more likely to live within extended families than white, West Indian, Chinese, African and Arab populations (Haskey, 1989).

It is equally difficult to forecast what medical advances there may be which will enable people to live longer or help them to be less disabled. On the other hand, there may be a swing in public opinion against positive medical intervention to help keep elderly people alive.

INTRODUCTION

It is remarkable that although the elderly population more than doubled between 1901 and 1945 very little information was gathered in these years on either elderly people at home or in residential care, 'A dearth of published information and, apparently of interest too' is how Townsend and Wedderburn (1965) described the situation [doc 7].

To obtain a complete picture of what has been written about elderly people one must search a number of different sources. The medical profession, sociologists, psychologists, geographers, social workers and many others have looked at this group from their own different viewpoints. Similarly, research has been undertaken by a variety of bodies: central government, local authorities, voluntary societies and political parties as well as by individuals.

SOCIAL SURVEYS

One of the first large-scale social surveys was undertaken in 1944–6 for the Rowntree Committee on the *Problems of Ageing and the Care of Old People* and published in 1947. As this was a pioneering study the terms of reference to the report are given [doc 8]. Details of this survey and others carried out between 1945 and 1964 are also given [doc 9]. This list of social surveys has been updated by the author [doc.9].

A high proportion of the surveys carried out in the 1940s and early 1950s was concerned with the medical aspects of ageing, although some, such as that by Walker (1952) and Sheldon (1948), while starting from a medical viewpoint, went on to consider further issues. Others were restricted in geographical scope.

The social surveys of the late 1950s, the 1960s and 1970s concentrated on the frail, sick and needy. They were concerned in the main first with the relationship between need and provision, and second with the importance of taking into account informal networks (particularly the family) as well as statutory provision.

In the 1950s and 1960s a growing number of studies, such as Bracey's *In Retirement* in 1966, began to look at questions connected with retirement rather than dependent elderly people, and suggested that more thought should be given both by society and the individual to where and how elderly people might live (Bracey, 1966). At the same time sociological studies were throwing new light on the place of elderly people in the family. One of the earliest and most important was Townsend's study of *The Family Life of Old People* in 1957 (Townsend, 1957). Although there are certain factors peculiar to Bethnal Green, where the research took place, the findings about the close links between the generations surprised a good many people. Willmott and Young's subsequent study of Woodford, *Family and Class in a London Suburb*, in 1960 was an attempt to compare middle-class families with the working-class ones of Bethnal Green (Willmott and Young, 1960). They found that the ties between relatives were much looser, but none the less still quite considerable.

All the research relating to social provision showed that this was not as effective as many had supposed. One of the first, published in 1965, was Townsend and Wedderburn's *The Aged in the Welfare State* which was part of a cross-national survey to find out how effective social services were in meeting the needs of elderly people (Townsend and Wedderburn, 1965). The authors set out in particular to discover whether certain functions formerly performed by the family had been taken over by the social services. Their findings did not support this view. The cross-national survey itself, by Shanas *et al.*, *Old People in Three Industrial Societies*, came out in 1968 (Shanas *et al.*, 1968). It was important not just for the information it gave on health, incapacity and so on, but in clarifying and substantiating certain concepts related to the family and to isolation among elderly people. They found, for example, that there was flexibility in the patterns of relationships which existed in families between the generations. Even when families were small, they noted, elderly people would adapt and substitute and could often turn to their siblings or the children of siblings for support.

Tunstall's *Old and Alone* in 1966 was another part of the cross-national survey (Tunstall, 1966). As well as his conclusion that social policy must do more to help old people remain independent, his findings and subsequent discussion about living alone, social isolation and loneliness are as relevant now as when they were published.

A much more general survey was carried out by Harris in 1968 for the Government Social Survey and published as *Social Welfare for the Elderly* (Harris, 1968). There seemed some doubt as to whether planning was being based on the needs of elderly people or on what the local authorities thought they could afford.

In the 1970s both academic and the more popular literature turned to the particular problems of very elderly people. Two major social surveys were published in 1978 which made some comparisons. Hunt in *The Elderly at Home* surveyed 2,622 elderly people living in private households to provide information on their social circumstances as a base for social policy (Hunt, 1978). Abrams in *Beyond Three Score and Ten* surveyed 1,646 elderly people to discover more about their needs, conditions and resources (Abrams, 1978 and 1980). Both Hunt and Abrams brought out the differences between the under 75s and those over this age.

In the 1980s there were very few national surveys. One of the main sources of information came from the 1985 *GHS* (OPCS, 1989). The 1980 *GHS* had an extensive series of questions to elderly people and these were repeated with some minor changes in 1985. This survey has been a rich source of data for secondary analysis. Another survey which yielded a great deal of data was that on disability undertaken by OPCS. Of particular interest are *The Prevalence of Disability among Adults* (Martin et al., 1988), *The Financial Circumstances of Disabled Adults Living in Private Housholds* (Martin and White, 1988) and *Disabled Adults: services, transport and employment* (Martin et al., 1989). These surveys confirmed that the overall rate of disability rises with age, slowly at first then accelerating after 50 and rising very steeply after about 70. *Life after Ninety*, a national survey of 222 people in 1986, was a pioneering study of this age group (Bury and Holme, 1991).

After the earlier bursts of work on the general circumstances of elderly people and their health and use of various social services it is interesting that housing is coming to the fore. Two large national surveys were carried out by the Department of the Environment (DOE) in conjunction with the DHSS. The first was a study of innovatory ways of enabling elderly people to stay in their own homes, *Staying at Home: helping elderly people* (Tinker, 1984) and the second *An Evaluation of Very Sheltered Housing* (Tinker, 1989b).

The DOE also started a large study of the housing needs of, and provision for, elderly people in 1990.

A survey by OPCS of 3,500 elderly people in 1988–9 on retirement and retirement plans is expected to yield much data on jobs, pensions and support given and received.

MEDICAL AND PSYCHOLOGICAL ASPECTS

It is interesting to note that the medical aspect still continues to take a central place in the literature. Some classics, such as *The Social Needs of the Over Eighties* (Brockington and Lempert, 1966), and *Survival of the Unfittest* (Isaacs, Livingstone and Neville, 1972) and *The Care of the Elderly in the Community* (Williams, 1979), are primarily concerned with a medical perspective but are also highly relevant to other professions. Others, such as *Geriatric Medicine* (Anderson and Judge, 1974) and *Health Care of the Elderly* (Arie, 1981), have chapters which are concerned with other aspects of care of elderly people. Subsequent books on geriatric medicine contain chapters which are also important for social scientists (e.g. Pathy, 1985, and Andrews and Brocklehurst, 1987).

Books such as *Life Before Death* (Cartwright, Hockey and Anderson, 1973), while written mainly from a medical angle, are important in enhancing our understanding of a specific period in an old person's life. *The Hospice Movement in Britain* looked at the role and future of this form of care (Taylor, 1983) and *A Safer Death* examined multidisciplinary aspects of terminal care (Gilmore and Gilmore, 1988).

A particular medical problem revealed in this growing collection of written material is that of elderly mentally disordered people. Studies on this subject have been made from different standpoints. Robb's *Sans Everything* in 1967 painted a black picture of conditions in psychiatric hospitals (Robb, 1967). It attracted a lot of publicity although many of the allegations were found not proved by an official investigation. *Taken for a Ride* was also a description of institutions for mentally infirm elderly people (Meacher, 1972). The discipline of psychogeriatrics has developed during the last few years and some of the books, e.g. *Recent Advances in Psychogeriatrics* (Arie, 1985), *Living with Dementia* (Gilleard, 1984) and the *International Journal of Geriatric Psychiatry*, which started in 1986, combine medical and non-medical content.

A welcome addition to the literature has been a growing number of publications on preventive care and promotion of good health.

Preventive Care of the Elderly: a review of current developments is specifically about the role of the Primary Health Care Team in screening and case finding (Taylor and Buckley, 1987). *Promoting Health Among Elderly People* offers pointers derived from practice and research (Kalache *et al.*, 1988). Another welcome addition is interest in medical ethics and books like *Medical Ethics and Elderly People*, which resulted from collaboration between medical specialists and moral philosophers, demonstrate a valuable approach (Elford, 1987).

Much more attention is being paid to the psychological aspects of ageing (Birren, 1964; Comfort, 1965; Bromley, 1966, revised 1988; de Beauvoir, 1972; Coleman, 1986; Bromley, 1990; and Birren and Schaie, 1990.) Psychologists are concerned with 'the effects of ageing upon learning, memory, intelligence, skills, personality, motivations and emotions' (Harris, 1990).

THE DEVELOPMENT OF GERONTOLOGY

Gerontology, the scientific study of ageing, is in its infancy in the UK. In the United States of America services are less developed, but the scale of research and publications and the number of gerontology courses and institutes are more developed than anywhere else in the world (Warnes, 1989). Perhaps the most encouraging development is the growth of multidisciplinary research and teaching in gerontology. Bringing together the psychological, social and cultural study of ageing with biomedical knowledge and clinical application should enable a far greater understanding of its processes and problems (Tinker, 1990a). There were early examples of this approach in the 1970s. The British Council for Ageing's report *Research in Gerontology* (1976) and the British Association for the Advancement of Science's *Old Age – today and tomorrow* (1976) were two such reports. *Human Ageing and Later Life* edited by Warnes (1989) brings in a wider number of disciplines. Advances have also been made in the field of social gerontology, where the focus is on the social aspects of ageing. The British Society of Gerontology, whose membership has increased rapidly since its creation in 1973, has published a series of books based on its annual conferences which have been helpful in bringing together a number of papers (Jerrome, 1983; Bromley, 1984; Butler, 1985; Phillipson *et al.*, 1986; di Gregorio, 1987; Bytheway and Johnson, 1990). They have now sponsored two books which will help those with an interest in ageing and particularly those who teach gerontology. *Ageing in*

Society is an introduction to social gerontology and covers a wide range of topics to explain ageing within the perspective of the whole life span (Bond and Coleman, 1990). *Researching Social Gerontology* offers an introduction to key concepts, methods and issues in research (Peace, 1990).

In specific areas of social gerontology the majority of books are still American (e.g. *Sociology of Aging*, Harris, 1990) but a growing number of British academics are beginning to write books in particular disciplines. In social policy the first edition of *The Elderly in Modern Society* (Tinker, 1980a) was followed by *Ageing and Social Policy: a critical assessment* (Phillipson and Walker, 1986) and *Old Age in Modern Society* (Victor, 1987). *The Sociology of Old Age* has also been a helpful addition to the literature (Fennell *et al.*, 1988). Sociology has been defined as 'the scientific study of human interaction' (Harris, 1990). A relatively new area of study is educational gerontology. In 1986 the editorial in the first issue of the *Journal of Educational Gerontology* distinguished between educational gerontology (the education and learning of older people) and gerontological education (education about ageing and teaching gerontology) (April 1986). In the latter area the pioneering courses put on at the Age Concern Institute of Gerontology, King's College London, the Centre for Extra Mural Studies, Birkbeck College, University of London, and the University of Keele should be noted. Other disciplines where there has been a growth of interest have included geography, economics, demography, law and anthropology.

In geography the pioneering work of Warnes and Law has particularly focused on migration (see Warnes, 1982 and 1987). Warnes has pointed out that, while studies of the geographical aspects of elderly people's social and environmental circumstances have been numerous and diverse, only a few geographers have made successive contributions (Warnes, 1990).

Economic aspects of ageing, especially the costings of alternative types of provision have been noticeably sparse. Wager in 1972 produced an innovatory exercise in cost benefits, *Care of the Elderly* (Wager, 1972) and Davies has also done much work (Davies *et al.*, 1971). More recent work is referenced in Davies and Challis, (1986). Other work on costing alternative patterns of care have been done at the University of York (Wright *et al.*, 1981) and by DOE (Tinker, 1984 and 1989b). The Audit Commission has carried out costings specifically on services for older people (1985) and more generally on community care (1986). Knapp's *The Economics of Social Care* has many illustrations of services for older people (Knapp, 1984). An economist and social administrator have combined to write *The Economic Approach to Social Policy* and this too has illustrations from the field of ageing (Charles and Webb, 1986).

Demographers are another group who are increasingly turning their attention to ageing, especially to the implications of an ageing population (see Grundy, 1983, 1987, 1989, 1991a, 1991b; Joshi, 1989; and the work of the Suntory-Toyota International Centre for Economics and Related Disciplines). Particularly useful is the dialogue between demographers and medical specialists, as in *Research and the Ageing Population* (Evered and Whelan, 1988).

Possible changes in law and practice which might help to represent and protect the interests of this group of older people were considered in *The Law and Vulnerable Elderly People* (ACE, 1986). *The Law and Elderly People* covers most of the services which older people may need and states the legal position (Griffiths *et al.*, 1990). Bridging law and medicine ethical issues are beginning to come to the fore. *The Living Will*, about consent to treatment at the end of life (Kennedy, 1988) and *Medical Ethics and Elderly People* (Elford, 1987) open up discussion about the inability of certain groups of elderly people to speak on their own behalf in certain circumstances. Both these books are examples of collaboration between groups of professionals such as medical specialists, lawyers and moral philosophers. In the field of anthropology, notable contributions have been made by researchers such as Jerrome, Wenger and Kellaher.

INDIVIDUAL SERVICES

There is an increasing amount of specialist literature on particular services. Much of this will be referred to in the appropriate chapters. There is scarcely a service now which has not been explored from the perspective of older people although not all of this is up to date. Particularly fruitful areas for study in the 1980s were housing and community care services. Studies of particular groups, such as elderly people found dead (Bradshaw *et al.*, 1978), have been fewer recently possibly due to financial constraints on surveys. However there have been a number of studies of both elderly dementia sufferers and their carers (e.g. Askham and Thompson, 1990) and others on carers in general (e.g. Wright 1986; Thornton, 1989). The classic study in 1978, *Old and Cold* (Wicks, 1978) is being replicated in 1990–1 (Salvage, 1989 and 1991). One of the current gaps in our knowledge is of elderly people from ethnic minorities. These are now the subject of two studies at the Age Concern Institute of Gerontology both of which started in 1990.

LOCAL STUDIES

Local studies provide a rich source of data on ageing. An early example of research undertaken by an academic was Shenfield's *Social Policies for Old Age* (1957). More recently Wenger's study of areas in North Wales *The Supportive Network* has provided useful evidence about informal patterns of care (Wenger, 1984). The research team at the Open University in collaboration with Gloucester Health Authority have written extensively about the provision of care co-ordinators in Gloucester (Dant *et al.*, 1989). Probably the best known example of a local study was the community care project in Kent, which has now been replicated in a number of other areas (Challis and Davies, 1986 and Davies and Challis, 1986). Many reports in the 1970s came from local authorities, especially social services departments, and a growing number came from joint health care planning groups.

In the 1980s fewer reports emanated from local statutory bodies possibly because of shortage of finance for research but there were a number of useful studies dealing with local innovations. Some of these (e.g. Isaacs and Evers, 1984 and Ferlie *et al.*, 1989) are much more analytical than some of the earlier descriptive studies of services.

Some of the local studies, such as *The Needs of Old People in Glamorgan* (Watson and Albrow, 1973), were used centrally to draw more general conclusions in *The Elderly and the Personal Social Services* (DHSS, 1976a). The model of the Kent community care project has also been instrumental in moulding central goverment's policies.

PRACTICAL ADVICE

Another noticeable feature of the literature of the last 20 years has been the growing number of books offering practical advice either to elderly people or to their relatives and friends. The Consumers Association published *Arrangements for Old Age* in 1969 and *Where to Live after Retirement* in 1977. Brandon compiled a handbook *Seventy Plus* in 1972 with chapters on living options, keeping fit, aids and safety in the home and finance (Brandon, 1972). Many more such publications were produced in the 1980s.

There has also been a steady stream of popular books about retirement. *Thinking about Retirement* (Wallis, 1975), *Caring for Elderly People* (Hooker, 1976), *Action with the Elderly* (Keddie, 1978) and *Understanding Ageing* (Hardie, 1978) were early examples. In the 1980s Age Concern England and others have published on a wide range of topics from incontinence to loneliness. Some are very detailed and particularly aimed at carers. One such is *The 36 Hour Day* (Mace and Rabins, 1985). David Hobman, the former Director of Age Concern England, edited *Coming of Age* which was subtitled 'a positive guide to growing older' (Hobman, 1989).

THE VIEWS OF POLITICAL AND VOLUNTARY BODIES

Some interesting studies, which probably reached a wider audience than some of the more weighty academic books, were produced in the late 1960s and early 1970s by the Fabian Society, the Bow Group and the Conservative Political Centre. Four of the major ones concerned with elderly people were *Old People in Britain* (Weston and Ashworth, 1963), *Old People: cash and care* (Bellairs, 1968), *The Care of the Old* (Agate and Meacher, 1969) and *New Deal for the Elderly* (Bosanquet, 1975). These attracted a good deal of publicity. Less has been produced in the 1980s from the political parties and it is interesting that there was very little mention of older people in the Party manifestos in the elections in 1983 and 1987.

Research has always been one of the main contributions of the voluntary sector to social policy (but see subsequent chapters for their growing contribution to the provision of services). The Manifesto series in 1974 by Age Concern England comprised excellent accounts by experts on particular problems. Particularly interesting when considering the kinds of policies likely to find favour with elderly people was a study of the attitudes of 2,700 pensioners (ACE, 1974). Age Concern's *Profiles of the Elderly* in 1978 was also a useful series.

In 1986 Age Concern England moved their research unit to King's College London where it became the Age Concern Institute of Gerontology. Apart from the usual publications of an academic group a series of research publications has been produced in conjunction with Age Concern England. The implications of research for policy and practice have also been publicised in a series of *Ageing Updates* (Morton, 1989a,b,c, 1990a,b, 1991). Age Concern England marked its Golden Jubilee in 1990 by publishing a major review of the vital issues which affect older people (ACE, 1990b).

The Centre for Policy on Ageing have produced an impressive list of publications in the 1970s and 1980s (referred to in individual chapters and summarised in Midwinter, 1987) as well as their widely acclaimed periodical *New Literature in Old Age*. Help the Aged have also produced helpful publications and sometimes sponsored research.

THE VIEWS OF OLDER PEOPLE

What older people themselves wish and their views should be a main strand in the literature but there is a remarkable lack of this. Elder in *The Alienated* explains very vividly why many members of her generation feel as they do (Elder, 1977). More recently Stott (1981) also described her feelings on growing older, as has Kroll in *Growing Older* (Kroll, 1988). Two recent Committees have described the influence which the views of older people themselves had on their findings. The Wagner Committee on residential care appealed for people to write to them (Wagner 1988a and b). While they had some reassuring letters they also had some which, they said, 'none of us who read those letters could remain unmoved by the depth of unhappiness and despair revealed by the writers' (Wagner, 1988a, p. 2). The Working Party set up by the Board for Social Responsibility of the Church of England to look at ageing had the same experience. In their report *Ageing* they say: 'A distressing number of respondents had felt patronised or scorned on the grounds of their age' (Board for Social Responsibility, 1990; p. 9).

INTERNATIONAL STUDIES

It is beyond the scope of this book to do more than make brief mention of studies made abroad. Those who want to pursue comparative studies will find that comparative social policy is beginning to emerge as an interest. Jones's *Patterns of Social Policy* is an introduction to comparative analysis (Jones, 1985) and does describe and compare policies. Many books are collections of papers by different authors in various countries without any attempt to compare and contrast. For comparative information publications of the United Nations (UN) and the Organisation for Economic Co-operation and Development (OECD) are among the most helpful. Research undertaken by the European Foundation for the Improvement of Living and Working Conditions specifically on ageing is now beginning to come to fruition (e.g. *Meeting the Needs of the*

Elderly, Fogarty, 1987). Work sponsored by the European Commission can be helpful when trying to compare policies and services. Some examples are *Social Developments Affecting Elderly People in the EC Member States* (Drury, 1990), a study of the financial position of older women in Europe (Harrop, 1990) and *Contrasting European Policies for the Care of Older People* (Jamieson and Illsley, 1990). The case study approach is sometimes useful, as in a comparison of residential care *Social Care for Elderly People* (McDerment and Greengross, 1985). An outstanding source of research information is given in supplements to the *Danish Medical Bulletin*. They produced compilations of research data on a wide range of topics in the late 1980s, from falls and hearing problems to primary health care and Alzheimer's disease (*Danish Medical Bulletin Supplements*, 1985–9).

Part two
NEEDS AND HOW THEY ARE MET

Chapter four
A CRITICAL NARRATIVE OF THE MAIN DEVELOPMENTS IN SOCIAL SERVICES FOR ELDERLY PEOPLE

It is easy to rationalise when looking back at social provision for any group of people and to see a pattern in what has happened. In practice the directions taken by social policy are often in response to all kinds of events and personalities. A crisis, war, the action of a pressure group or the influence of a dominant person may all change policy, as will the overall political philosophy of a political party.

Policies for elderly people as for other groups have evolved as a result of many different factors. Some of these directions will be explored briefly in this chapter to provide a framework for a more detailed account of individual services later.

THE GROWTH IN SERVICES

Greater concern

The needs of elderly people in this country have traditionally been the concern both of central and local government and of voluntary agencies. All of these have paid increasing attention to how appropriate policies and administrative structures may be developed.

Setting up a Royal Commission or a Committee to investigate a topic is one conventional way of showing concern. It is interesting that one of the first, which reported in 1895, was the Royal Commission on the Aged Poor. This provided evidence about the poor conditions in which many old people existed. In 1909 both the majority and the minority reports of the Royal Commission on the Poor Laws painted a bleak picture of life for elderly people. Townsend has commented: 'Both reports recommended improvements in institutional conditions and an extension of separate provision for the old, but little was done for many years to carry out these recommendations' (Townsend, 1964, p. 16). He went on to argue that as far as 'the infirm aged and chronic sick' were concerned, far less information on these people was made available to the public between 1910 and 1946 than was available between 1834 and 1909. No official inquiries were instituted and hardly any books or pamphlets were published which contained more than a few fleeting references to their circumstances or their needs. He believed that the reason for this was the low priority that the welfare of elderly people had in British society. It is pertinent that an official publication maintains that provision for elderly people is largely based on legislation passed since 1945 (Central Office of Information (COI), 1977).

Since 1945 many important Commissions and Committees have paid particular attention to elderly people. Notable Reports from three of these were the Guillebaud Report on the cost of the National Health Service (NHS) (Ministry of Health (MOH), 1956), the Cullingworth Report on council housing (Ministry of Housing and Local Government (MHLG), 1969) and the Seebohm Report on personal and allied social services (Home Office, Department of Education and Science, MHLG, MOH, 1968).

In 1978 the Labour government produced a Discussion Document, *A Happier Old Age* (DHSS, 1978a), which looked at services for older people. In 1979 the Conservatives came to power and the new administration's White Paper *Growing Older* in 1981 was noticeably less optimistic (DHSS, 1981d). Few major changes in policy were outlined but the emphasis was rather on what could be achieved within existing resources. There was stress on the contribution of the private and voluntary sectors – an important theme of the last few years. *The Guardian* in a leader (6.3.81) criticised the White Paper, saying it 'makes no attempt even to identify the nature and scale of the problem. Its message is plain: the Government has no intention of spending any more money at all to cope with the extra demand. It is all up to the community.' Similar criticisms came from organisations representing elderly people. Most of the disappointment centred on the absence of any concrete proposals. The main aim of government policy in relation to elderly people as expressed in *Ageing in the United Kingdom*, produced in 1982 for the World Assembly on Ageing, was 'to enable them to lead full and independent lives in the community to the greatest possible extent' (DHSS, 1982a, p. 1). This is almost identical to the words of the 1981 White Paper, which said policies were: 'to enable elderly people to live independent lives in their own homes wherever possible – which reflects what the majority themselves want' (DHSS,

1981d, p. 6). Similar policies continued with the Conservative victories in the 1983 and 1987 elections, although it is doubtful if the other parties would have adopted a different stance.

In 1988 the Church of England set up a Working Party to consider the major issues of ageing, to offer a Christian contribution to the debate and to evaluate the Church's ministry in this field. Their report in 1990, *Ageing*, received widespread media coverage (Board for Social Responsibility, 1990). The report challenged negative attitudes to ageing and produced detailed recommendations aimed at the nation and the church.

In 1990 The Carnegie Inquiry into the Third Age was set up. The Third Age was defined as the active independent stage in life after a person has finished his or her main career or job, or bringing up children, or both. The Inquiry covers issues affecting the life, work and livelihood of people in this age, and reports in 1992.

The last 50 years have also seen the birth of major voluntary organisations. The National Old People's Welfare Council (NOPWC) started in 1940 and became Age Concern in 1971. The National Corporation for the Care of Old People (NCCOP) started in 1947 and subsequently became the Centre for Policy on Ageing (CPA). Help the Aged started in 1962. As well as acting as pressure groups these organisations undertake research and policy analysis and are regularly consulted by official bodies.

The development of research

In the review of the literature (Ch. 3) it was noted that increasing attention has been paid to finding out the facts about elderly people. This has taken the form of social surveys, medical enquiries and sociological studies which have often attempted to measure need and provision.

It is worth remembering that increased provision has been accompanied by a more satisfactory data base on which to base policies. But there are still many gaps in our knowledge and as a report from the United Nations put it: 'However, there is no general theory or unified body of knowledge on ageing' (United Nations, 1975, p. 7).

Much of the research has been very specific and has concentrated on particular groups of old people. For example Townsend wrote about those in residential institutions and homes in *The Last Refuge* (Townsend, 1964), as have many other researchers (see Ch. 8).

Bradshaw, Clifton and Kennedy researched those *Found Dead*

(Bradshaw *et al*., 1978) and Wicks in *Old and Cold* (Wicks, 1978) did the same for elderly people with hypothermia. Others have chosen to look at recipients of particular services such as home helps (Hunt, 1970), telephones (Tinker, 1989a), alarms (Research Institute for Consumer Affairs (RICA), 1986), food (Dunn, 1987) and leisure (Midwinter, 1990).

Major national surveys sponsored by the government since 1945 have included the Phillips Report on *The Economic and Financial Problems of the Provision for Old Age* (Chancellor of the Exchequer, 1954); the Boucher Report on *Services Available to the Chronic Sick and Elderly 1954–55* (MOH, 1957); the Ministry of Pensions and National Insurance (MPNI) Report, *Financial and Other Circumstances of Retirement Pensioners* (MPNI, 1966); *Social Welfare for the Elderly* (Harris, 1968); *Handicapped and Impaired in Great Britain* (Harris, 1971); *A Nutrition Survey of the Elderly* (DHSS, 1972); *The Elderly at Home* (Hunt, 1978) and a number of surveys undertaken by the MHLG and DOE of the housing conditions of elderly people.

The 1980s also saw the completion of some major pieces of research which were brought together for discussion in an important seminar organised by DHSS in 1982 (DHSS, 1983a). While no new major general survey of elderly people was carried out, the *General Household Survey* 1980 contained questions, some repeated in 1985, to elderly people which enabled some of the Hunt data to be updated. In fact, very few changes were shown in levels of disability or of services received (Ch. 6 and 8 and [doc 10]). The 1981 Census has also yielded information, as will the 1991 one. What has been missing from research has been any longitudinal studies which would greatly help an understanding of ageing.

Widening scope and changes in organisation

The development of the Welfare State At the beginning of the century there was little provision for elderly people apart from the Poor Law, charities and almshouses. These services were largely looked on as being for second class citizens. But even before World War I, social services were beginning to be regarded not as a form of charity but rather as one of the rights available to citizens as were services for defence, justice, law and order. During World War II the feeling grew that society was not automatically divided into the rich and poor or givers and receivers. A neat summary of the effects of the war is given in DHSS *Collaboration in Community Care*:

The effects of the war were threefold. First, a degree of physical fitness was required in the entire population. Second, the war had an equalising effect on all classes of society which made selective provision of services less acceptable. Third, the cause of social problems, such as unemployment or handicap, was no longer seen to be the individual's fault but to lie in the social context. (DHSS, 1978b, p. 4)

The term 'Welfare State' has been defined as a 'state which has a policy of collective responsibility for individual well-being' (Clegg, 1971). The foundations were laid during World War II where a landmark was Beveridge's 1942 report *Social Insurance and Allied Services* (Beveridge, 1942). As Thane has noted: 'More than any other wartime blueprint for post-war social reconstruction the Beveridge report caught the popular imagination and came to symbolise the widespread hopes for a different, more just, world. These hopes were embodied in the term which, although not quite new, came into wide currency after the publication of the Report' (Thane, 1982, p. 253). It should be noted, incidentally, that Beveridge preferred the term 'social service state'. Again to quote Thane: 'The term welfare state expressed the desire for a more socially just, more materially equal, more truly democratic society, in short, everything that pre-war society had not been' (Thane, 1982 p. 253).

One of the most striking subsequent developments was the widespread adoption of comprehensive services. No longer were the major services, in particular health, provided for different categories of people depending on how much they could pay and from what source. Where a universal service was provided everyone was entitled to use it. For a generation of people used to highly selective services this was a major change.

The state has never been the sole provider of welfare in this country, as voluntary bodies, and to a lesser extent private provision such as in health, have played a role. What has come to the fore since the 1970s, and especially since the Conservatives came to power in 1979, has been the questioning of the role of the state. State provision is particularly important to older people as over half of expenditure on social security, health and personal social services is spent on them. The so-called Thatcher years from 1979 to 1990 have been ones where the emphasis has changed to more reliance on the private and voluntary sectors and on the private individual. The term 'mixed economy of welfare' is commonly used to describe provision by different agencies. This is a form of provision which lies between the extremes of a *laissez-faire* model, with minimal government and maximum market forces, and the Marxist model, with an absolute commitment to state-controlled provision (Pinker, 1979).

The late 1980s saw major changes away from state provision and towards the contracting out of services by local and health authorities and the encouragement of the private sector through legislation and tax incentives. The compulsory selling-off of council houses to tenants and tax incentives to encourage the purchase of private health care are examples. The vision was that an enterprise culture and property-owning democracy would replace the welfare society and dependency. The challenge is not just over the provision of services but about state regulation of private activities and giving more freedom to individuals. Indeed Gough has pointed out that any definition of the Welfare State must incorporate both provision and regulation (Gough, 1979).

Part of the reason for the questioning of the growing role of the state has been the cost, but partly there has been the view that personal responsibility must be encouraged. 'We believe the well-being of individuals is best protected and promoted when they are helped to be independent, to use their talents to take care of themselves and their families and to achieve things on their own,' declared the Secretary of State for Social Services in a speech to the Conservative Political Centre (John Moore, 26.9.87.). There is also the view that state provision is too bureaucratic (Day and Klein, 1987). However, despite the questioning of the role of the state gross expenditure has risen rapidly. Between 1979–80 and 1987–8 expenditure in Great Britain on local authority domiciliary care services rose from £464 millions to £1,167 millions and on community health services from £135 millions to £320 millions (Secretaries of State (Sec of St) for Health *et al.*, 1989b, p. 99). Over the same period gross public expenditure on community care services rose from £1,169 million to £3,444 – an increase in real terms of 68 per cent (Sec. of St. for Health *et al.*, 1989b; p. 3).

There are three main models of the Welfare State:

– A collectivist one where provision by the state is the norm.
– A reluctant collectivist or liberal one where the state takes responsibility for some aspects of provision but in such a way as to encourage individuals to help themselves.
– A residual model where the state provides minimal services.

However, as Glennerster has pointed out, a crucial distinction is between finance and provision (Glennerster, 1985). A service may be:

- Publicly provided and publicly funded, e.g. NHS hospitals (though even here there may be some voluntary and private input).
- Publicly provided and privately funded, e.g. private pay beds in NHS hospitals.
- Publicly provided and partly funded publicly and partly privately, e.g. local authority old people's homes which charge fees.
- Privately provided and privately funded, e.g. private sheltered housing.
- Privately provided and publicly funded, e.g. day care by voluntary bodies.
- Privately provided and partly funded publicly and partly privately, e.g. private old people's homes when some residents receive public support and others pay for themselves.

Discussions about the Welfare State must necessarily take into account that the position is a complicated one and naïve assumptions should be avoided. Among recent books which give different perspectives on the welfare state are Glennerster, 1983; George and Wilding, 1984; Glennerster, 1985; Klein and O'Higgins, 1985; Riddell, 1985; Hill and Bramley, 1986; Lee and Raban, 1988; Bulmer, Lewis and Piachaud (eds), 1989; and Williams, 1989.

At a national level Looking back on provision this century there are some notable landmarks. In terms of central services one of the most important Acts was the 1908 Old Age Pension Act. This was an attempt to make some provision for elderly people outside the Poor Law. It gave elderly people over 70 a small non-contributory pension but applicants had to undergo a means test, and to begin with, provide evidence that they were of good character. Better provision was made in 1925 under the Widows, Orphans and Old Age Contributory Pensions Act. During World War II the Unemployment Assistance Board took over the Poor Law responsibility for outdoor relief of the elderly. The Beveridge Report in 1942 recommended [doc 11] that elderly people, and other groups, should be covered by an insurance scheme while an assistance board should provide for those who were not covered. However, after the war pensions were provided on a universal scale (with certain exceptions) out of general taxation, but amounts were not high enough to prevent many having to apply for extra means-tested assistance. Since 1945 a series of Acts have extended pensions to nearly all elderly people. In 1961 graduated pensions were introduced and in 1975 pensions became earnings-related. These measures have enabled elderly people to be financially independent and, in particular, not to be dependent on their children. However, large numbers have had to have their pensions augmented by the state through income support (formerly called a supplementary pension) (see Ch. 5 for details of later legislation).

Under the National Health Service Act 1946 a comprehensive health service was set up for everyone regardless of means. The object was to promote the establishment of a comprehensive health service designed to secure improvements in the physical and mental health of people and the prevention, diagnosis and treatment of illness, and for that purpose, to provide or secure the effective provision of services. This service has been largely free of charge for those in medical need, and even where charges have been made (e.g. prescriptions) some groups, including pensioners, have been exempt. It has enabled elderly people to be spared the kind of indignities remembered by Elder where 'doctors bills had to be avoided' (Elder, 1977, p. 62). There were three main divisions after 1946: the hospital and specialist services administered through regional hospital boards; the general practitioner services administered by local executive councils; and the domiciliary services (such as home nursing and domestic help) administered by the major local authorities. The NHS was reorganised in 1974 with the intention that expertise in health care should be concentrated in the NHS and expertise in social work in social services departments.

Under DHSS came 14 Regional Health Authorities, then 90 Area Health Authorities and then District Health Authorities. In April 1982 the Area Health Authorities were abolished largely on the grounds that there was one tier too many. In the NHS and Community Care Act 1990 major changes took place in organisation, hospital management and finance and family practitioner services (see Ch. 6).

At a local level For local services the Local Government Act 1929 was a milestone because it transferred the powers and duties of the Poor Law Guardians to the county councils and county boroughs. They took over some of the Poor Law institutions and ran them as hospitals. Those that were left were managed by the public assistance committees of the local councils. Conditions in both types of institution, however, remained poor.

The development of local services after 1945 is referred to in

Chapter 8, but 1946, 1948, 1962 and 1968 were important dates when the powers of local authorities were extended. Services for elderly people have expanded greatly, particularly since 1945. Some, such as holidays, telephones and free transport, were scarcely thought of as public services even 20 years ago. But it is likely that the cost of these services combined with the belief of some that the state should play a smaller role may restrict any large-scale future expansion and some contraction did take place in the late 1980s and 1990.

In a perceptive article in *Public Administration* on the future of local government, Clarke and Stewart (1990) raised a number of issues for discussion. They identified the various roles which local authorities have played including direct service provision, regulation, contracting out, community role and representation. Although one of the main roles in the past has been the direct provision of services the authors state that local government has probably always involved a combination of roles. What varies is the emphasis given to each one.

On the issue of central control Clarke and Stewart identify three possible models. The first is the relative autonomy model where the emphasis is on giving freedom of action to local authorities within a widely defined framework of powers and duties. The second is the agency model where local authorities are mainly agencies for the carrying out of central government's policies mainly through detailed controls. Third there is the interaction model where there is a complex pattern of relationships in which the emphasis is on mutual influence. In many ways the 1980s were a time when more local freedom was given, e.g. to choose how central government grants were spent. But in other ways such as rate and poll tax/ community charge capping central government has laid down firm boundaries especially over spending.

In any discussion about local services for elderly people the effect of local government reorganisation must be taken into account. Many attempts were made from 1945 onwards to change the structure for a number of reasons. Some local authorities were thought to be too small, some boundaries seemed meaningless and the division of responsibility between different types of authority hindered the provision of effective services. Under the Local Government Act 1972 the old all-purpose county boroughs disappeared and a tiered system of local government set up. In 1986 Metropolitan County Councils and the Greater London Council were abolished (Table. 4.1).

Table 4.1. The structure of local government in England since 1986: responsibility for housing and social services

Non-metropolitan County Councils (39)	Metropolitan District Councils	London Boroughs (32) City of London (1)
Local social services	Housing and local social services	Housing and local social services
County District Councils (296) | Housing		

At the same time two other changes have occurred that have affected local provision. Following the reorganisation of local government in 1974 the NHS, as already mentioned, was also reorganised. Some services were taken over by the NHS (such as home nursing) and others, formerly under the NHS (such as medical social work) were transferred to local authorities. Then in 1970 the Local Authority Social Services Act created social services departments in local authorities, bringing together many functions which had previously been scattered between health, welfare and other departments.

Responsibility for services for elderly people is therefore still split between different agencies with the major division being between NHS (health) and local authorities (local social services). Outside London and the metropolitan areas different authorities are responsible for housing and social services. It has been argued by some that a more effective service could be provided if only one authority was involved. On the other hand it is maintained that division does not matter as long as there is co-ordination of services. However, in the late 1980s and early 1990s both Conservative and Labour politicians were discussing the advantages of all-purpose local authorities and the possible abolition of County Councils.

By voluntary bodies Voluntary bodies have pioneered provision for elderly people. Almshouses, charities and trusts to help elderly people date back at least as far as the Middle Ages. Old people's homes, financial help and the provision of meals are all examples of this.

Local authorities have sometimes used voluntary bodies instead of making provision themselves. Under the National Assistance Act

1948, for instance, a local authority may use accommodation such as a hostel provided by a voluntary body and make payment for it. They may also contribute to the funds of a voluntary body that provides recreation or meals for elderly people. What developed rapidly in the late 1980s was the contracting out by local authorities of services to the voluntary sector. For example ACE has become involved in providing services to older people such as day and residential care. In a similar way housing associations have found themselves taking over some public housing. The sudden acquisition of services has not been without its problems. These particularly concern the contraction of choice for the consumer, controlling standards and the difficulties small organisations may have in taking over new, and possibly larger, tasks than they have undertaken before (Morton, 1990a).

SOME CHANGES IN THE NATURE OF SERVICES

Greater entitlement as of right

Some of the services for elderly people, such as pensions and health, are provided as of right. There is no question of pensions or access to a general practitioner (GP) being restricted to a limited number of people. Every old person (with a few exceptions in the case of pensions) has a right to these national services. The same is true in some areas of certain local services such as bus passes for free travel.

Eyden in *The Welfare Society* distinguished between three main types of service (Eyden, 1971). First, services which are financed wholly or mainly out of general taxation and are used at will without any test of contribution (e.g. health). Second, services framed on a contractual basis with entitlement to benefit being dependent on being within the scope of a particular scheme and satisfying its relevant contribution test (e.g. pensions). Third, services where there is a needs test (e.g. local authority housing). As Glennerster has shown (see previous section), there are now other models.

This provision for everyone in a particular age category (regardless of means) was part of the general change in outlook since World War II noted earlier. However, some services are provided on a selective basis – that is certain criteria are laid down and people are invited to apply. Services provided in this way include meals on wheels, chiropody, aids such as Zimmer frames, and adaptations to houses. The arguments in favour of this sort of approach are that it ensures that those with specific needs have them met, that scarce resources can be rationed and that services are not 'wasted'. Against this it is held that there may be a low take-up if it is left to individuals to apply, there may be a stigma attached if only a few people receive the service and that such schemes are expensive to administer. An increase in selective services, referred to more often in the late 1980s as targeted, was evident during this period, e.g. the new home improvement system which started in 1990. Whichever system is adopted, comprehensive or targeted services, there still remain the practical problems of access to services. These are explored by Foster in her study of welfare rationing (Foster, 1983).

Moves to prevention

Those responsible for many services, for elderly people as well as for other groups, are attempting to move away from the sort of provision which aims to solve particular problems, i.e. is crisis centred, and goes no further.

This is specially noticeable in medicine where people are being persuaded not to drink or smoke and to take greater care on the roads. This approach is in contrast to the provision of a health service which picks up the casualties after the damage has been done. Thus, it can be argued that chiropody and greater attention to the care of the feet may prevent elderly people becoming housebound. In DHSS, *Prevention and Health: everybody's business* it is stated that: 'Prevention is the key to healthier living and a higher quality of life for all of us', and ways are outlined related to elderly people (DHSS, 1976c, p. 96). The question that has to be asked is what is the object of prevention? Not the avoidance of death, because this is inevitable. One answer is that it may be possible if certain measures are taken early enough to prevent people from going into expensive forms of care. It is also held that preventing an accident or entry to institutional care saves money and human suffering. A strategy for prevention is laid out in *The Health of the Nation* (Sec. of St. for Health, 1991).

In social work, too, the tendency has been to try to work with people before a crisis develops, although staff shortages may make this difficult. Leonard in an article in Social Work Today (3.6.71) suggests that:

Primary intervention which concentrates on identifying the pre-conditions of social problems and acting to remedy them, is now seen as a potential further field for social work not only in the form of community work and social policy and planning but as one to which social workers in general can contribute even though they work mainly at other levels of intervention.

COMMUNITY CARE

One of the main developments has been the shift in emphasis in policy away from institutional care to what is loosely called community care or care in the community. This shift and the reasons for it are not confined to elderly people but apply also to other groups such as children, offenders and mentally disordered people.

There seems to be a lack of a satisfactory definition of community care and some confusion as to its meaning. This may be partly because a number of different theories and facts came together at roughly the same time. First, there were views about the positive value in terms of quality of life of being at home. There was also a general reaction against institutional care which led to the belief that alternatives ought to be made available for both existing and potential inhabitants of institutions. Second, there were practical problems increasingly associated with institutions such as the difficulty of getting residential staff. Third, there was less need to keep some people (including elderly people) in an institution away from society because much behaviour that was disturbed or bizarre could be controlled by drugs and other methods. Fourth, there was the cost of institutional care. Finally, there was a growing recognition that people had a right, where possible, to live among ordinary people in society and not to be in a separate institution. The institution was seen as a barrier to normal living.

In short, for both positive and negative reasons the fashionable swing towards attempting to look after people within society (or the community as it was usually put) snowballed. There can be scarcely a group of people now who do not have some form of 'community' service, whether it is community (children's) homes, community health councils or (offenders') community service.

In the past it seems that community care has meant very much what people have wanted it to mean. There are two extremes of meaning. There is the narrow definition of community care as the provision of domiciliary rather than institutional services and there is the ill-defined cosy picture of a group of local people 'caring' for their neighbours.

The official view for a long time was nearer to the first description and has equated the concept with the provision of services by local authorities. The Ministry of Health (MOH) 1962 *Hospital Plan*, for example, was intended to be complementary to the local services 'for care in the community' (MOH, 1962). Similarly, when local authorities were asked to produce plans along these lines the title of the official publication was *Health and Welfare: the development of community care* (MOH, 1963) and so was the revision (MOH, 1966). The introduction to the 1963 edition states: 'At the reorganisation of 1948, local government, while losing responsibility for any part of the hospital service, retained the environmental services, and took on much wider responsibilities for the prevention of ill-health and for care in the community.' But it went on to include a short section headed 'Voluntary Effort' which was an indication that something other than statutory help could be included in the definition.

A wider definition of community emerges from the Seebohm Report, although even here the official definition was: 'Community care has come to mean treatment and care outside hospitals or residential homes' (Home Office *et al.*, 1968). It is this concept of community which is so difficult to define and perhaps contributes to the extreme view of a caring group of people given above. As Clegg points out: 'There is no agreed definition of "community" among academic sociologists, social workers or the makers of social policy' (Clegg, 1971, p. 16). She indicates that the sociological concept relates to: 'a small population in a defined geographical area whose social relationships are distinguished by the fact that they share a common culture which has emerged over a long period of time' (Clegg, 1971, p. 16).

The chapter on 'The Community' in the Seebohm Report starts with the definition of community both in the physical sense of location but also 'the common identity of a group of people' (Home Office *et al.*, 1968, p. 147). However, it then goes on to introduce yet another factor: 'The notion of a community implies the existence of a network of reciprocal social relationships which among other things ensure mutual aid and give those who experience it a sense of well-being' (Home Office *et al.*, 1968, p. 147). Although official thinking has moved beyond the narrow concept of domiciliary provision there is still need for a working definition of community care which needs to be spelled out with precision.

Major reports and legislation concerning community care are to be found in the Chapter on Health (Ch. 6) and that on Personal and Other Social Services (Ch. 8). The focus of them has been on enabling elderly people, and other vulnerable groups, to remain in their own homes for as long as possible and also to allow people in institutions to return to the community. Key reports were that of the Audit Commission, *Making a Reality of Community Care* (Audit Commission, 1986), the Griffiths Report *Community Care: agenda for action* (Griffiths, 1988), and the government White Paper *Caring for People* (Sec. of St. for Health *et al.*, 1989b).

It will be suggested in Chapter 12 that any redefinition of community care needs to take into account in a realistic way the role both of the family and of elderly people themselves.

Chapter five

THE FINANCIAL AND EMPLOYMENT POSITION

THE FINANCIAL POSITION

Introduction

Financial security in old age is a fundamental need because few elderly people are able to continue to earn their living. An adequate income may be secured from a number of sources including personal savings and state and private pensions. In the past elderly people who could no longer work and had no savings were thrown on the resources of the Poor Law or of their families.

Landmarks in legislation

The development of statutory provision of pensions from 1908 has been outlined in Chapter 4. Some points are elaborated below.

A major initiative was the Committee of Inquiry set up by the government in 1941 and chaired by Sir William Beveridge, to look at the whole system of social security. Its terms of reference were: 'to undertake, with special reference to the inter-relation of the schemes, a survey of the existing national schemes of social insurance and allied services including workmen's compensation, and to make recommendations' (Beveridge, 1942, p. 5). The Committee's proposals for pensions must be seen against the background of an overall strategy for a system of insurance covering everyone whatever their income, and for benefits including pensions to be paid to everyone who contributed based on a national minimum [doc 12]. Contributions were to be compulsory and benefits universal and not means tested. The responsibility of the state was seen to be the provision of a minimum income, while people were encouraged to supplement this on a voluntary basis. The monetary benefit was to be seen as just one part of 'a comprehensive policy of social progress' which included provision of better services in health, education and housing.

The Beveridge Report was published in 1942 and accepted with one important exception. This was the rejection of the 'national minimum' standard of benefits, which would have meant frequent changes to keep up with the cost of living. Benefits were to be fixed and reviewed at intervals. National insurance became compulsory for everyone of working age except married women. Pensions were to be paid on retirement (65 for men and 60 for women). To encourage people to work beyond this age an addition to the basic rate was given for each year of deferment.

In 1948 the National Assistance Act set up the National Assistance Board (NAB) with a duty to assist persons in need, i.e.: 'who are without resources to meet their requirements or whose resources (including benefits receivable under the National Insurance Act 1946) must be supplemented in order to meet their requirements.' For those who were not insured, or who needed additional help, this Act laid down the machinery. It was the last break with the Poor Law [doc 13].

One of the provisions of the National Insurance Act 1957 was to enable retirement and widowed pensioners under the age of 70 (65 for women) to revoke their declaration of retirement if they wished and to earn additions to their retirement pensions to be paid when they ceased working.

A major change of principle was embodied in the National Insurance Act 1966. In order that people might be able to receive a pension more closely related to the level of what they had been earning, as distinct from a basic minimum, a Graduated Pensions Scheme was brought in. Higher pensions were to be payable in return for higher contributions related to higher earnings. Employees might, however, be contracted out if their employers provided a comparable or better occupational scheme. Another change was the granting of a standard addition for supplementary pensioners and some other long-term cases. This was intended to reduce the number of discretionary additions to the weekly rate of benefit and to limit the need to ask detailed questions about special expenses.

In 1966 the NAB was merged with the Ministry of Pensions and National Insurance to become the Ministry of Social Security, and a semi-autonomous board, the Supplementary Benefits Commission (SBC) (which replaced the NAB) was set up under this Ministry.

The National Insurance Act 1970 provided three new social security cash benefits, one of which was for old people aged 80 or over who were too old to come into the National Insurance Scheme when it began in 1948. About 110,000 old people benefited. The National Insurance Act 1971 authorised a further payment above the normal retirement pension for the over 80s. And the following year a tax-free Christmas bonus for pensioners, and some others, was provided under the Pensioners and Family Income Supplement Payments Act 1972. This bonus has been paid in most subsequent years.

Following the Social Security Act 1975 the State Earnings Related Pension Scheme (SERPS) began in 1978 to provide pensions based on earnings, regardless of whether there were company schemes. Contributions to the former Graduated Pension Scheme ceased in 1975. One of the main features was that pension rights should be protected during absence from work to look after children, the old or the sick. This was thought to be particularly beneficial to women. There is provision for members of occupational pension schemes to be 'contracted out' of the additional pension of the state scheme by their employers.

The 1980 Social Security Act amended the Social Security Act 1975 so that in future benefit increases were to be related to the movement of prices, and not of earnings. The Social Security Advisory Committee, which replaced the Supplementary Benefits Commission, said in their first report in 1982 that they regretted the decision to break the link between the growth of earnings and pensions (Social Security Advisory Committee, 1982, p. 2). Pensioners, therefore, no longer had a guarantee that their living standards would rise in step with those of wage and salary earners. While the Advisory Committee did not single out benefits for retired people as a priority topic, they emphasised their concern that the benefits for this group should be protected and improved as resources permitted. The Social Security and Housing Benefits Act 1982 provided for a change in the way in which pension increases were calculated.

In 1984 the DHSS announced that there was to be what the Minister, Norman Fowler, called 'the most substantial examination of the social security system since the Beveridge report'. In 1985 the results were presented in a government Green Paper *Reform of Social Security* (Sec. of St. for Social Services, June 1985a). A particularly controversial proposal was to withdraw SERPS only six years after its introduction. However, the subsequent White Paper *Reform of Social Security: programme for action* in 1985, which virtually mirrored the Green Paper, proposed to modify rather than withdraw SERPS (Sec. of St. for Social Services, December 1985b).

The aims of the White Paper were to achieve a simpler system of social security, to give more effective help to those who needed it, to reduce the poverty trap, to give individuals more choice and to take account, especially over pensions, of 'the very substantial financial debt that we are handing down to future generations' (Sec. of St. for Social Services, 1985b; p. 1). The way this was to be done was to modify the SERPS scheme and to encourage the spread of occupational and personal pensions. The change took place after the Social Security Act 1986. These recent modifications represent substantial reductions in the benefits that will be paid out.

The Social Security Act 1986 also brought changes in the supplementary benefits system. This Act, which took effect in April 1988, replaced supplementary benefit with income support, changing the kind of help that had been available to people on long-term benefit. The additional requirements based on individual need for heating, special diets, laundry and so on were abolished. The normal and additional requirements were replaced by personal allowances and client group premiums. An innovation was the introduction of the social fund which was to help people on low incomes meet exceptional circumstances. The reason was that Ministers had concluded that the costs of previous systems of exceptional needs payments between 1966 and 1980 and single payments after 1980 were out of control (National Audit Office, 1991). Critics of the 1986 Act claim that the emphasis on targeting means-tested benefits marked a shift away from the aims of the Beveridge Report which guaranteed security against want without a means test (Social Security Consortium, 1986). The *right* to single payments was replaced by discretionary ones from the social fund (see also p. 61).

Some poverty and other studies

A noticeable feature of much research into poverty is how prominent elderly people are. Some of these studies will now be referred to in chronological order.

The studies As early as 1895 a Royal Commission had investigated 'the Aged Poor' and recommended some alterations to the Poor Law system. Then a notable researcher, Seebohm Rowntree, carried out a survey of poverty in York in 1899 and again in 1936 and 1948. He concluded that the main causes of poverty had been low wages in 1899, unemployment in 1936 and old age in 1948. In 1947 Rowntree chaired a Committee on the problems of ageing and the care of old people (Rowntree, 1947) [doc 8]. One of their main conclusions was that acute poverty had been substantially abolished among the aged and that state pensions were 'now probably adequate' (Rowntree, 1947, p. 99). They felt that there was still a considerable measure of austerity, but the flexible administration of the Assistance Board had been successful in adjusting benefits to need in a humane but not unreasonably extravagant manner. The year 1953 saw the setting up of an official Committee chaired by Sir Thomas Phillips: 'to review the economic and financial problems involved in providing for old age, having regard to the prospective increase in the numbers of the aged, and to make recommendations' (Chancellor of the Exchequer, 1954). They considered the economic problems to be those resulting from the need to accumulate or free resources out of which adequate provision could be made for the old, and the financial problems to be those arising from the need to transfer to the old the purchasing power that would give them the appropriate command over those resources (Chancellor of the Exchequer, 1954).

In 1962 Cole and Utting in a study, *The Economic Circumstances of Old People*, noted that all the problems they looked at – loneliness, ill health and poverty – appeared to be suffered in *extreme* form by only a relatively small minority (Cole and Utting, 1962). Two periods were examined by Abel-Smith and Townsend and reported on in *The Poor and the Poorest* (Abel-Smith and Townsend, 1965). Comparing 1953–4 and 1960 they found that 7.8 per cent of people in the United Kingdom (4 million persons) were living below 'national assistance' level in 1953–4. About half of them were living in households whose heads were retired. In 1960 they found that 14.2 per cent of people in the United Kingdom (7.5 million persons) were living below 'national assistance' level. About 35 per cent were living in households primarily dependent on pensions. One of the reasons for the apparent increase from 7.8 to 14.2 per cent living at this low level appeared to be the relative increase in the number of old people in the population. Another reason was the slight relative increase in the number of chronically sick middle-aged men and the relative increase in the number of large families. Abel-Smith and Townsend concluded: 'On the whole the data we have presented contradicts the commonly held view that a trend towards greater equality has accompanied the trend towards greater affluence' (Abel-Smith and Townsend, 1965, p. 66).

Townsend and Wedderburn in their survey, *The Aged in the Welfare State*, in 1962 of over 4,000 people, found that in general the elderly had income levels of half or more below the levels of younger persons in the population (Townsend and Wedderburn, 1965). Few old people had substantial assets and over one-third were solely dependent on state benefits. About two-fifths of the men and of the couples and one-tenth of the women received a pension from their employers, but these were relatively small. The very old were worse off as a result of inflation and because they were less likely to work.

There was mounting evidence that some old people were living on a smaller income than the scale provided by the NAB. The MPNI, in co-operation with the NAB, carried out an enquiry in 1965 to find out their numbers and the reasons why they did not apply for assistance. The report, *Financial and Other Circumstances of Retirement Pensioners*, was published in 1966 (MPNI, 1966).

The enquiry consisted of a survey of nearly 11,000 pensioners and the findings were similar to those of other researchers. Incomes of pensioners were low. Nearly one-half of the men had occupational pensions. The corresponding proportions were one-quarter for single women other than widows, and one-ninth for widows.

Turning to the main purpose of the enquiry it was estimated that rather more than 700,000 pensioner households (about 850,000 pensioners) could have received assistance if they had applied for it (MPNI, 1966, pp. 83–4). The main reasons why pensioners did not apply for assistance were: lack of knowledge, the dislike of 'charity', a feeling that they were managing all right on what they had and (a small proportion) a dislike of going to the NAB (MPNI, 1966, pp. 84–5).

The Townsend and Wedderburn survey and that of the MPNI both found that the older the person the smaller the income, that few old people had substantial assets or savings, and that single and widowed women were the worst off. In Townsend's 1968–9 national sample, elderly people comprised one-third of those in poverty. One of his findings, reported in *Poverty in the United Kingdom*, was that: 'People tend to separate into two groups, one anticipating a comfortable and even early retirement, the other dreading the prospect and depending almost entirely for their livelihood on the resources made available by the State through its social security system' (Townsend, 1979, p. 820).

The 1976 OPCS survey for DHSS gives further data about the financial position of elderly people (Hunt, 1978). Many of the findings, such as the dependence of elderly people on state benefits and the decline of income with age, were similar to previous surveys. It is interesting, however, that financial difficulties did not figure prominently in the list of things they disliked, although suggestions about ways in which they could be helped *did* include a number having financial implications. The 1980 *GHS* showed that almost three-fifths (59 per cent) of the sample of elderly people in 1980 had no income other than that provided by the state. For three-quarters the retirement pension was their largest single source of income (Victor and Vetter, 1986).

Useful information was gained from a study by Market and Opinion Research International (MORI) commissioned by London Weekend Television. This was a survey of 1,174 people in Great Britain in 1983. The results were published in *Poor Britain* (Mack and Lansley, 1985). The central idea of the study was similar to that of Townsend and provided information on the comparative living standards of the poor and attitudes to them. In the Townsend study elderly people represented about one-third of all those in poverty. In the 1983 study the proportion was about one-fifth. Moreover, it was not only the case that elderly people formed a smaller proportion of those in poverty generally, they also formed a smaller proportion of those in intense poverty. The researchers put the decreased proportion down to higher pensions, including a higher proportion having an occupational pension, but also attributed it to the dramatic rise in the numbers of unemployed people.

A similar finding about the drop in the proportions of pensioners in poverty was established in a special analysis of the *Family Expenditure Survey* which the government conducted for the 1984–5 *Social Security Review* (see Social Security Advisory Committee, 1988). This revealed that there had been a shift in the composition of the lowest fifth of the income distribution, with a reduction in the number of pensioners and an increase in the number of families falling in the bottom group (Social Security Advisory Committee, 1988, p. 50).

The OPCS surveys 1985–8 also shed light on poverty. *The Financial Circumstances of Disabled Adults Living in Private Households* showed that a high proportion (69 per cent) of disabled adults were over the age of 60 compared with 29 per cent in the general population (Martin and White, 1988). However, disabled pensioners had similar incomes on average to those of pensioners in general since all pensioners were largely dependent on state benefits and had on average lower incomes than non-pensioners. But the research makes it clear that disabled people have extra expenditure, although for disabled pensioners this was less marked than for non-pensioners.

Attempts are now being made to make comparisons with other countries. Laczko concludes that it is difficult to draw firm conclusions about poverty among elderly people in the European Community (EC) because of lack of comparative data (Laczko, 1990). He states that on the information available old age is still more associated with dependence on social assistance in Britain than in other northern countries of the EC. This, he says, is partly because the state pension in Britain is much less generous than in other EC countries.

Some definitions The strict definition of poverty as below subsistence level, i.e. absolute poverty, is not normally one used today. Some researchers have used as a guide supplementary benefit, now income support, level, which is higher than would be needed for sheer physical survival. Others have claimed that a better yardstick would be a certain percentage above that level. Thus Abel-Smith and Townsend added 40 per cent, taking into account discretionary payments and statutory disregards (Abel-Smith and Townsend, 1965).

These differing definitions make strict comparison between the poverty studies difficult. Taking gross or net incomes alone reveals only a crude indication of poverty. Even more sophisticated analyses which incorporate indirect taxes and make allowance for use of services funded through public expenditure, such as health, have their drawbacks. Any study relating to the incomes of elderly people has to start from the premise of caution. Evidence is conflicting (for example different conclusions are presented by Fiegehen, 1986; Thomson, 1986, and Dawson and Evans, 1987) and sometimes this is because some researchers use incomes of individuals and some of households. DHSS have abandoned the notion of a poverty line based on income support and replaced it with proportions of mean/ median income and analyses of the bottom fifth of the household income distribution.

It is generally accepted that any definition must take account of more than just financial matters. Abel-Smith and Townsend considered that income and expenditure should be regarded as only one of a number of indicators of poverty and that differences in home environment, material possessions and educational and occupational resources must also be included. Townsend suggested a definition based on 'relative deprivation' – that is: 'the absence or inadequacy of those diets, amenities, standards, services and activities which are common or customary in society' (Townsend, 1979, p. 915). A great deal of the debate on poverty since this study has been about the kinds of services and items which are essential to avoid poverty/ deprivation. Mack and Lansley adopted this approach and noted the correlation between the lack of items and the level of income (Mack and Lansley, 1985). This wider definition of not just material deprivation but taking account of a person's place in society and how far they are excluded from taking part in the normal pursuits of their peers is an advance on previous measures.

Some studies are now asking questions about both income and expenditure and also about people's feelings about being poor. For example, the OPCS disability surveys used two subjective measures of financial position and standard of living (Martin and White, 1988). These were how people managed and how satisfied they were with their standard of living. They also asked about lack of particular items, as had Townsend and Mack and Lansley. But they went further and asked if this was because they did not want them or could not afford them.

A useful discussion of absolute and relative poverty, relative deprivation and inequality can be found in Alcock (1987) and details of the poverty debate in Oppenheim (1990).

The present position

There seems little disagreement about the importance of state income to old people. For example, in a comparative study of the last 50 years it was found that at no time in recent years has the state played a subsidiary role (Falkingham and Gordon, 1988). These researchers found that the role of the family has always been minimal. In 1987 16 per cent of pensioner units (i.e. single pensioners and married couples where the husband was aged 65 or over) were dependent on state benefits for 100 per cent of their income and 54 per cent for 75 per cent of their income (House of Commons written answer, 21.2.91, Column 264). There are powerful voices maintaining that poverty and deprivation in old age has persisted despite social recognition for over a century and more than thirty years of welfare provision (e.g Walker, 1990a). For some, however, the combination of a private pension and home ownership will mean greater affluence in old age. But Falkingham and Victor argue that the number of affluent elderly people is relatively small but highly visible with the danger that the reality of later life as experienced by the poor majority of pensioners may be obscured (Falkingham and Victor, 1991, p. 30).

Pensions and personal savings The current pension system is one where there is a universal flat-rate pension and a second-tier system where a person may belong to an approved occupational scheme, may belong to the state SERPS scheme, or may have a personal pension. A retirement pension is payable to people of pensionable age provided that they have paid sufficient national insurance contributions. Before 1989 pensioners did not receive their full pension if they earned over a certain amount but this so-called 'earnings rule' has now been abolished. (Details of all benefits are given annually by ACE in their *Your Rights* booklet.) Anyone over 80 who is not getting a contributory retirement pension, who satisfies certain residence conditions, is entitled to a non-contributory pension. In 1988–9 it was estimated that 9.2 million pensioners in Great Britain were receiving a retirement pension and in 1987–8 1.8 million a supplementary pension (CSO, 1990, pp. 88–9).

Income support Income support, formerly supplementary benefit, is available to home owners, tenants and to people living with families. It may also be a passport to other benefits such as free dental treatment, grants for insulation and grants from the social fund. Figure 5.1 shows that retirement pensions and other social security benefits have provided the major source of incomes from 1971 to 1987, although their share has declined slightly during the 1980s. The drop in income from employment is because fewer pensioners are now economically active. This drop has been more than counterbalanced by the increasing importance of occupational incomes which accounted for one-fifth of income in 1986 (CSO, 1991). Numbers of pensioner households claiming supplementary benefit/income support have remained relatively stable between 1970 and 1987–8, although they have declined as a proportion of claimants (Falkingham and Victor, 1991, p. 61).

Occupational pensions Many public services and commercial organisations now run occupational pension schemes with pension based on final salary. There has been a major expansion of personal pension plans following the Social Security Act 1986. The 1988 *GHS* showed that about three-fifths of the workforce, 64 per cent of men and 54 per cent of women, were covered by this sort of scheme in 1988 (OPCS, 1990). But not all the present pensioners, and in particular few women, were covered. Of existing pensioners 52 per cent received an occupational pension in 1987 (Twigger, 1989). However, the amount was not very much. In 1986 the weekly

Figure 5.1 Income of pensioners[1]: by source

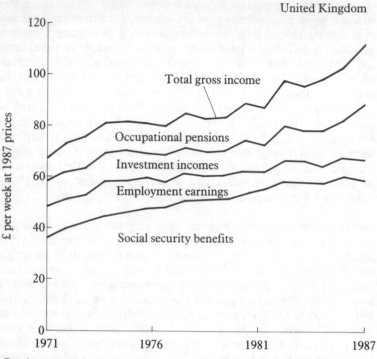

United Kingdom

Source: *Social Trends*, No. 21, HMSO, 1991, Figure 5.6, p. 86.

[1] Pensioner tax units

average (arithmetic mean) was £43.30 for single men and £33.80 for single women (House of Commons written answer, 27.3.90; Col.163).

Other ways in which people can provide for their old age is through *personal saving*. The 1965 MPNI survey showed that few old people had much in the way of savings (MPNI, 1966) and the position in 1976 was very similar (Hunt, 1978). In part this may be due to low levels of wages and to unemployment in the past, but in part it may also be due to the effect of inflation which erodes the value of savings. In 1982 two-thirds of pensioners received income from their own savings and investments, though often this was a small proportion of their total income (Fiegehen, 1986). Looking specifically at pensioners with savings income, their income from savings and occupational pensions (the amount is not disaggregated) rose from 53 per cent with savings income in 1974 to 73 per cent in 1987; however the average amount received at 1988 prices was only £20.50 in 1974 and £28.40 in 1987 (House of Commons written answer, 25.7.90, Column 308). Personal pensions which bring tax advantages are not very widespread but could become more important and have been encouraged by the government.

Other forms of financial help

There are other ways in which financial help is given, apart from pensions, and some of these are listed below.

The social fund The social fund has both non-discretionary and discretionary elements. The former provides entitlements to help with funeral and maternity expenses and with the cost of heating during periods of cold weather for people on certain social security benefits. The discretionary element, from a fixed budget, provides budgeting and crisis loans (about 70 per cent of the budget) and non-repayable community care grants (about 30 per cent of the budget). The purpose of community care grants was: 'to help people re-establish themselves in the community, to avoid institutional care, or to ease particular exceptional pressure on families' (Sec. of St. for Social Services, 1985a, p. 42). They are available for help with moving out of institutional or residential care, help to remain at home (such as minor house repairs), help with certain travel expenses and help with exceptional pressures on families caused by disability, chronic sickness or a breakdown in a relationship.

Help with health charges Pensioners and others on income support are entitled to help with certain NHS charges. They are eligible for free prescriptions and for remission of charges for glasses, dentures, dental treatment, wigs and fabric supports.

Help with heating costs Housing surveys show that elderly people tend to live in older, poorer accommodation than other households. This means that they will need to spend a higher proportion of their income on fuel than most households and therefore need heat for longer periods. These facts, as well as the great increase in the cost of fuel, have given rise to widespread concern about the many elderly people who are living in homes which are cold (see Ch. 6). Supplementary pensioners used to be eligible for help with extra heating costs but this amount has now been subsumed into the general amount given in income support. However, cold weather payments can be claimed from the social fund in certain very limited circumstances.

Help with housing costs Financial help is available from local authorities for housing benefit which replaced the two previous schemes of supplementary benefit for rent and rebates and local authority rent and rebates and rent allowances. It is available for help with rent and certain service charges. A new system of housing benefit was introduced in 1988 and it was claimed that pensioners would be one of the largest groups of losers (Social Security Consortium, 1986).

A major problem faced by elderly owner-occupiers is the cost of repairs to the home. Income support can cover certain housing costs for home owners, including mortgage interest payments and interest on some repairs and improvements. Some building societies and a small number of local authorities make available interest-only 'maturity loans' to older people who need to carry out bigger repairs and improvements. The capital is recovered from the sale proceeds of the property. Full interest has to be paid monthly, but in some circumstances income support assistance from DHSS may be available to cover some or all of the interest. In certain circumstances a grant may be given by the local authority to repair or improve the home (see Ch. 7).

Community charge/Council tax The community charge, or poll tax as it is more often called, started in Scotland in 1989 and England and Wales in 1990 and replaced local rates. Pensioners with low incomes were eligible to have community charge benefit and some people were exempt altogether. They included people who lived permanently in hospital, a residential or nursing home or certain people who were 'severely mentally impaired'. The community charge will be replaced by a council tax.

Income tax People aged 65 or over receive a higher tax allowance than younger people and allowances are still higher at age 75. However, these increased allowances are subject to an income limit. Older people may also qualify for other allowances such as the blind person's allowance or widow's bereavement allowance.

Attendance allowance A tax-free attendance allowance is payable for people who need frequent attention or continual supervision by day and at night. A lower amount is payable if the help is needed only for the day or the night. Many of those who receive this are elderly people.

Mobility allowance The Social Security Act 1979 extended the upper age limit for mobility allowance which can be claimed by people who cannot walk, or have great difficulty in walking. When the scheme was introduced in 1979 it was progressively phased in by age. Once a person receives this allowance it can be continued up to the age of 80. However, no one over the age of 65 who has not claimed by their 66th birthday can do so. It is argued that this allowance should be available to everyone, whatever their age, if they are disabled (e.g. by Walker, 1990b, p. 67). (NB: In 1991 it was proposed that attendance and mobility allowance be extended a little to help less severely disabled people and merged in 1992 into a single benefit called the disability living allowance.)

Paying for residential and nursing home care Income support is available for elderly people with low incomes for both these forms of care (see Ch. 8).

Other financial concessions Travel at a reduced rate, or free between certain hours, is subsidised by some local authorities. Some also give concessions for other services such as for pensioners attending further education courses or public entertainments. There is much variation between local authorities. British Rail allows pensioners to travel at reduced rates with a special railcard. Television licences at a reduced rate are available for pensioners in old people's homes and sheltered housing.

Expenditure

Pensioners have a slightly different pattern of expenditure to other households. The 1987 *Family Expenditure Survey* showed that they spent more on fuel, light, food and housing and less on clothing, footwear and transport (CSO, 1990, p. 99). Low income households, including pensioners who came into this category, spent over half their expenditure on such necessities as food, housing, fuel and light compared with just over one-third of those with higher incomes. The 1985 *GHS* showed that households containing at least one elderly person were less likely to own a deep freezer, washing machine, tumble drier or car than households containing no elderly persons (OPCS, 1987, p. 188).

Some issues

Level of pensions The main need for elderly people is for an adequate income when they are no longer able to earn their own living. The breaking of the link between the level of the pension and that of prices or earnings, whichever is the greater, in 1979 has been widely criticised (e.g. Atkinson, 1991). Since 1980 earnings have tended to rise faster than prices. Had the pensioners' earnings link not been broken it is estimated that the single pension in 1990 would be £13.10 higher and the married pension £20.70 higher (Twigger, 1989). Earnings have grown faster than prices and in 1989 were 29 per cent higher in real terms (Tompkins, 1989).

Many academics and others have argued for an increase in the basic level of the pension. For example, Midwinter in *The Wage of Retirement: the case for a new pensions policy* suggests a single retirement wage in place of the contributory pension and means-tested benefits (Midwinter, 1985). He argues for a wage based neither on an earnings or prices index but on a spending index. He estimated that in 1985 this would be £80 per week per person. Interestingly he argues for this on the basis that many elderly people are excluded from 'what a majority of people would now consider a normal lifestyle' (Midwinter, 1985, p. 1). As was seen above, this is very much in line with current definitions of poverty. He goes further and says that older people should be treated as citizen-pensioners rather than welfare beneficiaries and their income should be looked on as a wage of retirement.

Public expenditure on pensions In Great Britain expenditure on retirement pensions rose from £5,662 millions in 1976–7 to an estimated outturn in 1988–9 of £19,237 millions (CSO, 1991, p. 87). At least part of this is accounted for by the rise in the number of pensioners and pressure will grow in the first quarter of the next century for the same reason. Of all social security benefits, retirement pensions are by far the largest, accounting for 40 per cent of total expenditure.

Age for retirement Men and women may now retire at the minimum state pension age, i.e. 60 for a woman and 65 for a man, but organisations should have equal retirement ages. A few continue for longer (e.g. clergy, judges, those in domestic service, the self-employed) but they are the exception. Some people, especially those in heavy manual jobs, may wish for early retirement, while others would prefer to stay on for longer. The Sex Discrimination Act 1986 makes it illegal for men and women to be forced to retire from work at different ages. A flexible age for retirement may be more in keeping with the varying physical and mental capacities of old people and the case for this has been carefully set out in *Flexibility and Fairness* (Tompkins, 1989). The disparity between the ages at which men and women are eligible for a state pension is another factor. Other countries also have unequal pension ages, although within the EC 7 out of the 12 have equalised (France at 60, Germany, Ireland, Luxembourg, Netherlands and Spain at 65, and Denmark at 67) (Tompkins, 1989). A draft Directive from the Commission proposes full equality for men and women in pensions and other benefits in 1992.

Dependence on income support It has been seen that the original Beveridge plan was for the national insurance retirement pension to be sufficiently high for pensioners not, in general, to have to rely on means-tested assistance. This has not happened and so large numbers of elderly people have had to apply for the latter. The safety net of income support has become an important element of pensioners' resources.

The social fund In contrast to single payments which were a legal entitlement governed by regulations, there are no legal entitlements to the discretionary parts of the social fund. The only part of the fund which is not cash limited and which is based not on discretion but on regulations is for grants for funerals, maternity and cold weather. Although an applicant can ask for a review by a social fund officer, and then an inspector, if a grant or loan is refused there is no right of appeal. As ACE has pointed out, although the total allocated to the fund in 1988–9 (£203 million) was slightly higher than the single payment expenditure in the previous year, 70 per cent of the budget is allocated for loans and not grants (ACE, 1989). Research undertaken by ACE in 1988 among its groups showed that loans were unacceptable to most elderly people as they were often frightened of getting into debt. ACE reported: 'Government figures for the first 6 months of the social fund back up these views. Of the £61 million spent on crisis and budgeting loans up to 30 October

1988, only 4 per cent of the expenditure went to pensioners' (Hansard [Commons] 20.2.88, quoted in ACE, 1989). Great variations in the success of applications for grants were also noted, as was general ignorance about these grants. In 1989–90 more than half of applicants (53 per cent) were turned down for community care grants (NAO, 1991, p. 27).

Take-up of benefits   One of the regular findings of surveys has been that elderly people do not all claim the benefits to which they are entitled. In 1985 retirement pensions were claimed by virtually all those eligible. But for supplementary pensions only 79 per cent claimed this benefit (CSO, 1990, p. 90). This means that one in five (380,000 pensioners) were not claiming. In 1983 the weekly entitlement of pensioners failing to claim supplementary benefit was £3.40 per week. However, the value of this small weekly entitlement, stretching over years, may not be inconsiderable. A study of non take-up of supplementary benefit, housing benefit and family income support by a sample of 300 non-claimants in the London Borough of Hackney showed that among those most likely to resist claiming were those approaching, or well over, pensionable age (Davies and Ritchie, 1988).

Abuse   There is great public concern about wrongful claims to social security and in 1971 the Fisher Committee was set up to report on this form of abuse. In 1973 they produced *Report of the Committee on Abuse of Social Security Benefits* (DHSS, 1973). In one area (non-disclosure of earnings) the Committee found that there was abuse 'to a substantial extent' though no evidence is given about the extent among pensioners. The Committee considered how the DHSS attempted to make sure that pensioners were aware of the earnings rule and correctly reported any earnings which might affect the amount of benefit payable. The Committee felt that there was little public sympathy for those who both worked and drew benefit, but they added: 'More sympathy is felt for pensioners, for disabled men and for women without male support who do part-time or casual work and earn a little over the "disregard" limits. Though this is "abuse" it could take a lower place in the attentions of the Departments' (DHSS, 1973, p. 277). Since this date there has been little in the way of systematic monitoring of abuse among elderly people, but the abolition of the earnings rule may have made this less relevant. During the 1970s there was a 'vigorous, and at times strident, public campaign against social security abuse' but in the early 1980s, possibly due to the use of special claims control and regular fraud teams, there was a sharp decline in the number of cases of prosecutions for suspected social security fraud (Barker *et al.*, 1990).

EMPLOYMENT

Introduction

Retirement from work can be viewed from a number of different standpoints – economic, medical, administrative and social. Economically, it implies the loss of trained and experienced workers and also considerable expenditure by the state on pensions. Medically, there may be the effect of ageing on productivity, although there is little evidence about this, and of retirement on the individual's health. Administratively, there is the problem of deciding what type of retirement policy should be adopted. Socially, it can be examined for its impact on the happiness of the individual.

Decline in proportions of economically active elderly people

An important change took place in the economic activity rate (i.e. the percentage of the age group gainfully employed) of most elderly people between 1951 and 1989 in Great Britain. In 1951 31 per cent of men of pensionable age were economically active, but in 1989 this had dropped to 9 per cent (CSO, 1979, 1991). The decline for single women of pensionable age was from a rate of nearly 5 per cent in 1951 to 3 per cent in 1988 (CSO, 1979, 1990). The rate for married women rose to a peak in the mid-1970s but has now dropped too.

The rise and fall in the number of elderly people in paid employment is to some extent related to the state of the economy. Changes in government policy have been made thus: 'twenty-five years ago the labour shortage led to official encouragement of older people remaining at work, *inter alia* by promoting research to show that their capabilities were on a par with others; now the situation is different. The point has been made that official interest in the elderly employed has tended to be influenced by the state of the economy so that voluntary early departure from the labour force is now regarded as worth encouraging' (Jolly *et al.*, 1980). In 1988 and 1989 there was a slight increase in economic activity rates for both male and female pensioners which may partly reflect the expected drop in the younger working population (see Ermisch, 1990). In some cases older people are being wooed back to work and this is particularly noticeable in the retail trade. The House of Commons Employment Committee in *The Employment Patterns of the Over-50s* put it thus:

When we began to plan the inquiry [1987], interest still centred on the development of schemes to ease older workers into early retirement. By the time we had finished taking our evidence there had been a dramatic shift of emphasis and there was a growing discussion of ways in which older people could be persuaded to stay at work in order to offset the impending shortage of young workers. The pendulum has rarely swung so swiftly. (House of Commons, 1989, p. ix)

They later argued that the nature of work would change as well as the nature of the workforce. 'As part-time work, self-employment and career mobility increase, the post-industrial revolution pattern of a lifetime of paid, full-time work in a single trade or occupation, frequently for one employer, becomes less dominant' (House of Commons, 1989, p. ix).

Phillipson argues that the treatment of elderly people as a reserve workforce has led to confusion about the value of retirement. He also makes a useful distinction between the experiences of men and women in retirement. He and Dex believe that there should be a major initiative to assist older employees which distinguishes between policies needed for men and women (Dex and Phillipson, 1986). Phillipson also suggests that the experience of growing old 'as a period where the biological process of age assumes a primary role is to ignore the cumulative power and significance of life in a class society' (Phillipson, 1982, p. 167). However, class, while important, is only one element in a person's history.

Why elderly people stop working　As might be expected, the percentage of people working decreases sharply with age. Most elderly people have to leave their jobs on reaching the official retiring age, unless they are self-employed. Some leave earlier. Surveys, such as *Reasons Given for Retiring or Continuing at Work* (MPNI, 1954), and subsequent research have confirmed that many who retired early did so for health reasons. However, this seems less the case more recently. In an analysis of a sample of men formerly in paid employment who retired early, Laczko found that only 7 per cent of non-manual and 8 per cent of manual workers retired for health reasons (Laczko, quoted in Victor, 1987, p. 175). He found that while voluntary retirement was about two-thirds for both groups,

15 per cent of non-manual men were retired compulsorily and 24 per cent of manual workers were made redundant. Although there are no detailed figures for the age of people who were made redundant before the Redundancy Payments Act 1965, there is some evidence that prior to the Act age played a rather less significant part in redundancy selection than it has subsequently.

Another reason why elderly people stop working may be because of the views of society. The House of Commons Social Services Committee said: 'The strongest pressure (for early retirement) comes from the high rates of youth unemployment leading to individual and collective beliefs that older workers should retire to make way for younger people' (House of Commons Social Services Committee, quoted in Victor, 1987, p. 174). It is also worth noting that ending paid employment for a minority of people does not always mean that status is lost. Doctors and clergy, for example, can continue to use their titles.

Elderly people who want to continue to work Work provides income, status, interest and companionship and the need for these does not necessarily become less on retirement. People may wish to continue in work for all these reasons. Showler, and others, have argued that while many older people prefer to retire rather than continue in work, others would suffer a substantial fall in living standards and prefer to work. For people who are self-employed this is easier than for employees. The self-employed are more likely to be in work over retirement age than employees. In the combined data for Great Britain, 1987 and 1988 in the *GHS* 5 per cent of self-employed men and 10 per cent of self-employed women were over state retirement age compared with only 1 per cent of male and 4 per cent of female employees (OPCS, 1990, p. 183).

Even those who have been compulsorily retired from their jobs may seek another one, and for those who have to retire in their 50s (e.g. from the police or armed services) a long spell in another occupation may be possible. The most likely outcome is part-time work. Some have suggested that jobs suitable for older people should be kept open for them and that special training should be provided. This, however, assumes that elderly people are alike and can be provided for as a group, whereas all the evidence shows that each is an individual with particular skills and differing levels of performance.

Some have argued that work after retirement should be encouraged. The Rowntree Committee, for example, pointed out that from the economic standpoint it was important for people of pensionable age to remain at work so long as they could make a worthwhile contribution to the creation of wealth (Rowntree, 1947). However, these views have to be considered against the background of the current unemployment situation, since a high level of unemployment may make it less likely that people will argue along the lines of the Rowntree Committee's Report. The case for more flexibility over work patterns is persuasive (e.g. Mellor, 1987). Voluntary work should also be considered in this context. A detailed discussion follows in Chapter 11.

Some problems

Attitudes In Chapter 2 reference was made to society's perceptions of ageing and it was remarked that elderly people are often regarded as second-class citizens unable to make much contribution to the world around them. A blanket approach like this is unhelpful and inaccurate. Research in two particular spheres, the physiological and psychological aspects of ageing, demonstrates this in relation to employment.

Research into the physiological aspects of ageing is clearly important for the light that can be shed on physical and mental performance. The general conclusion seems to be that while performance in certain ways, e.g. physical strength, does decline with age, yet chronological age is by no means an accurate indicator of capacity to perform a task (Straka, 1990). Psychological evidence is just as important because the way in which both prospective employee and employer view the older worker will affect their attitudes. There is evidence that stereotypes are common about ageing and that these influence the behaviour of people in the employment market. These beliefs can affect recruitment, transfer, training and redundancy policies.

Age bars Evidence drawn from advertised job vacancies has shown that the incidence of age-qualified vacancies is fairly widespread (Equal Opportunities Commission, 1989, quoted in McEwen, 1990, p. 88). A number of reasons for this practice has been suggested; the presence of career structures and internal labour markets (people may be recruited and trained to fit in with the structure of a particular organisation); the likely age at which the peak of professional output is reached; the standard of health and fitness required; restrictive practices; length of training required; wage-for-age scales; a filter mechanism (to reduce the number of applicants); and problems over pension funds.

In 1978 legislation in the United States outlawed discrimination on grounds of age among workers up to the age of 70, but no similar legislation has so far been passed in this country. Whether a change in the law would help is debatable. Laczko and Phillipson have shown that the impact of the American legislation must not be exaggerated (Laczko and Phillipson, 1990). Legislation there has not reversed the trend towards earlier retirement and age discrimination is still a major problem in the workplace. Phillipson and Laczko nevertheless suggest that, while a variety of strategies may be needed, legislation would 'be important in terms of setting an agenda for change, challenging stereotypes, and for highlighting particular areas of injustice faced by older workers' (Laczko and Phillipson, 1990; p. 93). ACE have also argued that upper age limits in recruitment advertising should be made illegal (Greengross, 1990, p. 11).

The House of Commons Employment Committee in their report *The Employment Patterns of the Over-50s* recommended a number of other things such as:

- the Employment Service should always ask employers seeking to impose age restrictions on recruitment if these are strictly necessary;
- the Government should mount a campaign with the Confederation of British Industry to encourage awareness among employers of the potential worth to them of older workers and to challenge on practical grounds the discrimination being practised and should try to persuade employers of the benefits of considering older workers (House of Commons, 1989, pp. xvii–xviii).

Preparation for retirement More attention is now being paid to the need for preparation for retirement. Some firms organise courses for their employees and some adult education institutes do the same for a wider constituency. The Pre-Retirement Association offer seminars, courses and individual counselling and publishes a monthly magazine, *Choice*.

Studies of elderly people, however, show clearly that many are ill-prepared to cope with what may be one-third of their lives. In one of the classic studies, *Work, Age and Leisure*, Le Gros Clark argued that for most men the end of their working life no longer coincides with physiological old age (Le Gros Clark, 1966 [in doc 7]). He believed that advances in technology would mean fewer jobs and that other methods for prolonging working life outside industry,

71

such as sheltered workshops, were little more than pilot schemes. He ended with a plea for active pursuits in retirement to be considered in the wider context of increasing leisure for people of all ages.

What is missing from much of the debate is any mention of gender differences. Women in later life may either wish to start a career, retrain or come to terms with a continuation of a domestic life. The experiences of retirement and the need for preparation may be very different for a man who has spent his whole life in full-time employment and a woman whose work-pattern may be very uneven or non-existent. Some men are now calling for 'portfolio careers' in which different jobs and unpaid work can be done at different times in their lives. Handy has argued that the portfolio approach with a combination of part-time jobs, and perhaps voluntary work, means that no one need finally 'retire' (House of Commons, 1989). This pattern is, of course, well known to many women already.

Current focus on the Third Age may mean that we should think of retirement *to* something rather than retirement *from*.

CONCLUSIONS

It is clear that older workers are not a group who can be neatly categorised according to skill, ability or physical strength. It would be helpful if employers could choose people for a particular job regardless of their age and train them accordingly. But for those older people who are disabled, special policies may be appropriate.

There may, however, be practical difficulties for employers. For example, an employer undertaking to train someone for a job expects that person to work in it for sufficient time to pay off the cost of the training. Again, an employer may have to weigh up the cost of additional safety measures such as extra lighting that may be required against the value of the end product. On the other hand, the employer may find that older workers provide stability and do not move on so quickly from one job to another as younger people sometimes do.

What has also to be remembered is that employment policies cannot be considered in isolation. Pension transfer schemes and the effect of the state pension age all have a bearing, both on what the individual elderly person chooses to do and on the retirement policy of employers. The issue is also part of the wider debate on the value that society currently puts on paid employment rather than the contribution which people make to society in an unpaid capacity. Midwinter calls for a sharing for everyone throughout life of 'A harmonious balance of work-sharing and non-work (or free time or leisure)' as the long term ideal (Midwinter, 1985, p. 44). Martin argues that older people may be able to retire with the opportunity to pursue the mainstream activities of family, home and self-satisfaction now that the 'work ethic' is disappearing (Martin, 1990). It is also part of the debate about opportunities for older people which is explored in Chapter 11.

INTRODUCTION

Health is a matter of prime importance for elderly people because it is staying reasonably well, among other things, that helps them to remain independent. As has been seen in Chapter 2, a common view of ageing is of a steady decline in physical and mental powers. Professional workers can be particularly prone to this negative view, since it is the ill and the frail whom they normally meet.

THE HEALTH OF ELDERLY PEOPLE

General

There is clear evidence of a greater incidence of both acute and chronic sickness among elderly people than in other age groups, as the 1988 *GHS* shows (OPCS, 1990). For acute sickness the average number of days of restricted activity for people aged 65 and over in 1988 was 39 for men and 54 for women. The average for all ages was 20 for men and 28 for women. For chronic sickness 60 per cent of men and 65 per cent of women reported a long-standing illness. The average for all ages was 33 per cent for men and 34 per cent for women. Figure 6.1 and [doc 14] show the estimated rises with age of limiting long-standing disability.

Elderly patients differ in three major ways from the young: in the type and number of diseases and accidents, in their reactions to disease and in special features to do with their background (Hodkinson, 1975). They often have a multiplicity of diseases, partly accounted for by the accumulation of non-lethal diseases such as osteo-arthritis and deafness. They are more likely to fall than any other age groups except the under fives (Department of Trade and Industry, 1990) often with serious consequences (Askham *et al.*,

Figure 6.1 GHS estimates of prevalence of limiting long-standing disability by age (Great Britain 1985) compared with disability survey estimates: adults in private households

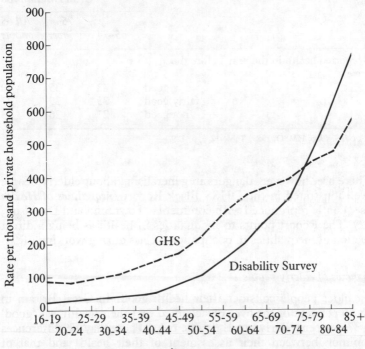

Martin, J., Meltzer, H. and Elliot, D., *The Prevalence of Disability among Adults*, OPCS Surveys of Disability in Great Britain, No. 1, HMSO, 1988, Figure 3.4, p. 20.

1990). On the other hand diseases such as infective hepatitis are less common among elderly people and so is severe bronchitis – probably because 'susceptible individuals are eliminated at earlier ages' (Hodkinson, 1975, p. 6). There are also differences in the way elderly people react to disease (e.g. pain mechanisms and temperature response). General background, too, has an effect, for poverty, lack of status and disability can all lead to depression. Coronary heart diseases and many cancers, while strongly age-related, also have important environmental causes. Many researchers have also pointed to the dangers to elderly people of potential toxic effects of the many drugs they have to take.

Table 6.1.   A comparison of health in the year before interview between the under and over 75s

	Great Britain 1988		
	65–74	75 or over	All 65 or over
Self-reported health in the year before the interview			
good	43	35	40
fairly good	35	39	37
not good	21	26	23

OPCS, *GHS*, *1986*, HMSO, 1989, Table 12.6, p. 189.

There are, however, dangers in generalising about elderly people as well illustrated in the DHSS Black Report *Inequalities of Health* subsequently reproduced with comments (Townsend and Davidson, 1982). The Report points to inequalities in health as being a direct reflection of inequalities in occupational class during working life.

The views of elderly people

Most older people consider their health good. In Great Britain in 1988 40 per cent of the over 65s claimed that their health was 'good' and 37 per cent 'fairly good' (Table 6.1). There may be differences of opinion between their assessment of their health and that of doctors. Commenting on this Johnson argues that self-referred illness is only the tip of the iceberg and is likely to have reached a fairly advanced state before consultation with a doctor is considered necessary (Johnson, 1972). Increasing attention is being paid to measuring health status and various measures of function and disability, broader measures of health status and psychological well-being are included in an assessment of their use and validity (Bowling, 1991).

Because there is a stereotype of old age which promotes expectations of ill-health and decrepitude it is little wonder that old people refuse as long as possible to be labelled as sick. In the OPCS disability surveys, commenting on the lower prevalence estimates of limiting long-standing disability of the *GHS* compared with their survey, the authors say that: 'many elderly people do not think of themselves as having health problems or being disabled; they

Table 6.2   A comparison of chronic and acute sickness between the under and over 75s

	Great Britain 1988		
	65–75	75 or over	All ages
Chronic sickness – self-reported	60	68	33
limiting long-standing illness	40	53	19
restricted activity	15	20	12
Acute sickness – self-reported average number of restricted activity days per person p.a.	40	59	24

OPCS, *GHS*, *1988*, HMSO, 1990, Table 4.1 p.71, Table 4.19 p.79.

consider limitations of activities a normal consequence of old age' (Martin *et al.*, 1988, p. 21). In a study of over 90 year olds only 8 per cent rated themselves as either unfit or very unfit although only 7 per cent had no chronic conditions (Bury and Holme, 1991).

The very old and least mobile

In general there is an increase in ill health among the over 75s. In the 1988 *General Household Survey* 68 per cent of the over 75s reported that they suffered from a long standing illness compared with 60 per cent of the under 75s (Table 6.2). Table 6.2 also shows that limiting long-standing illness and average number of restricted activity days also rises with age. There is also a substantial difference over falls. Among women aged over 75 falls were the cause of three quarters (73 per cent) of all home accidents treated in hospital compared with 57 per cent for those 65 to 74 in GB in 1988 (CSO, 1991, p. 125). For men the comparable figures were 66 per cent for those over 75 and 39 per cent for those under 75. For eyesight and hearing there is a similar pattern with 29 per cent of the over 75s wearing glasses but still having difficulty with their eyesight compared with 17 per cent of those aged 65–74 (Table 6.3). Fifteen per cent of the over 75s had a hearing aid and 27 per cent did not wear an aid but still had difficulty hearing compared with 6 and 19 per

Table 6.3.   A comparison of eyesight and hearing between the under and over 75s

	Great Britain 1988		
	65–74	*75 or over*	*All 65 or over*
Wears glasses, still has difficulty with eyesight	17	29	22
Wears a hearing aid	6	15	10
Does not wear a hearing aid but has difficulty	19	27	22

OPCS, *GHS, 1986*, HMSO, 1989, Tables 12.11 and 12.13, pp. 191–2.

cent respectively. For cognitive function *The Health and Lifestyle Survey* in 1984–5 showed that, in general, older groups performed more poorly than younger groups, but age differences were reduced when differences in education were taken into account (Cox *et al.*, 1987).

Surveys show that the main causes of loss of mobility are arthritic and rheumatic conditions, followed by cardiac and pulmonary conditions (e.g. Hunt, 1978). Evidence about the least mobile is given in the study of disabled adults by OPCS. Figure 6.1 shows that the overall rate of disability rises with age, slowly at first then accelerating after 50 and rising very steeply after about 70. In the survey almost 70 per cent of disabled adults were aged 60 or over and nearly half were aged 70 or over. Among the most severely disabled adults the very elderly predominated.

Surveys also show that women are more likely than men to suffer impairment or disability in later life. For both chronic and acute sickness the 1988 *GHS* showed that there were higher rates for women than for men (OPCS, 1990). The OPCS disability surveys, which, unlike the *GHS*, included people in institutions found that for the over 75s the prevalence of disability, particularly severe disability, was higher among women than men. However, the study also showed that for the under 75s the prevalence of mild, and therefore overall, disability was slightly higher for men. Grundy suggests that possibly men of this age are more conscious of health limitations than women because of the effect on their ability to work (Grundy, 1991a).

What is 'normal' is a moot point. Does society distinguish

between some sort of 'norm' and older people's perceptions of what is normally acceptable? ACE, for example, took issue with the Minister of Health when the disability surveys were published and he implied that it was 'normal' for older people to accept higher levels of disability without remedial measures. Grimley Evans argues that there is at present no way of identifying those processes which constitute intrinsic ageing whose effects it might even be reasonable to designate as 'normal' (Evans, 1988, p. 45).

The previous OPCS study had measured impairment and handicap (Harris, 1971). Impairment was defined as 'lacking part or all of a limb, or having a defective limb, organ or mechanism of the body.' Handicap was the 'disadvantage or restriction of activity caused by the loss of functional ability.' The later survey, which was of adults and children between 1985 and 1988, decided to use disability as its concept. They defined this as 'a restriction or lack of ability to perform normal activities, which has resulted from the impairment of a structure or function of body or mind' (Martin *et al.*, 1988, p. xi). Based on 1985–8 disability surveys it is estimated by OPCS that there were just over 6 million people with one or more disabilities in Great Britain of whom 7 per cent lived in a communal establishment. Nearly 4 of the 6 million were estimated to be over the age of 60 years.

Use of services

Table 6.4 shows the use of health and other services by elderly people. The 1985 *GHS* shows that for all the services, except visits to the doctor's surgery and visits to a day centre, there is a steady increase in services the older the person. For all the health services women are greater users than men (OPCS, 1989, p. 210). Table 6.5 shows the increased use by very elderly people of the services of a district nurse, health visitor and chiropodist. There was little variation in the use of services between 1976 and 1985.

People living alone also make greater use of services. It should also be noted that although there are references to families and other carers in this chapter many elderly people live on their own and may have different kinds of problems in dealing with disabilities such as incontinence.

SOME RELATED HEALTH ISSUES

Some health problems faced by elderly people have attracted a good deal of multidisciplinary research and have a particular relevance to

Table 6.4. Use of health services by the under and over 75s

	Great Britain 1988		
	65–74	*75 or over*	*All ages*
Consultation with an NHS GP in the 14 days before interview: percentage consulting GP	16	20	14
Average number of NHS GP consultations per person p.a.	5	6	4
Percentage of persons who reported attending an outpatients or casualty department in a 3-month reference period	18	20	14
Average number of inpatient stays per 100 persons in a 12-month reference period	16	23	13
Average number of outpatient attendances per 100 persons p.a.	156	183	117
Percentage with inpatient stay	12	17	10

OPCS, *GHS, 1988*, HMSO, Tables 4.12–4.16, pp. 76–8.

social policy. Four of these are nutrition, incontinence, hypothermia and osteoporosis.

Nutrition

The health of individuals is clearly affected by what they eat. The early poverty studies (e.g. those by Rowntree) showed that many old people did not enjoy a diet which enabled them to remain healthy. More recent evidence suggests that this is now no longer the case.

Surveys in 1952 and 1962 indicated that the popular idea that many old people who live alone exist almost entirely on bread, butter, jam, biscuits and cups of sweetened tea was not substantiated. In 1972 *A Nutrition Survey of the Elderly* found that elderly people followed a dietary pattern that was similar to that of the general population except that they ate smaller quantities (DHSS, 1972). There was no evidence to suggest that those elderly people in the survey who ate a less good diet did so for economic reasons.

Table 6.5. Use of some health services in the month before interview

	Great Britain 1985 Percentage		
	65–74	75 or over	All 65 or over
District nurse	2	9	5
Health visitor	1	3	1
Chiropodist[1]	4	11	7

[1] Excluding private treatment.
OPCS, *GHS*, *1986*, HMSO, 1989, Table 12.40, p. 211.

There was little overt malnutrition and where it did occur the cause was usually an underlying medical condition rather than a poor diet. Nevertheless, some old people were malnourished. The researchers felt that elderly people at risk should be identified through regular visits by community nurses. Similar findings were reported in 1979 (DHSS, 1979). A study of the nutrition and wellbeing of elderly people in *Three Score Years . . . and Then?* by Davies rejected the simple approach to nutrition needs (Davies, 1981). She pointed out for instance, that the provision of meals on wheels will not automatically increase the food intake in those who are ill or neglecting their diet.

MacLennan argues for a variety of ways of identifying those at risk of subnutrition and points to the lack of evidence about the pros and cons of nutrient supplements and diet supplementation (Maclennan, 1986). Swift also points to the lack of knowledge about those at risk, and indeed about the prevalence of subnutrition (Swift, 1987). Scrutton suggests a role for social workers in advising older people about diets and for social services in the provision of meals (Scrutton, 1988). In 1990 a Working Group was set up by the DOH under the chairmanship of Professor Hodkinson to review the diet of elderly people. The Chairman was reported as believing that some of the main areas for consideration are the nutritional status of people in institutional care, bone disease, bowel disorders and nutritional assessment (DOH, 1990b, p. 46).

Nutrition for older people is an under-researched area. There is, for example little knowledge about the nutritional needs of older people compared with younger and the nutritional needs of different kinds of older people such as active, bedbound or terminally ill.

Incontinence

In 1980 it was estimated that urinary incontinence affected 11.6 per cent of women and 6.9 per cent of men over the age of 65 (Thomas *et al.*, 1980). It is now thought that numbers are higher. In one study faecal incontinence was found to affect 10 per cent of residents in local authority residential homes (Tobin, 1987). Often sufferers do not get assistance because society treats it as a taboo subject; sufferers themselves are reluctant to discuss this problem. But incontinence can prevent an old person from living an independent life. For instance it is sometimes laid down that no one who is incontinent can be accepted in sheltered housing. Unresolved problems related to caring for an incontinent person can also lead to stress on relatives and may be the determining factor in whether or not a family feels able to continue to care for an older person.

It is therefore important to identify the cause of the incontinence and to treat it or take other steps. There is need for careful diagnosis and then both medical and social factors to be taken into account. Practical considerations like steps to negotiate or the absence of a conveniently placed lavatory may suggest the need for adaptations to the home. Good practice by health authorities should include the availability of a continence advisor, provision for regular and adequate supplies of continence aids and reasonable access to a urodynamic unit. Although there is much more awareness by local authorities now (e.g. Norton, 1989), the fact that both they and health authorities have discretionary power to provide incontinence supplies, aids and services does not always help. There is wide variation in the provision of incontinence services by health authorities. It is hoped that DOH sponsored research will lead to recommendations which will reduce these variations.

Hypothermia

Unlike incontinence hypothermia is a subject which is discussed in public. Hypothermia means low body temperature. It is usually defined as the condition present when the deep body temperature falls below 35°C, or 95°F, but there is no sharp cut-off point at this temperature. There are two main causes: diseases and conditions in the body (such as a failure in the temperature-regulating system) and environmental factors such as cold winters and lack of heating.

Hypothermia is a dangerous condition with a high mortality rate. Information on the numbers of deaths with any mention of hypothermia on the death certificate, irrespective of whether it did or did not appear as the underlying cause of death, shows little change in numbers. There were 913 deaths in 1978 and 1,057 in 1985 in Great Britain (*Population Trends*, Summer, 1986, p. 2). Nearly all these deaths were of people aged 65 and over.

The importance of hypothermia as a medical condition seems to have been noted only comparatively recently. In the 1950s articles appeared in medical journals reporting hypothermia in babies and these were followed by accounts relating to old people. The British Medical Association (BMA) reviewed existing knowledge and the Royal College of Physicians undertook a screening survey. The Medical Research Council and the Centre for Environmental Studies then combined to undertake a joint research programme. The aim was to measure the body temperatures and the social and environmental conditions of a sample of old people and 1,020 were interviewed. The results can be found in Wicks, *Old and Cold* (Wicks, 1978). This study was replicated in the winter of 1990-1 at the Age Concern Institute of Gerontology. A review of the literature has been published (Salvage, 1991).

Although there are few deaths diagnosed as due to hypothermia there is considerable evidence that large numbers of people suffer from cold conditions and some die from them. For example the increase in deaths from coronary thrombosis occurs mainly 24-48 hours after a cold day. In Great Britain mortality statistics for elderly people show that a larger proportion die in winter compared with summer and this proportion increases with age (McManus, 1985). In countries with similar or colder winters, such as Sweden and Canada, numbers are spread more evenly throughout the year. This suggests that there are special factors at work in this country. Collins concludes that winter mortality may be due *both* to outdoor exposure and cold indoor temperatures – outdoor exposure being associated with deaths related to heart conditions and cold indoor climates being responsible for deaths related to respiratory conditions (Collins, 1989).

Many people lack adequate heating facilities in the home. The Hunt survey found that a high proportion of elderly people had no means of heating their bedroom, and that a majority of halls, passages and lavatories, and many kitchens were unheated. Although more widespread use of central heating would help, it is clear that other things are important. Wicks concluded that while specific policies such as using electric blankets and insulating housing would help a more general approach was needed. He emphasised the need for more small units of accommodation and housing specially built for older people and for a significant increase in pensions to enable them to meet heating bills. Gray *et al.* also stress the importance of training for all who have contact with elderly people especially home helps (Gray *et al.*, 1977). Kafetz advises general practitioners (GPs) that there should be prompt treatment of acute illness (visiting today and not tomorrow) and monitoring function (Kafetz, 1987). The new GP contract should help identify illnesses.

Osteoporosis

Osteoporosis, the loss of bone tissue resulting in the thinning and weakening of bones, is one of the most important age-related diseases (Riggs and Melton, 1988). Not only may osteoporosis contribute to fractures, including the hip, but it can also cause painful and disabling fracture of the wrist and spine. Described 'as the geriatric iceberg' (Leader *Care of the Elderly*, Oct. 1989, p. 207) and the 'silent epidemic' (Riggs and Melton, 1988, p. 129), prevention, especially attention to diet and exercise in early life, is recommended and the advantage of hormone replacement is also emphasised.

GROUPS WITH SPECIAL NEEDS

There are some groups of elderly people about whom there is particular concern. Five of these are those people who are dying, bereaved, mentally disordered, abused and those from ethnic minorities.

Dying elderly people

Over one-third of those who die do so in their own homes, and many of those who die elsewhere may have spent many months seriously ill at home before they went to hospital. Over half a million people die in Great Britain each year and a high proportion are in the upper age ranges.

The care of dying people is a major social challenge, not only for those faced with death but for those who attempt to provide support and help. Until recently there was little in medical or social work education about the care of the dying nor was there much public concern. Now the subject is more openly discussed. A pioneering study was that of Kübler-Ross who enunciated the likely responses from someone who is dying as denial, anger, bargaining, depression and acceptance (Kubler-Ross, 1970). Another study is Hinton's book *Dying* (Hinton, 1972). Hodkinson points out that the attitudes towards death of staff, patients and the community at large have a considerable bearing on terminal care: 'Thus doctors and nurses are at risk of being so geared to the philosophy of cure that death is regarded as a humiliating failure' (Hodkinson, 1975, p. 61).

In *Life Before Death* the last 12 months in the lives of 785 adults is described (Cartwright *et al.*, 1973). This study shows that relatives often struggle on with inadequate help from the professionals and community services. The message is for more and better co-ordinated services. A recent example of this is a conference on multidisciplinary aspects of terminal care. The subsequent publication is aptly called *A Safer Death* (Gilmore and Gilmore, 1988).

One of the pioneers in this country in care of the dying is Dr Cicely Saunders. Her approach, outlined in *The Management of Terminal Disease* is based on the control of pain, allaying the fear of a painful death, and a positive and caring approach to patients who are encouraged to feel that their lives are still worth living (Saunders, 1978). The hospice movement has grown rapidly in the last decade and some of the issues are outlined in *The Hospice Movement in Britain* (Taylor, 1983). Many people seem to equate 'terminally ill' and hospices with people in the final stages of cancer. Less attention seems to be paid to the needs of people dying from other causes. The NHS is paying more attention to terminal (palliative) care and in 1987 issued guidance (Circular (HC) 87/4 *Terminal Care*) and requested health authorities to undertake joint planning with the voluntary sector. (NB. Circulars are listed in full in the text but are not in the bibliography.) The National Association of Health Authorities (NAHA) also produced guidance *Care of the Dying: a guide for health authorities* (King Edward's Hospital Fund and NAHA, 1987). There has been a phenomenal growth in the provision of palliative care since 1980. The number of NHS patient units rose from 59 to 121, the total number of beds doubled and home care teams increased from 32 to 261 (DOH, 1990b).

Another aspect of dying is about the use of life-sustaining treatment for patients who are no longer able to consent to, or refuse, medical therapy. *The Living Will* is the Report of a Working Party on the current legal and medical practice (Kennedy, 1988). It examines the potential for competent individuals to make certain stipulations about their future health care. The report highlights the range of options available and calls for changes in current practice so that advance directives can be made for those who wish to use them.

The growing technological ability to 'save' life or to intervene also raises questions about euthanasia and the quality of life. The UK contribution to the World Assembly on Ageing stated: 'There is a small body of opinion which believes that euthanasia should be legalised. Most people believe that legalised euthanasia could expose very vulnerable people to undesirable pressures, and would not wish to see it made possible. The Government considers euthanasia unacceptable, and is firmly opposed to changing the law to allow it' (DHSS, 1982a, p. 11).

Bereaved elderly people

To bereave is defined as 'to rob of'. Elderly people are more likely than other age groups to be robbed of the life of someone close to them. Those who lose a partner or who see their contemporaries dying may feel grief, shock, anger and bitterness. In 1989 2.4 million women over the age of 65 were widows in England and Wales, whereas only 550,000 men were widowers (*Population Trends*, Winter 1990, p. 45).

The importance of understanding mourning and the need for skilled professional help is underlined by Parkes in his book *Bereavement* (1975) and by Pincus in *Death and the Family* (1974). A comprehensive book on the subject is *The Anatomy of Bereavement* by Raphael (1984). Older people may need counselling to face their own and others' dying, as do their families. It is also helpful to understand the ways in which death and bereavement are treated in different cultures, as Neuberger has demonstrated in *Caring for Dying People of Different Faiths* (Neuberger, 1987).

Mentally disordered elderly people

One of the most difficult situations facing families and professionals alike is in caring well for the mentally disordered elderly person. The term 'mentally disordered' is usually taken to cover both mentally ill and mentally handicapped people.

The World Health Organisation has suggested a broad definition of mental illness which covers all forms of illness in which psychological, emotional or behavioural disturbances are the predominating features. The DHSS have distinguished three main groups among elderly people with mental illness symptoms to whom the term 'psychogeriatric' is often loosely applied (DHSS Circular HM (72)71 *Services for Mental Illness Related to Old Age*, Oct. 1974). These are patients who entered hospitals for the mentally ill before modern methods of treatment were available and have grown old in them, elderly patients with functional mental illness and elderly people with dementia.

It is difficult to estimate the number of elderly people who are mentally ill, but 34 per cent of admissions to mental hospitals and units in England in 1986 were of people aged 65 and over (Taylor and Taylor, 1989, p. 15). The OPCS disability surveys showed that the prevalence of problems with intellectual functioning in Great Britain in 1985–8 was 40 per 1000 for people aged 60–74 and 152 for those aged 75 and over compared with 20 for those aged 16–59 (Martin *et al.*, 1988, p. 26).

Dementia involves the irreversible degeneration of brain tissue and resultant loss of intellectual function. There are two main types: cerebrovascular (or multi-infarct dementia), progressive brain damage often resulting from something like a mini-stroke, and neurodegenerative. The best known example of the latter is Alzheimer's disease. The prevalence of dementia increases with age. A rate of 4 to 5 per cent of people over the age of 65 is estimated (Taylor and Taylor, 1989, p. 13) and 20 per cent for people over the age of 80 (Roth and Wischik, 1985). Recent estimates are that about half a million people suffer from dementia in the United Kingdom but that the growth in the population aged 80 and over could increase this by 20 per cent in the early years of the next century (Taylor and Taylor, 1989, p. 11). One of the most encouraging developments in dementia has been the growth of academic interest in the subject (e.g. Arie, 1985 and 1988) including a multidisciplinary approach (e.g. *Danish Medical Bulletin*, 1985).

Much that has been written about mental disorder in old age has focused on dementia. Work done by Levin has shown that there is a heavy burden upon families supporting demented elderly people at home (Levin *et al.*, 1989 and Askham and Thompson, 1990). Over one-third of the supporters in the Levin study were so stressed as probably to be in need of psychiatric help themselves. Bergmann and Jacoby say that until scientific research provides a means of altering the prognosis of dementia fundamentally, the main focus has to be on maintaining the autonomy and viability of the elderly person for as long as possible (Bergmann and Jacoby, 1983). In the absence of the family, or when it collapses, homelike institutional settings in the community can substitute. Arie has argued that there are some patients, and he includes some with dementia, for whom institutional care is the only humane and proper answer (Arie, 1986). Norman, in *Severe Dementia: the provision of long-stay care*, looks at a number of establishments which aim to provide high quality specialist care (Norman, 1987).

Some of the symptoms of dementia are associated with other problems. For example, confusion, which may be the result of dehydration, adverse drug reactions or a chest infection.

Depression is another state which needs careful investigation to find out the causes which may or may not be due to physical symptoms. Murphy concludes that adverse life events, lifelong personality traits, and lack of self-esteem may also play a role but the relationship between social factors and genetic and biological ones needs further exploration (Murphy, 1986b). There is little evidence that elderly people are *per se* more vulnerable to depression than younger adults. Extreme depression may lead to suicide. Death rates from suicide increase with age but not so steeply as rates for other causes of death (Bulusu and Alderson, 1984). For females, the rates fall after the age of 70 but rise slightly for males.

Mentally handicapped people, now usually referred to as people with learning difficulties, have been defined as 'those whose intelligence in relation to their age is so far below average that they are incapable of assuming the kind of responsibilities accepted as normal' (Clegg, 1971). Numbers of people with learning difficulties are difficult to estimate.

The DHSS expect that the number of elderly people suffering from mental disorder will grow (DHSS, 1978a). This increase will have to be accompanied by careful planning so that families and services are prepared to meet the challenge. In the past the care of mentally disordered people has been mainly by the family and in institutions, often isolated from society. In the 1950s, however, a number of factors combined to emphasise the trend away from hospitals. There was dissatisfaction in many quarters about the effects of institutional care. There were also major developments in drug treatment allowing for symptoms of mentally ill patients to be controlled so that their behaviour became less disturbing. So the underlying trend was to community care. The aim of the Mental Health Act 1959 was to establish a comprehensive commmunity care service for mentally ill people who did not need hospital treatment.

In 1971 *Better Services for the Mentally Handicapped* (DHSS, 1971) explained why services needed to be extended and improved. It showed that there had been a large growth in numbers of elderly people in hospitals, but also that considerable numbers had been discharged: 'Many of these probably required residential rather than hospital care.'

In 1972 the DHSS, in a circular, *Services for Mental Illness Related to Old Age* (DHSS HM (72) 71), stressed the importance of assessment, defined the groups involved and examined their needs in turn. It advised that those needing hospital treatment were best treated in the psychiatric departments of district general hospitals. For the rest the emphasis was on rehabilitation with the use of day hospitals and, where necessary, residential care. The importance of co-ordination and joint planning with local authorities was stressed. The eventual closure of hospitals for the mentally ill was envisaged.

In 1975 the White Paper *Better Services for the Mentally Ill* (DHSS, 1975) recognised that adequate support facilities in the community had not generally become available owing to the limits on resources and increasing and competing demands for new developments. In 1978 *A Happier Old Age* acknowledged that places in some large mental hospitals were being reduced ahead of alternative provision in local hospitals (DHSS,1978a) and a DHSS National Development Group gave advice [doc 15]. In 1981 *Care in the Community* gave estimates of how many mentally ill and handicapped people could be returned to the community if services were available (DHSS, 1981c). In 1982 the Mental Health (Amendment) Act expanded the range and degree of safeguards for patients and set up the Mental Health Commission as a watchdog on the new legislation.

The Rising Tide in 1982 was an aptly named report by the NHS Health Advisory Service (HAS) which claimed that rising numbers and increased expectations meant that 'the flood is likely to over-whelm the entire health system' (HAS, 1982, p. 1). Particular emphasis was given to stressing that the problem was not just one for specialist psychiatric services. The difficulties of people attempting to care for elderly people at home, in private nursing homes or residential homes were acknowledged. The report called for extra resources and in 1983 an extra £6 million was given by the government to finance 30 demonstration projects in the community. The subsequent evaluation showed their value (Cambridge and Knapp, 1988).

The effect of changes in policy can be demonstrated by the fact that at the end of the 1950s about 40 per cent of NHS hospital beds were occupied by people suffering from mental illness. In 1986 the figure was 20 per cent (Taylor and Taylor, 1989, pp. 14–15). Mental illness outpatient attendances, on the other hand, have risen by 50 per cent in the last decade and there has been a significant rise in short-stay admissions and in numbers of consultants and nurses in the field of psychiatry (Taylor and Taylor, 1989, p. 15). The case for a comprehensive psychogeriatric service geared to the needs of elderly people and their carers has been forcibly put (Royal College of Physicians and the Royal College of Psychiatrists, 1989).

The emphasis on community care was endorsed in the Short report *Community Care* which called for a wide variety of facilities in the community and stressed that none of this would be cheap (House of Commons, 1985). A further influential document was the Audit Commission's *Making a Reality of Community Care* (Audit Commission, 1986). The House of Commons Social Services Committee advocated a range of policy changes in *Community Care: services for people with a mental handicap and people with a mental illness* (House of Commons, 1990b). These included the need for some form of 'asylum' service provision, adequate financial provision for community care to be transferred to local authorities from the Social Security budget, and the need to monitor the community care programme. The NHS and Community Care Act 1990 introduced a specific grant to local authorities for the development of social care services for people with a mental illness. Community care for mentally disordered people is discussed further in Chapter 8.

Elder abuse

A group who have received increasing attention are elderly people who are assaulted by families and other carers. First called 'Granny battering', it is now usually referred to as elder abuse. It took its place in the matters of concern taken up by journals in the 1980s and especially the media. Non-accidental injury to children has long been a subject researched and written about, but the identification of elderly people as objects of abuse is relatively new. Its discovery owes much to Mervyn Eastman, a social worker. In a survey of the literature it was concluded that despite concern expressed in this country over a period of almost fifteen years almost no systematic or reliable research has been carried out, in contrast to North America (McCreadie, 1991). There is no standard definition but abuse can include physical and psychological abuse, neglect and sometimes financial abuse. A distinct phenomenon is institutional abuse. Nothing is known in this country about the incidence of abuse.

Some guidelines have been produced for those working with elderly people (British Geriatrics Society, 1990).

Ethnic elders

The projected increase in numbers of ethnic minority elders has implications for health services. Little is known nationally about the specific ways in which health (and social services) are planning to meet the health and social care needs of this group (Tarpey, 1990). The provision of and need for separate special and mainstream care and the advantages and difficulties surrounding each of these three different forms of care are currently being researched in the Age Concern Institute of Gerontology.

TRENDS AND PRIORITIES IN HEALTH CARE

Health care

The growing interest by doctors from many different disciplines in the treatment of elderly people is illustrated by Arie's *Health Care of the Elderly* (Arie, 1981). Arie admits that 'very aged people get a poor deal from services; not all the services which we disburse, often enthusiastically and almost always expensively, have been shown to be effective' (Arie, 1981, pp.12–13). On the other hand, he points to the great advances made in treatment in some areas; for example, the growing clinical and epidemiological understanding of mental illness which is often treatable. On high technology intervention there does not seem to be evidence that elderly people are being denied treatment (see Tinker, 1990a). Less dramatic interventions like hip replacement and cataract operations can vastly improve quality of life but do not always receive high priority.

The development of geriatric medicine, defined by the British Geriatrics Society as: 'that branch of general medicine concerned with the clinical, rehabilitation, social and preventive aspects of illness and health in the elderly', has been rapid. The differing views about the pros and cons of an 'age-related' or 'integrated' service have been summarised by Hall (Hall, 1988).

Health promotion and prevention of ill health

'Current policy reflecting both modern medical practice and the wish of most elderly people to remain in their own home is to promote an active approach to treatment and rehabilitation' (DHSS, 1978a). This statement, taken from *A Happier Old Age*, is an indication of a positive approach towards the health of elderly people. *The Health of the Nation* was a consultative document published in 1991 by DOH to develop a health strategy for England (Sec. of St. for Health, 1991). A main objective was 'to focus as much on the promotion of good health and the prevention of disease as on the treatment, care and rehabilitation of those who fall ill or who need continual support' (Sec. of St. for Health, 1991, p. vii). It has, however, been criticised as putting too much emphasis on individual responsibility and less on wider issues such as poverty and housing.

To enable elderly people to remain healthy attention has to be given to prevention, detection and rehabilitation. Prevention has already been mentioned (Ch. 4) as an objective of many services. The pioneering work by Gray on the importance of paying attention to the old person's ability to function has been refreshingly practical (for example, Gray, 1987). Measures to prevent unfitness (e.g. encourage exercise: the motto is 'use it or lose it') and social problems are outlined. To get over these messages he favours a normal primary care consultation (because most elderly patients will contact the practice at some time during the year) rather than full-scale screening. The opportunity for that consultation is now given in the GP contract. From 1990 patients over the age of 75 must be offered a consultation and a domiciliary visit to see whether medical or other services are needed.

Detection to pick up early signs of illness is important because not all old people report their medical conditions. This can lead not only to serious illnesses being unnoticed in their early stages but also to failure to treat minor conditions which later can have a cumulative effect. Reliance on patient initiated contact with GPs has resulted in health problems remaining unrecognised until a crisis occurs but a screening programme can anticipate problems. In 1987 an Age Well campaign was set up by the Health Education Authority in collaboration with Age Concern England. It was designed to increase the expectations of good health among older people themselves and all those who come into contact with them, e.g. health professionals, carers and families. Practical examples of health promotion are given in *Promoting Health Among Elderly People* (Kalache *et al.*, 1988).

Recent research underlines the importance of rehabilitation, which is generally defined as the achievement of the optimum level

Table 6.6. Health and social services expenditure on elderly people in 1989–90

	£million gross, England		
	Expenditure on elderly people 1989–90	Expenditure on elderly people as % of expenditure on all age groups	Increase in real expenditure on elderly people 1979–80 to 1989–90
	£m	%	Ave % change pa
Hospital and community health services	7154	51.9	2.3
Family health services	1303	25.0	4.5
Personal social services and Income Support for private nursing home and residential care	2893	56.4	6.1
Total	11350	47.0	3.4

DOH, Economic Advisor's Office, 1991, Table 1.

of independence for the individual. Most experts agree that a successful outcome owes more to mental factors than to the degree or nature of the physical disability (Hodkinson, 1975). Good motivation may lead to recovery in the face of quite severe physical difficulties.

Expenditure

Costs of health services are greater for elderly people than other age groups. While people over the age of 65 represented 15.8 per cent of the population in England in 1989 (*Population Trends*, Winter 1990), Table 6.6 shows that expenditure on hospital and community health services for this group was 51.9 per cent and 25 per cent for family health services. Comparative annual costs of hospital and community health services and family health services per person in 1989–90 were:

- aged 16–44   £187
- aged 45–64   £306
- aged 65–74   £730
- aged 75–84   £1,409
- aged 85+   £2,407

(DOH, Economic Advisers' Office, 1991, Table 2).

One contributory factor to cost is that older people are more likely to spend longer in hospital. The mean length of stay in hospital in England and Wales in 1985 was 14.4 days for people aged 65–74 and 24.7 for those over 75 compared with an average for all ages of 10.7 (Bosanquet and Gray, 1989, p. 16).

When considering future expenditure it is clear that the projected increase in numbers of very elderly people means that extra resources will be needed just to maintain, let alone improve, standards. DOH economists estimate that expenditure on elderly people will need to increase by around 0.7 per cent over the next 10–15 years just to keep up with demographic change (DOH, Economic Advisers' Office, 1991).

In early cost benefit analyses of health there was a tendency to measure the output of intervention as the ability of patients to return to work and contribute to the economy. Cost effectiveness procedures now use the health state of patients as the value so that elderly people are not disadvantaged (DOH, Economic Advisers' Office, 1991).

Performance indicators and QALYS

The use of performance indicators arose from concern by the Public Accounts Committee in 1981, and subsequently by DHSS, about the monitoring of activities by health authorities (House of Commons, 1981). The purpose of the indicator is to provide health service managers with systematic information so that they can compare their performance with other areas. Criticisms of them have been on the grounds that they do not measure performance, that they do not compare like with like, that the data used is inaccurate and that, even if the indicators were accurate, there would be variations between districts because of random factors (Allen, 1987). Research has shown that, despite these criticisms, they did result in districts changing their performance; however they are blunt instruments and need to be supplemented by other means (Allen, 1987).

One measure which can help health authorities direct resources to areas which will derive most benefit is the QALY measure. QALY (quality-adjusted-life-years) is an estimation of expected life years gained from consumption of a health care procedure, in addition to a judgment on the quality of expected life years gained. It has been argued that QALYS are not an appropriate way of measuring quality of life of elderly people requiring long-term care, mainly because it is based on a scale (Rosser) which uses disability and distress as its main indicator and it has never been studied in people over the age of 60 (Donaldson *et al.*, 1988). Others have shown the dangers of relying on a single measure of the quality of life and question economic approaches (Baldwin *et al.*, 1990). (For a wider discussion about the quality of life of elderly people see Ch. 13.)

Medical audit is the systematic critical analysis of the quality of medical care, including the procedures used for diagnosis and treatment, the use of resources and the resulting outcome for patients. A Standing Medical Advisory Committee has recommended what the obligations of doctors are and how medical audit can be organised (DOH Standing Medical Advisory Committee, 1990).

THE DEVELOPMENT OF SERVICES

General

The origins of the NHS were described in Chapter 4. Specific general points relating to the development of services are now discussed. The development of services for people with mental disorder were described earlier in this chapter.

An early matter of concern was the cost of the service which in 1946 had been estimated a £110 million, but by 1951–2 had grown to £384 million. The Guillebaud Committee in their *Report of the Committee of Enquiry into the Cost of the NHS* had concluded that in practice there was no objective and attainable standard of adequacy in the health field, that there was no evidence of extravagant spending, and that in some cases (e.g. hospitals, capital expenditure) more money needed to be spent (MOH, 1956). For elderly people they drew heavily on a paper on costs prepared for them by Abel-Smith and Titmuss which concluded that: 'by-and-large, the older age groups were currently receiving a lower standard of service than the main body of consumers and that there were substantial areas of unmet need among the elderly' (MOH, 1956, p. 40). The Committee examined the pattern of care between the different parts of the NHS and laid down guidelines.

The Guillebaud Committee referred to a survey on chronic sick patients which was then being carried out and which was published in 1957. The Report was called *Survey of Services Available to the Chronic Sick and Elderly 1954–55* (MOH, 1957). The wide ranging conclusions of this survey covered both medical and other provision. In regard to the former the report indicated that the number of hospital beds for the chronic sick was sufficient in total but needed to be properly used and better distributed. Their recommendations about other provisions arose out of their conviction that 'the key to the problems stemming from an ageing population lies with preventive and domiciliary services' (MOH, 1957, p. 37).

The *Hospital Plan* 1962 (MOH, 1962) laid down standards for geriatric patients (1.4 beds per 1,000 total population) and it was visualised that the main hospital services would be brought together in district general hospitals (of 600–800 beds) designed to serve a population of 100,000–150,000. Although the plan was subsequently modified in 1966 many new hospitals were built and conditions for patients and staff greatly improved. More of these general hospitals had geriatric units providing treatment and rehabilitation so that the elderly people would not need long-term hospital care. More day hospitals were established.

In 1962 local authorities were asked to take part in a long-term planning exercise similar to that for the hospitals (MOH, 1963 and 1966). Wide variations were disclosed in what they planned to provide for health and welfare services.

The administration of the NHS had since its inception been the subject of much comment and criticism and it was reorganised in 1974. Then followed what Abel-Smith has called 'the lean years following reorganisation: 1974–8', with a shortage of resources and criticisms of the new tiered system of administration (Abel-Smith, 1978, p. 42). Geographical equity was one matter of concern: the Resource Allocation Working Party (RAWP) made suggestions for financial allocations to be based on criteria which included age and mortality (DHSS, 1976b). The question of priorities formed the subject of two consultative documents – *Priorities for Health and Personal Social Services in England* in 1976 (DHSS, 1976e) and *The Way Forward* in 1977 (DHSS, 1977). Both consultative documents visualised an expansion in community services, and advice by the

DHSS to local authorities and health authorities in 1979 acknowledged the growing pressure on services.

The Royal Commission on the NHS, which reported in 1979, had a great deal to say about the demands of elderly people on health and local authorities for the rest of this century (Royal Commission on the NHS, 1979). They agreed with current national priorities, including the emphasis on elderly people and community care for them [doc 16], but found that there were considerable practical difficulties to be overcome in shifting the resources from one patient or client group to another.

In 1982 the NHS was reorganised following the Health Service Act 1980. The main effect was to reduce the tiers of management from five to three.

A positive flood of documents came from DHSS in the early 1980s, most with community or care in the title and all concerned with two issues. One was the need to give priority to increasing and improving provision for elderly people and the other to promoting care at home rather than in institutions. These documents continued the theme of the mid-1970s following the concentration in the 1960s and early 1970s on hospital provision.

In February 1981 *Care in Action* was published (DHSS, 1981a). This was a handbook providing national guidance for health and personal social services. It stated that priority was to be given to four groups one of which was 'elderly people', especially the most vulnerable and frail (DHSS, 1981a, p. 20). Four objectives were given (DHSS, 1981a, p. 32). First, to 'strengthen the primary and community care services, together with neighbourhood and voluntary support, to enable elderly people to live at home.' Second, to 'encourage an active approach to treatment and rehabilitation to enable elderly people to return to the community from hospital wherever possible.' Third, to 'maintain capacity in the general acute sector to deal with the increasing number of elderly patients.' Fourth, to 'maintain an adequate provision for the minority of elderly people requiring long-term care in hospital or residential homes.' In December 1982 the Government stated that these priorities had not changed (DHSS, 1982b). *Care in Action* drew on material included in a *Report of a Study on Community Care* written by DHSS officials based on research and published in September 1981 (DHSS, 1981b). It concentrated on assessing whether there had been any shift away from long-term hospital or residential provision for those people whose needs put them on the boundary between institutional and non-institutional care and also the contribution of the voluntary sector to all forms of community care. Some interesting findings and expressions of doubt emerged. The authors found little shift from hospital and residential care for elderly people on the margins of institutional and community-based care and they noted that there may have been a tendency to underestimate the number of elderly people who will always require long-term residential care. There was an acknowledgment that 'community-based packages of care may not always be a less expensive or more effective alternative to hospital or residential provision, particularly for those living alone' (DHSS, 1981b, p. 3). They also made some salutary points about the voluntary sector, which they wanted strengthening, and included the warning that 'it is important not to assume that the amount of informal care can be limitlessly increased' (DHSS, 1981b, p. 5). Some of the general pointers to emerge from this study were that it may be necessary to shift NHS expenditure from hospital in-patient to community health services, that manpower constraints (e.g. a shortage of district nurses) may become as important as financial constraints, that social and demographic changes may reduce the number of people who have traditionally provided the mainstay of informal care and finally that demand for all community-based services was likely to continue to increase over the next decade.

Published simultaneously were two complementary studies on hospitals. *The Respective Roles of the General Acute and Geriatric Sectors in the Care of the Elderly Hospital Patient* indicated that an important area of concern was the impact on the acute sector of the shortfall in provision for elderly patients in departments of geriatric medicine (DHSS, 1981f). *The Report of a Study on the Acute Hospital Sector* also showed that between 1968 and 1978 most of the increase in activity rates throughout the acute sector were accounted for by services to elderly people (DHSS, 1981e). In between *Care in Action* and the three reports came (DHSS 1981d) the White Paper *Growing Older* (see p. 36) with its firm commitment to community care, but again with the warning that community services and families 'cannot be expected to provide a solution to every problem and should not normally be used to support people who can only properly be cared for elsewhere' (DHSS, 1981d, p. 32).

Then in July 1981 *Care in the Community* was published (DHSS, 1981c). This was subtitled 'A consultative document on moving resources for care in England' and it was concerned with how patients, 'together with resources for their care', may be transferred from the NHS to the personal social services in addition to existing joint finance arrangements. As a subsequent DHSS note explained (*Explanatory Notes on Care in the Community* (DHSS, 1983b), the policy thrust was different from before:

The joint finance arrangements have assisted the development of community care and in doing so have contributed to the important objective of enabling people to *remain* in the community instead of having to be taken into hospital. But the *Care in the Community* initiative has a different and quite specific aim: to help long-stay hospital patients unnecessarily kept in hospital to *return* to the community where this will be best for them and is what they and their families prefer. (DHSS, 1983b, p. 1)

While no estimate could be given of numbers of elderly people who might be more suitably cared for by the personal social services, it was stated that each patient cost the NHS on average about £8,000 in 1979–80.

A number of suggestions were put forward including the transfer of hospital buildings, lump-sum or annual payment, central transfer of funds and extending joint finance arrangements. In a subsequent DHSS circular in March 1983 *Health Service Development: care in the community and joint finance* (DHSS, 1983 HC (83)6 and LAC (83)5) District Health Authorities were empowered to offer lump-sum payments or continuing grants to local authorities or voluntary organisations for people moving from hospital into community care. In addition joint financing was extended from 7 to 13 years. A further decision was the extension of joint financing to housing departments and housing associations. This needed legislation and was part of the Health and Social Security Adjudications Act 1981. A programme of pilot projects was started.

It is clear that joint financing has provided a welcome additional source of funds for elderly people. Money allocated for joint finance rose from £8 million in 1976–7 to £105 million in 1985–6 (National Audit Office, 1987). About 40 per cent of this money was spent on services for elderly people in 1981 (DHSS, 1981c). While attempts have been made to change policies and to direct resources away from hospital to health services in the community an analysis of costings shows that there has actually been very little variation in percentages spent (DHSS, 1983c). In England in 1974–5 hospital services absorbed 63.1 per cent of health service expenditure and in 1981–2 62.8 per cent. The National Audit Office noted that there had been a rise in the proportion of joint finance funds being spent on NHS schemes. This is probably because of the reluctance of local authorities to take up joint finance (NAO, 1987).

But a simple shift of resources away from hospital care may not always be in the best interests of elderly people. More advanced and safer anaesthetic procedures, together with more refined surgical techniques, have enabled surgical treatment to be given to patients who would previously have been considered too frail for major surgery.

In 1983 a Management Inquiry Team chaired by (Sir) Roy Griffiths reported (Griffiths, 1983). The team's view was that a small, strong management body was needed at the centre and that responsibility should be passed down the line as far as possible. They recommended a Health Services Supervisory Board at the centre to decide overall objectives and budgets, an NHS Management Board to run the Health Service and, at Regional and District Health level managers to take charge of services. At District level each Unit was to have its own manager too. In 1984 the new system was set up and in 1985 most managers were in post. Aimed mainly at hospitals the new system seemed torn between the political imperatives of the NHS and the principles of business management and between the new managerial values and the caring values necessary for the health needs of the population (Leathard, 1990).

In 1986 and 1987 a consultation paper and then proposals for changes in primary health care were published by the government and these are discussed in the next section.

In 1989 the government's proposals for a review of the NHS were published in a White Paper *Working for Patients* (Sec. of St. for Health *et al.*, 1989a). The objective was to give patients better health care and greater choice of services and to give greater satisfaction and rewards for those working in the NHS. It was stated that the founding principles of an NHS open to all, regardless of income, financed mainly out of taxation and generally without charges at the point of service would remain.

On organisation a new Policy Board was to replace the Supervisory Board and a new Management Executive was to replace the NHS Management Board. There was to be delegation of power and responsibility as far as possible. The District Health Authority (DHA) was to have an enhanced purchasing role and would enter into contracts or agreements with those hospital and community health units which could best provide high quality, value for money services. A key principle was the separation of the responsibility for managing services and for purchasing those services. The DHAs were to assess the health needs of the population, decide the pattern of service provision, appraise service options, choose between providers and place contracts, monitor the contracted services and control expenditure within the District. A central feature was that hospitals and units would be funded for work they actually did, i.e. the money would follow the patient.

Service providers would include the District's directly managed hospitals and units, those from other Districts or the private sector, and the proposed NHS Trusts. The latter were to have greater freedom than directly managed hospitals, for instance to determine the pay and conditions of their staff, borrow money and acquire, own and dispose of assets. They were to earn revenue for the services they provided through contracts with health authorities, GP practices with their own budgets, private patients and insurance companies. Another change proposed was to make Family Practitioner Committees accountable to Regional Health Authorities and to rename them Family Health Services Authorities (FHSA). Other changes were planned for GPs who could apply to manage their own general practice funds.

The proposals were made law in the National Health Service and Community Care Act, 1990 (Ham, 1991) (Figure 6.2). Critics point to the upheaval of yet another reorganisation, the danger of treating health as a business and not a service, the emphasis on management and the encouragement of private provision, all of which may lead to a two-tier service.

Primary health care

General practitioners (GPs) play a crucial role in maintaining the health of older people but they may not always take a positive approach. Elderly people account for about 20 per cent of all general practice consultations and are likely to need more home visits than average. Two-thirds of consultations with older people take place at home. This may be partly due to difficulty in getting to a surgery because of lack of transport. A number of different developments have taken place since the early days of the NHS which have affected elderly people.

The number of patients per doctor has dropped from 2,250 in 1961 to 1,910 in 1989 (CSO, 1991, p. 129). There has been a shift away from single-doctor practices to group practices and health centres. These make it possible to experiment with different methods of providing primary health care, and they can also house a wide range of services, such as consultant out-patient clinics and diagnostic and paramedical services. For elderly people their advantage is

Figure 6.2. The organisation of the National Health Service, 1991

PARLIAMENT

SECRETARY OF STATE FOR HEALTH

DEPARTMENT OF HEALTH
Function Make policy, issue advice to authorities, allocate resources, monitor the performance of authorities and hold them to account

NHS POLICY BOARD
Chaired and appointed by Sec. of State for Health
Function: Determine strategy, objectives and NHS finances

NHS MANAGEMENT EXECUTIVE
Chaired by Chief Executive appointed by Sec. of State for Health
Function Responsible for all operational matters within the strategy of objecteves established by the Policy Board

REGIONAL HEALTH AUTHORITIES
SPECIAL HEALTH AUTHORITIES   NHS TRUSTS
Chairman appointed by Sec. of State for Health
Function Plan the development of services within the context of national guidelines, allocate resources to DHAs, FHAs and GP fund-holders, monitor the performance of DHAs and FHAs and hold them to account

DISTRICT HEALTH AUTHORITIES (DHA)	COMMUNITY HEALTH COUNCILS	FAMILY HEALTH SERVICES AUTHORITIES (FHSA)
Chairman appointed by Sec. of State for Health *Function* Ensure health needs of population are met, purchase services for their residents, manage units which remain under their control, public health	*Chairman* appointed by Regional Health Authority *Function* Represent community interests to health authorities	*Chairman* appointed by Sec. of State for Health *Chief Executive* to be appointed by Chairman and lay members *Function* Manage the contracts of family practitioners, assess the population's need for health care, plan services to meet these needs, manage GP development funds

UNITS
General Manager
appointed by DHA
Function day-to-day
management of service

This Figure draws on information in Ham, C., *The New National Health Service*, Radcliffe Medical Press, 1991.

that they are more likely to be purpose-built premises which are more comfortable and have better facilities, and it is more likely that a range of both medical and non-medical staff are employed. The elderly person may therefore be able to see a nurse for dressings and not join the queue to see the doctor. Home nurses also do much of value in visiting the elderly people at home and make follow-up visits on a regular basis. However, there are disadvantages. The grouping of doctors in one building inevitably means that it is less likely that elderly people will have their own GP just 'round the corner'. A group or health centre practice is also likely to run an appointments system, although there may be an open surgery as well. A rigid appointments system may cause problems for elderly people who are less likely to be on the telephone than the rest of the population and who may just 'turn up' at the surgery. Elderly people may also feel that they get a more personal service from a doctor practising alone whom they will see on every occasion except when he or she is ill or on holiday. Some single-handed doctors are, however, in poor, lock-up premises in inner city areas and may not be as accessible as a group practice.

Another development has been the growth in the number of staff other than doctors who are involved in the primary health care team. In 1980 over 80 per cent of district nurses and health visitors worked with GPs and their patients. It is not known how many social workers are members of primary health care teams, but progress has been slower, possibly due to a different approach to patients between the two professions and some mutual distrust. The importance of receptionists and secretaries is also being increasingly recognised for they can act as 'gatekeepers' – that is, be a help or a barrier to contact between the elderly patient and the doctor. In a thoughtful review of the primary health care team two experts claim that there is a general growth in awareness of the particular needs of elderly people in recent years despite the multiple and often complex problems (Freer and Williams, 1988).

In 1986 the government published *Primary Health Care: an agenda for discussion* (Sec. of St. for Social Services *et al.*, 1986). As a result of discussions *Promoting Better Health: the government's programme for improving primary health care* came out in 1987 (Sec. of St. for Social Services *et al*,. 1987). The aim was to shift the emphasis from the treatment of illness to the promotion of health and the prevention of disease (see also Ch. 4 on *The Health of the Nation*, Sec. of St. for Health, 1991). One of the ways this was to be achieved was by giving incentives to GPs, proposing help with premises and ensuring that patients got a wider choice of doctors and more information about them. Large GP practices (those with over 11,000 patients) could apply for their own budgets to cover certain diagnostic, outpatient, in-patient and day care costs together with practice team staff costs, improvement to practice premises and prescribing costs. Other GPs would have a drugs budget set by the FHSA. In response to criticisms that GPs would not want to take on elderly people or would be reluctant to prescribe expensive drugs the Minister said that there was no question of GPs having to stop treating their patients but, if they exceeded their budget they would have to justify this (Kenneth Clarke, 9.3.89). As noted before, patients aged 75 years and over must be offered a consultation and domiciliary visit by the GP to assess whether personal medical services are needed.

The new GP contract, which came into force in April 1991 following the NHS and Community Care Act 1990, implemented these proposals.

The structure of the NHS in 1991 is given in Figure 6.2.

Community and other services

Community services include community nursing, occupational and speech therapy, physiotherapy and pharmaceutical, ophthalmic, chiropody and dental services.

Community nurses include district nurses, health visitors, community psychiatric nurses, school nurses and their support staff of registered and enrolled nurses and nursing auxiliaries.

District nurses, many of whom work in group practices or health centres, are state registered nurses who provide care for people in their own homes. In some areas this extends to a night nursing service. In 1986–7 in England 30 per cent of the district nursing budget went on the age group 65–74 and 45 per cent to the over 75s (Bosanquet and Gray, 1989, p. 31). There were 5.3 district nurses per 1000 population of the over 75s in 1985 in England which was virtually the same as 1980 (National Audit Office, 1987, p. 32). Expenditure on district nurses rose by £50 million in England between 1976–7 and 1984–5 (National Audit Office, 1987, p. 44).

Health visitors are nurses with additional training, who are concerned with the promotion of health and the prevention of ill health. They usually work in an advisory supportive role rather than in a nursing capacity. In 1986–7 in England 3 per cent of their time was spent with the 65–74 age group and 7 per cent with the over 75s (Bosanquet and Gray, 1989, p. 31).

The Cumberlege Report in 1986 was about community nursing (Cumberlege, 1986). The Review Team, chaired by Julia Cumberlege, were asked by DHSS to study the health services provided outside hospitals and to report on how resources could be used more effectively. Their major recommendation was that nurses outside hospitals should come under a neighbourhood nursing service, which would plan, organise and provide community nursing services, and that subsidies to GPs enabling them to employ staff to perform nursing duties should be phased out. The Government's response in 1987 was that: 'there is no single right way of organising services and the decision about what is appropriate in different localities remains one for the Health Authority concerned' (Sec. of St. for Social Services *et al.*, 1987, p 41). The government also produced *A Strategy for Nursing* in April 1989 which set 44 targets for action related to practice, manpower, education and leadership (DOH, 1989c).

An expansion of the role of district nurses and health visitors had been recommended by the Royal Commission on the NHS and this was also a theme of the Cumberlege Report which included the adoption of nurse practitioners into primary health care. The eventual merging of GP practice nurses with community nursing services was predicted by DOH's chief nursing officer (*Health Service Journal*, 8.11.90). Nurse prescribing was accepted in principle by the Government but legislation was needed (Virginia Bottomley, *Hansard* 23.1.91, vol. 184, no. 41, col. 220).

The Cumberlege Report included a useful checklist of ways of monitoring and improving community nursing services (Cumberlege, 1986, p. 44). Stilwell discusses the demarcation between nurses and doctors and highlights the role of nurses as health educators (Stilwell, 1986).

Another invaluable service is *occupational therapy* (OT). This is usually arranged through a hospital, but many local authorities have occupational therapy services associated with the provision of aids and appliances. Occupational therapists now play an important role in assessment of levels of independence, maintenance of these levels and of rehabilitation, as well as providing advice on, and arranging for, aids and adaptations. Although numbers of OTs have grown rapidly in recent years there has also been a serious drain of qualified staff. Shortages are widespread as demand for their services grows.

Speech therapy is another profession which is increasingly being regarded as one with a contribution to make to the wellbeing of elderly people. Speech therapists are concerned with communication and speech problems.

Physiotherapists usually work in a hospital rehabilitation unit, but are sometimes available to treat a patient at home. Their main concern is with mobility. They play a crucial role in the assessment, rehabilitation and treatment of illness and conditions that affect elderly people (Wagstaff and Coakley, 1988).

For *pharmaceutical services* two matters are of particular concern – access to the service and the role of the pharmacist. Both these were considered by the Royal Commission on the NHS (1979). They found that while few people experienced difficulty in getting a prescription dispensed there were some problems in rural areas. Problems have subsequently been reported in other areas. The role of the pharmacist has traditionally been to dispense medicine on the prescription of doctors. The Royal Commission on the NHS found that this role had expanded and that the pharmacist was now regarded as a main source of advice in relation to minor ailments. An extended use of the pharmacist's skills was also recommended by the Nuffield report (Nuffield Foundation, 1986) and the White Paper, *Promoting Better Health* (Sec. of St. for Social Services, 1987).

Many elderly people have eye problems and these increase with age (Weale, 1989). They may be dealt with under the NHS by hospitals or by the general *ophthalmic service*, which provides sight-testing and the supply, replacement and repair of spectacles. A particular need, however, of many old people is for a domiciliary consultation.

National surveys have confirmed that one of the greatest unmet needs of elderly people is *chiropody*. Foot conditions affect mobility inside and outside the home. A detailed survey which investigated foot problems and treatment among elderly people found that one-quarter reported severe or moderate pain or discomfort with their feet and almost half should have been referred to a chiropodist (Cartwright and Henderson, 1986). The study recommended a doubling of current facilities, a screening service for the over 65s and a foot care clinic at health centres employing better trained foot care assistants. Quite apart from medical conditions which need treatment cutting toenails can present major difficulties (Hunt, 1978). The importance of this service has also been emphasised by researchers.

Dental services are also important to elderly people. In 1985 nearly three-fifths of people between 65 and 74 and four-fifths of the over 75s in England and Wales had no natural teeth (Sec. of St. for Social Services *et al.*, 1987, p. 26). There is evidence, too, of poor dental health among elderly people. The Royal Commission on the NHS noted that many elderly patients need special dental care (Royal Commission, 1979, p. 118). In general there is a lack of awareness of regular dental care for older people both with and without their own teeth, and of the relationships between dental health and comfort and nutritional wellbeing.

Hospital services

Very few old people (2.5 per cent) are in hospital at any one time, but they occupied 43 per cent of all acute beds in 1985 and hospital admission rates increase significantly with age (OPCS, 1987). The effect on hospitals of the increasing number of very old people in the next 20–25 years will be marked.

Elderly people now go either to geriatric hospitals (some of which were formerly workhouses, though some are modern), to psychiatric hospitals or to general medical or geriatric or specialty wards (such as orthopaedics) in acute types of hospitals. One of the objectives of policy has been to bring the three types of hospital together. This has been for a number of reasons; not least to even up standards and to bring the first two types of hospital into the mainstream of modern medicine. The development of geriatrics – which is the study and treatment of diseases common to old age – as a medical speciality also has a bearing on the service provided. The Royal Commission on the NHS felt that the development of geriatrics had in many places enhanced the quality of care of elderly people but that it had also influenced some physicians to take less interest in elderly people and to look to geriatricians excessively for their care (Royal Commission, 1979, p. 216).

Another development has been connected with maintaining elderly people in their own home while at the same time providing them with hospital treatment. This can often relieve the pressures on a family who are looking after a frail elderly person. It can be achieved through short-term care in hospitals, for example admitting an old person for a specified period on a regular basis, or through day hospitals where treatment is given on certain days to patients who continue to live at home.

There is general agreement that conditions for elderly people in hospitals have improved greatly. New buildings, more patients being nursed in wards of acute hospitals and growing medical interest in old age have all contributed to this improvement. Nevertheless, there are still some problems and these are mainly to do with buildings, staff and lack of suitable accommodation for patients who should be discharged. The problem of old buildings and the lack of small community hospitals for people who do not need the facilities of the district general hospital is still acute. Staff problems are related to shortages, lack of trained personnel and negative attitudes towards the benefits of working with older people. Redfern, for example, explains reasons why nurses choose not to work with elderly patients (Redfern, 1989).

A further dilemma is 'bed-blocking' which comes about when a patient cannot be discharged from hospital because no suitable accommodation is available (see Victor, 1990). The development of other forms of housing such as very sheltered housing (see Ch. 7) and NHS nursing homes is helpful but there is only limited provision of either (Tinker, 1989b and Bond *et al.*, 1989). An evaluation of the first three experimental NHS nursing homes found that residents were 'not disadvantaged in terms of outcomes; this form of care was preferred by both residents and their relatives; and it was no more expensive than continuing care provided in NHS hospitals' (Bond *et al.*, 1989, p. 3).

Private health care

Private medical insurance was taken out by over 5.3 million people in the UK in 1987. In the 1986 *GHS* only 11 per cent of policy holders in GB were over the age of 65 (OPCS, 1989, p. 157). The number of NHS beds authorised for private inpatients' care dropped from 4,400 in 1971 to 3,000 in 1988–9 but the numbers of private nursing homes, hospitals and clinics, which older people are likely to use, went up from 25,000 to 94,500 (CSO, 1991, p. 128). It seems unlikely that elderly people will contribute much more to the costs of their health care over the next 10 to 15 years (DOH, Economic Advisors' Office, 1991). Tax relief on private health insurance for elderly people, introduced from April 1990, may encourage some increase in the number of policy-holders; but premiums for elderly people are high, such that only a minority are likely to be able to afford them, and conditions requiring long-term care, often the most costly conditions, are in any event generally excluded from coverage (DOH, Economic Advisors' Office, 1991, p. 6).

COLLABORATION BETWEEN SERVICES

Teamwork and co-ordination within the NHS

It is vital that there is co-operation between the various parts of the NHS. A few examples demonstrate the need for co-operation. When an elderly person is referred to hospital the latter must be made aware of all the relevant medical and social circumstances which only the GP will know. When the patient is discharged the primary health care team needs to be alerted in good time and advised what, if any, treatment is needed. Those working in community nursing and other services also need to be kept in the picture and the development of primary health care teams should aid this.

Links between health and other services

Links between health and other services are crucial in a number of situations. For example when elderly people are discharged from hospital they probably need the support of some of the domiciliary services. Equally there can be occasions when an elderly person is incapable of remaining either at home or in residential care and the hospital is unwilling or unable to admit them. The closure of long-stay hospitals without adequate community provision is a matter of deep concern.

After the reorganisation of the NHS in 1974 the health of elderly people became the responsibility of the NHS and welfare that of local authority social services departments. The latter took the responsibility for the medical social workers employed in hospitals and certain other services. The importance of housing has never been fully recognised (see Ch. 7).

The new local and health authorities were required to set up joint consultative committees, made up of members from both authorities, to advise on arrangements for collaboration and the planning and operation of services of common concern. Authorities were recommended to set up joint care planning teams, one of whose tasks was to plan and co-ordinate for groups like elderly people. Joint finance, which was introduced in 1977 (DHSS, *Joint Care Planning: health and local authorities* Circular HC(77) 17/LAC(77) 10, 1977), has helped this co-operation (see earlier section). A working party representing Local Authority Associations and the National Association of Health Authorities with full participation from DHSS produced a report *Progress in Partnership* (DHSS, 1985). But, as Westland commented, joint planning requires at least two willing parties and this cannot be achieved by legislation (Westland, 1986). Later developments are discussed in Chapter 8.

INTRODUCTION

Any discussion about housing for elderly people should have as its starting point the fact that most of them live in homes of their own and not in any form of residential care. There has been little change since 1948. Approximately 90 per cent live in ordinary accommodation either owned by themselves or rented, 5 per cent live in their own home in sheltered housing and 5 per cent live in some form of institutional care – mainly old people's homes or hospitals. Exact numbers are difficult to obtain. DOH statistics on residential care, nursing home care and long stay hospital care suggest that 5 per cent in institutional care is a reasonable estimate.

Adequate housing is of importance to elderly people in many ways. Such features as the absence of stairs and the presence of an indoor lavatory may enable even a very frail person to continue living independently. Warmth, too, is particularly necessary for less active people. Familiar surroundings and nearness to shops, post office, pub and church also contribute to their ability to live alone. What is shown more clearly than anything else by surveys is the desire of elderly people to be able to live in the way they want in their own home. The psychological aspects of home are also increasingly being recognised (Sixsmith, 1988). At the same time community physicians have been pointing to the benefits of the physical and mental activity involved in housework, shopping and generally caring for themselves. Those who have been concerned with the financial aspects of old age, such as the Phillips Committee in 1954, have stressed the need for suitable housing on the grounds of both social happiness and finance (Chancellor of the Exchequer, 1954).

Many old people, however, live in less than desirable housing and some groups have particular problems. There is evidence, too, that some people remain in residential care only because alternative accommodation is lacking (Wagner, 1988b).

THE DEVELOPMENT OF POLICIES

Policies for elderly people

There has been remarkable consistency in policies for housing elderly people irrespective of which political party has been in power. Advice from central government, given mainly in circulars, has emphasised the need to provide small units of accommodation, to allow elderly people to maintain independent lives in their own homes and make movement from larger to smaller dwellings easier. Other points made have been the importance of siting dwellings near amenities and, between 1944 and the early 1980s, the value of grouping accommodation, usually referred to as sheltered housing, with communal facilities and a warden [doc 17]. Another piece of advice regularly given is the need for effective co-operation between all the authorities and departments concerned.

In 1956 the Ministry of Housing decided to find out whether old people were receiving a reasonable share of the accommodation provided and whether this was of the kind best suited to their physical needs and financial circumstances (Circular 32/56, *The Housing of Old People*). The following year advice was given (Circular 18/57, *Housing of Old People*) which stressed the need for adequate provision of small dwellings and a sympathetic and an efficient system for moving tenants from larger to smaller homes. Observations were made about the success of local authority and housing association schemes for accommodating less active elderly people in bedsitters or flatlets in converted large houses where some shared facilities could be provided. Handbooks were then issued (*Flatlets for Old People* and *More Flatlets for Old People*, Ministry of Housing, 1958 and 1960) illustrating sheltered housing schemes and the hope was expressed that councils would consider carrying out such schemes. In 1961 general advice was given in a joint MHLG/ Ministry of Health (MOH) circular, *Services for Old People* (Circular 10/61) [doc 18].

The ministry then became involved in an interesting experiment in which they built (for Stevenage Development Corporation) a prototype sheltered housing scheme and monitored reactions to it. The results were published in three MHLG Design Bulletins (No.1,

Some Aspects of Designing for Old People in 1962, No.2, *Grouped Flatlets for Old People* in 1962 and No.11, *Old People's Flatlets in Stevenage* in 1966).

The following year Circular 36/67, MHLG, *Housing Standards, Costs and Subsidies*, established what have become known as the Parker Morris Standards (these were minimum standards of design and construction). Then in 1969 the principal circular (MHLG/Welsh Office (WO), *Housing Standards and Costs: accommodation specially designed for old people*, Circular MHLG 82/69, WO 84/69) came out [doc 19]. In that circular two types of accommodation were declared eligible for subsidy. Category 1 was self-contained dwellings for old people who were more active. The standard was Parker Morris with some additional features. Limited communal facilities could be provided and so could a warden. Category 2 accommodation, for less active elderly people, was smaller than Parker Morris standards and comprised grouped flatlets with full communal facilities and a warden. The circular was withdrawn in the 1980s (but still technically lies on the table of the House of Commons) and is no longer a standard to be adhered to by local authorities. However, housing associations still have design guidance relating to these categories of accommodation.

As a preliminary to a new circular *Housing for Old People: a consultation paper* was issued in 1976 (DOE, DHSS, WO, 1976). This particularly stressed the importance of widening the choice of accommodation available for the elderly.

General housing policies

General housing policies have also had an effect on provision, for example the 1963 White Paper, *Housing*, laid great stress on new building and in particular of small units for elderly people (MHLG, 1963). A White Paper, *The Housing Programme 1965 to 1970*, in 1965 set out the first stage in formulating a national housing plan but stated that more needed to be known about the needs of elderly people (MHLG, WO, 1965). Meanwhile a committee was set up by the MHLG to review the practice of authorities in allocating tenancies. Their report, *Council Housing Purposes, Procedures and Priorities* (the Cullingworth Committee), appeared in 1969 (MHLG, 1969). Concern about the need for more and better homes led to another White Paper (in 1973), *Widening the Choice: the next steps in housing*, which expressed disquiet about the many people who had no choice at all (DOE, WO, 1973a). When considering the way in which provision could be made the government proposed a range of measures to expand both owner-occupation and the role of housing associations. However, the view was expressed that local authorities had a special responsibility for groups who had 'general needs or suffer from special disadvantages'. Included among these were elderly people. A further White Paper, *Better Homes: the next priorities*, in 1973 proposed a range of measures to tackle the worst housing conditions and in particular outlined changes in the improvement grants system (DOE, WO, 1973b). The setting up of housing action areas and general improvement areas, recommended in the White Paper, took place after the Housing Act 1974 which also expanded the role of the Housing Corporation. The importance of these changes was the attempt to help urban areas with poor property (where incidentally many elderly people lived) and to expand the role of housing associations (which were fast becoming major providers of accommodation for elderly people). The Rent Act 1974 gave security of tenure to tenants in furnished accommodation, many of whom were elderly.

The growth in small households, including elderly people, was one of the reasons for *Housing Needs and Action* (DOE Circular 24/75) in 1975 which stressed the need for more small accommodation and showed how better use could be made of existing dwellings. The latter theme was expanded in 1977 in *Better Use of Vacant and Under-Occupied Housing* (DOE Circular 76/77) which sought to bring into full use empty and under-occupied dwellings, whether or not they belonged to the local authority, and to ensure that the accommodation people occupied accurately reflected their housing requirements. In the same year the new system for deciding on capital allocations to local authorities by central government was put forward by the DOE in *Housing Strategies and Investment Programmes* (DOE Circular 63/77). In the annual strategy statement which local authorities were requested to complete, they were asked to include any measures 'to meet the housing requirements of groups with special needs, for example, the aged and disabled'.

In 1977 a Consultative Document, *Housing Policy*, was published (DOE, 1977). Previous policies for elderly people were endorsed, but the proposed abolition of local authority residential qualifications was stressed as was the need for co-operation between authorities.

Of major importance was the Housing Act 1980 which affected people in all tenures. The right-to-buy provisions enabled council (and some housing association) tenants to buy their homes at a discount from the local authority or housing association. Over one million dwellings have now been sold (Whitehead, 1989). Purpose-built or adapted accommodation was specifically excluded, but this covered only a small proportion of the stock. Opponents of the Act argued that council housing would become a residual service and that some families would lend or give their parents the money so that they could eventually sell the home at a profit or use it as a second home.

Elderly people gained from some of the other provisions of the Act such as security of tenure, greater freedom over conditions (e.g. the right to take in lodgers) and the statutory duty of authorities to give information about allocations and to consult tenants. The Act also widened the grant system so that more owner occupiers became eligible for improvement and repair grants and grants were made more flexible.

The mid and late 1980s saw the publication of a number of important reports, surveys and also legislation relevant to the housing needs of elderly people. The Housing Act 1984 extended the right to buy. The 1985 Green Paper on home improvement policies stressed the importance of targeting grants to those in need partly to help elderly owner-occupiers (DOE, 1985). The basic thrust of policy in the early 1980s concentrated on controlling public sector spending and providing incentives for privatisation (White-head, 1989). Neither of these measures were particularly helpful, probably the reverse, to older people.

In 1985 the influential report of *An Inquiry into British Housing*, chaired by the Duke of Edinburgh, declared that there were deep-seated problems in housing which were the product of policies going back over several decades (National Federation of Housing Associations, 1985). The authors stated that old and poor owner-occupiers emerged as a clear target for assistance and encouragement.

The 1987 White Paper, *Housing: the government's proposals*, set out the government's proposals. These were to:

- reverse the decline of rented housing and improve its quality
- give council tenants the right to transfer to other landlords if they choose to do so
- target money more accurately on the most acute problems
- continue to encourage the growth of home ownership.

These led to the 1988 Housing Act.

The main thrust of policy since 1988 has been designed to limit the role of local authorities and to stimulate an independent rented sector. Under the Housing Act 1988 provision was made to deregulate new lettings in the private rented sector, finance for housing associations was restructured, public sector tenants were offered the opportunity to change landlords, and Housing Action Trusts could be established. The Local Government and Housing Act 1989 made certain changes to the right to buy as it related to housing for older people. Sheltered housing, and other housing deemed to be particularly suitable for older people, was still excluded from the right-to-buy unless it was first let after 1 January 1990. The Act also stipulated that local authorities seeking to exempt a property from the right-to-buy must first seek the approval of the Secretary of State.

The Local Government and Housing Act 1989 also introduced a new mandatory grant system to bring properties up to a new fitness standard with discretionary grants for work above this. However, the level of income threshold and the treatment of savings are likely to mean that many elderly people are excluded from a grant or eligible only for a reduced one (Mackintosh *et al.*, 1990). A useful addition though was the introduction of minor works grants for certain items like insulation. Since 1988 elderly home-owners in receipt of income support have also been eligible for grants from the Department of Social Security's social fund for essential repairs, although provision of these varies considerably between areas.

Amenities and the condition of housing

The poor state of housing of some elderly people was confirmed in the 1981 and 1986 *English House Condition Surveys* (DOE, 1983 and 1988). Overall the condition of the stock had improved between 1981 and 1986. There was a substantial fall in the number of dwellings lacking amenities, a small reduction in unfit dwellings but no significant change in the proportion of the stock in serious disrepair. The greatest improvement in conditions between 1981 and 1986 was in homes occupied by people aged 75 and over. However, this group were more likely than other groups to have homes which were unfit or lacking amenities (Table 7.1) [doc 20].

New build

Another factor which has affected elderly people has been the decline in house building. There were 377,607 houses and flats completed in England and Wales in 1976 but this had halved to

Table 7.1. Long-term residents in[1] housing in poor condition by age of head of household

	Percentage households in each age group in dwellings in poor condition			
	Lacking basic amenities	Unfit	In poor repair	All households resident 20 years and over
Aged 17–39	2.5	2.0	1.3	0.7
Aged 40–59	12.9	18.5	24.8	27.2
Aged 60–74	38.4	41.4	46.9	52.6
Aged 75 and Over	46.2	38.1	27.0	19.5
All households resident 20 years and over	100	100	100	100

[1] Defined as living in their homes for more than 20 years.
DOE, *English House Condition Survey, 1986*, HMSO, 1988, p.42, Table 6.1.

181,579 in 1989. However, the proportions of one- and two-bedroom homes have increased in all sectors. In 1989 78 per cent of local authority and new town, 88 per cent of housing association and 42 per cent of private new-build homes were one or two bedrooms compared with 58 per cent, 78 per cent and 27 per cent respectively in 1976 (CSO, 1991, p. 137). Specialised dwellings completed for elderly people in England show an overall drop between 1981 and 1989 from 12,576 to 8,865 (a fall of 29 per cent) as Table 7.2 indicates. Over the period completions by the private sector increased substantially but were offset by a 65 per cent decrease in the number of completions by local authorities.

Tenure

For all households the major change has been the rise in owner-occupation and the decline of the private rented sector. Whereas 44 per cent of all households owned their own homes in 1959 that figure had risen to 64 per cent in 1988 (CSO, 1983 and 1990; OPCS,

Table 7.2.   Number of specialised dwellings completed for elderly people in 1981 and 1989

	Sheltered			Other			England All			
	Priv	HAs	LAs	Priv	HAs	LAs	Priv	HAs	LAs	Total
1981	130	1,929	5,558	62	261	4,636	192	2,190	10,194	12,576
1989	3,289	1,101	2,590	552	344	992	3,841	1,445	3,582	8,868

Priv – Private sector
HAs – Housing associations
LAs – Local authorities and new towns
DOE, *Housing and Construction Statistics*, 1981–9.

1990). Figures from the *General Household Survey* in 1988 indicate that there was a much higher level of satisfaction with owner-occupation than with other tenures (OPCS, 1990, p. 254). A lower proportion of elderly than all households were owner-occupiers but more elderly households were outright owners and fewer had mortgages. Overall it would appear that whereas 64 per cent of all households were owner-occupiers in 1988, 60 per cent of people aged 65–69, 50 per cent aged 70–79 and 46 per cent of the over 80s owned their own homes. These findings are shown in Table 7.3.

Older people are not only less likely to own their own homes but less likely to have considered buying their council home. The combined figures for 1987 and 1988 show that whereas 24 per cent of all households had considered buying in the last two years only 10 per cent of the over 65s had (OPCS, 1990, p. 233).

New forms of owner-occupation have been developing whereby older people can buy part of their home and rent the rest. A study of some of these schemes (flexible tenure, shared ownership and leasehold) was undertaken by Oldman who concluded that they were particularly valuable for a significant group of elderly people who were 'not rich, not poor' (Oldman, 1990). They allowed older people to use their own resources supplemented by public subsidies for the rented part.

More older people were local authority or housing association tenants and a higher percentage rented unfurnished private accommodation than in the population as a whole in Great Britain in 1988 (Table 7.3). In the council sector research now indicates that older people make up an increasing percentage both of council tenants and of those on waiting lists (Means, 1990). Means suggests that

Table 7.3. Age of head of household by tenure – percentages 1988 – Great Britain

Age of head of household	Owner-occupied owned outright	Owner-occupied with mortgage	Rented from local authority or New Town	Rented from housing association or co-operative	Rented privately furnished	Rented privately unfurnished	Rented with job or business
Under 25	1	(35)	32	2	7	20	4
25–29	1	(61)	24	3	4	6	3
30–44	5	(74)	17	2	2	2	3
45–59	22	(73)	21	1	2	0	2
60–64	44	(62)	31	1	3	1	2
65–69	52	(60)	32	2	6	0	1
70–79	46	(50)	39	4	7	1	0
80 or over	45	(46)	35	6	13	0	0
All	24	(64)	26	2	4	2	2

OPCS, *General Household Survey, 1988*, HMSO, 1990, p. 240, Table 11.20.
0 Less than 1

being old was perhaps once an automatic guarantee of the label of 'deserving' rather than 'undeserving' but there are problems, especially over 'hierarchies of desirability' of accommodation, now that overall demand exceeds supply (Means, 1990). A special analysis of the 1980 *General Household Survey* showed that elderly council tenants were more likely to report physical disabilities and to receive domiciliary help than people living in other accommodation and were four times as likely to receive a supplementary income than owner-occupiers (Evandrou and Victor, 1988).

There is very little research on older people in the private rented sector. In one of the few studies Smith found that tenants were living in very poor conditions but 81 per cent preferred to stay in their own homes and were reluctant to move from familiar surroundings (Smith, 1986).

A new feature has been the growth of housing association tenancies. Housing associations are non-profit-making organisations providing low-cost housing for people in housing need. Some go back to the beginning of the century. Their expansion dates from 1964 when the Housing Corporation was set up to make loans to cost-rent and co-ownership housing associations. Under the Housing Act 1974 the Housing Corporation was given wider powers which included the supervision and registration of housing associations. English housing associations have produced more than 600,000 homes in their 700-year history – two-thirds of them in the past 20 years. In 1989 housing associations in England managed or owned half a million homes and accounted for nearly a quarter of all public capital expenditure on housing (Housing Corporation Annual Report, 1988–9). Local authorities often nominate the tenants in housing association schemes. In a national survey of new housing association tenants in 1988 34 per cent of all new lettings were to elderly people aged 60 and over (Randolph and Levison, 1988).

Types of accommodation

Housing and flats   The majority of elderly people live in houses. In 1988 83 per cent of households containing two adults, of whom one or both were aged 60 or over, lived in houses, 15 per cent in a purpose-built flat or maisonette and 2 per cent in a converted flat, maisonette or rooms (OPCS, 1990, p. 246). Fewer single people of that age occupied houses (65 per cent) and more occupied purpose-built flats or maisonettes (30 per cent) or a converted flat, maisonette or rooms (5 per cent). In the 1986 *GHS* 2 per cent of households containing at least one elderly person lived in a flat without a lift (OPCS, 1989, p. 187).

What many old people, though by no means all, seem to want, is somewhere small and easy to manage. In one survey of preferences of older people wishing to move half would have liked a bungalow. As has been seen, a higher proportion of new-build is now smaller accommodation following a swing away from the concentration on building three-bedroom houses that took place between the wars.

Sheltered housing In 1989 there were nearly half a million sheltered housing units. They were provided as follows:

– local authorities	303,061
– housing associations	120,911
– other public sector	2,905
– private	38,798
Total	465,675

(DOE, Housing Investment Programme Statistics, 1.4.90)

The 5 per cent of elderly people who live in sheltered housing have many advantages. They have their own flat (although not all – particularly in early schemes – are self-contained) or a bungalow with communal facilities and a warden on hand for emergencies. For those who enjoy living in groups with people of their own age this type of living arrangement seems very satisfactory.

Most of the early literature concerned design features, but in the 1970s and early 1980s a more critical approach to the social implications became apparent. This can be seen both in academic research such as that of Boldy, Abel and Carter (1973), Page and Muir (1971), Bytheway and James (1978) and Butler *et al.* (1983) and research sponsored by government departments (Griffin and Dean, 1975; Attenburrow, 1976; Wirz, 1982). The research showed that sheltered housing, although ideal for some people, was not quite the panacea that some had envisaged. In the late 1980s there was a national study of sheltered housing in Scotland (Clapham *et al.*, 1988) and a study of Anchor housing association schemes in England (Fennell, 1986) and in two housing associations in Scotland (Fennell, 1987) where there were similar findings.

Three crucial questions relate to the purpose of sheltered housing, its design and layout, and the problem of frail tenants. It is clear from Circular 82/69 that sheltered housing was conceived as a form of accommodation where elderly people could maintain independent

121

lives. The less active were supposed to form the main body of tenants although there was believed to be value in mixing ages and states of dependence. Sheltered housing has been seen as having a preventive role (to prevent people going into residential care), a social role (primarily for those who are isolated and have no or few relatives) and a housing role in offering an attractive alternative to elderly people who were under-occupying or who needed to be rehoused for some other reason. In reality research has shown that clear criteria for selection do not appear to be applied. The national study by Butler *et al.* queried the lack of clarity about the purpose of sheltered housing and disproved some of the benefits claimed (e.g. that it increased longevity and broke down isolation of elderly people) (Butler *et al.*, 1983). The national study in Scotland suggested clear grounds for reviewing the concept of a balance of tenants and recommended allocation on grounds of need (Clapham and Munro, 1990).

On design and layout, questions have been asked about the need for communal facilities and research indeed seems to indicate that their use depends to some extent on the warden. The Scottish study found under-use of communal facilities, especially the common room, and recommended using them as a local resource (Clapham *et al.*, 1988). The study by Butler *et al.* (1983) concluded that while most tenants were satisfied with their housing, this satisfaction was generally linked to the wish for small, warm, easy-to-run accommodation rather than the provision of an alarm and warden. In the Anchor study the need for more suitable rather than sheltered housing was evident. Research has not found that the size of schemes is an important factor in their success or otherwise (Griffin and Dean, 1975).

The question of what should happen to tenants as they become older and more frail is a difficult one. The Butler study showed that on average tenants were not more dependent than other old people in the community, but the situation might have changed in the ensuing ten years. Fennell's study of Anchor tenants also found a low degree of physical disability. Those who are frail cannot be forced to move (because they are either tenants with rights or owners) even though they might need to be in residential care or hospital. The answer seems to be to provide extra care in the existing scheme (see next section).

Private sheltered housing has developed rapidly during the last ten years. Reasons for the growth include the growing number of elderly owner occupiers who want to remain home owners in smaller homes and the growing realisation among developers of the possible size of this new market (G. Williams, 1990). The latter was fuelled by a number of reports which estimated a huge market (Baker and Parry, 1983, 1984, 1986).

Research reveals general satisfaction with schemes but, as with public sheltered housing, it was generally the wish for more suitable housing rather than the sheltered features which were important (Fleiss, 1985). There were problems, especially over management charges and the small size of units. In the DOE study almost one-fifth of owners said that they would consider moving again, while one in six said that they would not have moved if they had known as much about their sheltered scheme as they did when interviewed (Fleiss, 1985). The building industry has responded to criticism in a positive way and has drawn up a *Sheltered Housing Code of Practice* (National House Building Council, 1990) which is complemented by a *Guidance Note on Management and Services* (House Builders Federation, 1990). Guidance on the location and design of private sheltered housing has also been produced (House Builders Federation (HBF)/National Housing and Town Planning Council (NHTPC), 1988). ACE, with the NHTPC, has published *A Buyer's Guide to Sheltered Housing* (ACE and NHTPC, 1989). ACE has also set up a Sheltered Housing Advisory and Conciliation Service for residents in private sheltered housing schemes.

The role of the warden has been the subject of some research and comment. The original idea was that the warden would be a good neighbour and, despite evidence that some wardens perform more duties than others, the general conclusion is that the warden should be the enabler and should not perform duties, such as home nursing, that are the responsibility of others. A Working Party on sheltered housing laid down useful guidelines about warden services (ACE, 1984).

Very sheltered housing   Very sheltered housing is sheltered housing with extra facilities, usually extra communal rooms, some meals and 24 hour cover by staff. A study for DOE, *An Evaluation of Very Sheltered Housing*, showed that schemes have developed rapidly and in 1985 17 per cent of local authorities and 11 per cent of housing associations in England and Wales made this kind of provision (Tinker, 1989b). In addition 24 per cent of the non-providing local authorities and 14 per cent of the non-providing housing associations planned to provide very sheltered housing (Tinker, 1989b). A national evaluation of schemes which included interviews with 1,089 elderly people, showed that they were popular with management, elderly people and staff. Because of its expense it was considered that it should only be provided for people who both wanted and needed it (Tinker, 1989b) [doc 21]. Such needs might be high dependency, strain on relatives or lack of ability to live in ordinary non-specialised accommodation. Bringing extra care to existing sheltered housing was one way of making provision.

There are a number of problems which need to be taken into account and these include dissatisfaction of some staff with pay and conditions of work and unrealistic expectations by some elderly tenants, relatives and other professionals.

Alternatives to sheltered housing

Much more attention has been paid recently in policy and research to alternatives to sheltered housing (Butler and Tinker, 1983). Butler and colleagues have identified some of the reasons which include danger to health and psychological well-being because of relocation, creation of geriatric ghettoes, cost, over-provision of support, schemes beginning to resemble the institutions they were intended to replace and independence undermined rather than fostered among tenants (Butler *et al.*, 1983). Not all the criticisms are proved, as Butler points out, but these are nevertheless some of the reasons for a changed view of sheltered housing.

Research for DOE and DHSS, *Staying at Home: helping elderly people*, looked at some innovations by housing and social service departments to enable elderly people to remain in their own homes (Tinker, 1984). The evaluation focused on a variety of care and alarm schemes. The sample of 1,310 elderly people were found to be, on average, more dependent than elderly people in sheltered housing. Nearly all the elderly people wanted to stay in their own homes and the innovatory schemes were successfully providing help to enable them to do this. However, the schemes needed to be provided as part of a package of statutory and informal support. The findings of the research supported a growing body of other evidence that for some frail elderly people who do not need full-time surveillance these innovatory schemes provided a successful option [see also doc 21].

Other research which also pointed to ways in which elderly people could remain at home were the Kent Community Care Scheme (see Ch.8) and agency schemes for owner-occupiers (see p. 132).

Granny annexes Another form of special housing is granny annexes. These are self-contained homes next to a family home. The idea is that the elderly person will be able to live independently yet be able to give and to receive help from their family next door. In an evaluation of local authority schemes some problems of flexibility were found when either the family had to move or the grandparent died (Tinker, 1976). Should the family be asked to move out, or should an unrelated person be moved in? Most local authorities took the latter course and, although relations generally proved good, there were rarely close links between the two households. Private schemes seem to be becoming increasingly popular as families see the advantages of having a grandparent next door. Some owner-occupiers use the granny flat for a nanny, au pair or teenager when they do not need it for a grandparent, or else they just let it.

Hostels In hostels shared rather than self-contained accommodation is provided. One variety is that run by Abbeyfield societies where 8–10 elderly people live in bedsitters in one house. A housekeeper provides the main meals.

Comparisons between different types of accommodation

Comparisons between different kinds of housing for elderly people are in their infancy. Pioneering work was done by Wager (Wager, 1972) and Plank (Plank, 1977). The DOE study, *Staying at Home: helping elderly people*, produced costings of alternative forms of housing (Tinker, 1984) and these were updated in *An Evaluation of Very Sheltered Housing* (Tinker, 1989b). These showed that staying at home with a package of innovatory and other statutory services was about £1,000 cheaper on average per annum than very sheltered housing [doc 21]. It was also cheaper than sheltered housing and residential care and hospitals. Costings were also produced by the Audit Commission which showed that staying at home options were cheaper than alternatives (Audit Commission, 1986). Caution is, however, needed in any costings exercise because, if the cost of informal care was added, or if the salaries of the mainly low-paid women working in various housing situations was increased, the position would change dramatically. It is also possible that the cost of providing 24 hour surveillance and services for people in their own home could exceed that of alternatives.

SOME ISSUES

Assessing and meeting needs

One dilemma facing central government with its allocation of public money is how to assess what sort of housing is needed and by whom, and then how these needs may be met. It is also an issue faced at a local level by local authorities and housing associations and a problem which private developers are increasingly facing.

There is very little national guidance on how much housing is needed by elderly people and what form this should take. The National Housing Forum, in *Housing Needs in the 1990s* discussed the complex matters that have to be taken into account when assessing needs (Niner, 1989). These include the number of existing, potential and concealed households, the condition and suitability of the housing and homelessness. The study suggested a likely pent-up housing need in England and Wales of about half a million. While not giving figures for older people, they were stated to represent 'a considerable challenge for the future'.

In Scotland the Scottish Development Department undertook a piece of research based on interviews with 1,750 people over the age of 65 to estimate their requirements for housing and support (Hart and Chalmers, 1990). There was a high degree of satisfaction with existing housing and only one-quarter of the sample expressed a wish to move. As a result of the research the department issued guidelines of:

- sheltered housing – 46 dwellings per 1,000 elderly population
- other medium dependency housing – 80 dwellings per 1,000 elderly population
- very sheltered housing – 20 dwellings per 1,000 elderly population

There is no such guidance in England and Wales but the DOE commissioned research on the housing needs of older people in 1990. This included a survey to assess the numbers of existing kinds of specialised housing.

At local authority level the Cullingworth Committee in 1969 put forward certain criteria to be used as a basis for assessing housing need (MHLG, 1969). This included some of the ideas now current in social services departments such as looking at the needs of the whole community and not just those with whom they were in contact (i.e. the housing waiting list) and regardless of whether the solution to any problems lay in their own hands or elsewhere. As early as 1978 the DOE, in *Organising a Comprehensive Housing Service*, pointed out that needs are not necessarily best met by the local authority itself (DOE, 1978).

Local authorities use a number of different methods for allocating accommodation. Some work on a points basis, some work strictly on a date order of first come first served, while others have separate categories for different people and different kinds of accommodation. In 1978 the DOE Housing Services Advisory Group in *Allocation of Council Housing* suggested various criteria such as the need to treat all applicants equitably and to be easily understood by both applicants and staff (DOE, 1978). Under the Housing Act 1985 councils must publish a summary of their rules relating to allocations, transfers and exchanges.

It may be necessary to treat particular groups in a special way for housing, but that does not necessarily mean that they will need special types of housing. Some may need a special design, or special location, or to be grouped in some way, but not all. Nor should the assumption be made that those who are already housed are necessarily in the most appropriate form of accommodation. Most surveys of elderly people in whatever situation find a proportion who appear to be in the wrong place. For example, both the Butler *et al.* (1983) sheltered housing and the very sheltered housing (Tinker, 1989b) research showed that one quarter would have preferred to have stayed where they were. The latter study also showed that 15 per cent had no physical or mental disability. Studies of residential care invariably show a proportion of people who do not need to be there (see Ch.8). In addition, research on people who shared accommodation showed that a majority of the over 60s, in common with other age groups, would have preferred separate accommodation (Rauta, 1986).

It may be possible to solve some housing problems simply through a more flexible and sensitive use of existing stock. Even a small amount of building of one- and two-bedroom homes may lead to a general shifting round of people to a more appropriate size of accommodation. But this raises the question of under-occupation, where accommodation is located and whether elderly people should be encouraged to move.

Under-occupation

Many elderly people occupy only a part of their home after their family move away or a spouse dies. This can be a problem when it comes to repairing, decorating, cleaning and heating the home. 'Under-occupation' is usually defined as having two or more bedrooms above the bedroom standard. In 1988 28 per cent of households in England under-occupied their homes compared with 25 per cent in 1981 (*Labour Force Survey*, unpublished statistics). The figures for people over the age of retirement in England in 1988 who were under-occupying were:

	Owner-occupiers	Local authority tenants	Unfurnished rented tenants
1 person alone	16	31	31
Couple	26	38	26

(Labour Force Survey 1988, unpublished statistics).

There may be a shortage of accommodation for families in those same areas where elderly people are under-occupying. Yet many local authorities may do nothing to encourage elderly people to move. The reasons are not hard to seek. There is a general reluctance to persuade elderly people to move from a home in which they have lived for many years.

Moving

General The 1981 *Census* showed that 10 per cent of the whole population moved in the previous year whereas only 5 per cent of people over the age of 65 had moved (Grundy, 1987). Most moves are of short distances. In 1981 at least half of all moves were of 4 kilometres or less and only a little over 10 per cent of elderly migrants moved more than 80 kilometres (Victor, 1987, p. 123). A recent analysis of the NHS registration data reveals that migration rates were falling in the late 1970s and then increased strongly during 1982–8. They fell sharply in 1988–9, no doubt as a result of difficulties in the housing market. Migration around retirement age conformed to this pattern, but a notable feature was a strong increase of mobility among the 75+ group. It appears that there is a slight peak in migration at 65 and then a second peak in later old age.

While many elderly people move willingly, this is not always the case, as has been seen in the previous section.

To another tenure There are several reasons why people may wish to switch tenure as they become elderly. They may, for example, have to give up tied accommodation when their employment ends. They may be worried about the upkeep of their home and garden and willingly accept a council or housing association tenancy. They may need some special form of accommodation only provided in the public sector. However, most changes in tenure are associated with changes in domestic circumstances: such as moving to live with relatives. In 1981 80 per cent of women aged 85 or over living in a son or daughter's household were in the owner-occupied sector, compared with 40 per cent of those living alone (Grundy, 1989). Some of the new forms of tenure such as equity share and housing co-operatives may prove attractive to elderly people.

To a retirement area While the majority of older people remain in the same neighbourhood area, others may choose to move to the seaside, country or other retirement area. Recent years have seen a clear dispersal of the most favoured destinations for retirement-age migrants. East and West Sussex and Dorset have declined in their relative popularity as Norfolk and Cornwall have climbed. During the 1980s, Lincolnshire, Powys in central Wales and North York-shire emerged as attracting high rates of people of retirement age. Retirement communities are beginning to be developed by the private sector.

Retirement migration may have some effect on the recipient area and therefore on elderly people who move there. Karn found that while the majority of her sample were happy in their new environment, and would have made the same decision again, there were problems for health and social services (Karn, 1977). Karn (1977) and Law and Warnes (1982) in their retirement studies have established that elderly migrants were less likely to have younger relatives to help them. These elderly movers were predominantly owner-occupiers, childless or had few children, and they had retired at or before pensionable age. Other research indicates that institutionalisation rates were slightly above average in 1981 in counties with large proportions of retirement migrants and high rates were found in areas with high densities of elderly people (Harrop and Grundy, 1991).

Very little is known about retirement migration to other countries. In 1987 458,646 people were claiming a UK pension abroad; of these 103,599 were in European Community Member States (*Euro-link Age*, 1990). If the existing rights of free movement for workers and their families in EC countries extends to retired people more older people may want to settle abroad.

To be near relatives   One of the groups identified by the Culling-worth Committee as wanting to move was elderly people wishing to join their relatives (MHLG, 1969) [doc 22]. In most cases this was to enable them to give mutual support. In Hunt's survey the major reason given for moving (by 40 per cent of all movers) was to be near relatives. In research on every housing authority in England and Wales and a number of housing associations, *Housing the Elderly near Relatives*, it was found that although many elderly people already lived near their families, there was a demand from those who did not to move closer (Tinker, 1980b). Two groups of elderly people who faced particular problems over moving were owner-occupiers who wanted to move into council accommodation in their own area and people from any tenure who wanted to rent in another local authority area. A number of schemes sponsored by central government exist to help local authority and housing association tenants move and wishing to receive support from, or give support to, relatives is one criterion.

Some groups in need

Six groups of elderly people who may be particularly vulnerable in the housing market are those who are disabled, owner-occupiers, private renters, homeless, tenants in tied accommodation, and people from ethnic minorities.

Disabled people   Elderly people figure prominently among the disabled, but their housing problems may differ widely. Early evidence was given in the OPCS study, *Work and Housing of Impaired Persons in Great Britain* (Buckle, 1971). The OPCS surveys of disability between 1985 and 1988 included some questions on the proportion of disabled pensioners who were owner-occupiers (50 per cent for married pensioners and 39 per cent for unmarried) and showed that this was not very much lower than in the general population of pensioners (57 per cent and 42 per cent respectively) (Martin and White, 1988, p. 12). The DOE Housing Services Advisory Group's *The Assessment of Housing Requirements* advised that for many disabled people the adaptation of the home in which they live usually provides the quickest, cheapest and best solution (DOE, 1977). That has become more possible with greater powers given to housing departments, especially since the Housing Act 1975, now consolidated into the Housing Act 1985.

In a circular published in 1978, *Adaptations of Housing for People who are Physically Handicapped*, housing authorities were asked to take responsibility for structural modifications and social services, under the Chronically Sick and Disabled Persons Act 1970, for non-structural features and aids. New disabled facilities grants were introduced following the joint DOE/DOH circular *House Adaptations for People with Disabilities* (DOE 10/90 and DOH LAC(90)7). The OPCS disability surveys showed that of all disabled adults 31 per cent of those with a locomotor disability and 38 per cent of those with a personal care disability had some adaptation to their home (Martin *et al.*, 1989, p. 59). Of these 41 per cent had paid for all their adaptations themselves, 41 per cent had had all their adaptations provided for them by a statutory or voluntary body, 8 per cent had paid for some themselves and some had been provided, while the remaining 10 per cent lived in accommodation which already contained adaptations when they moved in. Thirty-five per cent of those with locomotor disabilities and 42 per cent of those with personal care disabilities thought they might be helped by some sort of adaptation which they did not have. All the research on adaptations shows the crucial role, and shortage, of occupational therapists.

The advisory group in 1977 also argued that 'mobility housing', that is normal housing with low-cost adaptations such as level thresholds and ramped access, was a sensible form of provision (see Goldsmith, 1974). They considered that for very disabled people 'wheelchair housing', which has extra space and other provisions, might be needed (see Goldsmith, 1975).

A good deal of practical advice has come out in the 1980s. This included a free booklet, *Housing Services for Disabled People* (DOE, DHSS, Welsh Office, 1984) and *House Adaptations for People with Physical Disabilities* (Statham *et al.*, 1988). The latter included plans and case studies. It is important to consider not only the home of the disabled person but ways of making all housing more accessible so that the disabled person can visit other people.

Owner-occupiers Elderly owner-occupiers may face particular problems. Among those identified as early as 1969 by the Cullingworth Committee were physical inability to cope with maintenance, cleaning, stairs or garden, too large accommodation, financial problems of upkeep, the need to move to a more convenient area and inability to cope with improvements (MHLG, 1969). Some specific problems faced by this group, in addition to those mentioned above, are lack of knowledge about the grant system, lack of money, difficulty in finding builders to carry out the work and dislike of the upheaval of having workmen in the house. Help may be needed to improve, repair and adapt the home. In addition to the main housing renovation grants, other grants including minor works assistance to help elderly people remain in their own homes or move in with relatives, have become available from local authorities. Most are discretionary.

A great many schemes have been developed to help with the problems of owner-occupiers in the last ten years. The biggest development has been in the setting up of home improvement agencies, usually called agency services. These provide advice and practical assistance to householders seeking to repair and maintain the fabric of their homes. Their help is usually technical and financial and can include assistance with raising money (through grants, loans, etc.) for the work, help with choice, organisation and supervision of builders and checking the work has been satisfactorily completed.

Agency services can be provided by local authorities, housing associations, voluntary bodies and the private sector. Thomas had pointed to the role of local authority schemes (Thomas, 1981) and the first scheme provided in the voluntary sector was in Ferndale (Morton, 1982). This was quickly followed by others. Some of the first schemes provided by Anchor Housing Trust were evaluated by Wheeler in her study *Don't Move: we've got you covered* (Wheeler, 1985). Her research stressed the poor housing conditions of applicants to the schemes but they were not, on the whole, unaware of or satisfied with this. Most had low incomes and were unable to pay for repairs. The research confirmed the value of these schemes and recommended that more should be provided. In 1986 the DOE announced a £6 million initiative with the Government offering half the costs of setting up around 50 new services. More help was given subsequently. A large number of publicly funded agency services was monitored and further expansion was encouraged (Leather and Mackintosh, 1990). Long-term funding through local authorities was agreed in 1990 and Care and Repair Ltd were given a national co-ordinating role.

Another development which has helped owner-occupiers has been the development of schemes allowing older people to use the equity in their homes (Leather and Wheeler, 1988). The contrast between low-income home-owners has become known as 'house rich, income poor'. Of course older home-owners can realise their equity by selling and trading down to a cheaper home but, if they want to stay where they are, some form of re-mortgage is possible. Home equity release schemes, often called reverse mortgages in the United States, allow some or all of the value of the home to be realised to generate a lump sum or regular income at the same time enabling the owner to stay in their own home (Hinton, 1991). The most widely available type involves an insurance company providing a mortgage loan on part of the value of an elderly owner's home. The loan is used to purchase an annuity, part of which goes to paying off the loan interest, the remainder providing the elderly owner (annuitant) with an income for life. Research has shown that these schemes had on the whole successfully provided an additional source of income for elderly owners (Fleiss, 1985). Subsequent research looked at home income, maturity loans and home reversion schemes (Leather and Wheeler, 1988). ACE produces an annually updated guide on the schemes available and they stress the need to take professional advice.

Homeless elderly people Surprise is often expressed that some elderly people are homeless. But in one of the most detailed studies carried out in the sixties, elderly people figured prominently (National Assistance Board (NAB), 1966). The survey for the NAB, *Homeless Single Persons*, found that of those sleeping rough (nearly 1,000) 18 per cent of the men were aged 60 and over. Research has continued to highlight the problems of elderly people who are homeless. A survey published in 1981, *Single and Homeless*, found that 8 per cent of the sample were over retirement age (Drake *et al.*, 1981). In a survey of rehoused hostel residents, *A Home of their Own*, 39 per cent of the sample were 60 or over (Duncan *et al.*, 1983). Under the Housing (Homeless Persons) Act 1977, later consolidated in the Housing Act 1985, with minor amendments in the Housing and Planning Act 1986, local authorities in Great Britain were given a statutory duty to secure accommodation for applicants who are homeless and who are in priority need. In 1989 6 per cent of homeless households found accommodation by local authorities were in the category of vulnerable because of old age (CSO, 1991, p. 140). In research on policies and practices of local authorities variations were found in the age at which elderly applicants were accepted as being in a priority need (Evans and Duncan, 1988). For the majority this was retirement age but some used 60 for men and women. The Audit Commission pointed to the need for more affordable permanent housing, a lack of co-ordination between agencies and the need for changes in practice (Audit Commission, 1989). The government's *Review of the Homelessness Legislation* (DOE, 1989) has led to a revised *Code of Guidance*.

Ethnic minority elders Little attention has been paid to the housing conditions of ethnic minority elderly people partly because they form such a small group. However, what little evidence there is confirms that many live isolated and often unhappy lives in inappropriate accommodation and circumstances. A Working Party concluded that common assumptions regarding the ability of families to care for their elders and the accepted policy of integration combine with racial disadvantage and discrimination to deny an appropriate response from housing and care providers (ACE and Help the Aged Housing Trust, 1984). The research of the Working Party concluded that there was little attempt to assess and meet the special needs of ethnic elders. What also emerged from the findings was that few providers were prepared to consider the possibility of providing separate housing even though the present generation of ethnic elders often found it difficult to integrate because of language, cultural and other difficulties, including their experiences of prejudice and discrimination. Recommendations included the plea for sensitivity to different ethnic groups and different needs, employment of ethnic minority staff, separate provision in some cases, monitoring provision and good information.

Tenants in tied accommodation Those who live in accommodation provided by their employers generally lose their right to their home when they stop working. Their employer may try to find them alternative accommodation, but will need their home for the next employee. Some elderly people will have managed to save for a retirement home, but others will have to apply to a local authority or housing association for a tenancy. The 1988 *GHS* showed that about 2 per cent of the population lived in tied accommodation in 1988 and they included people like farm workers, clergy and the police (OPCS, 1990, p. 140).

Affordability

Affordability of rents is important to older people because nearly half of them rent accommodation. The Housing Act 1988 and the Local Government and Housing Act 1989 are likely to result in higher rents in both the public and private rented sectors. In the public sector local authority rents are likely to rise and there is concern whether the new funding arrangements for housing associations will force rents up beyond the reach of older people, even with housing benefit support (Mackintosh *et al.*, 1990). While existing private renters will retain their present arrangements, once properties are vacated when 'market rents' take over higher rents can be charged. This is likely to reduce opportunities for older people to move into this tenure. Since 1988 housing benefit has been available to people with less than £8,000 capital. While most attention tends to be focused on rich and poor elderly people, the housing options for those on middle incomes should not be forgotten and is examined in *Not Rich Not Poor* (Bull and Poole, 1989).

Paying for Britain's Housing, a nationwide survey of 100,000 households in 1988, concluded that savings of elderly local authority and housing association tenants were very small (MacLennan *et al.*, 1990). They point to the devastating correlation of old age, social rental status, low incomes and negligible assets – assets that are barely enough, they say, to cover the cost of a pauper's funeral.

The need for advice

Over many of the issues just discussed, such as whether to move or not and how to get repairs done, advice is important. It is important to ensure that staff in housing departments, housing advice centres and housing associations are fully briefed on the needs of elderly people and the means available to help them. Publications such as ACE's *Housing Options for Older People* fulfil an important role in giving information to old people (Bookbinder, 1987).

Links with other services

To offer choice and to avoid duplication and omissions, housing and social services departments and health authorities need to collaborate to plan whatever services are appropriate for their areas. The recognition that housing is 'the foundation of community care' (to quote from the title of a book – NFHA/MIND, 1987) is taking a long time. The Griffiths report (see Ch.8) played down the role of housing. However, in the NHS and Community Care Act 1990 there is a requirement for local authorities to consult every housing authority and 'such voluntary housing agencies and other bodies as appear to the local authority to provide housing and community care plans'. A DOH circular on *Community Care and Housing* was planned for Autumn 1991. In the overall planning of particular forms of housing, and especially over the criteria for acceptance to sheltered housing and residential care, co-operation is essential. Staff in each agency must be clear about this policy.

Chapter eight

PERSONAL AND OTHER SOCIAL SERVICES

THE DEVELOPMENT OF LOCAL SOCIAL SERVICES

Before 1971

In comparison with services concerned with income maintenance, health and housing, local personal social services are of more recent origin. Much of the provision before 1946 was by voluntary bodies. One of the first post-war Acts to give local authorities powers to intervene in this field was the National Health Service Act 1946 which among other things allowed local authorities to employ home helps [doc 23]. It also gave very general powers for the care and aftercare of persons suffering from illness and preventive measures relating to health. So services such as chiropody and laundry became possible.

Under the National Assistance Act 1948 local authorities were enabled to make arrangements for 'promoting the welfare' of people who were deaf, dumb, blind or substantially handicapped [doc 24]. The provision of workshops, hostels and recreational facilities were specifically mentioned. Elderly people who came into any of these categories benefited from this legislation. Power was also given to local authorities to make contributions to the funds of voluntary bodies providing meals or recreation for old people [doc 24].

Under the 1948 Act a duty was laid on local authorities to make accommodation available for all persons who by reason of age, infirmity (amended to illness, disability in the NHS and Community Care Act 1990, p. 50 para 42), or any other circumstances are in need of care and attention not otherwise available to them [doc 25]. Because residential accommodation is provided under Part III of this Act it is usually just referred to as Part III. Some local authorities had been providing residential care on an experimental basis, but they now inherited from public assistance committees large workhouses. Local authorities were also given power to provide residential care in homes run by voluntary bodies.

Under the National Assistance Act 1948 (Amendment) Act 1962 local authorities were themselves enabled to provide meals and recreation for old people in their homes or elsewhere, as well as day centres, clubs and recreational workshops. They might, however, continue to employ voluntary bodies as agents, if they so wished.

It has been noted (Ch.4) that the development of local services was seen as being complementary to the hospital service. In 1962 local authorities were asked by the Ministry of Health to draw up plans for local health and welfare services for the next 10 years. The advice given (in Circular 2/62, *Development of Local Authority Health and Welfare Services*) was that:

Services for the elderly should be designed to help them to remain in their own homes as long as possible. For this purpose adequate supporting services must be available, including home nurses, domestic help, chiropody and temporary residential care. These supporting services will also often be needed for those who live in special housing where there is a resident warden. Residential homes are required for those who, for some reason, short of a need for hospital care, cannot manage on their own, even in special housing with a resident warden.

Specific standards were not laid down.

The general power for local authorities to provide welfare services for elderly people was not given until the Health Services and Public Health Act 1968 [doc 26]. These powers did not come into force until 1971. They include powers to provide home helps, visiting, social work and warden services, arrangements to inform elderly people about services and to carry out adaptations. Local authorities may use voluntary bodies (widened in 1990 to include private organisations) as agents and may make charges. Another section of the 1968 Act which came into effect in 1971 made mandatory the provision of domestic help on an adequate scale. Power was also given to provide laundry services.

Concern about the lack of a co-ordinated approach to the family by the local authority which meant that welfare departments were responsible for elderly and mentally disordered people, children's departments for children and health departments for home helps and other domiciliary provision, was one of the reasons for the appointment of a committee in 1965 'to review the organisation and responsibilities of the local authority personal social services in England and Wales, and to consider what changes are desirable to secure an effective family service.' Its report, *Local Authority and Allied Personal Social Services* (the Seebohm Report) was published in 1968 (Home Office *et al.*, 1968). Its main recommendation concerning administration was the establishment of a single social services department in each authority. This took place in 1971 following the Local Authority Social Services Act 1970.

The overall philosophy of the report was that the new departments should be less concerned simply to meet individual needs in crises and more concerned about ensuring a co-ordinated and comprehensive approach to people's problems [doc 27], detecting need and encouraging people to seek help. In this way they would be better able to attract and use scarce resources and to plan systematically to best advantage for the future (Home Office *et al.*, 1968). The need to support families caring for old people was also a consideration [doc 27].

Following the Act the main services for elderly people for which social services departments became responsible were: provision of domestic help, residential accommodation, general welfare, meals and recreation, registration of old people's homes and social work support. Another change which came about as a result of the Seebohm Report was the focus on the number of generic social workers instead of specialists (see social work section).

Developments since 1972 have included further attempts at long-term planning. In 1972 (Circular 35/72) 10-year plans were requested by the DHSS for health and social care and in 1977 3-year plans were introduced. Financial constraints have subsequently made planning more difficult.

In Chapter 4 the reasons for the development of community care policies were given. There was a number of subsequent initiatives by the DHSS to promote these policies. These included legislation in 1974 imposing a duty on health and local authorities to co-operate in planning services (joint planning), the introduction of joint finance in 1976 to enable NHS funds to be used on collaborative projects with local authorities and the introduction of financial arrangements in 1983 to enable the transfer of funds from the NHS to local authorities to pay for services for people moving from hospitals to the community. These and other measures are discussed in Chapter 6.

The 1980s brought a number of very influential reports which, together with a new thrust to Government policies, brought about legislation to change the role and funding of local social services departments. A report of the House of Commons Social Services

Committee, chaired by Renee Short MP, *Community Care*, presented a critical picture of services for people, many of whom were elderly, who were mentally ill and mentally handicapped (House of Commons, 1985). The Committee argued wholeheartedly for community care policies but were concerned at the lack of local services. They expressed particular worries about people discharged from institutions and quoted one of their witnesses who said: 'patients should not be removed until the alternative facilities actually exist in the community. It seems to me it is like asking a passenger to jump off an elderly ship into the stormy sea with the assurance that the lifeboat will be along in a few months time' (House of Commons, 1985, p. lviii). They maintained that no one should be discharged without an individual care plan. They also said that some people would need institutional care.

The Audit Commission's *Making a Reality of Community Care* was highly critical of community care policies (Audit Commission, 1986). Their grounds for concern were the slow progress that had been made and the uneven response of authorities despite some very encouraging local schemes. Pointing to some fundamental underlying problems [doc 28] the Commission suggested a number of courses of action. At the core of their recommendations was the principle that the 'perverse incentives' (created by DHSS funding for care in residential and nursing homes, with no similar level of funding for people in their own homes) must be removed. Drawing on this study the National Audit Office (NAO) examined progress in implementing community care policies, including that of shifting support from long-term hospital care to community-based care (NAO, 1987). They found that there had been a shift from long-stay provision and an increase in community facilities but it was less clear whether this had gone far enough, particularly with regard to the unknown numbers of people in the community who formerly would have been admitted to long-term care.

The Secretary of State for Social Services then asked Sir Roy Griffiths to 'review the way in which public funds are used to support community care policy and to advise me on the options for action that would improve the use of these funds as a contribution to more effective community care' (Griffiths, 1988, p. iii). Building on both the Short and Audit Commission reports the conclusion of Griffiths was that 'community care is a poor relation; everybody's distant relative but nobody's baby' (Griffiths, 1988, p. iv). The keystones of his proposals were:

- the appointment of a Minister for Community Care;
- a clear framework for co-ordination between health and social services with ring fencing of funds for community care and the transfer of any necessary resources between central and local government;
- local social services departments to be in the lead over planning and providing community care;
- at a local level social services departments should be responsible for ensuring that packages of care are devised for individuals and, where appropriate, a care manager is assigned; they should also be responsible for assessing moves to residential care where public funding is required.

Other proposals included one for public housing authorities to be responsible only for 'bricks and mortar' and not for care through wardens or other means.

After some delay the White Paper, *Caring for People*, subtitled 'community care in the next decade', was published at the end of 1989 (Sec. of St. for Health *et al.*, 1989b). This report acknowledged that progress in community care had been 'slower and less even than the Government would like, and the arrangements for public funding have contained a built-in bias toward residential and nursing home care, rather than services for people at home' (Sec. of St. for Health *et al.*, 1989b, p. 4). The major objectives of policy were affirmed as enabling people 'to live as normal a life as possible in their own homes or in a homely environment in the local community; provide the right amount of care and support to help people achieve the maximum possible independence and, by acquiring or reacquiring basic living skills, help them to achieve their full potential; give people a greater individual say in how their lives and the services they need to help them to do so' (Sec. of St. for Health *et al.*, 1989b, p. 4). The key objectives of the proposals were:

- to promote the development of domiciliary, day and respite services to enable people to live in their own homes wherever feasible and sensible;
- to ensure that service providers make practical support for carers a high priority;
- to make proper assessment of need and good case management the cornerstone of high quality care;
- to promote the development of a flourishing independent sector alongside good quality public services;
- to clarify the responsibilities of agencies and to make it easier to hold them to account for their performance;

– to secure better value for taxpayers' money by introducing a new funding structure for social care (Sec. of St. for Health *et al.*, 1989b, p. 5).

Reference was made to housing in the White Paper which went beyond the 'bricks and mortar' approach of Griffiths, but it was not clear what action was to be taken.

The key proposals were given force of law in the National Health Service and Community Care Act 1990. This did not include the suggestions in the Griffiths Report for a Minister of Community Care or for ring fencing of funds. It was subsequently decided that the provisions in the Act would be introduced in three phases. Policy guidance was issued by the DOH, *Community Care in the Next Decade and Beyond: policy guidance* (DOH, 1990a).

There has been a general welcome for the emphasis on community care and the eventual removal of the perverse funding incentives. Sceptics have suggested that financially stretched local authorities will find it difficult to provide a reasonable standard of community care without the injection of large amounts of extra money. Critics also question whether social services departments will have the ability to draw up community care plans and whether social workers have the skills to manage care packages. Local information and research and training for social services staff need to be a priority. CPA have produced a useful code of practice (CPA, 1990). While many would agree with a variety of local providers, critics point to the dangers of over-dependence on the private sector (e.g. Glennerster *et al.*, 1990) and the problems for voluntary bodies (see Ch. 10). The importance of carers in the White Paper does not seem to have been translated into much practical help (see also discussion of community care in Ch. 12).

DISABLED ELDERLY PEOPLE

Evidence has already been presented that the incidence of disability increases with age (Ch. 6). Because elderly people are the largest proportion of physically disabled people, 65 per cent in a sample in 1965 (Harris, 1971) and 69 per cent in 1984–6 (Martin *et al.*, 1988), it is appropriate to consider any special provision that has been made for this group. Generalisations about disabled people are as dangerous as those about other elderly people. Elderly people with impaired hearing or vision may need different services to those in wheelchairs. There are also the distinctions discussed in Chapter 6 between impairment, handicap and disability. Most services are based on the degree of disablement, e.g. mobility allowance on impaired locomotor mobility.

The main way in which provision can be made by social services departments is under the Chronically Sick and Disabled Persons Act 1970. This Act extended the powers of local authorities and placed a duty on them to find out the numbers of disabled people in their area, to publicise the services available and, where there was need, provide the services described in the Act. These included practical assistance in the home (including aids such as walking frames – see OPCS disability surveys for a comprehensive picture; Martin *et al.*, 1989), television and radio, help with travel, holidays, meals, telephones and adaptations to the home. The latter is now the main responsibility of housing departments (see Ch. 7). A DHSS circular (12/70) stated that local authorities were to assess need in the light of their resources. Charges may be made for services. Occupational therapists are skilled at assessing needs and are valuable, though scarce, members of social services teams.

The International Year of Disabled People was designated as 1981. Some have argued that, although attitudes may have been changed, little was achieved in practical terms. Despite attempts in the 1980s to enforce the 1970 Act provision is patchy. The 1986 Disabled Persons Act was an attempt to give more power to disabled people. The parts that have been implemented include the duty placed on social services departments to decide about the needs of disabled people for welfare services, the duty when assessing these needs to take into account the carer's ability to continue to care and the duty to give disabled people information about relevant services. The Government announced in 1991 that it was not planning to implement the sections giving rights to disabled people to have an advocate, who would have right of access to meetings, and the right of a disabled person to make their views known to social services and have account taken of these views. Ministers argued that the NHS and Community Care Act 1990 would enhance the rights of service users through community care plans and complaints procedures. Disability groups did not agree.

The minister's title was changed in 1990 when he became Minister for Social Security and Disabled People (instead of the Disabled). Also in 1990 a seminar supported by the EC produced *A European Code of Good Practice* in meeting the needs of disability and ageing (Eurolink Age, 1990).

ETHNIC MINORITY ELDERS

The needs of elderly people from ethnic minorities have come more into prominence. Although it was seen in Chapter 2 that numbers of people in this group are small they are expected to grow as the present generation of middle aged people reach old age. As with any group there are dangers in generalising. While most studies concentrate on black elders there is also need to consider other groups such as the Chinese who, because of their ethnic origin, language, cultural or religious differences share a common experience (Williams, 1990; National Association of Health Authorities, 1988). Barker's account of the different groups of people who came to this country from the Caribbean and South Asia is revealing (Barker, 1983) (Fig. 8.1). Not only have people come for different reasons and from different parts of the world but their experiences here vary too. Many of these differences for people of working age will have an effect on them when they are older. For example West Indians are more likely to be single than their white counterparts (in 1986–8 58 per cent compared with 38 per cent of the white population, CSO, 1991, p. 25). Pakistani and Bangladeshi women are less likely to be in paid employment than white women (21 per cent in 1987–9 compared with 70 per cent, CSO, 1991, p. 69). West Indians are less likely to be owner-occupiers (in 1988 42 per cent compared with 66 per cent of white households and 80 per cent of Indian households, CSO, 1991, p. 146).

A number of studies have highlighted the problems which some members of ethnic minority groups face. Alison Norman's *Triple Jeopardy: growing old in a second homeland* (Norman, 1985) paints a vivid picture of some of these problems and so have other researchers (e.g. CPA, 1982; Bhalla and Blakemore, 1981; Barker, 1983; Blakemore, 1985; Donaldson, 1986; Fennell *et al*, 1988). These include language difficulties, negative attitudes, isolation, a marked under-use of some mainstream services and a lack of knowledge of services. Housing problems and how they might be overcome were discussed by a working party (ACE and Help the Aged Housing Trust, 1984).

Cultural or religious customs may be different from those of the indigenous population and may mean that there are particular needs, such as dietary requirements or support in certain circumstances. For example meals need to reflect these differences and so does design in sheltered housing where different forms of cooking and worship should be taken into account. Assumptions should not be

Figure 8.1 Ageing cohorts of black and Asian-origin people in Britain: a study of people aged 55 and over from the Caribbean and South Asia in 1982

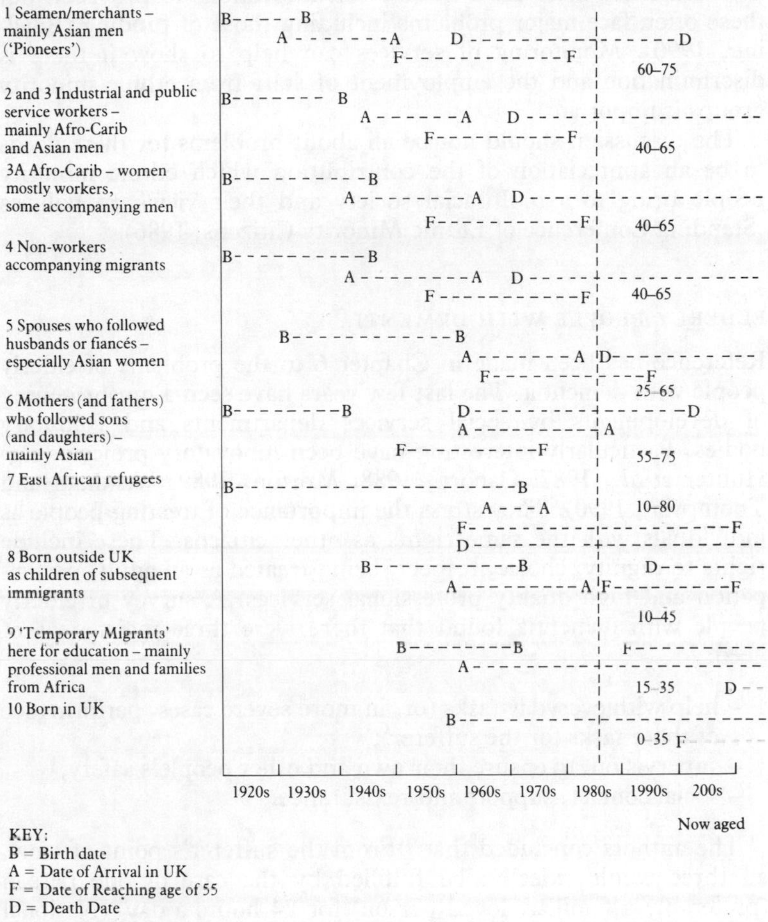

KEY:
B = Birth date
A = Date of Arrival in UK
F = Date of Reaching age of 55
D = Death Date

Source: Barker, J., *Black and Asian Older People in Britain*, Age Concern England, 1984, Figure 1, p. 19.

made that services are not needed. For example the myth that 'ethnic minorities look after their own' can result in a lack of awareness and sensitivity in the provision of services to a multiracial society (DHSS, Social Services Inspectorate (SSI), 1988b, p. 1). A major part of the debate is whether a segregated or integrated approach will lead to provision of better services (Williams, 1990). Encouragingly there are a number of innovations in provision but these often face major problems including those of funding (Bowling, 1990). Monitoring of services can help to show if there is discrimination and the employment of staff from ethnic minority groups is important.

The discussion should not be all about problems for there needs to be an appreciation of the contribution which ethnic minority people bring to a multiracial society and their views on policies (Standing Conference of Ethnic Minority Citizens, 1986).

ELDERLY PEOPLE WITH DEMENTIA

Reference has been made in Chapter 6 to the problems of elderly people with dementia. The last few years have seen a mushrooming of developments by social services departments and voluntary bodies. Particularly interesting have been innovatory projects (e.g. Hunter *et al.*, 1987; Osborn, 1988; Morton, 1989a; Askham and Thompson, 1990). They stress the importance of treating people as individuals with the same rights as other citizens. These include rights to dignity, choice, respect, being treated as an adult, participation and high quality professional services. A survey of elderly people with dementia found that there were three main areas of need:

– help with everyday tasks (or, in more severe cases, performance of those tasks for the sufferer);
– supervision, to ensure their own and other people's safety;
– social contact, support and reassurance.

The authors concluded that: 'From the sufferer's point of view, all three would, ideally, be fulfilled by the care of one person (preferably a familiar, loved person) for 24 hours a day' (National Consumer Council (NCC), 1990). The most important issue which they and other researchers have identified is how to support the carer. The particular gaps in provision for carers appear to be early diagnosis, information and advice, especially at the early stages, counselling, a sitting service, information about possible residential care (for long-term planning) and a prompt reliable transport service for the those needing day care (NCC, 1990, p. 29).

DOMICILIARY SERVICES

General

Surveys consistently show the inability of a minority of elderly people to perform domestic tasks. The purpose of domiciliary services is to provide help to people in their own homes. Townsend and Wedderburn commented: 'The domiciliary services therefore perform two main positive functions. They furnish expert professional help which the family cannot supply, and they furnish unskilled or semi-skilled help for persons who do not have families and whose families living in the household or nearby are not always able or available to help' (Townsend and Wedderburn, 1965, p. 135). This role of providing services for older people who have no relatives and of supplementing what the family does comes out in many studies.

No norms are laid down by the Department of Health for these services, but they suggested in 1977 that the need for meals, home helps and chiropody services would be greater than previously envisaged because of the difficulties in increasing the supply of residential care (DHSS, 1977).

The 1985 *GHS* showed that most domiciliary services are used more by the over 75s, by women and by people living alone. This is true of home helps, meals on wheels, and visits to day centres (OPCS, 1989, p. 183). The greater use by women is partly explained by the greater number who live alone. Charges are referred to at the end of the chapter.

Home helps and home care

The mandatory duty to provide a home help service was imposed on local authorities by the Health Service and Public Health Act 1968, as part of their general responsibility to promote the welfare of elderly people. There is evidence from numerous studies that home help and home care services are among the most popular and effective elements of community care (summarised in Sinclair and Williams, 1990).

Home helps undertake a range of tasks including cleaning, laundering, shopping and cooking, and sometimes give help with dressing and washing. They also often informally provide companionship and advice. Almost 90 per cent of the users of home helps are elderly. Home carers are relatively new (see below) and

147

Table 8.1. Use of some services by elderly people aged 65 and over

	1985* GB	1980† GB	1976‡ England
Doctor at surgery	26	27	not given
Doctor at home	11	11	33
District nurse or health visitor	6	6	12
Chiropodist[1]	11	11	not given
Home help	9	9	9
Attendance at day centre	5	5	17 } social centre for the elderly
Lunch at lunch club or day centre	4	3	
Meals on wheels	2	2	3

* In the month before interview. OPCS, *GHS, 1986*, HMSO, 1989, p.210 and p. 212.
† In the month before interview. OPCS, *GHS, 1980*, HMSO, 1982, p.211 and p.213.
‡ Visits received during the past six months. Hunt, A., *The Elderly at Home*, HMSO, 1978, p.87 and p. 103.
[1] Excluding private treatment.

their role is to provide a more intensive service which may include care which is of a personal rather than a domestic nature.

By 1949 all the English and Welsh local authorities provided home helps. There has been little variation in the percentage of people over 65 who receive the services of a home help. It was 9 per cent in 1976, 1980 and 1985 (Table 8.1).

The OPCS disability surveys showed that 12 per cent of disabled people aged 65 to 74 and 31 per cent aged 75 and over received a home help (Martin *et al*, 1989, p. 37). However, this service gives an example of uneven provision. In 1984–5 provision of home helps varied by a factor of six or more among authorities – from under 7 full-time home helps for every 1,000 people aged over 75 to 44 (Audit Commission, 1986, p. 24). Research in the 1960s, 1970s and more recently suggests that there is a substantial amount of unmet need. In 1976, for example, Hunt commented: 'Although those groups who appear on the face of it to be in the greatest need of the help are most likely to receive it, in all these groups a majority do not do so' (Hunt, 1978, p. 89). The SSI stated: 'If increasing numbers of very elderly people are to be enabled to continue living in their own homes, or in sheltered housing, rather than having to move into residential care, either a higher volume or domiciliary services will be necessary, or the currently available resources will have to be more specifically targeted on those in most need, and those for whom most can be achieved (DHSS, SSI, 1987, p. 26).

Problems identified in the 1970s and early 1980s included the number of visits elderly people received per week (i.e. the service was spread too thinly) and restrictions on what home helps could do. Research raised questions over whether home helps should be domestic cleaners or personal carers (Hedley and Norman, 1982). It was partly to meet these criticisms and partly because of the growing frailty of clients that home care or intensive domiciliary care schemes developed. Aimed at elderly people who needed more than a cleaning service innovatory schemes grew up around the country. Some of the early ones were evaluated and found to be a popular and cost effective element in a package of care (Tinker, 1984). In some areas it is now difficult for elderly people to find help with the 'traditional' home help tasks, such as cleaning or shopping, if they do not have more intensive care needs.

Most recent work has focused on management issues (DHSS, SSI, 1987 and 1988a) and these are important. The SSI identified three strategies for home care services: incremental change; radical change towards a more professional, flexible and targeted service; and parallel change with a new type of service developed alongside the traditional home help service (DHSS, SSI, 1987; see also Morton, 1989b). Particularly acute are political issues. A service which changes from one provided for a large number of people and targets it on a few may not endear itself to councillors.

Meals

Meals, usually lunch, are provided for some older people either at day centres or clubs or are delivered to their homes. Sometimes a meal is cooked by a neighbour who may receive payment from the local authority. The meals service is a good example of co-operation between local authorities and voluntary bodies. As has been seen earlier, voluntary provision came first and local authorities were given powers to contribute to their costs under the National Assistance Act 1948. In 1962 this Act was amended to allow local authorities to provide meals themselves, as well as widening their powers to help voluntary bodies with the cost of vehicles, equipment, premises and staff.

The percentage of people over the age of 65 receiving meals on wheels has changed very little. In 1976 it was 3 per cent and in 1990 and 1985 it was 2 per cent (Table 8.1). Many more very old people now receive the service. Hunt found that while 2.6 per cent of all old people received meals on wheels, for those aged 85 and over it was 11.5 per cent. In 1985 the figures were 2 and 11 per cent (OPCS, 1989, p. 212).

Among the reasons stated for the provision of meals are the nutritional one and that of enabling someone to keep an eye on recipients to make sure all is well. However, research raises doubts about the nutritional value of the meals, about the value of the surveillance when visits only take place infrequently, and also more fundamental questions about whether provision of meals can sometimes increase dependency. Johnson *et al.* in *Ageing, Needs and Nutrition* argue that an extension of luncheon club provision might be a better use of resources given that few meals recipients are house-bound (Johnson *et al.*, 1981). In a review of provision of all kinds of meals Dunn's starting point was to consider why an elderly person might be in temporary or permanent need of a meal provided by someone else (Dunn, 1987). She looked at possible problems of finance, isolation, environment, cooking and cultural barriers. Only when these are analysed can an appropriate response be made; this may be help with shopping, advice on cooking or equipment or the provision of a microwave oven rather than meals on wheels.

Day care

Day care is care provided on a daily basis not in the elderly person's home. Attendance may be daily or less frequently. Sometimes this is provided in a day hospital where it is usually short term and with a specific clinical or rehabilitation aim (see Ch. 6), sometimes in a residential home and sometimes in a day centre or club. Voluntary organisations are the biggest providers of clubs for elderly people and a wide range of recreational facilities are offered. Both in 1980 and 1985 5 per cent of elderly people attended a day centre (Table 8.1).

The purpose of day centres and clubs is to provide a means of social contact and recreation, and in some of the former other services such as meals, laundry facilities and chiropody are available. Services provided may be for different sorts of need, including physical (meals, chiropody, etc.), emotional (companionship, advice, etc.), recreational (drama, choir, etc.) and further education. Day care may also be helpful in relieving relatives of their care of an elderly person for a few hours each day. A more recent innovation is care in the evenings or night.

The value of day care is underlined in research but so are a number of problems. In 1974 Morley in *Day Care and Leisure Provision for the Elderly* pointed to problems of transport, location and type of buildings (Morley, 1974). A national study was carried out by Carter, *Day Services for Adults: somewhere to go* (Carter, 1981), and this was complemented by a number of local studies. Goldberg and Connelly have summarised research up to 1981 and they concluded that the most important issue was how to integrate day care into a continuum of community services (Goldberg and Connelly, 1982). The second main issue concerned the effective organisation of day care and the third related to staffing.

The last ten years have seen a renewed questioning of the role of day care. Pahl's study, for example, found little difference between users of hospital and other kinds of day care (Pahl, 1988). This is clearly an anomaly as hospital care is more expensive to provide and yet free to the user. Tester's national survey in 1989 showed the variety of provision, the problems and some of the anomalies (Tester, 1989). Other current issues such as timing, transport and who should provide are raised in Morton (Morton, 1989c). Both Pahl and Tester argue for clarity of purposes of day care but while Pahl veers towards a general kind of provision with a range of activities Tester would like to see services become more specialist.

Good neighbour and similar schemes

Although the official Good Neighbour Campaign sprang into life in 1976 good neighbour, street warden and similar schemes had been in existence for many years. Some are run entirely by voluntary bodies, often churches, but some social services departments contribute money or staff to help.

The reasons for visiting elderly people may vary. They range from just talking to shopping and cooking. In some cases payment may be made to a good neighbour. Some of these schemes have been evaluated and been found to be popular and good value for money (Tinker, 1984). A more recent study acknowledged the role of paid care schemes in the provision of local and highly personal care, but showed that it was difficult to detail the contribution to total provision in terms of numbers or characteristics of clients served (Leat and Gay, 1987). The morality of paying some people to care, while other are expected to care for nothing and more often at a considerable loss, is also discussed by the authors.

Telephone and alarm systems

Old people, particularly those living alone and those who find difficulty getting out of their homes, may need to summon help in an emergency. They may also want to communicate with professionals such as their doctor or with relatives, friends and shopkeepers.

The most versatile means of two-way communication is the telephone. Many local authorities supply these to elderly people under the Chronically Sick and Disabled Persons Act 1970. The value of telephones for emergencies (Tinker, 1984), but also as a means of enabling elderly people to keep in touch with people outside the home (Tinker, 1989a), is well established.

A growing number of local authorities are providing alarm systems. Overall coverage is not known but it is known that 3 per cent of all disabled people have a personal alarm (Martin *et al.*, 1989, p. 56). A national survey showed their value especially those that can be worn on the person (Tinker, 1984). But the same research also showed that alarms need to be provided as part of a package of care. Subsequent research by the Research Institute for Consumer Affairs (RICA) offered advice on dispersed (i.e. not in sheltered housing) alarms to organisations (RICA, 1986) and to individuals (Consumers Association, 1986).

Holidays

Some elderly people, who might not otherwise have had a holiday, have been able to enjoy one through schemes organised by local authorities. Before 1962 there was no power to do this and any schemes there were were mostly organised by voluntary bodies. Some authorities meet the cost of a holiday taken independently, but most offer holidays for groups of old people. Some run their own homes but more use ordinary holiday accommodation, usually out-of-season, in the spring or autumn. In some schemes the organisation and accommodation are provided by voluntary bodies while the social services department selects the individuals and pays all or part of the cost.

SOCIAL WORK SUPPORT

Before the creation of social services departments most statutory work with elderly people was done by welfare officers, few of whom were qualified, from the welfare department of the local authority. In contrast most social workers working with children were trained and they were in the children's department. The Seebohm Committee recommended a radical alternative to the previous pattern of specialisation whereby social workers dealt with one client group only (Home Office *et al.*, 1968). They suggested that a generic training should be the norm. This was the subsequent pattern of training. The Younghusband Committee in the *Report of the Working Party on Social Workers* had previously also come down in favour of a generic approach (MOH *et al.*, 1959). However, they considered that some specialisation would be necessary above the basic field level.

A study for the DHSS, *Social Service Teams: the practitioner's view*, found that four types of specialisation had developed (Stevenson and Parsloe, 1978). They were informal specialisation within social work teams, formal specialisation at practitioner level, organisational specialism at team level (e.g. sub-teams concerned with particular groups of clients) and formal 'advisory' specialisms outside the teams (Stevenson and Parsloe, 1978). Despite the aims of the Seebohm reforms, a national survey in 1986 found a return to client group specialisation which 'reflects a desire to prevent the deskilling of social workers and improve professional standards in a hostile climate' (Challis and Ferlie, 1988, pp. 20–1).

Stevenson and Parsloe found social workers to be preoccupied with the needs of families and children to the exclusion of other groups such as elderly people. The Barclay Committee set up to review the role and tasks of social workers, commented: 'If an elderly person has problems of these kinds, we consider they are as much in need of social work help as a child might be. We cannot accept what in effect is rationing by age' (National Institute for Social Work (NISW), 1982, p. 47). Rowlings in *Social Work with Elderly People*, discusses some of the reasons for the reluctance of social workers to work with elderly people (Rowlings, 1981). An increase in legislation and more attention to child abuse have also led to a high priority being given to social work with children.

The nature and aims of social work are a matter of controversy. The Younghusband Committee saw the function of social workers as including the assessment of problems and the offer of appropriate help of a practical or supportive nature (e.g. practical assistance, giving information or bringing about environmental changes). Stevenson and Parsloe described case-work as 'broadly concerned with helping the individual or family with a range of problems rather than narrowly directed to discussing the client's emotional functioning and interpersonal relationships' (Stevenson and Parsloe, 1978, p. 133).

The debate about the purpose of social work continued with the Barclay Committee favouring a community, locally based approach (NISW, 1982). However, Pinker, in a powerfully argued note of dissent to the report, pointed out the dangers of this with the possibility of conflict between social workers as 'advocates' of 'community needs' and their employers. He also argued for the continuation of the trend towards specialised social workers rather than community workers.

The range and complexity of skills required by social workers have been spelt out in a number of helpful books about social work and older people (e.g. Bowl, 1986; Scrutton, 1989; Froggatt, 1990; Marshall, 1990).

A more detailed statement by the British Association of Social Workers (BASW) laying down guidelines for work with elderly people also gave a summary of the role of the qualified social worker [doc 29]. This role was based on social work values of acceptance, self-determination and confidentiality.

More recent policy developments have identified other potential roles including that of care manager responsible for organising packages of care. The White Paper *Caring for People* identified the need for a 'case' manager to ensure that the needs of individuals were regularly reviewed, resources managed effectively and that each service user had a single point of contact (Sec. of St. for Health *et al.*, 1989b, p. 21). It was envisaged that the case manager would often be employed by social services but not always. It was stated that: 'The Government does not wish to be prescriptive about the background from which the case manager should be drawn. A range of backgrounds could be possible, although social workers, home care organisers or community nurses, as the professionals in most regular contact with the client, may be particularly suitable' (Sec. of St. for Health *et al.*, 1989b, pp. 21–2). The policy guidance following the NHS and Community Care Act 1990 substituted 'care' for 'case' management (DOH, 1990a; Appendix B/2). The care manager was defined as: 'Any practitioner who undertakes all, or most, of the 'core tasks' of care management, who may carry a budgetary responsibility but is not involved in any direct service provision' (DOH, 1990a; Appendix B/2). The care manager was distinguished from the key worker who is to carry the main service providing role (DOH, 1990a, p. 25). It was considered that the skills of the care manager could be found in a number of professions in both statutory and non-statutory agencies.

Whether the social worker is the care manager or key worker or performs any other task, he or she must know about local resources and welfare rights and be able to negotiate with other agencies on behalf of elderly people. An enhanced role in supporting carers has also become apparent with the growing recognition of the importance of the latter. An expanding role is also likely in work with elderly people with dementia, those who are abused and those from ethnic minority groups. Social workers are also likely to have to pay more attention to user participation in services. All these elements in the social worker's job will call for new skills and must be reflected in training.

A discussion of the role of social workers cannot take place outside the context of the organisation of personal social services and in particular, from that of social services departments (Webb and Wistow, 1987).

The assessment of social work practice has only been attempted by a few researchers. One which took place between 1965 and 1970 found that trained social workers did not bring about any further change in physical circumstances but did create a general improvement in morale (Goldberg, 1970). A small study of older people living alone which compared those allocated to social workers with those in touch with home helps showed the complex nature of the tasks which the former undertook (Sinclair *et al.*, 1989). Social workers had not made much impact and users did not often understand what they were trying to do. However, in the Kent Community Care project elderly people with a social worker as care manager fared better on the criteria laid down compared with a control sample who did not have a care manager (Challis and Davies, 1986). One summary of research on the effectiveness of social work concluded that:

- social work and case management backed by practical resources can sustain or improve the morale of old people, reduce their practical problems and possibly lessen the likelihood that they will die or be admitted to residential care in a given period;
- social work is likely to be most effective with those who have particular difficulties but are either fit enough to manage on their own or, if severely dependent, have the support of a caring relative; and
- the likelihood of effective social work may well be reduced by the pressures on social workers in area offices, (Sinclair and Williams, 1990, p. 151).

Figure 8.2 Homes for elderly persons aged over 65, by number of residents and type of provision (England)

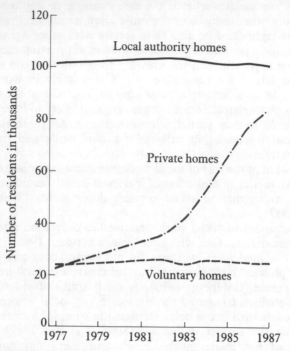

Source: HPSS Statistics 1989.
From: 'Epidemiological Overview of the Health of Elderly People', paper prepared by Dr Ruth Wallis, for DOH meeting on the Health of Elderly People 28.2.91, Figure 10.

RESIDENTIAL CARE

Provision and policy

Residential homes for elderly people are provided by local authorities, voluntary bodies and the private sector. While the overall proportion of elderly people in residential care has remained constant at about 2 per cent for some years there has been a dramatic shift towards private provision (Fig. 8.2). Between 1979 and 1989 there was an increase in numbers of residents over the age of 65 in England from 152,897 to 232,527 but whereas numbers in local authority and voluntary homes have remained almost stable those in private homes have risen from 26,095 to 111,391 (DOH, 1989b and [doc 30]). The Audit Commission concluded that, at best, there had been a shift from one pattern of residential care based on hospitals to an alternative supported in many cases by supplementary benefit payments, missing out more flexible and cost effective forms of community care altogether (Audit Commission, 1986, p. 2). Of the 97,337 people aged 65 and over in 1989 in England financially supported by local authorities 97 per cent were accommodated in local authority homes (DOH, 1989a, p. 5).

The main reason for the increase in private provision has been the availability of a board and lodging allowance by DHSS which has been paid to all those under certain capital limits without sufficient income to cover the fees but with no test of disability. Until 1980 most residents in voluntary sector homes received public funding from 'sponsorship' by local authorities in addition to the money that residents paid themselves. After this supplementary benefit board and lodging payments became available and 'there was an accelerating switch to this funding system accompanied by a massive increase in the number of private sector homes' (Peaker, 1988, p. 3; see also NAO, 1987, pp. 24–30, and Bradshaw in Baldwin *et al.*, 1988). DHSS social security expenditure on private residential care and nursing homes in GB was £10 million in 1979 and over £1000 million in 1989 (Sec. of St. for Health *et al.*, 1989b, p. 3). Numbers of people receiving this benefit increased from 12,000 to 90,000 between 1979 and 1986 (DHSS, Joint Central and Local Government Working Party, 1987, p. 6).

Residential care is for old people who, even with domiciliary support cannot manage to live in their own homes, but who still do not need intensive nursing care. Although the respective roles of residential home and hospital were laid down by MOH 15.9.65 in Memorandum for Local Authorities and Hospital Authorities, *Care of the Elderly in Hospitals and Residential Homes*, there is little current guidance. The boundary between very sheltered housing and residential care has also become blurred now that the former has to be registered under the Registered Homes Act, 1984 if care is provided (see Ch. 7 and NFHA *et al.*, 1987).

In 1980 the Residential Homes Act consolidated certain legislation relating to the registration, conduct and inspection of private and voluntary homes, but made no changes in powers. In 1982 DHSS issued a consultative document, *A Good Home*, which proposed a code of practice (DHSS, 1982c). Under the Health and Social Services and Social Security Adjudications Act 1983 a new classification of residential care homes, as distinct from nursing homes, was set up for establishments which provided residential accommodation with both board and personal care by reason of old age, disablement and certain other categories. Each home looking after four or more residents had to be registered with the local authority which might impose conditions and might refuse or cancel registration.

The Registered Homes Act 1984 defined a residential care home as: 'any establishment which provides or is intended to provide, whether for reward or not, residential accommodation with both board and personal care for four or more persons in need of personal care by reason of old age, disablement, past or present dependence on alcohol or drugs or past or present mental disorder.' The Act required homes to be registered with the local authorities and subject to inspection by them. The local authority may impose conditions and may refuse or cancel registration. Homes can have dual registration as a nursing home under the Nursing Homes Act, 1975 (see Jones, 1984). The Secretary of State has made the *Residential Care Homes Regulations*, 1984. In addition *Home Life: a code of practice* was published in 1984 as a result of a Working Party sponsored by DHSS and convened by CPA (CPA, 1984). Although it has no legal status DHSS asked local authorities to regard it in the same way as official guidance.

A working party report in 1985 recommended that local authorities' multidisciplinary assessment arrangements for admission to their own homes should be extended to those claiming supplementary board and lodging allowance for residential care in private and voluntary homes (DHSS, Joint Central and Local Government Working Party, 1985). A subsequent report (the Firth Report) of a joint central and local government working party, *Public Support for Residential Care*, was published (DHSS, 1987). It concluded that a system in which local government provided public support, rather than the social security system, for people in residential care homes offered the best way forward. They recommended that local authorities should take over assessment of need, setting of standards and responsibility for finance.

The Griffiths Report also recommended that local authority social services departments should be responsible for assessing the need for residential care (Griffiths, 1988). It also recommended that local social services departments should, if they judge it appropriate, meet the costs of caring for people who cannot pay themselves in residential (including nursing) homes above a basic level of support.

(This basic support should continue to be available as a social security entitlement, at a level broadly in line with that available to people in the community; Griffiths, 1988, pp. 1–2.)

The DOH White Paper *Caring for People* followed the recommendations outlined above and proposed that local authorities should take over responsibility for financial support of people in private and voluntary homes but that the new arrangements should not apply to existing residents (Sec. of St. for Health *et al.*, 1989b). Social services departments would become responsible for the assessment of people who sought care and wanted financial help. The subsequent National Health Service and Community Care Act 1990 formalised these proposals and also required the setting up of inspection units within local authorities to cover local authority residential homes, previously excluded from inspection, as well as those currently being inspected in the private and voluntary sector. Part III of that Act deals with community care. Its provisions are being phased in from 1991, with transfer of funds from social security to local authorities to begin from April 1993. In the meantime it is likely that some people will enter residential care inappropriately between 1991 and 1993.

Another development has been the transfer of Part III homes by local authorities to the private and voluntary sector. This has been mainly a result of Government policy. The White Paper *Caring for People* stated that social services departments should secure the delivery of services, not simply by acting as direct providers, but by developing their purchasing and contracting role to become enabling authorities (Sec. of St. for Health *et al.*, 1989b, p. 17).

Meanwhile in 1985 an independent review of residential care was set up by the Secretary of State for Health and Social Services. Its terms of reference were to review all forms of residential care and to make recommendations. The Committee, chaired by Lady Wagner, reported in 1988 (Wagner, 1988a). Some of their recommendations are referred to later in this section (and see [doc 31]). In a critical account covering every aspect of residential care for all groups they concluded that entry must be *A Positive Choice*, the title of their report. To make this choice, they said, there is need for:

- adequate information about options;
- realistic alternatives to choose from;
- help, if necessary, in making choices;
- the initial choice to be tested by a trial period with an option to return to the previous situation if possible, or to another setting;

159

- a review of the chosen service at appropriate intervals;
- ways to appeal against inadequate, inappropriate or enforced services (Wagner, 1988a, p. 26).

An accompanying volume to the Wagner report, *The Research Reviewed* (Wagner, 1988b), contains a summary of research on residential care for elderly people (Sinclair, 1988). The Wagner Development Group was formed in 1988 and the Caring in Homes Initiative set up by DOH in 1989 to carry forward the recommendations. The latter includes demonstration projects in five major areas and this will be followed by publication of models of good practice. More recently the Social Services Inspectorate of DOH have produced useful guidance on standards in homes (DOH, SSI, 1989 and 1990) and a helpful study has been made of regulatory practice for residential homes for elderly people (Kellaher *et al.*, 1988).

The residents

Evidence has already been presented that some elderly people have been in residential care only because of a lack of alternative housing (e.g. Townsend, 1964) [doc 32]. More recent evidence shows that some elderly people are inappropriately placed in most forms of care (e.g. Wade *et al.*, 1983). This is particularly so in the case of residential care (Audit Commission, 1985; DHSS, Joint Central and Local Government Working Party, 1987). Much of the evidence is summarised in Neill *et al.*, 1988. Research, mainly from the local authority sector, shows that the idea of residential care often begins with someone other than the applicant. Applicants have often not been given sufficient information to make an informed choice and only rarely do they make a positive choice (Sinclair, 1988, p. 264). Although a small pilot study for DHSS found that the proportion of elderly people in private and voluntary homes who were found to be in need of residential care at the time of admission was very small (Bradshaw *et al.*, 1987), Bradshaw has subsequently argued that there are still strong reasons for having an assessment procedure (Bradshaw, 1988).

The pressure for a move away from residential care is based on the views of elderly people themselves, the development of alternatives and the cost. However, some argue that an expansion of residential care is needed bearing in mind the expected growth in numbers of very elderly people. Table 8.2 shows the growing

Table 8.2. The growing percentage of very elderly people in residential homes 1980–1989.

	Percentage of residents aged 85 and over in local authority, private and voluntary homes
1980	37.6
1981	40.3
1982	41.0
1983	41.6
1984	42.8
1985	42.6
1986	43.6
1987	44.4
1988	45.6
1989	47.7

Source: DOH Personal Social Services *Local Authority Statistics, Residential Accommodation for Elderly and for Younger Physically Handicapped People. All Residents in Local Authority, Voluntary and Private Homes, Year ending 31.3.89*, RA/89/2, DOH, 1989, Table B.

proportion of very elderly people in residential care. Grundy and Arie have suggested that residential care is needed for those who need round-the-clock support and live alone (Grundy and Arie, 1982). Demand for residential care outruns provision and may be increased by demographic trends (Sinclair, 1988, p. 280) and stress on carers (F. Wright, forthcoming).

One of the key factors in the success of residential care should be the assessment of the elderly person. A useful summary of the literature and advice is given by the DHSS Social Services Inspectorate (SSI) (DHSS, SSI, 1985). The experience of a pilot study for DHSS concluded that there was no intrinsic barrier to employing social workers to assess elderly people's needs for residential care in the private sector (Bradshaw *et al.*, 1987).

Concern is growing over the frailty and confusion of residents in homes. The trend is for elderly people to be older on admission. In 1989 64 people aged 75 and over per 1,000 population in that age group were resident in a residential care home in England compared with 47 in 1980 (DOH, Personal Social Services, Local Authority Statistics 1989b, para. 9). One research project directly concerned with this was a feasibility study for NHS nursing homes which led to a number of experimental homes being set up (Wade *et al.*, 1983) and evaluated (Bond *et al.*, 1989).

Elderly people in modern society

Most elderly people move to institutional care voluntarily or with persuasion. But in certain circumstances – such as where an old person is physically incapacitated or is living in insanitary conditions and is unable to devote to herself, and is not receiving from other people, due care and attention – the local authority may apply for a court order for their compulsory removal to a hospital or other suitable place (under Section 47 of the National Assistance Act 1948). This power is rarely used.

Some important factors

Important aspects with residential care to be considered include setting up standards and monitoring the quality of care; staff training; numbers and deployment; design and adequacy of buildings, costs and the issue of unregistered homes.

Concern about standards in residential homes is considerable. These relate particularly to provision of privacy; the rights of the residents and their opportunities for self-determination; availability of choice over many everyday matters; and arrangements for health care. These were highlighted in the Wagner Report.

Many ways have been suggested to make life more satisfying and individual for both residents and staff. For example DHSS in *A Lifestyle for the Elderly* looked at ways in which staff and buildings could meet the real needs of residents (DHSS, 1976d). The point of the title of the report was that elderly people are not just consumers of a service but have a lifestyle which affects every aspect of living. How quality of care can be measured is discussed by Kellaher who then suggests that the available evidence indicates that residents are more satisfied with, and express definite preferences for, those care arrangements which allow a fundamental rather than a token measure of control over their range of life domains (Kellaher, 1986).

Availability of adequate numbers of staff may be related to the low status of residential social work and a lack appropriate training (Willcocks *et al.*, 1986; Sinclair, 1988). Among the recommendations of the Wagner Committee were that care staff should no longer be graded as manual staff but that their posts should be redefined as officers or the professional equivalent and that every establishment should have staff training plans. Perhaps more important was their recommendation that 'residential staff are the major resource and should be valued as such. The importance of their contribution needs to be recognised and enhanced' (Wagner, 1988a, p. 114).

One major study has widespread implications for buildings. *A*

Balanced Life is a consumer study of residential life in 100 local authority homes (Peace *et al.*, 1982 and Willcocks *et al.*, 1986). The researchers concluded that a major problem was lack of privacy and recommended that future homes should allow for more private and less communal space. They argued for residential flatlets which are more akin to very sheltered housing.

Few residential homes are now used exclusively for residential care. In some homes residents only stay for a short time, perhaps while relatives have a break, or for rehabilitation between hospital and their own home. Allen, in *Short-stay Residential Care for the Elderly*, found that the needs of short-stay residents were often different from long-stay and that the former seemed to be most successful when in a separate home or wing (Allen, 1983). The main beneficiaries seemed to be the carers. The use of residential provision as a community resource was supported by the Wagner Committee but with some reservations (Wagner, 1988a: Ch. 5).

On costs there is no doubt that institutional care is not cheap. The revenue costs for local authority residents was £118.48 per resident per week in 1986–7 (Tinker, 1989b). The overall public expenditure costs have already been given [doc 21]. It will be seen that Part III accommodation is less expensive than hospital care but more expensive than very sheltered housing and staying at home with a package of care (Tinker, 1989b, p. 114).

As has been noted (p. 158), residential care homes must be registered with their local authority if they care for four or more residents. Homes with three or fewer residents are not required to register (in England and Wales) and hence are known as unregistered residential care homes. Such schemes are likely to be seen as a business venture, although a small study found that there was little or no 'profit' in such small schemes (Young, 1988). Concern arises about standards in such homes when they are not inspected by the local authority.

A problem for residents in the private sector is the gap between income support levels and the fees charged so that they have to 'top up' their fees from relatives or charities (Peaker, 1986).

SUPPORTED LODGINGS SCHEMES

It has already been seen that both hospital (Ch. 6) and residential homes (above) provide short-stay and respite care for elderly people. Another kind of provision is supported lodgings, which is 'a general term covering a range of schemes such as: adult placement schemes, adult fostering, boarding out, home finding and so on. The common feature of all such schemes is that a care agency places people who need care (referred to as clients) in a living situation where they receive care or support as well as board and accommodation' (Young, 1988, p. 1). Where there have been schemes in the past they were often labelled by the press as 'rent a granny' or 'foster a granny'.

In a handful of towns voluntary organisations ran schemes like this is the late 1940s, but there was little public provision. A survey in 1977 of all social services departments in England and Wales revealed that less than 10 per cent had schemes operating (Rattee, 1977). A survey in 1980 found only 23 schemes in England and Wales. Some were long- and some short-term with a wide range of objectives from providing a cheap form of care, to enhancing the quality of life of elderly people (Thornton and Moore, 1980). The researchers reported satisfaction by both elderly people and their carers. They emphasised the importance of selecting and matching the elderly person and the person caring for them.

By 1982 just over one-third of English local authorities were running supported lodgings schemes (Tait, 1983) and by 1987–8 it had risen to 81 per cent in England, Wales and Scotland (Young, 1988). In the latter study 41 per cent of providers had only one scheme. Most schemes were quite small. Only 20 per cent had 20 or more carers and 40 per cent had under five. One-third of schemes placed elderly people and this was as follows:

	%
long-term care only	7
respite care only	62
respite and long-term care	31
	100

Carers were providing a high level of physical and personal care and many clients were receiving a level of care one would expect in a registered residential care home.

A slightly different kind of scheme is one using volunteers as opposed to employed individuals and research has found that the most likely model was an unpaid volunteer providing a regular daytime sitting service which was not necessarily what was wanted (Thornton, 1989).

In a summary of the research on all kinds of short-term care it is noted that spouses, who seem very reluctant to give up their caring role, rarely used it (Sinclair and Williams, 1990). The evidence also suggests a need to increase the quantity of short-stay care, increase the variety of ways it is provided, pay attention to the wish of carers for a shared approach, e.g. by passing on information about treatment, and ensuring that rotating care is part of a combination of services (Sinclair and Williams, 1990).

MOBILITY AND TRANSPORT

The mobility of elderly people, which affects their access to facilities, may decrease with increasing age. Not only do many of them become physically less able to move about but fewer own cars than other age groups. This may be less to do with age than with that generation of old people. In 1986 only 40 per cent of households containing at least one older person had a car, compared with 72 per cent containing no older people (OPCS, 1989, Table 12.4). The 1985 *General Household Survey* showed that elderly women, many of whom probably never learnt to drive, and people living alone were less likely to have a car than men (OPCS, 1989). It is estimated that walking accounts for about eight in ten of the journeys of pensioners without a car (Hillman and Whalley, 1979, p. 101). However, pedestrian casualty rates are much higher among people over 60 compared with younger adults and fatalities of people aged 75 and over account for a quarter of all pedestrian fatalities (ACE, 1990a). In 1985 about three-fifths of elderly people made use of public transport. The main reasons for not using it were related to not having a car and ill health and disability (OPCS, 1988, p. 182). The study of disabled adults, of whom the majority were elderly, found that for those in private households the largest number (76 per cent) had used a private car the previous year, 57 per cent a bus, 27 per cent a taxi and smaller proportions other forms of transport (Martin *et al.*, 1989, p. 24).

Suggestions made by ACE to improve access of older people include improving public transport, developing new forms of transport such as dial-a ride buses and taxi-card schemes and ensuring that older people can afford transport (ACE, 1990a). Concessionary fares (Ch. 5) are helpful, but less so for elderly people who live in areas with an infrequent bus service. One researcher has described 'the chaos of travel concessions' because of the complexity and unevenness of schemes (Norman, 1977).

Table 8.3.   Staffing trends in local authorities 1974–1987–88 England

Full time equivalents	*1974*[1]	*1979*[1]	*1984*[1]	*1987/8*[2]	*% increase 1974–87/8*
Home help service staff	42,400	46,700	53,100	59,500	40
Social workers	17,000	22,700	24,300	27,000	59
Occupational therapists	n/a	n/a	900	1,100	n/a
Adult training centre/day centre	8,100	11,400	15,000	27,200[a]	236

[a] Staff in day care establishments.
[1] Audit Commission, *Making a Reality of Community Care*, HMSO, 1986, p. 61, Table 22.
[2] Secretaries of State for Health, Social Security, Wales and Scotland, *Caring for People*, HMSO, 1989, p.17.

SOME ISSUES

Some of the points of concern about local social services are discussed elsewhere. These include variation between authorities (Ch. 12) and voluntary organisations (Ch. 10). Some which are more specific are discussed below.

Levels of provision

Comparative data about levels of provision of local social services are difficult to find. The National Audit Office commented that there was a general lack of information (NAO, 1987). In one comparison of social services for elderly people between 1965 and 1976 the conclusion was that there had been an enormous expansion in domiciliary services (e.g. twice as many people received a home help and meals on wheels) but for some services the expansion had been at the expense of people receiving it less frequently (Bebbington, 1979). This shows the need for caution with statistics. Nor does a comparison of expenditure necessarily give the full picture. For example while the expenditure figures in the White Paper *Caring for People* show that the gross expenditure on domiciliary care in Great Britain went up from £464 million in 1979–80 to £1,167 in 1987–8 (a growth in real terms of 37 per cent), this does not necessarily mean an expansion in services (Sec. of St. for Health *et al.*, 1989b; [doc 33]). It might mean that numbers of staff had risen (Table 8.3)

Table 8.4.   Personal social services 1976 to 1986

	1976	1986	% change 76–86
Meals 000s	40544.0	44110.8	+ 8.8
per 000 65+	6121.9	6139.8	+ 0.3
per 000 75+	17041.0	14453.5	−15.2
per 000 85+	89719.0	75922.1	−15.4
Home helps wte*	44.2	–	+23.8
per 000 65+	6.3	7.4	+17.5
per 000 75+	17.3	17.3	0
per 000 85+	91.8	89.3	− 2.7
Day care 000s	13.4	21.5	+60.4
per 000 65+	2.0	3.0	+50.0
per 000 75+	5.6	7.0	+25.0
per 000 85+	29.6	37.0	+25.0

* whole time equivalent
Source: DHSS Statistical Bulletin 3.5.88: *Personal Social Services for elderly and younger disabled persons England 1976–1986* (quoted in Henwood, 1990, p. 28).

or had received a rise in salaries. Nor does it relate expenditure to the growing number of vulnerable elderly people. In the absence of age specific statistics on the use of facilities it has been suggested that community services for the over 75s may have had difficulty in keeping pace with demographic change. This appears to be the case for the very old with meals and home helps, but not day care (Table 8.4). The NAO estimated that numbers of home helps per 1,000 people aged 75 and over in England dropped from 18.6 in 1975 to 17 in 1985, meals on wheels from 15.9 to 14.1 but local authority day centre places had risen from 6 to 10.2 (NAO, 1987, p. 32). They also pointed to the move to more short-term hospital care which indicated that elderly people are spending more time in the community with the consequent need for additional community services (NAO, 1987, p. 31).

One indication of unmet needs is in the OPCS disability surveys where disabled people were asked whether they needed some kind of domiciliary service they were not getting (Martin *et al.*, 1988). The most common service needed was a chiropodist (34 per cent) followed by a home help (21 per cent) (Martin *et al.*, 1988, p. 39 and p. 41).

Standards

One development in the 1980s has been the move away from norms (i.e. quantity) provision laid down by DHSS. Although these have not all been explicitly dropped much more recognition is being given to local conditions. In *Care in Action* it was stated that for personal social services: 'The Government indicates broad national policies, issues guidance where necessary and has a general concern for standards. There are only a small number of direct controls and these are being reduced as a matter of general Government policy towards local government' (DHSS, 1981a, p. 19). In 1982 the position was made even clearer when DHSS were asked by the House of Commons Committee on Social Services whether some indication could be given of the informal minimum personal social services standards which they used (House of Commons, 1982). They replied that they did not have any formalised or precisely quantified minimum standards.

The organisation of social services departments

A formidable problem of size was posed when local authority departments were not only amalgamated but took on fresh responsibilities at the time when the new social services departments were created. Most departments have attempted to get over the problem of size by creating area teams and patch organisations.

Staff

Numbers of staff in the personal social services have risen for all kinds of staff as Table 8.2 shows. Between 1981 and 1988 in the UK social work staff increased by 22 per cent and managment/administrative/ancilliary staff in local personal social services by 19 per cent (CSO, 1991, p. 132). Lack of trained staff is a major problem in social services departments. Residential staff, of whom few are trained, face particular problems. The Williams Report, *Caring for People: staffing residential homes* commented on the lack of a career structure, the variation in accommodation provided and the need for skills (NCSS, 1967). These views were endorsed by the Wagner Committee which particularly stressed the need for training (Wagner, 1988a). Demands on residential staff are likely to increase as a higher proportion of residents accepted are very frail and also possibly confused.

Another difficulty arises when jobs, such as those of social work, have no generally accepted job specification. It then becomes even more difficult to allocate work between the qualified professional, the unqualified social worker and the volunteer.

Innovatory schemes

As Isaacs has pointed out, an innovation has three components: a good idea, making it work, and demonstrating that it works (Isaacs and Evers, 1984). In *A Happier Old Age* stress was laid on exploring innovatory methods, especially in providing practical help to meet personal needs (DHSS, 1978a). In the 1980s many such schemes did develop and have since been incorporated in mainstream services. They included intensive home care and alarm schemes, the Kent Community Care project and others designed to help carers. A major finding of a national survey on innovatory schemes was that they needed to be provided as part of a package of care which included formal and informal services (Tinker, 1984). The lessons of the Kent scheme have been influential in policies to give a manager a budget to buy in care. In this scheme community care was targeted on people on the margins of residential care (Challis and Davis, 1986). Social workers with small caseloads were given a budget of two thirds the cost of residential care and were able to buy in services. The clients were matched with a control group who received the usual range of services. On various criteria, including cost and quality of life, the elderly people in the scheme were significantly better off.

Innovations need to be evaluated before it is decided whether they should be expanded, abandoned or incorporated into mainstream services. Interest is growing in the process of innovation and in the culture of the organisation to see why some become 'thrusters' and others 'sleepers' (Ferlie *et al.*, 1989).

Private and voluntary care

There is a great lack of hard information about the private sector but it is already known that it differs from public care in a number of ways including organisation, finance, use, regulation and the kinds of people it caters for (Parker, 1990 in Morton 1990b).

Private residential care is not new but private provision of other services such as domiciliary care is (Tinker, 1990b in Morton 1990b). Government policy in 1991 has been to put more weight on the independent sector. The White Paper *Caring for People* stated: 'The Government will expect local authorities to make use whenever possible of services from voluntary, 'not for profit' and private providers insofar as this represents a cost effective care choice' (Sec. of St. for Health *et al.*, 1989b, p. 22). Ways to develop this mixed economy of welfare include taking steps to stimulate the setting up of not for profit agencies, identifying areas of their own work which are sufficiently self contained to be suitable for 'floating off' as self managed units and stimulating the development of new voluntary sector activity (Sec. of St. for Health, 1989b, p. 23).

It is claimed, but with little evidence, that private care enables elderly people to be more in control and to be more able to choose the kind of service (including tasks done and timing) than in publicly provided services. The dangers are that there may be abuse unless standards are monitored and some kind of inspection takes place. There may also be problems where there are few competitors, when large organisations move into areas where profits are to be made, undercut their rivals and then raise prices (Glennerster *et al.*, 1990). Some have argued that regulation and inspection can be done by the providers as is done with private sheltered housing.

Charges for services

Charges may be made by local authorities for certain services. After the NHS and Community Care Act, 1990 it was stated that detailed guidance would follow on the powers and duties of local authorities to charge for personal social services, but 'it is expected that local authorities will institute arrangements so that the users of services of all types pay what they can reasonably afford towards their costs' (DOH, 1990a, pp. 28–9).

Little is known about these charges, which vary between areas, or how far they dissuade people from using services.

Links with other agencies

It is likely that more of all the supportive services are needed – more home helps, better laundry services, more adequate meals services and so on. But what is vitally important is that all the services should be planned together. Links between social services and health were discussed in Chapter 6 and housing in Chapter 7. Policy guidance from DOH in 1990 noted that the NHS and Community Care Act 1990 requires social services to bring apparent housing and health care needs to the attention of the appropriate authorities and invite them to assist in the assessment (DOH, 1990a, p. 29).

The other main agency with whom social workers come into contact is the Department of Social Security. This may be over eligibility for income support but also over the social fund.

CONCLUSION

At the beginning of the 1990s questions were being raised about the future of personal social services if they became enablers and managers (e.g. Allen, 1989). Would their own services become residual with all the likely stigma? Would contracting out mean more or less choice? How would social care be linked to health care and housing? And how would the link be made with informal care? It is to this last question that the next two chapters are addressed.

Chapter nine

COMMUNITY CARE – THE FAMILY

INTRODUCTION

When planning the provision of any social service three fundamental questions have to be asked. What is the need? How is it to be met? Who is to provide?

The first and second questions are discussed in Chapters 5–8 which dealt with particular needs and services, and a wider examination of need is to be found in Chapter 12. Chapters 5–8 paid special attention to developments in the statutory services. But there are other sources of help which are both more numerous and of longer standing. They are first the family, second the community expressed through voluntary organisations, volunteers and the wider network of neighbours and friends, and third elderly people themselves. These three will be examined in this and the next two chapters.

It is proposed to look first at the rise of the Welfare State and its effect on the family (in particular the extended family) and the three-generation household. Then some factors which are changing the pattern of family care will be discussed. Recent policy developments will be described. Evidence will then be presented about the degree of contact elderly people have with relatives and the extent of family care. Finally, questions will be asked about support for families in their caring role.

THE RISE OF THE WELFARE STATE AND ITS EFFECT ON THE FAMILY

Before examining the part that families play in providing help for elderly people some consideration must be given to the debate about the rise of the Welfare State and the alleged consequent decline of the family as a caring group.

If it is argued that the Welfare State is a 'state which has a policy of collective responsibility for the individual's well-being' (Clegg, 1971) with social services provided on behalf of society then, some have argued, the state must have taken over at least part of the role of the family. This issue was being debated in the 1960s and 1970s. For example Fletcher, while not holding this view himself, reported that some believe that 'since much is now publicly provided for old people . . . responsibility on the part of their families for the care of the aged has fallen away' (Fletcher, 1966, p. 160). Wright and Randall summarised the position of the family in pre-industrial England and gave some reasons why the state had taken over some (but not all) of the functions of the family (Wright and Randall, 1970). But after weighing the evidence they concluded that, in spite of all the forecasts about its imminent dissolution, the family continues to exist.

The conclusion of an extensive examination of the family and the state by Moroney is that: 'on balance, the evidence does not support the view that the modern family is giving up its caring function, or transferring its traditional responsibilities to the state' (Moroney, 1976). This view is supported by studies in the 1980s. For example Qureshi and Walker in their study in Sheffield said that they had found no evidence whatsoever that the family is breaking down (Qureshi and Walker, 1989, p. 244). This finding is echoed by other studies. In *Family Obligations and Social Change* Finch said: 'If anything it has been the state's assuming some responsibility for individuals – such as the granting of old age pensions – which has freed people to develop closer and more supportive relationships with their kin' (Finch, 1989, p. 243) [doc 34].

The difficulty in trying to make comparisons with the past lies in the lack of available data. Great care must be exercised in drawing conclusions when the picture of past conditions is so hazy. Finch says: 'If we take a fairly long historical perspective, we can see that people in the present are not necessarily any more or less willing to support their relatives than in the past; but the circumstances under which they have to work out these commitments themselves have changed and created new problems to be solved' (Finch, 1989, p. 242). Most of such evidence as there is about family care of old people relates to two separate concepts, the extended family and the three-generation household.

THE EXTENDED FAMILY AND THE THREE-GENERATION HOUSEHOLD

The extended family is not easy to define. Stacey attempts this definition: 'The extended family has generally been used for a persistent group of relatives, wider than the elementary family. Empirical evidence suggests that the numbers and categories of kin included in such social groups are highly variable. It is not therefore susceptible of precise definition' (Stacey, 1969, p. 36). A commonly used definition is that used by Rosser and Harris: 'Any persistent kinship groupings of persons related by descent, marriage or adoption, which is wider than the elementary family, in that it characteristically spans three generations from grandparents to grandchildren' (Rosser and Harris, 1965, p. 32). Many sociological studies, especially Young and Willmott's *Family and Kinship in East London*, have stressed the importance of the extended family in exercising a mutual caring role (Young and Willmott, 1957). Willmott subsequently described the typology of kinship as the local extended family, the dispersed extended family, the dispersed kinship network and the residual kinship network (Willmott, 1986).

The extended family is rooted in static and immobile patterns of society. Now younger people often have to move to where work is. If close links are to be preserved the elderly person may have to leave friends and neighbours and move as well to where their relatives have gone. Even if accommodation is available this solution may not always be the right one.

The second situation which is held to have a bearing on the family–old person relationship is the three-generation household. Much discussion has centred on the living arrangements of families and it is often assumed that the common pattern used to be one of three generations living together as one household. The further assumption is then made that if people live under the same roof they will care for one another. Whether many families did live like this is uncertain. There certainly have been many statements made that the three-generation household was fairly common. For example Cullingworth stated: 'The increasing break-up of three-generation households into two separate units . . . involves the provision of two or even three dwellings for every one that would have been required 50 years ago' (Cullingworth, 1960). Beyer and Nierstrasz likewise talk about 'the days when the three-generation household was the norm' (Beyer and Nierstrasz, 1967, p. 11).

But recent research casts doubts on whether the three-generation household ever existed widely, although there is no doubt that the size of households has declined. In 1961 12 per cent of all households in Great Britain were one person, but in 1989 they represented 25 per cent (CSO, 1991, p. 36). Hole and Pountney, in *Trends in Population, Housing and Occupancy Rates 1861–1961*, suggest that the larger households in Victorian times were due partly to a large number of children and partly to apprentices, domestic servants and lodgers. They say: 'Considerable doubt has been thrown on the popular conception of the Victorian household . . . it seems that a household consisting only of parents and children was as typical then as it is today' (Hole and Pountney, 1971, p. 27). They later conclude that the typical household was not an extended family, but one consisting of parent(s) and children only.

Laslett comes to a similar conclusion and suggests that the nuclear family was the normal arrangement even before industrialisation (Laslett, 1989). He points out how few old people survived to old age anyway, making the three-generation household a physical impossibility in most cases. His explanation of the myth of this type of household is that it was probably due to a cherished mythology and a wish to believe in the large and extended household.

In 1976 Hunt found that 12.5 per cent of elderly people lived with the next generation (Hunt, 1978). This figure compares with that of 7 per cent in the 1985 *GHS* (OPCS, 1989, p. 185).

CHANGING FACTORS

However, there are some qualifications arising out of all the research which must now be considered. These qualifications revolve around two points: whether close links are always desirable and whether this situation is likely to continue.

On the first point, little is known about standards of care by families. A number of authors have hinted at the tensions when families and older people live under one roof (e.g. Willmott and Young, 1960 and Brandon, 1972). Pruner claims that separate households do not mean the end of family ties and that living together is not necessarily a sign of family stability but can involve strain (Pruner, 1974). A study of 684 elderly people in Wales found that 133 (19 per cent) lived with their younger relatives (Wenger, 1984). Among this group living with younger relatives loneliness was more common than among other sub groups (Wenger, 1984, p. 190). Ungerson's qualitative study of 19 carers concluded that married women carers found care in the extended family was potentially destructive of the nuclear family of which they were a part (Ungerson, 1987). Elderly people living with their relatives may also find themselves less likely to get help from statutory services (Charlesworth *et al.*, 1984; Levin *et al.*, 1989 and Evandrou, 1987). Nor should it be forgotten, as Askham points out, that not everyone may be able to provide care for many reasons including lack of strength or knowledge (Askham, 1989, p. 112).

There is also the point raised by Fletcher that a high level of close family ties may not be as satisfactory as one which gives a greater degree of independence. He argues that: 'Close kinship relationships have their value but they can also be limiting, confining, frustrating, so that the loosening of these ties, for some people at any rate, may constitute a desirable improvement' (Fletcher, 1966, p. 171). There is little research on the preferences of older people for support from the various sources.

The second question is whether family links are likely to continue. Pessimists point to the reduction in the size of families which will mean that elderly people will have fewer children to turn to, the non-availability of the family when everyone is out of the house all day at school or work, the emergence of the four-generation family, and the mobility of families. Yet a closer examination of all these factors shows that the position is not as bleak as might be supposed and that there are other factors emerging that potentially may lead to more help being available.

Taking first the reduction in family size the most striking point is that it was between 1860 and 1910 that the average number of children born to a woman dropped most dramatically (from an average of 7 to 3). Since then the numbers have altered little. They dropped to 2.4 for women married in 1920 and 2.1 in 1940 and rose to 2.3 in 1950. Subsequent numbers, as far as can be ascertained where families have been completed, seem to be just about two children per married woman. This shows that smaller families are not a new phenomenon but have been in evidence since around the beginning of the century.

What is more significant is that today more children survive. A mother having seven children in 1860 would not expect that number to be still alive when she was old. There has been a remarkable decline in the infant mortality rate. This is most pronounced for infants under one year, but still appreciable for all ages of childhood. It is now the exception rather than the rule for a mother not to have her children survive to adult life.

Added to this is the fact that children live longer and therefore are more likely to be alive when their parents are old. The expectation of life at birth for a man in 1891–1900 was 44.1 and for a woman 47.8. In 1950–2 it was 66.5 for a man and 71.5 for a woman. In 1989 it was 72.4 for a man and 78.1 for a woman. This means that there will be more people in middle and early old age who may be able to assist their own parents as they move into extreme old age.

The alleged diminution in the pool of family care is also a more complex matter than would appear at first sight. On the one hand there are trends to suggest that sources of family help may be diminishing. There are fewer unmarried women to remain at home to care for aged relatives. There are also fewer married women at home because many more now go out to work. In 1921 8.7 per cent of married women were in paid employment (Moroney, 1976, p. 19) but by 1961 this had risen to 29.7 per cent (CSO, 1976, p. 19) and in 1981 this had gone up to 49.5 per cent (CSO, 1980, p. 58). The Department of Employment estimate that in the next ten years the female labour force in the UK will increase in all regions and by as much as 21 per cent in some areas (House of Commons, 1990a). So a lower proportion of potential carers *may* be available than in the past. On the other hand the decline in the number of single women means that more are marrying and therefore will probably have children to support them when they are elderly. And while there is a great increase in the number of married women working, many part-time, their greater financial independence may well enable them to buy in help for their elderly parents or give assistance with labour-saving devices.

Another potentially complicating factor is the growing complexity of family life. Growing rates of divorce, remarriage and co-habitation mean new sets of in-laws, step-parents and varying relationships. To which older people will the younger feel bound?

Another changing factor is the role of men as carers. A shorter working week, the increased possibility of flexible working hours and the greater sharing of tasks between men and women may all contribute to more men being able to help. Subsequent evidence presented in this chapter suggests that men are playing a role.

The emergence of the four-generation family must also be taken into account. The reduction of the age gap between generations may mean that a grandparent is far from being a dependent; she may be an agile woman who goes out to work full-time. A four-generation family can mean that a grandmother in her 60s is torn because her life is divided between the demands of her mother and her own children who may expect help with their children.

Family ties are also affected by mobility. A number of studies have found, not surprisingly, that the closer children live the more complete the assistance they are able to give in time of need (Jackson, 1968, Tinker, 1976). A specific question in the 1980 *GHS* directed to elderly people who lived alone showed that 30 per cent had relatives living nearby (OPCS, 1982, p. 169). Abrams found that nearly two-thirds of his sample of elderly people over 75 lived in the same dwellings, the same street or neighbourhood as their sons and daughters or only five to six miles away (Abrams, 1978, p. 22).

Another factor which may affect the future, and influence whether families continue to exercise a caring role, is the views of elderly people themselves. Age Concern England found that the expectation that children will look after their elderly parents was not accepted to any great extent. Sixty-seven per cent of the elderly people felt that 'old people should not expect their children to look after them' and elderly parents were most likely to agree strongly with the statement (ACE, 1978, p. 59). But when they speak of 'looking after' they may mean 'having them living in the same house'.

What is known about extended families and three-generation households does not provide enough evidence of greater family care in the past to justify the theory that the Welfare State has caused a decline in family care. Perhaps the factors mentioned in this section are the real reasons for any changes in family care rather than any theory about the consequences of the rise of the welfare state or the supposed breakdown of the extended family and the three-generation household.

POLICY DEVELOPMENTS

The family came into even greater prominence in the 1980s. The White Paper *Growing Older* not only recognised that families were still the principal source of support but held that there was 'no evidence to suggest that the modern family has given up its caring functions or transferred its responsibilities to the State' (DHSS, 1981d, p. 37). The emphasis in policy was to be on providing support for families. The family became a major theme for political speeches.

Among the actions taken by DHSS was the listing of initiatives (DHSS, Social Work Service Development Group, 1983), the issuing of models of practice for planners and practitioners (DHSS Social Work Service Development Group, 1984), the setting up of demonstration projects to support informal carers (Hills, 1991) and advice on setting up services for carers (Haffenden, 1991). It is argued that all these initiatives are but a drop in the ocean and what is needed is far greater provision of services (e.g. Hicks, 1988).

Both the Griffiths Report and the White Paper *Caring for People* (see Ch. 8) underlined the importance of carers. The Policy Guidance after the NHS and Community Care Act 1989 stressed the role of carers in assessing services for elderly people. It stated: 'The preferences of carers should be taken into account and their willingness to continue caring should not be assumed. Both service users and carers should therefore be consulted – separately, if either of them wishes – since their views may not coincide' (DOH, 1990a, p. 28).

The all-party House of Commons Committee on Social Services in its fifth report *Community Care: Carers* (House of Commons, 1990a) reported that the Minister had told them: 'we say very clearly and explicitly that we think practical help for carers is called for. . . . Although not enshrined in legislation, the role of the carer most clearly will be given the priority that they deserve in all our guidance about assessment, about community care plans and about all the other aspects of these proposals' (House of Commons, 1990a; para 4). The Committee replied that one of the reasons for their witnesses' dissatisfaction with the Government's plans for helping carers was that some of their needs were not ones which legislation or formal administrative structures could resolve. The Committee believed that the Government should set three long-term objectives for carers. These were improved income maintenance, improved opportunities to combine work with caring, and improved availability of domestic and nursing services (House of Commons, 1990a, para 104).

CONTACT WITH RELATIVES

Most social surveys find that elderly people have frequent contact with a relative [doc 35]. Willmott and Young found that 56 per cent of their sample in Woodford had seen a relative the previous day and in Bethnal Green it was 58 per cent (Willmott and Young, 1960 p. 43). Surveys of other areas which were not tight-knit communities in the sense that Bethnal Green was (and probably still is) show that family links are still very much alive. (N.B. Bowling has analysed the different ways in which researchers have measured social support; Bowling, 1991.)

With children

In most cases contact was with a child. This is as true now as it was in the earlier sociological studies such as those by Willmott and Young. In 1978 Hunt found that visits from daughters/daughters-in-law and sons/sons-in-law easily outstripped those of other relatives (Hunt, 1978, p. 96). Abrams found that three-quarters of those with children saw them once a week or more often. Frequent visits by children have been reported in studies of the community (e.g. Tinker, 1984; Wenger, 1984; Qureshi and Walker, 1989), sheltered housing (e.g. Butler *et al.*, 1983; Fennell, 1986) and very sheltered housing (Tinker, 1989b).

The general impression is that nothing really makes up for the loss of a member of the immediate family. Whether it is the death of a spouse, the loss of children (through death or emigration) or the pain caused in those rare cases where a child does not visit, the sadness is obvious.

It must also be remembered that some old people will have no children or will have outlived them. Abrams found that 30 per cent of his sample of the over 75s had no children (Abrams, 1978, p. 19). Wenger's study of the over 65s showed a similar picture with 15 per cent never having married and 15 per cent never having had, or having no surviving, children (Wenger, 1984, p. 72).

With other relatives

Nevertheless, old people do compensate for the lack, or the loss, of children. Willmott and Young (1960), Shanas *et al.* (1968) and Wenger (1984) have noted that older people provide replacements for intimate kin lost through death or in other ways. It seems that few people claim to have no living close relatives. Brothers, sisters, nieces and nephews can take the place of children and grandchildren.

EVIDENCE ABOUT CARE BY THE FAMILY

Research confirms that social services do not undermine self-help or responsibility. The family still plays a major role in meeting the needs of elderly people. Evidence accumulated in the sociological studies of the 1950s and 1960s. In 1957 Townsend published his famous study of Bethnal Green, *The Family Life of Old People* (Townsend, 1957). This concluded, first, that old people, particularly women, with daughters and other female relatives living near them, made least claim on the services of the state. Second, isolated old people made disproportionately heavy claims. A subsequent larger study of Bethnal Green, *Family and Kinship in East London*, showed a very close family network based on the mother, with a great deal of mutual help between her and her daughters (Young and Willmott, 1957). Subsequent studies in Woodford (Willmott and Young, 1960) and Dagenham (Willmott, 1963) confirmed the strength of family ties.

The next important study was part of a cross-national survey of about 2,500 old people in each of three countries (United States, Denmark and Britain). The findings which related specifically to Britain were published in *The Aged in the Welfare State* (Townsend and Wedderburn, 1965). The aim of the study was to find out how effective social services were in meeting the needs of elderly people, to find out whether certain functions formerly performed by the family had been taken over by social services, and to examine new needs and changing circumstances. The conclusion was that the family did play a positive role for many old people and there was little evidence that health and welfare services were misused or undermined family responsibilities. The role of the family as a supplier of services was dominant in all three countries. This was confirmed in the large national study in 1976 which showed that families were the main source of help for most personal and domestic tasks (Hunt, 1978).

The 1980s have brought new studies which have all shown the extent of family, mainly female, care. An Equal Opportunities Commission (EOC) report in 1980 found that two-thirds of their sample of carers were giving help to elderly people, mainly relatives (EOC, 1980). Only two fifths of carers lived in the same home and the others often had awkward expensive journeys to contend with before they could give help. Wenger's study of old people in Wales (Wenger, 1984) and one in Sheffield (Qureshi and Walker, 1989) together with the work of Finch and Groves (1980 and 1983) and Lewis and Meredith (1988) have all demonstrated the role that women play in caring.

The greatest source of national information results from a series of questions in the 1985 *GHS* to identify people looking after a sick, handicapped or elderly person (Green, 1988) [docs 36 and 37]. A 'carer' was defined as a person looking after, or providing some regular service for one of the groups just mentioned living in their own home or in another household. It was estimated that 14 per cent of adults were providing informal care and 19 per cent of households contained a carer [doc 37]. About one half of carers had dependants aged 75 or over. Green's report contains a wealth of material on the provision of informal care, who is caring for whom, the nature of care and who supports the carers (Green, 1988).

Who carers are

Allen, in a paper summarising research on elderly people and their informal carers, emphasised that carers do not constitute a homogeneous group of people, and failure to appreciate this can lead to inappropriate expectations of their role (Allen, 1983). For instance the duration and type of the relationship will affect what carers feel able to do. This point was underlined in a book by two carers. They said:

'A common fallacy is that the experiences of caring are similar to those of 'normal' child-rearing, and indeed there are shared problems – isolation, low income, lack of sleep. . . . The most important difference, however, is that of time-scale. The parent looks forward to the child leaving home, becoming independent, perhaps marrying. This is how parental success is measured and is the reward for years of caring and loving. The carer of a person with a disability can only see her task ceasing on the death of either his or her dependant, and this can bring with it the most crippling guilt' (Briggs and Oliver, 1985, pp. 112–13).

The preponderance of women as carers has been mentioned. The 1985 *GHS* found that women were more likely to be carers than men but the difference was not very marked, 15 per cent of women were carers compared with 12 per cent of men (Green, 1988). However, since there are more women than men in the total adult population in Great Britain, the number of women caring is considerably greater than of men – 3.5 million compared with 2.5 million. A closer look at the figures shows that female carers were more likely to be sole carers than male carers, and sole carers were more likely to provide a greater number of hours of care over a longer period with fewer opportunities for respite (Evandrou, 1990). Carers who were married women under 65 obtained the least domestic and personal health care support (Arber *et al.*, 1988). Research has also shown that discrimination by statutory services against women carers is primarily on the household composition of the elderly people rather than on gender *per se*.

Most of the literature has stressed the importance of the mother–daughter link but Bell, in his study of 120 middle-class families, found that there was also a strong father–son link (Bell, 1969).

Mutual care by elderly spouses is common. The extent of care by elderly spouses and the effect this subsequently had on their lives is documented in *Life after a Death* (Bowling and Cartwright, 1982). Elderly people who had cared for a spouse not only lose the person they cared for but may have to come to terms with anxiety, loneliness and adjustment to their lives. It must not be forgotten that elderly people do provide a substantial amount of informal care in the community including to spouses, brothers and sisters, parents and often to younger elderly people.

The nature of care

Attempts have been made to define exactly what care means. It may include physical, financial and emotional care. Parker makes the useful distinction between 'care' and 'tending' (Parker, 1981). He says that the word 'care' is used to convey the idea of concern about people. But it also describes the actual work such as feeding, washing, lifting, cleaning up the incontinent, protecting and comforting. He prefers the word 'tending' for these activities. The nature of the caring role will have an effect too. A son or daughter may feel embarrassed at performing personal tasks for a parent which may be easier for a professional. The parent may also feel embarrassed. Reviews of the literature provide a useful overview of family care (Parker, 1985 and Sinclair *et al.*, 1990). The latter considers the classification, types and patterns of care.

An analysis of the physical care, emotional demands and time spent caring has been given by the EOC together with the estimated costs involved (EOC, 1982). These included loss of employment opportunities. Similar findings are reported by Nissel and Bonnerjea (Nissel and Bonnerjea, 1982). The Family Policy Studies Centre estimated that in 1984 the minimum value of informal care was £5.3 billions per year (Henwood and Wicks, 1984).

Care for the carers

The last ten years have brought a growth of interest in the position of those who do the caring. Indeed the word carer was one increasingly used during the decade. It had not become familiar enough to be used in the 1981 White Paper *Growing Older* but it was used in *Care in Action* later that year. The formation of the Association of Carers (later to become the National Association) gave another boost towards recognition of this group of people, most of whom are family members. The media focussed on the problems of carers too and they figured prominently as a topic at conferences. These developments were helped by an upsurge of research reports, some of which have already been mentioned.

A recent review of research on services for carers (Twigg *et al.*, 1990, pp. 13–15) suggests that they fall into five broad categories. These are to:

- relieve the pressure of caregiving and help the carer to manage more adequately the emotional strains that arise from it;
- assist the carer with practical tasks;
- provide relief from caring;
- enable the carer to get more from the care system and from his or her own abilities;
- provide a high level and quality of services to the dependant.

Research on the 1980 *GHS* has shown that support to elderly people by statutory services was related to the household structure in which the elderly person lived (i.e. those living alone) rather than to whether or not they were able to carry out various activities of daily living without help (Evandrou *et al.*, 1986).

Practical suggestions about ways carers could be helped have been put forward and schemes started. These include self-help groups or opportunities to meet and discuss problems with fellow carers. The work of researchers on carers of dementia sufferers has shown not only that more services are needed but greater flexibility would help as would an explanation from a professional about what is happening to the person they are caring for (Levin *et al.*, 1989 and Askham and Thompson, 1990). Others simply want recognition of what they are doing. What is needed is a realistic assessment of how families willing to care for an elderly relative can be supported. Making it easier for families to move closer or enlarge their homes are two ways. Another is to give adequate professional support, such as extra nursing help, incontinence services and holiday relief. A night sitting service is often essential if a carer is to get her/his sleep. Alternating care in a hospice can prove to be another great support. Wenger's study, *The Supportive Network* (1984), calls for an inter-weaving of family and informal support which needs tact and diplomacy. Qureshi and Walker (1989) argue for shared care which implies the provision of resources to supplement and, where necessary, substitute for family care.

More practically there are strong arguments for more financial help. One victory was achieved in 1986 when the invalid care allowance was extended to married women. ACE are among those arguing for both the disabled person and the carer to be entitled to their own independent income. Others argue for a non-taxable non-contributory benefit, for a more flexible approach to the working week and domestic responsibilities, and for extended leave.

Giving up caring

There are some problems which may particularly lead to carers giving up their task. These include aggression, disturbance at night, and behavioural problems.

The sad fact is that the evidence points to families very reluctantly relinquishing the care of an elderly person when often a little more support would have tipped the balance. But it is only fair to recognise that other generations have their rights too. Who can argue that a disturbed grandparent in a family should be cared for at the cost of a mother's breakdown in health with the consequent effect on her children? Hopefully women's role will be shared more by men but even so it is likely that the future will continue to be one where middle-aged women look after other women a generation older. If present evidence is anything to go by they will receive less statutory help than their masculine counterparts. Finch and Groves raised serious question marks over community care based so much on families (e.g. women), claiming that equal opportunities were not being given (Finch and Groves, 1980). They felt that the forces pulling women back into the domestic caring roles were an inevitable consequence of community care policies. Unless there were a greater degree of financial and practical support for the carers and changes in employment patterns (e.g. the development of job-sharing, 'caring' leave, etc.) women will continue to be disadvantaged.

The dividing line between a family being able to cope or not is a narrow one. As Rapoport *et al.* concluded in *Families in Britain*: 'if the State shifts too much of a burden on to families themselves, it may produce another kind of erosion of its vast store of popular care-givers – erosion through overloading' (Rapoport *et al.*, 1982, p. 491). There is little disagreement that policies in the future must concentrate on a partnership between families and the statutory services. DHSS concluded in *A Happier Old Age*: 'Although family links are irreplaceable we cannot assume that the family can carry the whole responsibility for caring for the growing numbers of very old people. We may therefore need to look increasingly to the wider community to give more support of the kind traditionally expected of the family' (DHSS, 1978a, p. 6).

It is with this wider community that the next chapter is concerned.

Chapter ten

COMMUNITY CARE – SUPPORT FROM THE WIDER COMMUNITY

INTRODUCTION

In the last chapter it was suggested that, if family support is lacking, elderly people may turn to 'the wider community' (DHSS, 1978a, p. 61). But what do we mean by 'the wider community'? And, if it is possible to define this group, what is its role and what are its limitations?

Examining the literature it would appear that there are three seemingly distinct groups; voluntary organisations, volunteers and friends/neighbours. Each of these will be considered in turn. It is perhaps worth noting at this point that, while there have been great advances in practice there has not been a substantial increase in the literature in the last ten years.

VOLUNTARY ORGANISATIONS

Type

A voluntary organisation is defined by Clegg as: 'Any organisation which relies for its funds at least in part on voluntary subscriptions. . . . It is to be distinguished from (a) statutory authorities and (b) businesses run for profit' (Clegg, 1971). It is therefore not a statutory body like a local authority nor a commercial organisation such as those which run private nursing homes for elderly people. In the context of voluntary bodies concerned with the welfare of elderly people many would be known as charities whose prime purpose was to give 'charity' – money, goods or services – to the poor. A key element is that of voluntary management: in the case of charities it is their trustees or governors (of a charitable foundation).

The Wolfenden Committee, which was set up by the Joseph Rowntree Memorial Trust and the Carnegie United Kingdom Trust specifically to look at the role and functions of voluntary organisations, did not find it easy to establish a satisfactory definition: 'We decided that as a general guideline common sense or common parlance must prevail over verbal consistency or logical precision and that we would take as the centre or focus of our review voluntary organisations dealing with the personal social services and what is generally known as the "environment" (Wolfenden, 1978, p. 11–12).

Many of the early voluntary organisations, such as almshouses, were concerned primarily with providing for elderly people and so are many of those established more recently, such as Age Concern. The different origins of these groups give an indication of their strengths and weaknesses today.

Sometimes a benefactor has provided money for a very specific purpose. Some of the oldest charities were set up to provide money, fuel and food for such elderly people as satisfied certain conditions, usually relating to age, sex, place of birth or area of residence. These charities are often administered by churches which may interpret their brief widely. In place of the specified bag of fuel, money may be given to help pay the fuel bills. The modern counterparts, though often of a more transitory nature, are organisations giving food parcels to elderly people at Christmas, harvest, or other special times. The purpose of traditional charities concerned with older people has been, as now, to offer help to elderly people who are appropriate recipients of charity on grounds of poverty, disability or disadvantage.

A second type of voluntary organisation is that set up to further some particular cause or help some particular group and raise the necessary funds for it (e.g. Help the Aged).

A third type of voluntary organisation is the body which has one major objective but which also engages in voluntary social service. The churches, for example, have worship as their primary purpose, but they also provide many services for elderly people in such ways as sponsoring housing associations, opening church crypts, or providing food and shelter for those in need (many of whom are elderly). Probably their most important role is in visiting and maintaining contact with isolated older people amongst their own congregations.

A fourth type is the charitable trust set up with broad aims and little or no restriction on who may benefit. This gives the trustees considerable freedom to seek out and support worthwhile and often pioneering causes. The Nuffield Foundation, which has in the past given core funding to the Centre for Policy on Ageing, and the Joseph Rowntree Foundation are good examples of this type.

Some of these voluntary organisations are tiny charities while others, such as the City Parochial Foundation, handle millions of pounds a year. It is estimated that the total net income of registered charities rose by 32 per cent in real terms between 1980 and 1985 (Billis, 1989). Statutory grants were the fastest growing component of income although they only comprised about 11 per cent of total income against 61 per cent from fees and charges and 15 per cent from fund-raising and donations. These broad figures, however, disguise a very wide range of practice. A voluntary organisation may make a profit on some activities such as a service contract but, unlike a private organisation, the profit is not distributed. It is used wholly for the purposes of the charity. But whatever the size of voluntary bodies there is need to see what they do for elderly people in the widest context. In order to do that one needs to look at their functions and their problems.

Functions

Throughout the centuries individuals and groups have responded in various ways to the social conditions of their time. Some have worked through the state and tried to get services provided publicly (either by a statutory body or through public finance for non-statutory organisations). Others have set out, either alone or with others, to provide the service themselves. For elderly people this voluntary provision has embraced housing, residential homes, hospitals, pensions and many other kinds of service.

There has never been a time when it was foreseen that the state would take over total provision. Indeed Beveridge in his report, which formed the basis of much of post-Second World War provision, went out of his way to stress the need for voluntary action alongside that of the state (Beveridge, 1942, pp. 6–7). Subsequent investigations such as that by the Seebohm Committee have endorsed this view (Home Office *et al.*, 1968, pp. 152–4).

The Wolfenden Committee came to a similar conclusion: 'There is widespread voluntary involvement in caring for the elderly, for children and the handicapped. Some of this amounts to filling gaps in statutory provision but much of it is different in kind from statutory provision' (Wolfenden, 1978, p. 59). They went on to give evidence that, rather than declining, the amount and scale of voluntary provision was growing (Wolfenden, 1978: pp. 183–4).

What then is the special contribution of voluntary organisations to the care of elderly people? There are a number of functions that can be identified.

Filling gaps and supplementing services In some cases a voluntary body provides a service, or part of a service, which the state does not or cannot provide. Meals on wheels is probably one of the best known examples. Another is the loaning of medical equipment for old people at home by the Red Cross and the provision of many services for elderly people (and others) in hospital. These often include a mobile library and shop. In the early years of the post 1945 Welfare State the emphasis was on the State as a provider with voluntary organisations seen as fillers of gaps. Since the late 1970s there has been more emphasis on the role of voluntary organisations as professional providers and many services, such as day care, are now contracted out.

Giving a choice When a voluntary body gives a service slightly different from that provided by the state this in theory offers choice. The role of voluntary bodies in extending choice was an important theme in the Wolfenden Report (Wolfenden, 1978, p. 27). The various types of accommodation, for example, provided by voluntary bodies range from nursing homes, old people's homes and hostels to self-contained flats and bungalows. This should enable old people to choose what suits their wishes and their state of dependency. In practice there may be little difference in the kind of provision and the contribution of the voluntary organisation is that it adds to total provision. Voluntary bodies also offer choice to the staff, though this is less often noticed. Social workers who wish to specialise in older people may feel happier in a voluntary body team organised on a generic basis (although there is a good deal of specialisation now in local authorities).

Pioneering and experimenting Many social services for elderly people have been started on an experimental basis by a voluntary body. Chiropody, meals on wheels and good neighbour schemes are three examples. And sometimes it may be more appropriate for services to be provided by a non-statutory organisation. However, a word of warning was sounded by the Younghusband Report in suggesting that sometimes an evaluation of some services already provided might be more valuable than fresh experiments (National Council of Social Service (NCSS) and NISW, 1969). Pioneering and experimenting are not necessarily the prerogative of voluntary organisations. Sometime both statutory and voluntary organisations may be trying similar new schemes alongside each other. This was the case with sheltered housing in the 1950s and the early 1960s.

Harnessing individual and community enthusiasm Many voluntary bodies seem able to attract voluntary help through the personal appeal of the organisation concerned. Murray in *Voluntary Organisations and Social Welfare* pays tribute to the great benefit which the community derives from the involvement of large numbers of enthusiasts in voluntary activities (Murray, 1968). The many local branches of Age Concern, the numerous people involved in Help the Aged, and the young volunteers who work for various organisations are living examples of the commitment of many thousands of people of all ages to the welfare of elderly people.

Providing information and doing research Another traditional role for voluntary bodies has been the collection of information and the presentation of research findings. At the end of the last century voluntary bodies led the way in recording and analysing social conditions. This role has been continued in this century and was officially blessed by the Goodman Committee which was set up to examine the effect of charity law and practice on voluntary organisations. In their report *Charity Law and Voluntary Organisations* they said: 'Research has been recognised as a charitable object provided that it can be shown that the research is of educational value to the researcher and its fruits are disseminated to the public generally' (Goodman, 1976, p. 27). The Age Concern Research Unit, and its successor the Age Concern Institute of Gerontology, King's College London have undertaken a great deal of research. The Centre for Policy on Ageing concentrates a lot of their work on the dissemination of research, which is a much neglected area of social policy. It has a library and information data base and produces regular reviews of the literature as well as a directory of social research.

Acting as pressure groups Many voluntary bodies attempt to influence policy by acting as a lobby on special issues. When they are closely involved with the group they represent, like Age Concern, their views may carry considerable weight. A voluntary organisation may represent the needs and interests of a whole group (social advocacy) or a particular person (client advocacy).

The Aves Committee which looked at *The Voluntary Worker in the*

Social Services cited Age Concern, then called the National Old People's Welfare Council, as a body recognising a responsibility to involve the public 'in seeing where action is needed and bringing pressure to bear upon the authorities to make more adequate provision' (NCSS and NISW, 1969, p. 28).

Giving advice Not every elderly person likes to go to an official agency for advice. They do not, for example, use housing advice centres to any great extent. Voluntary bodies (such as the Citizens Advice Bureau) are often more acceptable as they are thought to be one step away from the agencies providing the services. The Goodman Committee considered that the giving of advice in appropriate cases was a charitable objective (Goodman, 1976, p. 32). But the Wolfenden Committee felt that 'the relationship between casework for individuals and wider ranging pressure group activities is a delicate one for organisations in this field' (Wolfenden, 1978, p. 49).

Others It could be argued that, apart from the functions just mentioned, voluntary organisations have other advantages. It is said that they save tax-payers' money, that their freedom makes them more flexible than statutory agencies, and that they perform a valuable role in supporting the informal caring system.

The flexible approach may be useful when the elderly person does not fit exactly into the rules for a particular state service. For example a local authority may exclude owner-occupiers from council accommodation while a voluntary body such as a housing association may feel able to accept them. It is also argued that flexibility may be more possible for bodies not subject to public election and the vagaries of party politics. However, voluntary organisations, which do not have external pressures to change, may themselves become traditional, set in their ways and inflexible.

Recent changes The growing number of voluntary organisations and the development of existing ones concerned with elderly people is illustrated by the increased activity in sheltered housing. However, the greatest change has been the growth of services contracted out by local authorities to voluntary bodies. As has been seen in Chapter 8 one of the objectives of the 1989 *Caring for People* White Paper was to promote the development of a flourishing independent (i.e. private and voluntary) sector. The policy advice following the NHS and Community Care Act 1989 encouraged the development of formal contracts for services. This could include contracts for client advocacy. Clear guidance about quality and details of contracts was given (DOH, 1990a). This role was differentiated from other aspects of work, such as social advocacy (i.e. speaking on behalf of older people) supported through grants.

Another feature has been the growing partnership between statutory and voluntary agencies. An illustration of this was the extension of joint financing to the latter and the encouragement given by DHSS to involving voluntary bodies. The Health and Social Services and Social Security Adjudications Act 1983 provided for additional members of consultative committees to be appointed by voluntary organisations. Participation in health authority joint care planning teams can be effective for joint planning. Voluntary organisations became eligible under the joint finance arrangements for pilot projects enabling elderly people to move into the community in 1983.

Various other initiatives in the 1980s impinged on the voluntary sector (Leat, 1990a). These included programmes such as the various Manpower Services Commission employment programmes and the Opportunities for Volunteering programme. A major reason for these programmes was to increase opportunities for unemployed people to undertake paid or unpaid work. This was often through a voluntary organisation.

Some problems

What is the role of voluntary organisations vis-à-vis statutory bodies? The question of which services can best be provided by voluntary bodies and which by statutory authorities is particularly difficult to determine. Jefferys has noted that the division may relate not to different sorts of needs but to which body first diagnosed the need and suggested the service (Jefferys, 1965). The Wolfenden Committee expressed the view that voluntary action should be evaluated in terms of the ways in which it complemented, supported, extended and influenced the informal and statutory systems (Wolfenden, 1978, p. 26). Questioning the expanding role of voluntary bodies, Leat maintains that it seems often to be based more on potential than actual strengths (Leat, 1990a). She points out that there are some weaknesses and failures in the voluntary sector.

The growing dependence on voluntary bodies to provide contracted out local social services (Ch. 8) is not without its dangers, especially when public funding becomes a main source of income (although it could be argued that there may be greater financial security arising from contractual agreements). Grants from public bodies inevitably mean that voluntary bodies have to tread a delicate line. Not only may they have to provide exactly what the local authority lays down, rather than experimenting (Harding, 1990) but they may be pressed to take on a task such as running a day centre which would otherwise be the local authority's responsibility and to do it more cheaply and with lower standards. The conclusion of a survey of County Councils was that trends towards more formal contracting arrangements will continue (Campbell, 1990). Financial insecurity and loss of autonomy could follow (Thomason, 1990), although the increase in fund-raising and marketing activity amongst voluntary organisations is enabling them to develop core activities which can enable them to retain some independence. Some of the new challenges to voluntary bodies have been spelt out (Harding, 1990). These include the need to:

- take into account the time and skills needed for the processes of planning, costing and tendering for services;
- consider their own management capacity and be prepared to learn new skills;
- obtain sources of advice and support;
- make clear distinctions between their different roles and to separate service provision from other development and advocacy functions (Harding, 1990, p. 30).

Harding also warns that voluntary bodies may find themselves changing in character and becoming more highly 'professionalised' – a potentially painful process. Professionalisation can mean increased reliance on professional staff and it is important to emphasise the continued importance of volunteers and volunteer involvement. It can also mean professional standards of operation and there is clearly a need for this. Another danger is that voluntary bodies may be loath to bite the hand that feeds them through taking a critical stance.

Are there variable standards?   When there are a number of different voluntary bodies working in the same field standards may be uneven. Such variation was seen by the Wolfenden Committee as a major weakness (Wolfenden, 1978, p. 88). However, standards also differ between local authorities.

A reason for the variation in provision by voluntary bodies is that so much depends on the energy and enthusiasm of individual people and committees. In an interesting study of the factors affecting the location of voluntary organisations, Hatch and Mocroft concluded that one of the most important was high social class which seemed to lead to a greater degree of provision (Hatch and Mocroft, 1977, p. 163).

To whom is a voluntary body responsible? Age Concern England in *Voluntary Organisations and the Retired and Elderly* alleged that voluntary bodies are often responsible only to a small self-selected group of people and that they are often not accountable to the people they attempt to serve (ACE, 1973, p. 4). They compared this with social services departments which are responsible to elected councillors. Two of the characteristics which differentiate statutory bodies from voluntary organisations are that they may work within legally authorised limits and they are accountable for the expenditure of public money.

These points were considered by the Goodman Committee which looked particularly at controls over fund raising and the wider question of the acceptability of charities (Goodman, 1976; Ch. 7, part 8). The Wolfenden Committee, taking into account also the evidence of the Goodman Committee, did not feel that the restricted acceptability normally led to serious problems, although they thought that some smaller organisations needed advice and help on how to keep and present accounts (Wolfenden, 1978, p. 148).

Are there overlaps? Critics of voluntary bodies sometimes point to the number of voluntary organisations apparently working in the same field and suggest that there is duplication. However, the Wolfenden Committee suggested that there may well be valid reasons why one organisation is more appropriate than another 'even if the outside world finds them almost indistinguishable' (Wolfenden, 1978, p. 191). There may be some duplication among providers but most people do not receive two services for the same need.

In the case of elderly people three of the major national organisations are Age Concern, Help the Aged and the Centre for Policy on Ageing. A closer look at them shows two things. First their aims and the way they carry these out are different. Second they have combined for various purposes when circumstances seemed appropriate.

Do they take the heat out of problems? It is argued that even the existence of a voluntary body, in however small a way, may give the impression that a need is being met. The voluntary body may be making only a minimal provision, but there is the feeling that something is being done and therefore others (perhaps the state) need not act. This allegation is very difficult to prove, but it is only fair to point out that some voluntary bodies are aware of the danger.

Do they have a 'charity' image? Some voluntary organisations founded as charities in previous centuries are said to have a lingering image of providing for the 'undeserving poor'. But this image may not be attached only to voluntary bodies since one reason why elderly people do not claim the statutory benefits to which they are entitled seems to be the feeling that they are accepting 'charity'.

What about lack of resources? The services that voluntary organis-ations can provide and their independence is partly affected by the amount of money they can raise. Salamon refers to 'philanthropic insufficiency' which is the inability of voluntary bodies to obtain adequate and reliable sources of funding (Salamon, 1987, quoted in Leat, 1990a). Money comes largely from voluntary and statutory sources and also from charitable foundations. A growing amount comes from government departments in the form of grants for running particular programmes. Not everyone is happy about this dependence on statutory funding.

Does what is provided depend more on the personal appeal of the voluntary organisation rather than the value of its work? Voluntary organisations concerned with elderly people, children and the blind attract a good deal of public support because there is much public sympathy for these groups. Older people are fortunate to come into this category for there is evidence that some organisations operating in difficult or contentious fields find virtually no public response. Salamon refers to the concentration on particular groups as 'philan-thropic particularism' (Salamon, 1987 quoted in Leat, 1990a).

Can an adequate supply of clients be found? In a summary of research on voluntary organisations, Leat maintains that some of the diffi-culties experienced by voluntary projects appear to be related not so much to the problem of recruiting sufficient volunteers, but rather to finding an adequate supply of appropriate clients (Leat, 1990a, p. 274). She feels this may be related to the wider issue of public knowledge of the voluntary sector and the acceptability or confi-dence in voluntary provision.

CONCLUSION

Despite the problems of voluntary organisations there are both positive and negative reasons for the continuation of their role in making provision for elderly people. What is essential is for them to be constantly questioning and redefining their roles. The crucial question is whether some of the potential advantages of the voluntary sector will continue to exist if its role is expanded to carry out more functions of the statutory sector (Brenton, 1985).

VOLUNTEERS

Introduction

Visiting an old person sounds a useful activity and seems to appeal to volunteers of every age. A recent survey found that elderly people were the largest client group (43 per cent) of all volunteers (MORI, 1990). In 1987 8 per cent of the population listed visiting elderly and sick people as their voluntary activity (CSO, 1991, p. 188). But who are these voluntary workers and what is their role? (see also Ch. 11). These were two of the questions examined by a committee under the chairmanship of Geraldine Aves. Its task was 'to enquire into the role of voluntary workers in the social services and in particular to consider their need for preparation or training and their relationship with professional social workers.' They reported in 1969. They did not find it possible to formulate any neat definition of a voluntary worker because, among other things, they did not want to rule out token payments. They concluded 'that there was no merit in attempting to restrict the term in any precise way' (NCSS *et al.*, 1969, p. 19).

Following the Aves Report there have been a number of research studies concerned with volunteers. Shenfield and Allen in *The Organisation of Voluntary Services* studied domiciliary visiting of elderly people by volunteers (Shenfield and Allen, 1972). In 1973 Kettle and Hart reported on an experiment in the voluntary visiting of old people in Newcastle upon Tyne (Kettle and Hart, 1973). Hadley, Webb and Farrell looked particularly at young volunteers working with old people in *Across the Generations* (Hadley *et al.*, 1975). This included a survey of 86 old people and 145 volunteers in four areas. In 1977 came a useful review of existing research and a discussion on how volunteers were organised (Leat and Darvill, 1977).

A study, based on interviews with over 2,000 people, provided

197

information for the Wolfenden Committee (Hatch, 1978). In this it was found that the largest group (35 per cent) of volunteers helped elderly people. Another study was primarily concerned with the use of volunteers by local authority social workers (Holme and Maizels, 1978). Another study was of the use of volunteer support to elderly people living in residential homes (Power, 1986). In a study of six residential homes it was found that there was a demand for volunteers but that they did not seem to make much difference to the quality of life of the elderly people.

Another important source of information is the Volunteer Centre UK which was set up in 1973 with funds from trusts and central government to promote and encourage the use of voluntary workers.

Much of the work of volunteers, and the research described above, was concerned with visiting services and practical tasks. Much more important now are voluntary work in hospital discharge and aftercare services, advocacy and counselling. Day care, including transport provision and luncheon clubs, is now the backbone of voluntary provision for older people.

The 1980s saw various programmes to encourage volunteers, many of which were specifically concerned with providing opportunities for the unemployed. The 1984 Helping the Community to Care programme was to help volunteers, families and others to care for people who needed support.

The contribution of the volunteer

Volunteers can add greatly to the well-being of elderly people, but what is their special contribution?

Supplementing the statutory services In her study of Buckinghamshire Jefferys found that there seemed to be a view that paid staff are always preoccupied with meeting material requirements while voluntary workers provide intangible services such as friendship (Jefferys, 1965, p. 294). In practice she found that quite often the reverse happened with paid staff giving friendship as well as professional help, and volunteers giving very practical help as well as friendship. In general, however, the role of the volunteer is seen as providing something that paid workers for various reasons, such as lack of resources or time, cannot offer. It is important to consider exactly what this may mean. The Aves Committee were clear that volunteers should not be used as substitutes for paid professionals (NCSS *et al.*, 1969, p. 195) and this was endorsed in guidelines drawn up by the Volunteer Centre UK in 1975 and reissued in 1990. The guidelines indicated that volunteers should not break strikes or be party to action to keep down the rate of normal earnings nor should they take away the more interesting parts of the work of professionals. In practice there is much blurring of the distinctions between professionals and volunteers.

Continuity Since statutory workers move jobs, especially in order to gain promotion, the volunteer may be in contact with an old person over a longer period of time. This will not, of course, always be the case since younger volunteers may also move frequently.

Less identification with authority Many people, elderly people included, seem reluctant to go to official sources for advice. They seem more likely to go to an organisation, such as the CAB, which is staffed almost entirely by volunteers. As ACE puts it: 'Volunteers may also offer, particularly when it comes to problems of welfare rights, a very useful independence from the relevant Government departments. They can therefore, if well-equipped with information, help claimants who might otherwise be reluctant to press for their rights' (ACE, 1973, p. 6).

Helping elderly people keep in touch with the outside world Elderly people in institutional care are surrounded by officials of various kinds and all of these occupy some part in the hierarchy. A volunteer coming in from outside represents a different perspective.

Type of help

A MORI survey found that the most common form of voluntary activity was fund-raising: this was undertaken by 47 per cent of volunteers (MORI, 1990). The Aves Committee considered that three sorts of activity were particularly useful. Work of a mainly practical kind was one, and many elderly people benefit from volunteers who decorate, do repairs, garden and cook for them. Another activity was work for which special skill or knowledge is required. Home nursing, first-aid and advice and information come into this category. The third area was work involving personal relationships. The Aves Committee felt that if volunteers worked under the guidance, and with the support of professionals, they need not limit their activities to practical tasks. Morris also felt that personal contact, especially if it was unhurried, was particularly valuable for elderly people (Morris, 1969, p. 227).

Who volunteers?

Before considering some of the problems about volunteers it is pertinent to examine who are the volunteers. The 1973 *GHS* showed that 8 per cent of a national sample had undertaken some form of voluntary work in the preceding four weeks (GHS, 1973 in Hatch, 1978). Hatch's survey for the Wolfenden Committee showed that 15 per cent had taken part in some form of voluntary work in the previous 15 months (Hatch, 1978, p. 2). A MORI survey found that 39 per cent of the general population had volunteered at least once during the previous year (MORI, 1990).

The image of the typical volunteer as a middle-aged middle-class married woman still has some truth in it, the Aves Committee found. But they also noted that men were 'playing a much greater part than was sometimes realised' (NCSS *et al.*, 1969, p. 26). However, in a study of social workers and their volunteers it was found that women were more likely than men to have helped elderly people (Holme and Maizels, 1978, p. 145).

As for the motives of volunteers these seem very mixed and range from a genuine desire to help others, to the wish to further a particular cause and the satisfaction of their own personal needs. Both the Aves and Wolfenden Committees agreed that motives are always mixed. The Aves Committee felt that most volunteers worked to meet some need or combination of needs, and the Wolfenden Committee felt that most of them would not understand about introspection or self-examination about motives. Before looking too deeply for motives it is worth noting that one research study showed that most people became volunteers by accident – they took it up on the spur of the moment because a friend or relative asked them to (Social and Community Planning Research (SCPR), 1990).

Some problems

The need to define the role of the volunteer   What seems to emerge from studies of volunteers are two clear recommendations. First, that the respective roles of paid and voluntary workers should be more clearly defined. It is especially important that unions are involved in discussions. Second, these definitions must be kept under constant review because the roles may change. Holme and

Maizels concluded: 'Taking into account the fact that, in our view, there are no fixed or settled roles for either professionals or volunteers and that any definition of the roles must be transient, the aim can only be to ensure the proper use of their respective contributions and a corresponding standard of service' (Holme and Maizels, 1978, p. 185).

Relations with statutory bodies Although most voluntary workers work for voluntary organisations some work under the umbrella of statutory bodies. When this is the case the role of the voluntary worker needs to be clearly defined and help and support given where necessary by statutory workers.

Training and organisation It is not enough for volunteers to know what their tasks are. They must also know how to go about them, what the limits of their job are and in what circumstances they should call on professional help. This particularly entails a knowledge of the needs of elderly people and of the services that can be called in to help them. The main reason why people drop out of volunteering is because of dissatisfaction with the way that voluntary organisations manage them and the lack of training and support, in effect the exploitation and the amateurishness (SCPR, 1990). However, in the major voluntary organisations there is a strong acceptance of the need for training, professional standards of management and competent evaluation.

Some feel that a paid organiser is necessary. Morris, commenting on old people's welfare organisations, felt that either a central bureau or at least a single person was needed to recruit and place volunteers, as well as to collect information about openings and to receive offers of help (Morris, 1969, pp. 232–3). ACE felt that one of the main jobs of a paid organiser was to prepare and support volunteers (ACE, 1973, p. 5). On the other hand, the Aves Committee found that not all volunteers felt the need for an organiser, so perhaps this will depend upon the task as well as the scale of the operation (NCSS *et al.*, 1969, p. 93).

Paying volunteers Payment of volunteers has been proposed for a number of reasons including the need to increase their numbers and to give them some recognition of their work. Leat, however, has pointed out the complex nature of transactions (Leat, 1990b). *For Love and Money* discussed the role of payment in encouraging the provision of care (Leat, 1990b). One group of paid volunteers are family placement carers. Leat felt that paid caring was useful because, although paid carers enjoyed doing something worthwhile they wanted recognition of their value; payment was part of such recognition.

Evaluation 'There is something almost improper about suggesting that voluntary social work ought to be evaluated. It is rather like proposing to measure the efficiency of concern or goodwill, when the most important thing is that they do or do not exist.' So wrote two researchers who had just completed a study of old people and young volunteers (*New Society*, 7.11.74, pp. 356–8). Yet evaluation there must be if money and effort are to be put into this form of help for older people. Despite the difficulties, some researchers have attempted to evaluate the work of volunteers and the results are almost entirely favourable. Leat and Darvill considered that schemes may be evaluated 'from at least three (sometimes conflicting) viewpoints – elderly people, volunteers and professionals; from each viewpoint it will be possible to specify a number of different criteria of success' (Leat and Darvill, 1977, p. 161). Shenfield also has suggested some ways in which the effectiveness of visiting elderly people can be assessed (Shenfield with Allen, 1972). She found that, if the results of her research are typical, large numbers of old people were being visited regularly and with considerable devotion. But, by her criteria, for over a fifth of old people the visiting which they were receiving was not apparently appropriate to their needs, and for 10 per cent the visiting seemed unnecessary and valueless (Shenfield with Allen, 1972, p. 163). Hadley, Webb and Farrell found an overall success rate which they considered quite respectable, although they suggested that refining the methods of selecting and matching clients and volunteers would raise the quality of the work (Hadley *et al.*, 1975; Ch. 8). Looking at the evaluation from the point of view of social workers, Holme and Maizels said: 'Generally social workers have a consistently favourable view of their experiences with volunteers, irrespective of the type of relationship they have with them' (Holme and Maizels, 1978, p. 106).

The volunteer, then, like the voluntary body, has a distinctive contribution to make to the care of elderly people. But, as the Aves Committee declared: 'We wish to make it abundantly clear that nothing we have to say about voluntary workers, their recruitment or their training, is intended to detract from the spontaneous contribution of the neighbour; indeed quite the contrary' (NCSS *et al.*, 1969, p. 19).

FRIENDS AND NEIGHBOURS

Who are they?

When studies are done of informal networks of caring, more often than not the local caring group for an old person turns out to be their family. Neighbours, too, although considered as a separate category, may also be relatives. Evidence has already been given (in Ch. 9) of the numbers of old people living near their relatives and it has also been seen how close some of their children live. It is clear from most of the studies that neighbours are not necessarily the people who actually live next door although many of them appear to live quite close. Neighbourly help that is spontaneous and unorganised is easier if people have some sort of link, and physical proximity may be the most important determinant. People who feel that they belong to a physical community may feel a sense of responsibility to one another, and it is interesting that in one study of the neighbourhood care of elderly people the help given by local shopkeepers and tradesmen is described (Cheeseman *et al.*, 1972, p. 75).

But a community which has physical boundaries may not be the only community network. Friends from many different groups – churches, former workmates, adult classes, and clubs of various kinds – form quite a different system from the world of clubs where elderly people meet only people of their own age. Friends are likely to be of similar age and life stage, and probably educational and social status, and are often a source of reciprocal support (Bulmer, 1987). Jerrome's extensive work on intimate relationships shows the importance to elderly people of friendship (Jerrome, 1990). She also shows that whereas men's relationships tend to be sociable rather than intimate and focus on shared activity women's friendships are characterised by emotional intensity and self-disclosure.

Evidence about help

Some studies show that friends and neighbours are relatively unimportant as a source of social care especially tending (Bulmer, 1987, pp. 76–7). However, they are complementary to kin ties. 'Ties with neighbours are face-to-face contacts and often time-urgent, as with borrowing small necessities or help in emergencies' (Bulmer, 1987, p. 78). But in addition to the evidence already cited in the previous section, many studies of elderly people do say something about care by neighbours and friends. In the cross-national survey of old people in Great Britain, the USA and

Denmark, considerable help was recorded from neighbours and friends (Shanas *et al.*, 1968). Ways in which social networks can be analysed are described by Bowling (Bowling, 1991).

In an interesting study of old people who had moved to the seaside resorts of Bexhill and Clacton, Karn found that the statutory health and social services were not seen as a major source of help (Karn, 1977). The most important group of people whom elderly people would call on for help were friends and neighbours. But it must be remembered that only 53 per cent of retired people in Clacton and 70 per cent in Bexhill had children. They had also moved away from their original homes where any children they had might have lived near them. This heavy reliance on neighbours and friends, Karn found, posed problems in areas where the neighbours and friends were also very likely to be old.

Hunt's study also found some disquieting factors about help from neighbours (Hunt, 1978). Although nearly three-quarters of the sample got on very well with all their neighbours, not all felt that they would be able to ask their neighbours for help in an emergency. In answer to the question: 'If ever you needed help urgently, how many of your neighbours would you feel able to ask?' 10 per cent said that they would not feel able to ask any (Hunt, 1978, p. 108). The most vulnerable group, the bedfast and housebound, were least likely to feel able to ask neighbours for help.

The 1980 *GHS* asked questions about contact between elderly people and friends and relatives. The overwhelming majority, about six out of seven elderly people, said that they saw relatives or friends at least once a week, and almost a third did so every day or nearly (OPCS, 1982, p. 174). Only 3 per cent said that they did not see relatives or friends at all. It is interesting that elderly people living alone were more likely than those living in other types of household to see relatives or friends daily or nearly every day (OPCS, 1982, p. 175). The national survey of carers showed that among those with dependants in other households about one-third (26 per cent) cared for friends or neighbours (Green, 1988, p. 16). Four per cent of those caring for a friend devoted at least 20 hours per week to this task (Green, 1988, p. 23) and 16 per cent said that no one else helped (Green, 1988, p. 29).

Wenger's research highlights the importance of family care (as does that of Qureshi and Walker, 1989) but her conclusions suggest that when this is not available friends and neighbours help and 'statutory services fill gaps in the fabric of informal care for a minority' (Wenger, 1984, p. 180). Contrasting friends and neighbours, Willmott suggests that, as probably most people would, most people turn to relatives first when care is needed and to friends only when relatives are not available (Willmott, 1986). Relationships with neighbours, he suggests, 'are characterised by a mixture of friendliness and trust and openness then takes over. Neighbours are an important source of certain kinds of help, most of which derive from the fact that they are close at hand. 'Surveillance is one example' (Willmott, 1986, p. 62). He concludes that 'for the great majority, ties with relatives, friends and others now extend far beyond the local area, and the neighbourhood or local community does not encompass the social networks of most people, not even among those identified earlier as relatively tied to the locality' (Willmott, 1986, p. 101).

FORMAL NEIGHBOURING SCHEMES

ACE claim that the terms 'good neighbour', 'neighbourly care' and 'neighbourhood groups' 'appear to be emotive and confusing expressions, with different meanings for different people' (ACE, 1972a, p. 2). They then attempted two broad definitions which could be established from the way the terms were already in use, i.e. the one-to-one relationship of a person helping a neighbour in a completely spontaneous way and a group of people arranging to help individual people – this is, community organised on a regular basis. They categorised schemes into:

– paid help: person-to-person
– voluntary help: person-to-person
– paid help: one person responsible for a group
– voluntary help: one person responsible for a group
– paid group help for individuals
– voluntary help for individuals.

DHSS launched an ambitious good neighbour scheme in 1976. A report on some good neighbour schemes, *Limited Liability?*, attempted to look objectively at the evidence and contained some useful case studies (Leat, 1979). Some interesting paid good neighbour schemes have developed and have been found to have been successful in helping to keep elderly people in their own homes (Tinker, 1984). It is natural that there should be so much more evidence about voluntary organisations and volunteers than about the help given by friends and neighbours. The most extensive study of neighbourhood care in this country is that conducted by Abrams and his colleagues (Abrams *et al.*, 1986 and 1989). Elderly people were the largest client group. Although the researchers found it difficult to construct objective measures of success, they nevertheless found that the care given did alleviate loneliness and did provide significant social contacts. The Wolfenden Committee suggested that it is so much taken for granted that it is scarcely mentioned in discussion about the provision of social services. This point will be taken up later (Ch. 12) in the discussion about the meaning of community care.

Part three
ASSESSMENT

Chapter eleven
THE CONTRIBUTION OF ELDERLY PEOPLE

INTRODUCTION

In the last two chapters attention has been focused on the help given to those elderly people who need some outside support. The main sources of help, apart from the statutory services, were described. In this chapter attention is turned to the help which elderly people themselves give to others. This is set in the context of the theory of the exchange relationship and of the stigma and dependency which are so often associated with services provided for elderly people. The help given by elderly people, both to their own families and to others, is examined. Then the wider role of elderly people in policy making is assessed.

Writers about elderly people tend to consider them almost exclusively as consumers of social services. But what is their role as contributors? Apart from their input in the past through rates and taxes, what they give through voluntary service is seldom mentioned in the literature.

THE EXCHANGE RELATIONSHIP

The exchange relationship can be defined as an encounter in which both giving and receiving takes place. It is nearly always assumed that it is more prestigious to give than to receive and that there is a clear economic and social distinction between the giver and receiver. Often there is stigma attached to receiving and, when elderly people are in this position, they are usually considered to be in a state of dependency. These concepts of the exchange relationship, dependency and stigma will now be considered briefly.

One of the most comprehensive analyses of the exchange relationship, as it relates to social policy, is given by Pinker (Pinker, 1971) who also comments on the theories of Titmuss (Titmuss, 1968 and 1970). This study is not concerned with the wider applications of the theory, but only with those that relate specifically to the social services as a whole as they affect the position of the individual. Whether people do in fact see themselves as involved in this way is, of course, another matter.

There is first the distinction between the exchange relationship in economic matters and that in social matters. Pinker points out that people know where they stand in an economic exchange relationship because money confers a recognised right to buy goods and services (Pinker, 1971). In social relationships the rate of exchange is not so clearly agreed.

Second, there is the exchange relationship which applies to all social services. The theory is that people pay a contribution in some way (e.g. taxes, rates, etc.) and therefore should feel as entitled to social services as they do to goods and services in an economic exchange. Pinker claims that this is unrealistic: 'The idea of paying taxes or holding authentic claims by virtue of citizenship remains largely an intellectual conceit of the social scientist . . . consequently most applicants for social services remain paupers at heart' (Pinker, 1971, p. 142).

Third, there is the exchange relationship involved in a specific (or particular) service. Forder states that it is, for example, the basis of schemes of national insurance (Forder, 1974, p. 68). People who are currently at work pay into a scheme which supports older people in the expectation that a similar exchange will take place when they themselves reach old age, although it could be argued that old people feel they have paid into a specially funded scheme.

Fourth, there is the exchange relationship on an individual basis. Services may be exchanged between individuals or between groups such as families. Sometimes there will be a real expectation that another service will be conferred in return, while at other times it may be given as a 'gift'. But, as Titmuss points out in *The Gift Relationship*, motives may often be mixed (Titmuss, 1970, pp. 210–24).

The position of elderly people is special because of a number of factors which can make them feel that they are receivers rather than givers. First, for many, there is a sudden ending of employment and of being productive members of the community (see Ch. 5). Many elderly people in pre-industrial society did not retire, but equally many did not survive to old age. Some people, like farmers, are able to 'taper off' in their particular professions, but for the majority the attainment of the age of 60 or 65 means the automatic end to a lifetime as an economic contributor to society. There may, however, be differences between social classes. In some middle-class professions people often do retain some status – the doctor keeps the title on retirement. But the working-class majority hold neither the 'power to strike nor the significant remnants of social acclaim and distinction that accrue to middle-class elderly' (Jones, 1976, p. 93).

Second, there is the current psychological atmosphere in which elderly people are regarded as being beyond the point when they have anything to contribute. It is part of the false sentimentality about old age where old people are 'frequently required to adopt a somewhat passive role and to express a sense of gratitude for what is provided' (ACE, 1972b, p. 49). Another aspect of this is the problem of older people in a youth-centred society.

Third, the emphasis on receiving is underscored because in economic matters most old people are dependent on a state pension for their main source of income. Fourth, Pinker argues that the growth of selective social services differentiates the recipients much more clearly than those social services which are universal and do not single out those who receive (Pinker, 1971, p. 151).

All these factors contribute to elderly people being looked on usually as a dependent group, if dependency is defined as being in a subordinate relationship. Whether older people are more or less dependent than in the past is arguable. Some maintain that a state pension lessens their dependence on their families, while others hold the view that they are now more dependent on social services. What seems to be ignored in most discussions about dependency, as Johnson has pointed out, is that we are all to some extent dependent on others (Johnson, 1990).

There is no doubt that elderly people themselves wish to be independent, although there are many differences in their interpretation of independence. Hunt found that it is often thought of in economic terms (Hunt, 1978, p. 130). For older people who worked it seemed to mean not being dependent on a supplementary pension, while for non-workers it meant being independent of the constraints of employment. Most surveys of elderly people find that the majority do not want to be dependent on other people. Even the elderly people who lived close to their own families in granny annexes stressed the importance of being 'independent' (Tinker, 1976).

Equally important is the feeling of having something useful to do. Age Concern in *The Attitudes of the Retired and Elderly* noted that over half felt that no one relied on them (ACE, 1974). It seemed that not being relied on by anyone was part of the poor health–loneliness–social isolation syndrome. Mochansky, a Russian physician, who analysed the emotional effect of the 17 months siege of Leningrad, attributed the lack of breakdowns to the fact that everyone, from the smallest child to the oldest inhabitant, had a job to do (NCSS, 1954, pp. 12–13). If people feel that they have no role and they also feel dependent, this may engender a sense of stigma.

Is there any evidence that older people wish to reverse the process of dependency and be more equal contributors to society? One recent inquiry on *Ageing* set up by the Church of England invited older people to write to give their views (Board for Social Responsibility, 1990). A distressing number of respondents felt patronised or scorned purely on grounds of their age and their letters to the Inquiry made it plain that they felt they had a lot to contribute. Age Concern maintains that there is need for older people to be convinced of their usefulness (ACE, Manifesto, 1975, p. 3). Titmuss argues that people have a social and biological need to help (Titmuss, 1970). It may therefore be right to take account of the needs of older people to contribute, not only from the point of view of their own welfare, but also of their use to society.

FACTORS AFFECTING THE ABILITY OF ELDERLY PEOPLE TO GIVE

Whether elderly people wish not only to remain independent but to give help to others in some form or other depends on a number of different things. Money and health have been discussed in previous chapters (Chapters 5 and 6). Also of importance are their abilities, how they choose to use their time, the opportunities given by society and the general concept of retirement.

Abilities

One of the most comprehensive discussions of the abilities of elderly people occurs in *Liberation of the Elders* (Jones, 1976). In this Jones shows how so-called objective tests are a less true measure of ability than the evidence coming from new interests, and the right kind of opportunity to learn. He points out that: 'It is not only an impoverished education which leads to an under-exploitation of potential; the circumstances of adult life, particularly the work undertaken, can compound and encourage the narrowing of interests' (Jones, 1976, p. 27). Thus someone in a clerical job may find that manipulative skills are left unused. Worse still, many women after years at home may become narrow in their interests and lacking in confidence. Jones gives evidence that where opportunities are offered, older people rapidly acquire new knowledge. He concludes that the majority of people can master new materials, irrespective of their age, and what prevents many from doing this is the limited expectation which they have of themselves and which others have of them. Many of the submissions to the inquiry on *Ageing* set up by the Church of England emphasised how much enjoyment there is in taking up new activities in later life.

Use of time and leisure activities

In 1989, of all the selected categories of people, retired people not surprisingly had the most free time, both during the week and at the weekend (CSO, 1991, p. 170). According to the 1987 *General Household Survey* the most popular home-based leisure activities for all age groups were watching television, visiting or entertaining relatives or friends and listening to the radio (CSO, 1991, p. 171). People over the age of 70 were much less likely than average to be involved in do-it-yourself activities and listening to records and tapes. People over the age of 60 in 1987 were less likely to participate in sports and physical activities, except for men in lawn or carpet bowls (CSO, 1991, p. 178). For open-air activities people over the age of 70 participated less than average in 12 of the 13 activities (OPCS, 1989, p. 240). For outings by car/motorcycle/boat the figures were the same.

Abrams, however, has shown that averages conceal wide differences and that for both 'passive' (e.g. watching television) and 'active' occupations (e.g. walking) there were sizeable minorities falling into extreme categories. The key to this variety in the use of time and behaviour by those reaching pensionable age lay, he felt, primarily in social class differences, and this was particularly so with men. While the average AB man on retirement reduced his paid work time and also reduced the hours he spent on passive leisure activities, the average DE man cut out paid employment almost entirely and increased the time spent on passive leisure activities. The transition for women on reaching old age was less dramatic because for all social classes there were still the same household activities to be undertaken.

Opportunities given by society

While some old people will wish to relax in their retirement and to remain as uninvolved as they were in their earlier years, others may wish to further their own education, to take up or develop former interests or to contribute to the community.

The number of those pursuing educational interests has increased rapidly as opportunities have expanded. Glendenning, writing of lifelong education and the over 60s, states that only recently have we begun to pay serious attention to the educational needs and potential of the over 60s (Glendenning, 1985). The University of the Third Age has been an important development. In 1980 Laslett argued on behalf of elderly people for the recognition of their cultural and intellectual importance and for their right to a fairer share of the budget, lifelong access to all institutions and to national distance learning (Laslett, 1980). Another landmark was the establishment of the Forum on the Rights of Elderly People to Education (FREE) in 1981. In their manifesto they stressed the benefits of education in later life. These included the fostering of self-reliance and independence, the growth in self-awareness and help in coping with problems in a rapidly changing world (FREE, 1983).

Midwinter says that the reluctance of elderly people to participate in conventional educational activities and their self-perception of what education and learning means stem alike from deep-set social and cultural factors and from weaknesses in the educational environment rather than, for instance, psychological or intellectual difficulties (Midwinter, 1982). His recommendations included the setting up of special schemes. There is now an extensive literature on the subject (Norton, 1987) and Educational Gerontology (learning in later years) has emerged as a discipline.

Others want opportunities for leisure and arts activities (Armstrong *et al.*, 1987; Midwinter, 1990). They look for the chance for really worthwhile things to do in the community, not 'pastimes or diversional therapy to fill in time till death comes' (Stewart, 1974, p. 8).

Retirement and its meaning

When Vic Feather retired as General Secretary of the Trade Union Congress he is reported to have analysed the theme of his retirement cards. The predominant motif was the setting sun closely followed by pictures of 'a decrepit old man sitting in an armchair with, beside him, his faithful hound, its head resting on his knee. From the soulful expression in its eyes the sentiment was clear. If only the dog could speak, it would be saying, "you've had it, chum'" (Pilch, 1974, p. vii). This conventional view of retirement is bound up with loss. People tend to retire from something rather than to another phase in life.

A more positive approach to retirement could be helped by preparation which would start early in life so that people could think about activities and lifestyles well before retirement. Pre-retirement education, while valuable, may be too short and too late for many people. However, new kinds of courses and approaches are developing (Coleman, 1983; Phillipson, 1983).

SOCIAL CONSTRAINTS, INCLUDING SOCIAL ISOLATION

Though elderly people may have both the time and the ability to give help to others, there may be other constraints over the degree to which they are able to do so. There are practical constraints such as whether they can be contacted readily and, in some cases, how mobile they are. One helpful development during the 1980s was the rise in the numbers of elderly households with a telephone. In 1988, 91 per cent of adult households with one or both members aged 60 or over in Great Britain had a telephone (the average for all households was 85 per cent) (OPCS, 1990, p. 253). But the percentage was only 78 for one adult aged 60 or over. It was noted in Chapter 8 that older people are less likely to own a car than other households. Women and those living alone are particularly disadvantaged.

Social isolation

It is often thought that isolation and loneliness are common problems in old age and that they are both a cause and a result of the lack of a contribution to society by elderly people. The concept of isolation is by no means straightforward. Shanas *et al.* considered it in four ways:

– by comparison with their contemporaries – peer-contrasted isolation;
– by comparison with younger people – generation-contrasted isolation;
– by comparison with the social relationships and activities enjoyed by [other younger or middle-aged people] – age-related isolation;
– by comparison with the preceding generation of old people – preceding cohort isolation–(Shanas *et al.*, 1968, p.260).

Isolation is clearly extremely difficult to measure. It may be objective (e.g. social contacts can be counted) or it can be subjective (people can be asked about their feelings). Most studies of social isolation have been concerned primarily with the first of the four types of isolation just outlined. Measurement usually consists of information about social activities as a way of estimating the number of 'social contacts' (e.g. Townsend, 1964; Tunstall, 1966; Shanas *et al.*, 1968). Approximately one-fifth of those interviewed in these three studies were isolated, or extremely isolated, and the majority were women without children. However, isolation does not necessarily increase with age. The likelihood of visiting family and friends declines with age but there is little variation in the likelihood of being visited by family and friends (OPCS, 1989, p. 201). Only 2 per cent of people aged 65 and over saw no relatives or friends.

Loneliness

There is a conceptual distinction between isolation and loneliness. Isolation relates to circumstances (which can usually be measured, however crudely), whereas loneliness relates to feelings (often about these circumstances). Care has to be exercised in measuring loneliness because self-perceptions may be unreliable since there is a stigma attached to the condition (Wenger, 1984, p. 141). A common dictionary definition of isolation is 'apart or alone'. One of the most important findings of all the recent studies of elderly people has been that loneliness appears to have little relation to lack of contact with relatives, friends, clubs or other social activities. That isolation and loneliness are not synonymous was one of the most important findings in the cross-national survey in 1968 (Shanas *et al.*, 1968). Tunstall made important distinctions between living alone, social isolation, loneliness and anomie (a feeling of 'normalness' or pointlessness) (Tunstall, 1966). As Jerrome has pointed out: 'We tend to think of widows, childless people and the never-married and those who live alone, as at risk. In fact the never-married tend to be less vulnerable, having well-developed strategies for establishing and maintaining social contacts' (Jerrome, 1990, p. 206). One of the less obvious groups who experience loneliness are elderly people who live with adult children (Wenger, 1984).

Not all the socially isolated in the various samples were lonely. Some seemed to enjoy being alone. In Abrams's study of the over-75s he commented: 'Some isolates are happy, satisfied with their lives and feel far from lonely; and at the same time some of those leading highly gregarious lives are not immune from a sense of loneliness and depression' (Abrams, 1978, p. 38).

Townsend has commented on the isolation and loneliness experienced by a high proportion of elderly people in residential care: 'The lack of even a single friend; a higher rate of severe or frequent loneliness; the discouragement of spontaneous social activity; the inability of visiting relatives and friends to adopt useful roles; the lack of satisfying, and sociable occupation' (Townsend, 1986, p. 38).

HELP GIVEN BY ELDERLY PEOPLE

Evidence has already been presented in Chapters 9 and 10 about the extent of help which elderly people receive from their families, from their neighbours and from the wider community. But elderly people also give help to all these groups and this will now be examined.

To families

Because there have been few systematic studies in the past of help given by elderly people it is impossible to make comparisons. Most current studies only touch on the subject in passing and do not have it as their main focus. Those who look back with nostalgia claim that the old kept a role right to the end; though it is to be hoped that it was not quite such a macabre one as that described by Simmons:

Even with their bent and nearly broken bodies the few surviving old people could be prized for their nimble fingers and ready wits – and above all for their knowledge, skills and experience. . . .

Old women too feeble to travel stayed indoors, attended to household chores, repaired garments, tanned leather . . . and shredded with their very worn teeth the sinew of dried caribou and narwhat. While a Chippewa family slept at night with their feet towards the coals, an old man kept watch, smoked and fed fuel to the fire. According to Inca law, elderly persons unfit for work should still serve as scarecrows to frighten birds and rodents from the fields. (Simmons, 1962, p. 42)

Shanas *et al.* question the view that intergenerational contact and mutual exchange of services is less today, even though the standard living pattern is now one of separate households. They say:

The traditional assumptions about the changes in modern societies have never been supported by empirical evidence. On the contrary, a number of studies have demonstrated that the generations, although preferring to live apart, maintain contact and exchange mutual services. What is found between the generations is 'intimacy' at a distance rather than isolation. (Shanas, *et al.* 1968, p.180)

The British studies of the 1950s and 1960s came to very similar conclusions about help given by elderly people, i.e. that it is still given, though more in areas where the families are housed near the elderly people. Migration of families impedes this flow of services between the generations (Young and Willmott, 1957, pp. 196–7). Evidence from the 1970s confirmed the extent of help given to families. Hunt found that nearly one-third of her sample of elderly people were able to give help when they visited relatives, but that this declined sharply with age (Hunt, 1978, p. 101). The *GHS* showed that 13 per cent of people over the age of 65 were carers in 1985 (Green, 1988, p. 8). For many this is likely to be care of an elderly spouse. As Wenger demonstrates: 'While elderly carers appear on average to provide care for shorter periods of time compared with younger carers, the care they do provide is likely to be more intense: in terms of the hours put in; in its intimate nature; and more likely to be done without help, compared with that given by younger carers' (Wenger, 1990, p. 210–11).

Bell has pointed out that there may be class differences in the kinds of help given (Bell, 1969). More financial help may be given by the older generation to the younger family in the middle classes, for example to help pay school fees.

One of the main ways help is given by elderly people is help with the care of grandchildren. This comes out in all the studies of elderly people and their families (e.g. Willmott and Young, 1960; Shanas *et al.*, 1968; Wenger, 1984). In a national study, *Women and Employment: a lifetime perspective*, it was found that the grandmother was the second most frequent source of child care for women in employment (Martin and Roberts, 1984, p. 39), the most frequent being the husband. For pre-school children, 34 per cent of working mothers used the grandmother and for school-aged children 25 per cent did. The use of formal care such as crèches, day nurseries and nursery classes was rare. But Harris has pointed out that the giving and receiving may blur into one: 'Whereas the daughter sees her visits as "keeping an eye on Mum", Mum may see the visits as the daughter turning to her for help and advice' (Harris, 1969, p. 204). He stresses that to be on the receiving end in old age amounts to an abrupt reversal of the parental role.

Until recently grandparenthood has been a neglected area of study (Cunningham-Burley, 1986). Academic interest has been much more widespread in the USA (e.g. Bengston and Robertson, 1985). Roles that have been identified are surrogate parent, formal, authoritarian, fun-seeker and distant figure (Neugarten and Weinsten, 1964 – quoted in Victor, 1987).

One matter of concern has been the lack of legal rights and obligations that grandparents have in relation to their grandchildren. Until recently grandparents could find that after death, divorce or separation had ended the marriage of their son or daughter there was no way, short of going to the High Court for a wardship order, by which they were legally entitled even to see their grandchildren.

To neighbours

Many elderly people give help to their neighbours. Sometimes the people helped are other old people. For example, in the granny annexe survey elderly people often gave help to other old people and it was found that the design of the accommodation was an important factor in bringing this about (Tinker, 1976). There was a good deal of keeping keys for one another, letting in meter readers and so on. This was particularly noticeable in flats where elderly people lived in a row (if, for example, they were in a block under family flats) or in a square or corridor (above the family flats). Other studies have noted the help given to neighbours and the reliance of old people in seaside resorts on their neighbours (usually also elderly) has already been noted in Chapter 10.

Voluntary work

The Aves Committee on volunteers thought that 'there may be considerable resources among the over 60s of both sexes' (NCSS and NISW, 1969, p. 120). The view that there are untapped resources among elderly people to help the community is now widely held. Some also believe that if a sense of purpose and of belonging to the community can be given, mental health can be considerably improved (Jones, 1976, p. 117). In a summary of research on older people as volunteers, it was found that a common objective was for them to feel useful, to meet and relate to other elderly people, and to support each other, rather than to take up issues with outside bodies or general problems (Goldberg and Connelly, 1982, pp. 173–4). Marshall has said that many old people can be inhibited through lack of confidence and also that they can be very short of money (Marshall, 1990).

Hunt found that over one-third (36.2 per cent) of her sample belonged to voluntary organisations (Hunt, 1978). In the 1981 *GHS* it was found that 23 per cent of respondents had participated in voluntary work in the year before the interview (OPCS, 1983, p. 166). For those aged 65–74 it was 21 per cent and for those over 75, 11 per cent. It is interesting that the recently retired participated less than any other group except those under 24 and the over 75s. One reason could be that help to families and friends was not included in the survey and, as has been seen, elderly people do give a great deal of help here. In 1990 it was estimated that 12 per cent of the over 65s were volunteers (Press release, Volunteer Centre, 1990).

One interesting development has been along self-help lines. An example of this is the University of the Third Age. Started in France, it now has many branches in this country and aims to provide educational opportunities for the retired as a group. Some of the tutors are retired and some groups are managed by retired people too.

Another development is groups to encourage the participation of older people in community projects and sometimes offer their services to voluntary organisations such as REACH (Retired Executives Action Clearing House). Schemes include linking older people with children, for example in schools.

ROLE IN SOCIAL POLICY

The challenge to society over elderly people comes not only through the outward pressure of events such as the rise in numbers of the very old and frail or the increased cost of services. It comes also from within through the growth of an increasingly articulate group of people speaking for themselves. In some cases they may be speaking about their own needs but in others about other aspects of society.

Social policy for elderly people

Organisations and individuals concerned about elderly people are becoming more forceful in putting forward their views. The acceptance of elderly people speaking for themselves was acknowledged in the DHSS in *A Happier Old Age*, which declared that its policies so

Table 11.1.   A comparison of the age of councillors in 1964, 1976 and 1985 (percentages in each age group)

	1964[1]	*1976*[2]	*1985*[3]
55–64	31	30	27
65–69	11	12	12
70–74	7	7	7
75 and over	4	2	3
Base (councillors of all ages)	3,970	4,648	1,534

[1] 1965 MHLG, *Committee on the Management of Local Government* (The Maud Committee), vol. 2, *The Local Government Councillor*, Moss L. and Parker, R. S., HMSO, 1967, Table 1.1, p.15.
[2] 1976 DOE, *Committee of Inquiry into the System of Remuneration of Members of Local Authorities (the Robinson Committee)*, vol. II, *The Surveys of Councillors and Local Authorities*, HMSO, 1977, Table 1, p. 8.
[3] 1986 Secretaries of State for the Environment, Scotland and Wales, *The Conduct of Local Authority Business* (The Widdicombe Committee). Research vol. II, *The Local Government Councillor*, HMSO, 1986, Table 2.3, p. 21.

Note The Maud Survey covered England and Wales, whereas the Robinson and Widdicombe surveys included Scotland.

far had two main aims but: 'Now we must add a third vital aim. Old people must be able to take their own decisions about their own lives. They must have the fullest possible choice and a major say in decisions that affect them' (DHSS, 1978a, p. 5).

Social policy in general

Elderly people are well represented both among MPs and among local councillors. Of those elected to the House of Commons in 1987, 23 per cent (compared with 13 per cent in 1974 and 10 per cent in 1977) were over the age of 60, compared with about 20 per cent of that age in the population. There is also above-average representation among local councillors (Table 11.1). Surveys for the Maud Committee on Management of Local Government in 1964, the Robinson Committee of Inquiry on the Remuneration of Councillors in 1976 and the Widdicombe Inquiry into the Conduct of Local Authority Business showed that there has been little change between 1964 and 1985, with around 22 per cent of councillors aged over 65 compared with 14 per cent in the population (Secretary of State for the Environment *et al.*, 1986, p. 21, Table 2.31). The Maud Committee saw value in a fairly high proportion of older councillors since they might bring wisdom and experience to local affairs. On the other hand, they declared that they were anxious about the high average age of members and thought that no one aged 70 or over should be allowed to stand for election.

In *Political Attitudes and Ageing in Britain* the conclusions from a National Opinion Poll survey were that elderly people were as likely as any other adults to have voted in a general or local election, stood for public office, paid individual membership to a political party and taken an active part in a political campaign (Abrams and O'Brien, 1981). They also found that in every general election since 1964, irrespective of which party had an overall victory, support for the Conservatives was highest in the 65 or more age group. Abrams and O'Brien speculate on why elderly people have not become a powerful pressure group. Among possible explanations are differences between elderly people (e.g. car owners may oppose free public transport on buses), dislike of being labelled old, and an awareness of lack of power (e.g. at being unable to withdraw their labour).

Research in 1987 showed that voters were as diverse as the rest of the population and they did not necessarily vote out of self-interest (Midwinter and Tester, 1987). Another interesting finding was that ageing was not an issue in the 1987 election.

In the United States elderly people are becoming increasingly involved in lobbying and advocacy and Oriel has speculated about the effect that this growing citizen participation will have on programmes (Oriel, 1981). Phillipson argues that older people in this country have been slower to become a political force but claims that there is a gradual emergence of more radical groups of pensioners (Phillipson, 1982, pp. 124–5). Whether they will ever attain the power of the American Association of Retired Persons (AARP) is doubtful.

CONCLUSION

Elderly people, then, can and do give service in various ways. The opportunities in the future may be even greater. For example, the increasing number of mothers who are in paid employment may lead to a demand for extra child care facilities. Grandparents, as has been seen, already play a major role in the care of their grandchildren. The increased emphasis on the value of voluntary help in many spheres may also lead to an expansion of help by elderly people.

On the other hand, there are other factors which should not be ignored. The numbers of young elderly people, who might be expected to contribute through part-time employment or voluntary work, will decline at least in the short term (see Ch. 2), nor may people want to become involved after a lifetime of work or caring. Society has also to be convinced of the value and usefulness of their contribution, for what everyone is able to contribute to society is determined in part by the social and psychological conditioning to which they are subjected. Those who feel wanted usually find it easier to give help than those who accept a public estimate of their own worthlessness.

What could be the greatest boost for the contribution of elderly people would be a re-thinking of what people do when they do not work and the whole concept of retirement. If a large proportion of people are going to spend long periods not in paid employment, because they are retired, caring or unemployed, then what they do, or can do, for the community has to be seen as valuable. Contributing in some way to society could give the self-esteem, status and role that many sadly only find now in paid employment. A more aggressive attitude by a new generation of elderly people who refuse to be treated as second-class citizens may make this hope a reality.

Chapter twelve

SOME GENERAL PROBLEMS

Many of the problems encountered in providing for elderly people are the same as, or similar to, those for other groups. Some old people suffer from physical impairment, and some who are housebound share some of the problems of parents with small children. Those who are deaf, blind or socially isolated present difficulties of communication similar to those experienced by ethnic minorities.

Some of these problems, which will now be discussed, are: differing perspectives of need; variations in services and the issue of inequalities; take-up of benefits and lack of knowledge of services; the evaluation of services; the meaning of community care; finance and the mixed economy of welfare.

DIFFERING PERSPECTIVES OF NEED

While theorists of social administration have become increasingly concerned with measuring needs there is a danger that those actually providing the service may become less so. If resources continue to be severely limited it is possible that agencies may deal solely with the obvious needs of which they are immediately aware. For example, a local authority with a lengthy waiting list for housing can perhaps be forgiven if it does not go out of its way to uncover any fresh needs. Yet it might be possible for some people on the list to have their needs met in a more appropriate way. An elderly person on a council list for sheltered housing, for example, may not have considered (or been offered) ways of improving or adapting their home. Similarly, there may be many in need who, for one reason or another, are not on the list. It might, for example, be more economic (and make for greater individual happiness) if some old people in residential homes had their needs examined more closely and, if it were found appropriate, offered an alternative form of housing. One of the most interesting ways of distinguishing types of needs is that developed by Bradshaw (Bradshaw, 1972). He divided needs into four types: normative, felt, expressed and comparative, and these will be discussed in turn.

Normative

This is need as defined by the experts. Examples of this concept of need, as used for elderly people, are the incapacity scale developed by Townsend (Townsend, 1964) and the measures of social isolation used by Tunstall (Tunstall, 1966). Subsequent researchers have constructed similar scales of disability by asking elderly people about their capacity to perform certain tasks. A scale based on questions about disabilities was used in the national disability surveys (Martin *et al.*, 1988). In these ways some attempt can be made to measure dependency. A critique of some of these methods has been undertaken by Wilkin and Thompson (1989) and Bowling (1991).

'Experts' may also be used directly to assess needs. But the expert may sometimes conceal needs. For example, a community physician has suggested that some old people are not put on a waiting list for accommodation by their professional advisers – health visitors and social workers – who wish to spare them from disappointment. Another disadvantage of this approach is that the views of experts are likely to be strongly influenced by their own perspectives (Forder, 1974, pp. 53–4).

Felt

Bradshaw's second category is felt need. This equates need with wants. Many services are based wholly or partly on this notion of self-referral. The problem here is that what people feel they want is governed very much by their previous experience and their knowledge of what is available. What one elderly person may feel he or she needs may be very different from what another feels. Rising expectations will mean that felt needs will keep on growing. Some elderly people today do not expect central heating in their homes, but it is likely that the next generation will.

Felt need is probably one of the least satisfactory ways of measuring need. A number of studies have shown that the less people have and the more deprived they are the less likely they are to feel the need for a service. Forder discusses the view that: 'a policy of provision based on felt need would require a wide dissemination of knowledge, and indeed a much greater openness about the criteria for decisions' (Forder, 1974, p. 52). However, subjective views can supplement more quantitative measures. For example, the disability surveys in 1984–6 asked about people's views on their financial situation, as well as measuring it by level of income (Martin and White, 1988).

Expressed

Bradshaw's third category is expressed need. This is when felt needs are turned into action. Need then becomes equated with demand, for it is those who express their need who are said to be 'in need'. But there may be many reasons why people do not demand a service. For example:

- they may not know the service exists;
- they may feel that they do not qualify;
- they may feel that the service is overloaded and they have no chance of obtaining it;
- the service may be very poor;
- there may be stigma attached to the service;
- the person may feel it beneath their dignity to apply.

On the other hand, the provision of a service – especially if it is of a high standard – will actually create a demand. The conclusion must be that any assessment of demands is hypothetical until a service is actually provided. When it is provided demand may rocket.

Comparative

The fourth definition Bradshaw used is comparative need. 'A measure of need is found by studying the characteristics of those in receipt of a service. If people with similar characteristics are not in receipt of a service, then they are in need' (Bradshaw, 1972, p. 641). This is the same basis used by Harris in *Social Welfare for the Elderly* (Harris, 1968). She examined the records of those getting a service or on live waiting lists. She then asked elderly people for details of the circumstances which led to their being given a particular service. From this she was able to make some assessment of need.

With the increased emphasis on the views of the consumers, for example in nursing (e.g. the Cumberlege Report, 1986) and health and social services (Secretaries of State for Health *et al.*, 1989a and b), it is likely that concepts of need will become more important. All four methods (normative, felt, expressed and comparative) have to be taken into account.

VARIATIONS IN SERVICES AND THE ISSUE OF INEQUALITIES

There may be variations in services and inequalities between individuals, between different groups of people and between areas. Numerous examples in welfare services have been documented (e.g. Sinclair *et al.*, 1990). Good reasons may well account for this variation. The personal circumstances of people are rarely identical, and likewise local conditions. However, there are signs that the government may be taking the matter of inequalities more seriously, for example as in *The Health of the Nation* (Secretary of State for Health, 1991).

Between individuals

There are numerous examples of inequalities between people in old age. Many, such as those between men and women, between ethnic minorities and the majority population and between rich and poor, existed before retirement. Only a radical change in society and a range of measures is likely to bring greater equality. For services there may be some which are laid down with great precision and where there is equality, for example over the amount of the basic old age pension. But for others where there is local discretion there may be considerable differences.

Between groups

The second sort of variation is that which occurs between different client groups. In the case of elderly people it is held that not only is there need to improve care, but provision must be made for the continuing increase in the elderly population. These points are developed further in Chapter 13 under Priorities.

Between areas and local authorities

Variations between areas, such as those noted by the Audit Inspectorate (1983) and Audit Commission (1985) occur largely because local authorities are elected bodies with considerable freedom of choice about what they do. For example, some give travel concessions for elderly people. This freedom of choice is given them so that they can take account of local conditions and so that they can experiment and pioneer with the services they provide. If successful, other authorities may copy. This may make for differences in provision as also may, for example, an unusually high proportion of elderly residents in a particular area. In the case of certain coastal areas and retirement towns and villages discrepancies over provision may widen (Allon-Smith, 1982).

Other reasons for differences and inequalities between local authorities are the political composition of the council, the demand for the service and the extent of provision in the past (Davies *et al.*, 1971; Bebbington and Davies, 1982). Wealth came out as important in two studies done for the Royal Commission on Local Government in 1968. The Maud Commission on Management showed the considerable impact of personalities, both elected members and officers (MHLG, 1967).

Variations and inequalities have led some to press for more central direction. Local authorities are subject to considerable central control, not least because most of their income comes from central sources. The controls exercised by central government include loan sanctions, subsidies, confirmation of plans, the right to vet certain key appointments and a whole range of informal advisory roles. The case for more guidance has sometimes come from researchers, for example over meals (Johnson *et al.*, 1981, p. 126) and home helps (Hedley and Norman, 1982, p. 36), though others have suggested that the central role should be monitoring and evaluation (e.g. Tester, 1989). Sometimes pressure has come from official sources. The Audit Commission, for example, wanted national guidelines about the appropriate forms of care for elderly mentally ill people but suggested that this should be prepared by the DHSS and professional bodies and local authority associations (Audit Commission, 1985). The Griffiths Report called for standards of service delivery to be laid down and for there to be ring fencing (i.e. a specific grant) for certain services (Griffiths, 1988).

An increase in central control would mean a shift away from the prevailing political attitude of central government in the 1980s and early 1990s which was to encourage local authorities to make their own decisions. However, it is interesting that detailed policy guidance has been laid down following the NHS and Community Care Act 1989.

Variations also occur in health provision (see Ch. 6). The DHSS Report of the Resource Allocation Working Party (RAWP) confirmed

Some general problems

the disparities in the way resources had traditionally been allocated
to different parts of the country (DHSS, 1976b). Following this the
DHSS stated that: 'there is also to be a shift of resources towards
those regions and localities which, historically, have received less
funds per head of population than others, and where standards of
service have suffered accordingly' (DHSS, 1976b, p. 13).

TAKE-UP OF BENEFITS AND LACK OF KNOWLEDGE OF
SERVICES

Access to benefits in the Welfare State is one of the most interesting
and relevant subjects.

One consistent theme running through social surveys in the 1960s
and 1970s was the reluctance of elderly people to take up benefits
which were theirs by right. Research showed underclaiming for
financial benefits (e.g. Townsend and Wedderburn, 1965), and
medical services (e.g. Isaacs et al., 1972). There has been less
evidence in the 1980s, probably because little research which might
have demonstrated this was undertaken. However, official statistics,
such as those for take-up of various kinds of income support (see
Ch. 5) indicate that the problem still exists. It would become a
subject of major importance again if people were to have more rights
to services rather than the latter being discretionary. It is therefore
worth exploring some of the reasons for non-take up.

One reason put forward is that of feeling a sense of stigma (Hill,
1976). But stigma is not the only reason why people fail to claim.
The attitude of the official to be approached, often referred to as the
'gatekeeper', may be equally important. It is also relevant to
consider the expectations of elderly people. Many have lived through
the privations of two World Wars and a depression and are grateful
for what they now have. Whether future generations of elderly
people, used to a higher standard of living, will take the same
attitude is doubtful.

Lack of knowledge of services can be another reason for non-take
up of services. Research has shown the lack of information (Tester
and Meredith, 1987). The need for more advice and information
services has been made by a long line of government and other
committees. One of the main roles of Age Concern is the giving of
advice about entitlements and in general about services through
their publications and information officers. Without the statutory
right to information, such as that in the Disabled Persons (Services,
Consultation and Representation) Act 1986, which remains to be

implemented, it is doubtful whether people will always know about their entitlements. It is, however, possible that complaints may be taken more seriously. For instance the policy guidance about community care has a detailed section on this (DOH, 1990a).

THE EVALUATION OF SERVICES

One of the most difficult tasks in social policy is how to measure the effectiveness of services. A study of research on welfare provision for elderly people concluded that evaluation was lacking in many services (Sinclair *et al.*, 1990). In some areas, such as carers, it is virtually non-existent (Twigg *et al.*, 1990). But evaluation there must be. In *The Effectiveness of Social Care for the Elderly*, Goldberg and Connelly suggest that as a 'safeguard against the new' (i.e. to assess the usefulness of new schemes which are being pushed but are not tested) and to get public accountability, to ensure that resources are so deployed that they achieve a measure of territorial and social justice, to determine what impact the service has on the well-being of its users, and to assess cost-effectiveness there must be evaluation (Goldberg and Connelly, 1982). There is no simple way in which this can be done, but some key questions must be asked.

Some questions

What is the total amount of provision? It is possible to measure total provision in a number of ways – amount spent, units provided, numbers of staff or man-hours allocated – and all these give some indication of the service. But even these figures do not allow for assessment of quality and may mask a poor or unequal service. A large amount of money may be spent but be wastefully used. There may be better, possibly cheaper, ways of providing the service. The amount may not be distributed evenly, either between individuals or between areas, so again the amount spent does not tell the whole story.

What is the range of provision? A wide range gives choice. For example there are many ways in which food can be provided for older people, but unless all the options, which include meals on wheels, clubs, day centres, allowing home helps to cook meals, having an arrangement with a local cafe, providing convenience foods possibly with a microwave oven or paying a neighbour, are offered the service is not necessarily an effective one as it may not meet the needs of everyone in need. A range of provision may mean that specialist services and workers are provided.

What is the quality of the service?   Quality is one of the most difficult things to measure. Some would argue that staff who are trained would provide a better quality service and this was borne out by a study which showed that trained social workers uncovered more of the needs of elderly people than untrained (Goldberg, 1970).

Does the service reach the people for whom it is intended?   An elaborate, expensive service may be provided but be totally ineffective if it does not reach the planned recipients. If this is because the elderly people do not know about it, the remedy is to find ways of ensuring that they do know. If, however, the elderly person does not in fact want it, that is a different matter. Elderly people, as other groups, have the right not to accept a service.

What are the aims and outcomes?   Evaluative studies have travelled a long way since it was thought sufficient to ask recipients of services simple questions about satisfaction. More searching questions are now being asked about what are the aims of the service and what are the outcomes. For example, if the aim is to keep people in their own homes, how many go into institutional care, what is the cost and what are the effects on carers?

Some problems

The subjective nature of evaluation   The process of evaluation necessarily entails, as the word suggests, the placing of goods, services or actions in an order of values. What these values are and what level of importance is given to them ought always to be openly stated and not, as so often happens, be left as a hidden assumption, since not everyone will necessarily accept the same scale of values. In some research, for example, the assumption is made that keeping elderly people in their own homes is to some extent a mark of 'success'. This solution may or may not be appropriate.

The views of the present consumers being used as a basis for provision for future generations   Even when it is possible to find out people's views and feelings one has to assess what weight should be given to the views of the present generation when planning for the next, whose expectations may well be different. It would therefore be unwise to plan solely on the basis of what today's elderly people think. It cannot, for example, be assumed that bedsitters and open fires, which find favour with some today, will do so in the future.

Comparisons between groups of elderly people   Another method of evaluation is to compare the information about elderly people in various studies. Comparisons are an important form of evaluation but there are problems to be faced (see Ch. 2). Problems may arise over different definitions, for example elderly people may be classified as over the age of 60, 65 or of pensionable age. Similarly, comparisons of dependency in studies is fraught with difficulties when different measures are used. Cross-national comparisons are even more complex because of the differing variables.

Evaluation still has a long way to go and often seems a relatively esoteric exercise to practitioners. Unless practitioners can become more involved and evaluation is built in as part of their normal work, there is a danger of them ignoring findings. Certainly better dissemination of evaluative studies could go a long way to spread the good news, but nothing brings home the value of research more than a small taste of it at first hand. Greater field involvement and peer reviews would enhance evaluation. It also has to be said that a number of other things are needed as well. Long-term follow-up and replication studies are needed to assess the impact of social intervention. Finally, when evaluations have taken place it is essential for policy makers and practitioners to be made aware of them. Whether it is good practice resulting in successful outcomes or the reverse, people need to know. They, professionals and elderly people alike, also have to be prepared to accept changes.

THE MEANING OF COMMUNITY CARE

The evidence of the previous chapters can now be brought together. The major findings are that some old people need some form of help and that this is substantial in the case of those who are frail. This help comes mainly from the family, but the statutory services, voluntary organisations and friends play an important role. They complement rather than compete. Many elderly people give help to others and it is suggested that more of them could if given the opportunity.

How do these findings contribute to a theory of community care? If we return to the definition of community care in Chapter 4, it was seen that the meaning is usually polarised between the provision of domiciliary services and a vague idea of caring by the community or society. Caring in this context is usually taken to mean the provision of help, support and protection. But, as a speaker to the Royal Society of Health said in 1972: 'Community care is a treacherous, seductive phrase which creates a warm glow like roses round the cottage door catching the rays of the setting sun.' The reality of care is usually a combination of the two extremes just mentioned. Domiciliary services are important and provide that care which a family is not able to give. But the support of the family is usually of crucial importance.

The concept of community care contains a number of different elements. First there is the public recognition of the importance of the family – usually referred to as informal care but in reality mainly the family. If the family still plays the major role then the aim of the statutory services ought to be to enable them to discharge their task more effectively. The community can care. It is up to the politicians and helping services to support it in doing so.

At the same time there will always be families who cannot or will not give help. It is not always possible for them to do so, nor is it always the right solution. It would be as foolish to ignore the limitations of the family as to undervalue its potential. Nor is it sensible to ignore the fact that family care, as has been pointed out, has up to now usually been provided by women and that equal opportunities may now mean that men will have to take a greater share in family caring. There are also elderly people without any relatives and for them family support is obviously impossible.

Second it is foolish and short-sighted to see elderly people (and probably any other group) as being always the recipients of services. The 80 year old running her son's household after the death of his wife and the 76 year old disabled man doing his 89 year old uncle's shopping found in the granny annexe sample (Tinker, 1976) are just as much part of the caring pattern as the family looking after a bedridden granny. Unless elderly people are seen as contributors as well as recipients they are unlikely to be considered equal members of society. This is relevant to the discussion (in Ch. 11) about loneliness which is particularly acute for those who feel that no one relies on them.

The third element in a social policy based on community care must be the role of neighbours and friends. Little is known about how commitment can be fostered. It is, however, probably unrealistic to expect help from this source to cover long-term care, especially that of a more intimate and personal kind. There is a difference between neighbours getting in shopping for an elderly person and going round to put them on a commode.

A fourth element in community care is the proposition that institutional care can be looked on as a (very necessary) form of community care. Under the NHS and Community Care Act 1990 (Section 46) the definition of community care services includes local authority homes. Where there is an easy exchange between the two, as in respite care schemes or the use of multi-purpose residential homes, it is easier to see institutions as part of the community. Some argue that when old people live in homes of their own these are becoming institutional with family members being 'trained up' to give nursing help, administer medicines and so on (Higgins, 1989).

Finally, there is need to see community care in less narrow terms than the provision of care services and the sole responsibility of social services departments. It needs to be seen in the widest possible context which particularly emphasises housing and income. This may mean giving more money to the elderly person rather than services so that, for example, taxis to a relative can be obtained rather than transport to day care. It also means starting with the needs of the individual old person and building on their strengths as well as focussing on crisis points such as bereavement and discharge from hospital.

In conclusion, the approaches outlined above are complementary and ought to dovetail into one another. It is the interleaving of informal, usually family, care with statutory services that is so necessary but so difficult to achieve. What does seem evident is that without good basic statutory services, such as community nursing and help in the home, informal carers will not be able to support elderly people without cost to their mental and physical health. It is no use paying lip service to support for informal carers if help from professionals is not forthcoming. This may mean a better use of existing resources but it may mean more resources.

FINANCE

Economic constraints and spending

Economic constraints have dominated social policy in recent years. On the positive side closer scrutiny of budgets can lead to a radical and valuable reappraisal of policies which might not otherwise have happened. Knapp, for example, argues that shortage of resources does not necessarily mean that the well-being of clients must take a back seat (Knapp, 1981). More than anything else it has been the continued growth in the number of very elderly people which has concentrated people's minds on finance since it is usually the care of this group which is the most costly.

What is very difficult to prove is whether public expenditure on social services for elderly people has risen in real terms recently (see also Ch. 8, pp. 166–7). For example a straightforward comparison given by the Government shows that gross expenditure on core community care services was £1,169 million in 1979–80 and £3,444 million in 1987–8 (Sec. of St. for Health *et al.*, 1989b, p. 99) [doc 33]. This they claim is an increase in real terms of 68 per cent. What this table does not show is how these figures relate to number of clients/patients. Also part of the increase is accounted for by increases in the salaries of people in the caring professions so there has not necessarily been an improvement in services. More helpful is to relate services to proportions of elderly people in particular age groups. On this basis it is possible to see that while there has been some expansion of services overall for elderly people for day care and domiciliary services this has not matched the growth in the population aged 75+ and 85+ (Henwood, 1990, p. 28). The National Audit Office also suggested that community services may have difficulty keeping pace with demographic change (NAO, 1987, p. 31). Others have shown how necessary it is to look behind crude figures to see what is happening to a service. One way is to use a constant level of service output as the benchmark against which standards can be assessed (Wistow and Webb, 1983).

In some services it is easier to see the drop in public provision as in local authority and housing association housing for elderly people (Ch. 7). The House of Commons Social Services Committee (1987–8) also claimed that there had been cumulative underfunding of health for a number of years but this was disputed by DHSS (DHSS, 1988).

Looking at manpower figures it is again difficult to come to firm conclusions about services. For example between 1981 and 1989 total NHS manpower fell by 3 per cent but this was partly a result of competitive tendering when numbers of ancillary staff fell by 38 per cent following the privatisation of laundry, catering and domestic services (CSO, 1991, p. 132).

Regardless of economic constraints it is not always easy to achieve any desired shift in resources. Research may show that it is both possible and cheaper to keep an elderly person in their own home

Table 12.1. Health and social services expenditure on elderly people in 1989–90

		£million gross, England	
	Expenditure on elderly people 1989–90	*Expenditure on elderly people as % of expenditure on all age groups*	*Increase in real expenditure on elderly people 1979–80 to 1989–90*
	£m	%	*Av. % change pa*
Hospital and community health services	7154	51.9	2.3
Family health services	1303	25.0	4.5
Personal social services and Income Support for private nursing home and residentail care	2893	56.4	6.1
Total	11350	47.0	3.4

DOH, Economic Advisor's Office, 1991, Table 1.

rather than in residential care but it may not be possible to switch buildings and staff at the drop a hat. The carrot of joint finance has been one way of attempting to bring about this switch.

There have been a number of factors which have contributed to the current interest in costs, such as variations in costs of apparently similar services, the growing interest generally in value for money, and the increasing number of economists and accountants becoming involved in social policy. In Government departments, the Audit Commission and bodies connected with local and health authorities' costings studies grew in the 1980s. But the problems should not be minimised. The methodological problems, as DHSS admitted to the House of Commons Social Services Committee in 1980, are difficult (House of Commons, 1980). The Committee recommended that 'high priority' should be given to research on the cost-effectiveness of different packages of care.

Wright's work has contributed much to laying the foundations of a methodology of costings; but he admits that the actual measurement of costs and benefits are 'fiendishly difficult' (Wright, 1982). His explanation of the methods of costing is one of the clearest expositions on the subject. He describes two major ways of measuring costs. The simplest is the public expenditures falling on public authorities. The other approach is the opportunity cost which arises from the premise that, as resources are limited, using them in one way means that a benefit is foregone for use for an alternative. Therefore cost is a measure of sacrifice or opportunity lost. The latter approach includes all the resources used in the provision of care, whether or not they belong to public authorities.

While caution should be exercised in any discussion of costs (for example capital costs are often left out of calculations) some comparative costs are significant. A public expenditure costings exercise for DOE, in conjunction with DHSS, which outlined some of the problems, showed that it is possible to cost a package of care for people of similar dependency levels (Tinker, 1984 and 1989b). This included the capital and revenue costs of particular schemes, such as alarms or very sheltered housing, and all the other public expenditure ones such as income. Doc 21 shows the relative costs and demonstrates that staying at home options, while not cheap, are very much cheaper than hospital care and cheaper than residential care. That is not to say that costs should be the only factor in decisions. Very few costings studies, for example, take account of informal care. It must also be recognised that costs for very dependent people following hospital closures may be more expensive than currently costed packages of care (Glennerster *et al.*, 1990).

The important work of the Audit Commission included identifying the balance of care between different services and care settings as well as between different authorities. They pointed to poor value for money with community care policies being in disarray (Audit Commission, 1986).

Other work on costings includes the Kent Community Care scheme evaluated by Challis and Davies (1986). This study, which was later replicated, demonstrated the cost-effectiveness of that scheme. The researchers also found that taking account of costs as well as welfare benefits did not distract social workers from their main objectives.

Another area of concern in value for money is over charges. The only free (to the old person) form of housing provision is the hospital; whereas in sheltered housing rent must be paid or the home bought, and for part III accommodation a person may have to sell their home or realise any other capital to pay for their stay.

237

Little research has taken place on the growing practice of charging for services and even less is known about rebates and their effect on demand.

Lack of information

A prerequisite to any understanding about patterns of expenditure is adequate information. Some of the most interesting evidence on finance in the last few years has come from the House of Commons Social Services Committee. For example in 1980 they examined the Government's White Paper on Public Expenditure relating to the social services and asked fundamental questions on spending plans and the impact of these policies (House of Commons, 1980). They also asked whether the information provided enabled Parliament to form judgments about the government's priorities and policies.

THE MIXED ECONOMY OF WELFARE

The previous chapters have shown the greater emphasis in the 1980s on private and voluntary provision. The growth of private sector pensions, sheltered housing and residential care has been particularly marked. So has the taking over of local authority services, such as day care, by voluntary agencies like Age Concern. Questions need to be asked about the effect on the statutory sector as well as on the private and voluntary.

One positive side to a lack of expansion of the public sector is, in theory anyway, that less taxes will be demanded and therefore people will have more of their own money to spend as they wish and so will have choice. In practice alternative services may not be available, for example the provision of private domiciliary help is very patchy. People need good information to know what is available. Also to be taken into account is the likely residualisation of services in the public sector if it becomes a sector which more and more serves those on low incomes. What public opinion polls in the 1980s were showing was the growing wish of people to spend money on statutory help to obtain better services. In the survey *British Social Attitudes* the question posed was: 'Suppose the Government had to choose between the three options on the card. Which do you think it should choose?' The three options were:

- reduce taxes and spend less on health, education and social benefits;

- keep taxes and spending on these services at the same level as now;
- increase taxes and spend more on health, education and social benefits.

The most popular option in 1987 was the latter – 50 per cent wanted to increase taxes and this compares with 32 per cent in 1983 when the majority (54 per cent) wanted taxes and spending at the same level (Jowell *et al.*, 1988).

The advantages of non-statutory help include choice, flexibility, and the encouragement of competition. However, one essential objective of the private sector is to make a profit and provision is not primarily a response to need. While the development of private sector provision has gone ahead and opened up more and different services to older people this has not been without criticism and questioning. Perhaps the most important of these relate to standards of care. Research on private residential homes shows that there are dramatic differences between the standards of the best and the worst. In private sheltered housing older people and their advisers need to look carefully at such things as the service charges. And in many areas of private care such as domiciliary help or chiropody little is known at present about standards. The particular problems in the voluntary sector were identified in Chapter 10. Another problem with a mixed economy of welfare is that planning a coherent social policy becomes difficult if providers are outside the state system.

There is also the blurring of the respective roles of public and private sectors. For example there are large numbers of state-supported elderly people in private old people's homes. While, as has been seen in the discussion of community care, dovetailing of services is clearly sensible there are researchers (e.g. Sinclair *et al.*, 1990) and Committees (e.g. Board for Social Responsibility, 1990) which argue strongly that savings in services can rarely be achieved without cutting services. The latter also argued for a high standard of basic statutory services such as adequate pensions. Some of these decisions need to be considered in the context of groups other than elderly people and this is one of the purposes of the concluding chapter.

Chapter thirteen

THE TOPIC IN PERSPECTIVE

In these chapters we have looked at the position of elderly people at the present time and at possible future developments. We have considered their needs and who might meet them. It is now possible to draw together some of the threads and come to some conclusions. But before doing so we must relate elderly people to other groups. This is important because a group should not be singled out for special policies without taking into consideration its position in relation to the rest of society.

It is easy to be aware that elderly people are a group which is increasing in size, while other groups, such as children, are at present declining in numbers. But it is not just this demographic fact alone that has caused an upsurge of interest in elderly people (as witnessed by official pronouncements, academic research, media stories and so on) (Tinker, 1990a). Although it is difficult to know exactly why this has happened, pressure groups and an increasingly articulate and educated group of elderly people must have had some impact. Some would argue, however, that this growing interest and public concern is not matched by increased provision of services. Nor is there as much competition for posts in geriatric medicine as in some other fields of medicine or a noticeable queue of people wanting to work in establishments that care for elderly people.

ELDERLY PEOPLE AND OTHER GROUPS

The majority of elderly people continue to live their lives with only marginal state intervention. While nearly all will receive a state pension and some form of state health care, it is only the minority who will receive the many other services available.

For those who do need help many of their problems, such as ignorance of benefits and feelings of stigma, will be the same as for other disadvantaged groups. The need for more information about benefits presented in a more lucid form (Tester and Meredith, 1987) is not peculiar to elderly people. Similarly, when sources of help are examined a pattern akin to that for other groups is found. This is particularly noticeable in the extent of family care. For mentally handicapped and physically disabled people the bulk of caring is also undertaken by kin (Green, 1988; Martin *et al.*, 1988).

The general approach to the delivery of services for elderly people is also similar in many ways to that being increasingly recommended for other groups such as children, disabled people and the homeless. All emphasise the importance of community care and joint planning and co-ordination between services.

Elderly people also share similar experiences with other groups. With the growth of unemployment they are sharing an experience of absence of paid employment. Is it too much to hope that this could bring about a change in the way in which people who are not in paid employment are seen? If more people could find status and satisfaction in their lives through activities other than paid work, then this would be bound to have repercussions on the way in which people see ageing. Instead of old age being the end of 'real life', it could be a more natural continuation of the life they have been living before the age of statutory retirement. Old people also share some of the uncertainties in social policy. What changes, for example, will be required in social policy when there are more ethnic minorities among elderly people? This group may compare the expectation of care that they would have received in their home country, possibly with an extended family system and with enhanced status, with the reality of care in Britain.

Nor is it at all certain what changes in law and/or public opinion over equal opportunities between men and women will mean. Not only is there the obvious difference in the age at which men and women are entitled to draw a pension; there are other anomalies. For example women have entitlement to free prescriptions at 60 compared with 65 for men.

PRIORITY FOR RESOURCES

A question that will be increasingly asked, particularly if resources continue to be limited, is what priority elderly people should have compared with other groups. In part the question is answered by demographic facts. The large increases in the numbers of very elderly people (Ch. 2) means, if present trends continue, a greatly increased demand for health and personal social services. Paradoxically, policies of prevention and care are enabling more people to live longer and in better health. But probably in the end there will be a period, perhaps only a short time, when they are more dependent and will need more services. Those who argue for priority to go to elderly people also point to the extent of unmet need.

The assumption has been made in many studies that the Welfare State will continue to expand and that the issue is largely about where priority for expansion should take place. Constraints were foreseen in 1975 by Klein who drew attention to the potential problems of inflation and lack of economic growth (Klein, 1975). It is these problems which have caused concern in all the major industrial countries in the last few years. Rising numbers of elderly people combined with a lack of economic growth have turned attention to what is usually the largest item in social welfare – pensions. Most state pensions are paid by the taxes of a working generation (known as pay-as-you-go finance) as part of an informal contract. The understanding is that the working generations will have their pensions paid by future generations in paid employment. When the numbers of people in paid employment decline, as will happen in the UK, then the proportion of their income required in taxation will increase to meet the pension costs of the larger number of pensioners.

What is happening abroad now, for example in the United States and New Zealand, are some bitter disputes over what has become known as inter-generational justice. This is illustrated in a book *Workers versus Pensioners: intergenerational justice in an ageing world* (Johnson *et al.*, 1989). The authors argue that younger generations see the present group entering old age as having benefited from economic growth, subsidised house purchase, large child benefits and other welfare help that are being increasingly denied to younger people now. In the United States older people have won many advantages in the field of social security and health care at the expense of other social groups (Berliner, 1988). It is understandable that younger age groups may feel reluctant to pay for such proportionately large pensions. Some governments at the end of the 1980s were beginning to raise retirement ages, introduce stiffer means testing for benefits and lower the relative level of others so that pensioners would not have the same benefits as previous generations.

While recent research in the United States and New Zealand has suggested that over the last two decades welfare systems have become increasingly generous towards older people and increasingly restrictive towards families with dependent children, this has not been shown to have happened in Britain. Examining direct Government expenditure on elderly people through pensions, health and social services, there is little evidence of any transfer of resources from young to old since the 1960s – any changes in the distribution of welfare payments and services has merely reflected changes in the age structure of the population (Johnson and Falkingham, 1988).

It is essential that those who argue for resources to go to one group or another do so on sound evidence. That is not to say that the weight of numbers will always be the most important factor. For example, cases of child abuse in the early 1990s have had an effect on public opinion and concentrated staff resources in this area.

INTEGRATION OR SEGREGATION?

Another basic issue in deciding social policies for elderly people is that of integration versus segregation. Should elderly people be (as the dictionary puts it) combined into the whole or should they be set apart? Should they be integrated into society through housing, new forms of employment and social activities, or should they be moved, or encouraged to move, away from the mainstream of life?

There are a number of different theoretical approaches to integration and segregation. First, there are those related to historical changes. These assume that while elderly people used at one time to be integrated into both society and the family, they are now much more likely to be segregated. However, as was pointed out in Chapter 9 when the family was discussed, evidence is lacking to substantiate such theories. What evidence there is does not support the view that the close three-generation family was the norm, and anyway few people actually survived into old age.

Second, there are theories about the advantages and disadvantages accruing to groups when they are singled out for special treatment. The advantages include the value of specialisation and a co-ordinated approach to provision. This has been argued strongly in the case of children. So it was for disabled people who since 1974 have had a minister to look after their interests. The plea for a Minister for the Aged is sometimes put but has been rejected by, among others, David Hobman. When he was Director of ACE he maintained that such an appointment would be psychologically damaging and could further disadvantage older people by setting them as a race apart. As far as administration is concerned, and particularly over the monitoring of services, it has been suggested that there should be an inspectorate based on client groups rather than on services. However, a service concerned solely with a client group risks the danger of being out of the mainstream of function-based services. There is also the problem that when a group is chosen for special treatment this can bring stigma. Also, as has been pointed out many times, elderly people are not a homogeneous group and may not gain from being treated as if they were.

The third approach is concerned with ageing and theories of disengagement. It is held to be normal for elderly people to disengage and therefore bring about their own segregation from society. The theory is that the individual's activities form a curve during their lifetime and gradually fall away. Preparation for death is made by withdrawing from previous roles and limiting social contacts. There is little evidence to support these theories and some writers suggest that insufficient attention has been paid to forms of compensation, replacement and substitution.

Probably the right basis for assessing the range of views is to note the evidence presented earlier that elderly people are a varied group. Some want independence with privacy. Others prefer the company of younger people. It seems more sensible to make varied provision in social policy so that, for example, elderly people can choose to live either in mixed communities or in special schemes for their own age group. The same course should be followed with other provisions such as clubs, since some will want to belong to those for their own age group while others will prefer ones without age restrictions.

ELDERLY PEOPLE IN MODERN SOCIETY: STRESSES AND COMPENSATIONS

Surveys of old people often concentrate on measurable needs and the extent of services provided. Many show up alleged deficiencies in services or focus on people found in particular situations – found dead, suffering from cold, lacking income and so on. A good deal, therefore, is known about the stresses of growing old but much less about its compensations. Nor is there a philosophy of retirement.

There is no doubt from recent evidence that for some old people life does present difficulties. In their own judgment the greatest problems are caused by ill-health, lack of income and loneliness. But for the majority of old people life continues to have a great deal of satisfaction. Hunt commented: 'looking at elderly people as a whole, it can be said that a great many appear to get a great deal out of life' (Hunt, 1978, p. 31). Abrams found this too when he measured life-satisfaction (Abrams, 1978) and so have subsequent surveys (e.g. Wenger, 1984; Bury and Holme, 1991).

Growing attention has been focused on measuring life-satisfaction and quality of life (Tinker, 1983; Hughes, 1990). Life-satisfaction is related to the degree to which people feel they achieve their aspirations, morale and happiness. How the quality of life is measured is difficult to decide. Some measures have been documented and criticised (Bowling, 1991). In a useful summary of ways of measuring quality of life Hughes includes:

- individual characteristics of old people such as functional abilities, physical and mental health, dependency, gender, race and class;
- physical environmental factors such as facilities and amenities, standard of housing, control over environment, comfort, security and regime in care settings;
- social environmental factors such as levels of social and recreational activity, family and social networks and contact with organisations;
- socio-economic factors such as income, nutrition, standard of living and socio-economic status;
- personal autonomy factors such as ability to make choices, exercise control and negotiate environment;
- subjective satisfaction: the quality of life as assessed by the old person;
- personality factors such as psychological well-being, morale, life-satisfaction and happiness (Hughes, 1990, p. 48).

Some research studies are based on the perceptions of professionals with questions asked of them rather than of the elderly people themselves. This may save time and achieve answers in a more standard form, but it may be dangerously misleading as a way of finding out how elderly people themselves really feel. Power, in his study of elderly people in residential care, showed how easy it is to be misled by appearances. Professionals in homes might see elderly people sitting apathetically but when they were interviewed nothing could be further from the truth (Power, 1981, p. 2).

When attempts are made to measure quality of life by asking elderly people themselves, there are different ways in which this can be done. In some cases direct questions, albeit open ones, are put, but others prefer a less structured biographical approach. Certainly there are some aspects of life which do not come out clearly in a questionnaire. No one who reads Ronald Blythe's *The View in*

Winter can fail to be moved by his chapter on prayer and the importance of a spiritual life to many elderly people (Blythe, 1979). The importance of this aspect of people's lives also came out clearly in the inquiry into ageing conducted by the Church of England (Board for Social Responsibility, 1990).

Coming to the fore now are other potentially life-enhancing aspects of life which were formerly scarcely touched on. One of these is sexuality and friendship in later life (e.g. Thienhaus *et al.*, 1986; Greengross and Greengross, 1989).

What is strikingly apparent is the variety of conditions of elderly people which give the lie to any attempt to generalise about them. As Brearley has said, each person's attitudes and life are unique and satisfaction for each of us is a highly personal experience (Brearley, 1975, p. 21). Differences between elderly people of different ages, between men and women, between social classes and between those living alone and those living with others are but four examples.

Of growing interest – and concern – is the first of these and in particular differences between the quality of life of what have been termed the young elderly and the old elderly. The dividing line between the two is often taken to be 75. Nearly all Hunt's data in *The Elderly at Home* is analysed on this basis and she found that one of the most interesting aspects of her findings was the extent to which many of the disadvantages were strongly age-related (Hunt, *Population Trends*, Spring 1978). In a profile of 11 risk groups it was found that the most disadvantaged risk groups were the very old, those who had recently moved or been discharged from hospital and the divorced or separated (Taylor *et al.*, 1983). On the other hand, some over-75s were doing very well. Bury and Holme's study of the over-90s also found large numbers of their sample who said that they were in good health and whose morale and well-being was high (Bury and Holme, 1991).

Hunt also made much of the differences between men and women in the quality of their lives as measured by health and access to services. In most cases women came off worse, though one can speculate that some of the disadvantages, such as lower income, were the result of fewer having been in paid employment or employment with equality of pay. The position of women may improve. The study of the over-90s also found that life satisfaction across the life course was higher for men than for women (Bury and Holme, 1991). Abrams has drawn attention to the striking differences between women who lived alone and women who lived with others (Abrams, 1980).

Abrams also considered class differences and found that among very elderly people those from a professional background led more active lives than those from a manual working-class background (Abrams, 1980). But he found no evidence that as a result middle-class old people found their lives more satisfying than working-class people. Where there were differences was in looking back and regretting what they did not do. Working-class people were more prone than middle-class people to look back on a period of frustrated aspirations and disappointed expectations.

The fourth situation in which there can be differences is in the quality of life of people living alone. Here the evidence is mixed. On the one hand common sense suggests that elderly people living alone will have no one to share their domestic tasks and will have less chance of contacting someone else in an emergency. But it is perhaps salutary to remember that Abrams found that satisfaction with particular aspects of their lives (e.g. health, financial position, income) was consistently greater among those living alone than among those living with others. And, in a follow-up study of his sample, he noted that more of those living alone had survived (Abrams, 1980).

Three overlapping problems identified are the restrictions resulting from poor material conditions and poor health, the effect of combinations of disadvantage (e.g. houses which are difficult to keep warm, frailty and low income) and disability or bereavement which may bring social isolation and which may make old people feel they have little to live for (Sinclair and Williams, 1990, p. 85). Although fears are often expressed about other aspects of life, it is important to remember these three. Some aspects of people's lives, for example as victims of crime, assume more publicity at certain times. Research, however, consistently shows that older people are the least likely to be victims of violent crime.

To allow elderly people to achieve their potential and to be valued members of society there may be a need for change in the mental picture that people have of old age. Comfort has said that men of his generation knew that their grandmothers dressed in black at 45 and looked like grandmothers, whereas today's grandmothers often wear shorts and play tennis (Comfort, 1965, p. 119). Twelve years later he stated that what was needed was a change of attitude (Comfort, 1977, p. 27). He thought that social gerontology would only have made an impact when an older person came to be seen not as old first and a person second, but as a person who happens to be old (plus experience and minus the consequences of certain physical accidents of time).

IMPLICATIONS FOR PROFESSIONALS

It is always important for professionals to remember that they will only be in personal contact with a minority of elderly people. And just as one cannot generalise from a study based on the 5 per cent in institutional care, so groups such as social workers should not generalise from those elderly people who present as clients, for they are bound to be those who have particular difficulties.

What it is hoped that this study has shown is that 95 per cent of old people live out their lives in their own homes supported in the main by their families. But this must not be taken to imply that there is no need to be concerned about them and about those services which they will all have recourse to, such as pensions and health care. There must be constant vigilance that these are adequate and, above all, provided in the most appropriate way with the elderly people having the maximum say in this. What is also crucial is that services for the growing number of frail elderly people should be adequate. These are vital to back up what their families can do and particularly vital for those old people who have no families to turn to.

One of the most encouraging developments is a growing awareness of the needs of elderly people by professionals. Part of this is a result of a multidisciplinary approach and part is an attempt by professionals to define what it is they are trying to do. And yet evidence continues to be produced about poor standards and a lack of understanding of the needs of elderly people. Elderly people have both legal and moral rights and exercising these may lead to voluntary and involuntary risks. Studies such as *Rights and Risk* show the need for a shift 'away from a patronising and paternalistic over-protection from risk and towards acknowledgement of their rights to as much self-determination as is possible for each individual within the limits of the resources available' (Norman, 1980, p. 8). Norman asks: 'should old people be allowed to live in squalor or danger if they refuse help? Should residential homes and long-stay hospitals protect old people from physical risk at the cost of depriving them of their independence? How can old people prevent medical treatment from being forced upon them?' (Norman, 1980; back cover). Writing in 1988, Norman claimed that there had been no significant improvement to elderly people's rights since 1980 (Norman, 1988).

The issues of rights and risks seem most acute in residential settings, and as Clough remarks, 'the more services staff provide, or the more they do for residents, the more power they have over their lives' (Clough, 1981, p. 162). It is a problem not only in institutions specifically for old people, such as geriatric hospitals, but for acute hospitals too since an increasing proportion of elderly patients are using beds in the acute sector. The widespread yet unfounded fear amongst the staff of residential and nursing homes that the Coroner's Court may apportion blame following a fatal accident continues to cause many staff to be over-protective, and thus to deprive elderly people of their liberty, self-responsibility and freedom of movement, claims Norman (1988). The Wagner Committee listed a number of rights which they thought that individuals should have in institutions (Wagner, 1988a). These included a trial period, retention of their pension book, a personal key to their room, a clear complaints procedure, and also that no one should have to share a bedroom as a condition of residence (Wagner, 1988a, p. 116).

This leads on to another point, that while professionals may not consciously opt for working with elderly people (e.g. medical students who declare adamantly that they wish to work with other age groups), most of them will in fact do so. For example, 40 per cent of acute beds are occupied by elderly people at any one time, and elderly people occupy nearly half of the NHS beds in hospitals. One geriatrician wrote: 'Like Peter Pan, British medicine wishes to stay with the young, dreaming of transplanting this and pioneering that – while avoiding the real health-care needs of our ageing population' (Livesley, 1982). And Grimley Evans, discussing the case for subsuming geriatric medicine as a speciality into general medicine asks, in view of demographic trends, whether there is a future for general medicine that is not geriatric (Evans, 1981).

Some would argue that a fundamental shift in society is needed for elderly people to have more rights and to be taken more seriously by professionals. Townsend argues that the dependency of elderly people is being manufactured socially. The major influences, he believes, are the imposition, and acceptance, of earlier retirement; the legitimation of low income; the denial of rights to self-determination in institutions; and the construction of community services for recipients assumed to be predominantly passive (Townsend, 1981). This argument that the experience of old age is determined more by economic and social factors and less by biological or individual ones is stressed by critical gerontologists (e.g. Phillipson and Walker, 1986). Wilding also takes a radical approach and suggests that the professions trample on people's rights, help some but disable others, have been guilty of serious failures of responsibilities and are an example of power without accountability (Wilding, 1982).

This widespread unease about the present attitude of our society to the care of elderly people has prompted many calls for more training. More specifically, professional education and training can enhance the understanding of staff who work with elderly people. Multidisciplinary degrees in gerontology, such as the one at King's College London, and the growing number of diplomas are also helpful in allowing professionals to learn from each other. Reports as diverse as the Wagner one on residential care (Wagner, 1988a) and one on training for doctors working in the field of the psychiatry of old age (Royal College of Physicians of London and the Royal College of Psychiatrists, 1989) have stressed training.

Another important area for professionals is attention to the legal rights of old people (ACE, 1986; Griffiths *et al.*, 1990). The Law Commission, in a consultation paper on mentally incapacitated adults, suggested that the options include:

– advance directives so that a competent person can give instructions about what should be done when capacity is lost to make decisions (ways include living wills and enduring power of attorney schemes)
– designated decision-making procedures such as substitute consent to treatment procedures;
– improving existing procedures for providing substitute decision-makers such as extending the scope of guardianship and the role of the Court of Protection;
– decision-making by a multi-disciplinary committee or tribunal;
– advocacy;
– a new statutory institution.

Professionals, whether administrators, doctors, social workers, health visitors, nurses or others in the caring professions, must aim to provide the sort of service which they themselves would wish for when they reach retirement. But the welfare of society is not exclusively the concern of the professional. There are many skills and resources available to help in the community, and some indeed are to be found among the users of services. It is the dovetailing of professionals with others that is of importance so that each may contribute to the maximum advantage of society.

THE INTERNATIONAL DIMENSION

Of growing importance in social policy is the impact of events abroad. Whether this is the effect of European Commission policies or comparative research (e.g. Jamieson and Illsley, 1990) the international dimension has to be taken in to account. For example, although very little is agreed yet about the European Social Plan, already decisions taken in the European Courts are affecting the matter of pensions and the legal position of carers. It is not just care delivery which may be affected but the possible migration of elderly people from one country to another which could have dramatic effects on policies. The constraints of this book mean that it is only possible to put up a marker about this area of policy.

CONCLUSION

It is ironic that the carefully measured speech of Prince Charles which stressed the diversity of older people should be headlined 'Prince seeks a dynamic role for the elderly' (*The Times*, 16.5.1990). Society swings between highlighting the third age type go-getter and the shivering, demented old person living alone. Both, of course, exist. But the majority are at neither of these two extremes. After all the discussion on research and the views of others, perhaps the last word is best left to Mary Stott. In a passionately written book, *Ageing for Beginners*, as she entered her eighth decade, she declared that ageing is not a 'condition' to be treated by doctors or social workers, but a process that brings with it possibilities of new experience and achievement (Stott, 1981). The next few years will bring problems, there is no doubt about that, but the most encouraging thing is that elderly people are more and more taking an active role in saying what sort of society they want. Long may it continue. And may professionals listen to, and learn from, them.

Part four
DOCUMENTS

THE NEW ELDERLY

Dr Mark Abrams discusses important demographic trends relating to the elderly:

So far and currently, society has the relatively easy task of providing support and care for a population of elderly people who for the most part are comparatively young, mobile, and healthy. From now on the balance of concern will have to shift in favour of the very old, the immobile and the frail.

He goes on to say why he thinks the focus will change in the future:

Since the 1960s the fortunes of the teenager have been the focus of discussion and research by those interested in age-stratification. He has had his day; from now on the centre of the stage is likely to be occupied by the growing millions who will live well beyond the traditional allotment of three score years and ten.

From: Abrams, M., 'The new elderly', *New Society*, 26.6.75, p. 778.

MYTHS AND REALITIES OF AGEING

The former Director of Age Concern describes some images of ageing:

The ageing process is deeply enshrined in a range of images leading to stereotypes based on notions of intense wisdom and even God-like proportions at one end of the spectrum, to uselessness and semi-idiocy at the other.

None of these extremes serve the elderly well. They are no more universally wise or nice or kind than they are stupid, but there are a range of half truths and fantasies about age, knowledge and experience which have become enshrined in the folk culture of ageing. Some of them stem from the professionals who practise in care. They also have their root in art and literature.

Perhaps the most important perception to be missing is that of the elderly themselves: People like a 60-year-old woman who wrote about her feelings on having reached the statutory retirement age. She said: 'Pensioners are being got at. We must prepare to do battle to maintain our independence and preserve our attractive personalities . . . now I am haunted by the fear that if I cannot dispel the assumption that I am a senior citizen, the following events may reasonably occur. (1) I shall have a gang of young thugs sent to my home to paint my kitchen instead of going to prison; (2) I shall have patients from the local mental hospital drafted to dig my garden; (3) I may be forced to go to suitable entertainments, drink tea and wear a paper hat; (4) I may receive vast boxes of assorted food to which I feel I am not entitled. We pensioners are in a terrifying position. We are *recipients* . . . hands off, please. I am in charge of my life.'

This person recognises, but does not accept, one widely held image of ageing full of assumptions and value judgements with its underlying theme of patronising attitudes, setting the elderly as a race apart to be pitied as people who are no longer capable of managing their own lives. It assumes that ageing is synonymous with a changing personality and that the retired adopt common characteristics with an incompetent level of social functioning. It also implies limited intellectual thresholds devoid of critical faculties.

Not only does this image suggest the old are incapable of exercising informed or rational choice and of maintaining a degree of control over their circumstances; but it also implies that they do not have sufficient resources to meet their own needs for recreation, or welfare when, in fact, the young retired now represent a very important resource which could well make a substantial contribution to the health and social well-being of the community as a whole.

From: Hobman, D., 'Myths and realities of ageing', *Social Work Today*. 3.1.78, p. 18.

Dr Alex comfort argues that the concept of ageism is part of the prejudice against the elderly:

AGEISM is the notion that people cease to be people, cease to be the same people or become people of a distinct and inferior kind, by virtue of having lived a specified number of years. The eighteenth-century French naturalist Georges Buffon said, 'to the philosopher, old age must be considered a prejudice'. Ageism is that prejudice. Like racism, which it resembles, it is based on fear, folklore and the hang-ups of a few unlovable people who propagate these. Like racism, it needs to be met by information, contradiction and, when necessary, confrontation. And the people who are being victimised have to stand up for themselves in order to put it down.

From: Comfort, A., *A Good Age*, Mitchell Beazley, 1977, p. 35.

The OPCs give census, estimated and projected numbers from 1951–2025.

Table 1.2 Age and sex structure of the population of the United Kingdom[1]

Millions

	Under 16	16–39	40–64	65–79	80 and over	All ages
Mid-year estimates						
1951	13.1	16.6	15.9	4.8	0.7	50.3
1961	14.3	17.5	16.9	5.2	1.0	52.8
1971	12.5	19.7	16.7	6.1	1.3	55.9
1981	12.5	20.6	15.7	6.9	1.6	56.4
1986	11.7	20.7	15.8	6.8	1.8	56.8
1989	11.5	20.4	16.3	6.9	2.1	57.2
Males	5.9	10.3	8.1	3.0	0.6	27.9
Females	5.6	10.1	8.2	3.9	1.4	29.3
Mid-year projections[2]						
1991	11.7	20.2	16.5	6.9	2.2	57.5
1996	12.5	19.8	17.0	6.8	2.4	58.5
2001	12.8	19.2	18.0	6.7	2.5	59.2
2006	12.6	18.4	19.4	6.6	2.6	59.6
2011	12.1	18.1	20.2	7.0	2.7	60.0
2025	12.1	18.6	19.0	8.5	2.9	61.1
Males	6.2	9.5	9.5	3.9	1.1	30.2
Females	5.9	9.1	9.5	4.6	1.8	30.9

[1] See Appendix, Part 1 Population and population projections
[2] 1988-Based Projections

Source: Office of Population Censuses and Surveys Government Actuary's Department; General Register Office (Scotland) General Register Office (Northern Ireland).

From: CSO, *Social Trends* (No. 21) HMSO, 1991, Table 1.2, p. 24.

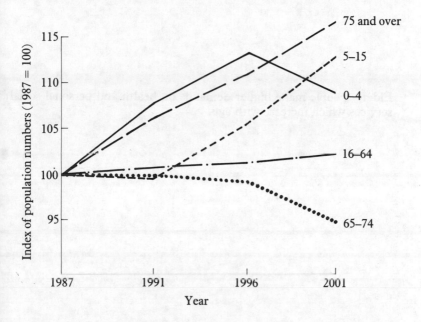

Figure 3.2 shows the projected change between 1987 and 2001 in population numbers of specific age groups. While a fall is expected in the number of people in the 65–74 age group, the numbers in the most 'expensive' age group, people over 75, are projected to increase by nearly one-fifth over the period

From: Fry, K., White, S. and White, J., *Pensioners and the Public Purse*, The Institute for Fiscal Studies, 1990, pp. 18–19.

THE DEMANDS WHICH DIFFERENT AGE GROUPS MAKE ON HEALTH AND PERSONAL SOCIAL SERVICES

Elderly people make higher demands on health and personal social services which increase with age.

Figure 3.1   Spending per head on Health and Personal Social Services

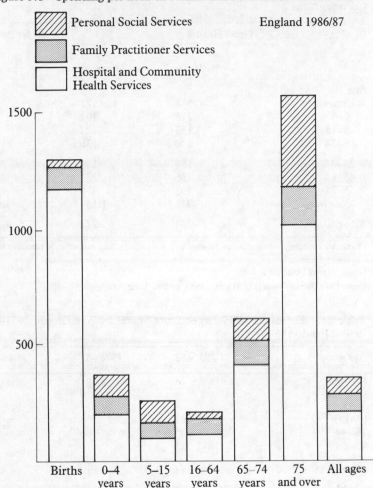

Source: *The Governments Expenditure Plans 1989–90 to 1991–92* Chapter 14 (Cm 614).

Figure 3.1 shows that use of health and social services varies greatly with age. Estimated spending per head on the 65–74 age group was three times the level of spending per head on the 16–64 age group, and spending per capita on those aged 75 and over was almost eight times as high as on these age 16–64.

From: Fry, V., White, S. and White, J., *Pensioners and the Public Purse*, The Institute for Fiscals Studies, 1990, pp. 17–8

Table 7.41   National Health Service – annual costs per person[1]: by sex and age, 1984

	Great Britain		£s per person
	Males	Females	All persons
Age			
Under 1	578	472	526
1–4	218	192	204
5–15	136	123	130
16–24	140	136	138
25–44	154	160	157
45–64	236	225	230
65–74	498	454	473
75 or over	945	1,159	1,087
All ages	234	272	254

[1] Excludes maternity (obstetrics, in-patients and out-patients, and midwifery), administration, and capital costs.

Source: Central Statistical Office

From: CSO, *Social Trends* (17), HMSO, 1987, p. 136, Table 7.41.

Table 24.   Estimated NHS Expenditure Shares by Age Group: 1951–52, 1980–81 and 1986–87.

Age group	1951–52	1980–81	1986–87
Births	–	7	7
0–4	–	6	6
5–15	–	7	6
(0–14)	21	–	–
16–44	35	–	16
45–64	25	–	16
(15–64)	–	34	–
65–74	11	18	17
75–84	–	–	23
85+	–	–	9
(75+)	9	27	(32)
Total	100%	100%	100%

Sources:
1951–2: Derived from Abel-Smith and Titmuss (1956), Tables 91, 106 & 107
1980–81 and 1986–87: DHSS correspondence

From: Bosanquet, N. and Gray, A., *Will You Still Love Me?*, National Association of Health Authorities, Research Paper No. 2, 1989, p. 30.

GROWING INTEREST IN THE PROBLEMS OF OLD AGE

Two researchers comment on the lack of interest in elderly people in the first half of the twentieth century and a resurgence from the late 1940s.

Between 1901 and 1947 the numbers of persons in Britain who were aged 65 and over grew from under two to five millions. Yet in that period very little information on the problems of the aged living at home or receiving treatment and care in hospitals and other institutions was published. It is an extraordinary fact. At the turn fo the century there had been a few studies on pensions and the effect of the Poor Law, three of them by Charles Booth.[1] In 1909 the reports of the Majority and Minority of the Royal Commission on the Poor Laws appeared, and they both contained sections on the aged.[2] In later years there were short passages on the problems of old age in various reports of general surveys.[3] Otherwise there was a dearth of published information and, apparently, of interest too.

Suddenly, in the late forties and fifties, or so it may seem to the historian of the written and spoken word, the problems of old age were discovered. The Nuffied Foundation pioneered the financing of a few studies, including the remarkable work of J. H. Sheldon.[4] The trickle of carefully documented studies became a modest stream, slightly preceding the floodwaters of interest and research in the subject which were released in the United States in the mid-1950s. Among some of the influential studies in Britain have been those of Dr Alex Comfort on the biology of senescence,[5] Dr Alan Welford and his colleagues on psychological adjustment in old age,[6] and Mr F. Le Gros Clark on ageing in industry.[7] There have been many sociological socio-medical and socio-economic surveys which have been based on interviews with samples of the elderly population.[8]

1. BOOTH, C., *Pauperism: A Picture; and the Endowment of Old Age: An Argument*, London, Macmillan, 1892; *The Aged Poor: Condition*, London, Macmillan, 1894; and *Old Age Pensions and the Aged Poor*, London, Macmillan, 1899.
2. *Report of the Royal Commission on the Poor Laws*, Cmnd 4499, London, HMSO, 1909.
3. See, for example, CARADOG-JONES, D., *The Social Survey of Merseyside*, London,

Hodder & Stoughton, 1934; ROWNTREE, B. S., *Poverty and Progress*, London, Longmans, 1941.

4. SHELDON, J. H., *The Social Medicine of Old Age*, Oxford University Press for the Nuffield Foundation, 1948.
5. COMFORT, A., *Ageing: The Biology of Senescence*, London, Routledge & Kegan Paul (revised edition), 1964.
6. WELFORD, A. T., *Ageing and Human Skill*, London, Oxford University Press for the Nuffield Foundation, 1958.
7. For example, LE GROS CLARK, F. and DUNNE, A. C., *Ageing in Industry*, London, The Nuffield Foundation, 1955.
8. A selected list is given in Appendix I for readers who may wish to learn more about old people in particular localities or regions.

From: Townsend P. and Wedderburn, D., *The Aged in the Welfare State*, G. Bell & Sons, 1965, p. 10.

TERMS OF REFERENCE OF THE ROWNTREE COMMITTEE

One of the first large-scale social surveys was undertaken in 1944–46 for the Rowntree Committee on the problems of ageing and the care of old people. The terms of reference of the Rowntree Committee, which was appointed by the Nuffield Foundation, were:

TERMS OF REFERENCE

1. The terms of reference under which the Survey Committee were appointed by the trustees of the Nuffield Foundation were:

'To gather as complete information as possible with regard to (i) the various problems – individual, social, and medical – associated with ageing and old age; (ii) the work being done by public authorities and voluntary organis-ations, and the public and private resources that exist, for the care and comfort of old people in Great Britain; (iii) the provision made for old people in those countries that have given special thought to this matter; (iv) medical research on the causes and results of ageing; and (v) the lines on which action might usefully be taken in the future by public authorities and private organisations, including the Foundation.'

From: Rowntree, B., *Old People. Report of a Survey Committee on the Problems of Ageing and the Care of Old People*, The Nuffield Foundation, Oxford University Press, 1947, p. 1.

A selected list of social surveys 1945–64 was given by Professor P. Townsend and Professor D. Wedderburn.

These have been updated to 1991 by Anthea Tinker.

Social surveys of old people 1945–64 (selected list)

Date of Survey	Area	Numbers interviewed	References
1945–46 (?)	Lutterworth, Midhurst, Mid-Rhondda, Wolverhampton, Oldham, Wandsworth and St Pancras	2,302 people of pensionable age	Nuffield Foundation, Survey Committee on the Problems of Ageing and the Care of Old People (1947), *Old People*, London, Oxford University Press
1945–47	Wolverhampton	477 people of pensionable age	Sheldon, J. H. (1984), *The Social Medicine of Old Age; Report of an Inquiry in Wolverhampton*, London, Oxford University Press
1948	Sheffield	1,596 people of pensionable age	Greenlees, A. and Adams, J. (1950), *Old People in Sheffield*, Sheffield
1948	Birmingham	2,230 people over 70	Shenfield, B. E. (1957), *Social Policies for Old Age*, London
1949–50	Plymouth	Chiefly 80 housebound on list of 350 kept by home help service	Plymouth Council of Social Service (1950), *Housebound*, Plymouth

Date of Survey	Area	Numbers interviewed	References
1949–51	Sheffield	476 living alone or with spouse (mainly health but also social)	Hobson, W. and Pemberton, J. (1955), *The Health of the Elderly at Home*, London; see also Bransby, E. R. and Osborne, B. (1953), *British Journal of Nutrition*, 7, 160, Osborne, B. (1951), *The Nutrition of Older People* (unpublished report of a government social survey)
1950	Northern Ireland	759 people aged 60 and over	Adams, C. F. and Cheeseman, E. A. (1951), *Old People in Northern Ireland, A Report to the Northern Ireland Hospitals Authority*, Belfast
1950	Great Britain	1,950 men and 482 women aged 55–74	Thomas, G. and Osborne, B. (1950), *Older People and Their Employment* (Social survey for Ministry of Labour and National Services. Report No. 150/1 – and unpublished). Summarised by Moss, L. (1955), A sample survey of older people and their employment in Great Britain in 1950. In: *Old Age in the Modern World* (Report of the Third Congress of the International Association of Gerontology, London, 1954), Edinburgh, Livingston, p. 353

Date of Survey	Area	Numbers interviewed	References
1951	Lewisham and Camberwell	1,082 households with at least one person over 65 being helped by domestic help and/or district nursing service	Chalke, H. D. and Benjamin, B. (1953), *Lancet*, 1, 588
1951–52	Liverpool	500 people of pensionable age in 5 selected districts	Liverpool Personal Service Society and Liverpool University, Department of Social Science (1953), *Social Contacts in Old Age*, Liverpool
1953	Hammersmith	100 people over 70 living alone	Sir Halley Stewart Trust and National Old People's Welfare Committee (1954), *Over Seventy*, National Council of Social Service, London
1954	Edinburgh	2,768 people aged 60 and over	Gordon, C., Thompson, J. G. and Emerson, A. R. (1957), *Medical Officer*, 98, 19
1954	Great Britain	120,000 people receiving assistance aged 80 years and over and living alone	Great Britain, National Assistance Board (1955), *Report for the year ended 31 December, 1954*, London, H.M. Stationery Office
1954–55	Rutherglen	323 men aged 65 and over	Anderson, W. F. and Cowan, N. R. (1955), *Lancet*, 2, 239

Date of Survey	Area	Numbers interviewed	References
1954–55	Bethnal Green	203 people of pensionable age	Townsend, P. (1957), *The Family Life of Old People; an Inquiry in East London*, London, Routledge & Kegan Paul
1955	Aberdeen	244 retired men aged 65–74	Richardson, I. M. (1956), *Scottish Medical Journal*, 1, 381
1955	Nottinghamshire (two areas)	340 people aged 65 and over	Marsh, D. C. (1955), *Elderly People*, Nottingham
1955	Dundee	400 people aged 65 and over	Mair, A., Weir, I. B. L. and Wilson, W. A. (1955), *Public Health* (London), 70, 97
1956–57	Stockport	2,073 people aged 80 and over	Lempert, S. (1958), *Report on the Survey of the Aged in Stockport*, Stockport, County Borough of Stockport
1957	Anglesey	160 persons aged 65 and over	Wynne Griffith, G., *The Needs of Old People in Rural Areas* (Paper read to the Royal Society of Health Congress, Eastbourne, 1958), *Journal of the Royal Society for the Promotion of Health*, July/August 1958

Date of Survey	Area	Numbers interviewed	References
1957	Orkney	233 people of pensionable age	Richardson, I. M., Brodie, A. S. and Wilson, S. (1959), 'Social and Medical Needs of Old People in Orkney: Report of a Social Survey', *Health Bulletin, Scotland*, Vol. 17, No. 4
1957	Woodford	210 persons of pensionable age	Willmott, P. and Young, M. (1960), *Family and Class in a London Suburb*, London, Routledge & Kegan Paul
1958–60	Aberdeen	474 people aged 60 and over	Richardson, I. M. (1964), *Age and Need*, E. and S. Livingstone, Edinburgh
1958	Great Britain	853 people receiving meals in areas with a meals service; 1,317 people of pensionable age living in private households	Harris, A. I., *Meals on Wheels for Old People; A Report of an Inquiry by the Government Social Survey*, London, The National Corporation for the Care of Old People, 1960
1958–59	Rural area in Shropshire	328 people of pensionable age	Miller, M. C. (1963), *The Ageing Countryman: A Socio-Medical Report on Old Age in a Country Practice*, London, National Corporation for the Care of old People

Date of Survey	Area	Numbers interviewed	References
1958–60	England and Wales	489 residents of Homes and Institutions who were of pensionable age (other information also about 8,000 persons of pensionable age in a random sample of 173 Homes)	Townsend, P. (1962), *The Last Refuge: A Survey of Residential Institutions and Homes for the Aged in England and Wales*, London, Routledge & Kegan Paul
1959–60	Seven Areas: Salisbury, Leicester, Hexham Rural District, Seaton Valley, Glasgow, Wimbledon and East Ham	1,078 'units' consisting of one person or a married couple of pensionable age	Cole Wedderburn, D. with Utting, J. (1962), *The Economic Circumstances of Old People*, Occasional Papers on Social Administration, No. 4, Welwyn, Herts, The Codicote Press
1960	Lewisham	1,370 people aged 65 and over	Harris, A. I. assisted by Woolf, M., *Health and Welfare of Older People in Lewisham*, The Social Survey, Central Office of Information, June 1962
1960	Swansea	1,962 individuals of all ages, including about 200 aged 65 and over	(Preliminary) Rosser, C. and Harris, C. C. (1961), 'Relationships through Marriage in a Welsh Urban Area', *The Sociological Review*, Vol. 9, No. 3, pp. 293–321

Date of Survey	Area	Numbers interviewed	References
1960–61	Newcastle-upon-Tyne	123 people aged 65 and over in geriatric wards of hospitals and in Residential Homes (together with other information)	Kay, D. W. K., Beamish, P. and Roth, M. (1962), 'Some Medical and Social Characteristics of Elderly People under State Care' in Halmos, P. (ed.), *The Sociological Review*, Monograph, No. 5
1962	Barrow	829 old people living at home (and other information about elderly hospital patients)	Edge, J. R. and Nelson, I. D. M. (1963 and 1964), 'Survey of Arrangements for the Elderly in Barrow-in-Furness, 1 and 2', *Medical Care*, 1964, Vol. 2, No. 1, p. 7.
1962	West Hartlepool	320 people aged 75 and over living alone	Bamlett, R. and Milligan, H. C. (1963), 'Health and Welfare Services and the Over 75's', *The Medical Officer*, CIX, No. 25
1962–63	Edinburgh	200 people aged 65 and over	Williamson, J. *et al.*, 'Old People at Home: Their Unreported Needs' (May 25th, 1964), *The Lancet*

From: Townsend, P. and Wedderburn, D., *The Aged in the Welfare State*, G. Bell and Sons, 1965, App. 1, pp. 140–3. Details of some major national social surveys of old people published since 1964 have been added by the author.

Some major *national* social surveys of old people published since 1964 compiled by Anthea Tinker

Date of Survey	Area	Numbers Interviewed	Purpose	References
1961–62	A stratified sample of local authorities in Great Britain	4,209 people aged 65 and over	A study to find out how effective social services were in meeting the needs of the aged, to find out whether it was true that certain functions formerly performed by the family had been taken over by the social services and to examine new needs. This is the British part of a cross national survey	Townsend, P. and Wedderburn, D. (1965), *The Aged in the Welfare State*, G. Bell and Sons
1962–4	Harrow Northampton Oldham S Norfolk	195 people aged 65 and over. This followed an initial screening of 538 people of this age	A study of old people who are isolated. It is concerned with those who live alone, are socially isolated, lonely or have a sense of anomie	Tunstall, J. (1966), *Old and Alone*, Routledge and Kegan Paul
1962	A stratified sample of local authorities in Great Britain	4,209 people aged 65 and over	A cross national study of old people in Great Britain, Denmark and the United States of America to describe the present capacities of the elderly including their economic and social circumstances	Shanas, E. et al. (1968), *Old People in Three Industrial Societies*, Routledge and Kegan Paul

Date of Survey	Area	Numbers Interviewed	Purpose	References
1965–66	Worthing Oakham (RD and UD) Salisbury Holyhead Sheffield Preston Maidenhead Kidderminster Gosport Dundee Coatbridge Buckie	9,866 people over retirement age in their own homes and residential care	The NCCOP sponsored this survey to try to measure need for given services. They had observed that local authority 10 year community care plans showed wide differences in planned provision	Harris, A. (1968), *Social Welfare for the Elderly*, HMSO
1966	A London Borough south of the river	300 people aged 70 and over referred to the welfare department	An attempt to measure the effectiveness of social work by comparing 2 groups of old people half of whom were allocated to trained case workers and half to untrained	Goldberg, E. M. (1970), *Helping the Aged*, Allen and Unwin
1968	Clacton Bexhill	1,000 people aged 55 and over	The main aim was to find out more about the process of retirement to the coast from the point of view of the retired persons themselves	Karn, V. (1977), *Retiring to the Seaside*, Routledge & Kegan Paul

Date of Survey	Area	Numbers Interviewed	Purpose	References
1976	Stratified random sample of 90 parliamentary constituencies	2,622 elderly people: 1,354 under 75 and 1,268 75 and over	To investigate the social circumstances of elderly people living in private households in the community. To enable health and social services to be deployed to the best effect and also to provide information which may make it possible to devise new forms of assistance. Comparisons are made between the under 75s and those over 75	Hunt, A. (1978), *The Elderly at Home*, HMSO
1977	Hove Merton Moss Side Northampton	1,646 elderly people: 802 under 75 and 844 75 and over	To discover more about the needs, conditions and resources of elderly people over 75 so that policies may be developed to enable the 75 and overs in the next 2 decades to lead satisfying lives. Comparisons are made between the under 75s and those over 75	Abrams, M. (1978), *Beyond Three Score and Ten*, Age Concern

Some general social surveys in the 1980s which yielded substantial data on elderly people compiled by Anthea Tinker

Date of Survey	Area	Numbers Interviewed	Purpose	References
1980	Stratified sample in GB	4,156 people aged 65 and over in private households	To monitor changes in dependency and use of services among elderly people	OPCS (1982) *General Household Survey*, 1980, HMSO.
1982	A sample of elderly people in a representative number of 10 local authorities in England and Wales	1,310 people aged 55 and over in private households	To evaluate a number of innovatory services for elderly people living in private households (For DOE in conjunction with DHSS)	Tinker, A (1984), *Staying at Home: helping elderly people*, HMSO.
1985	Stratified sample in GB	3,691 people aged 65 and over in private households	To monitor changes in dependency and use of services among elderly people	OPCS (1987) *General Household Survey*, 1985, HMSO.
1987	A sample of elderly people in a representative number of 10 local authorities and 10 housing associations in England and Wales	1,089 people aged 55 and over in private households	To evaluate very sheltered housing schemes (For DOE in conjunction with DHSS)	Tinker, A (1989), *An Evaluation of Very Sheltered Housing*, HMSO.
1986	A random sample of 8 areas in England	183 people aged 90 and over in private households and communal establishments	To discover the quality of life of people aged 90 and over in private households and communal establishments	Bury, M and Holme, A (1991), *Life after Ninety*, Routledge.

PERSONAL MOBILITY, SELF-CARE, AND SOME DOMESTIC TASKS

A comparison between 1976, 1980 and 1985 of those unable to manage on their own.

Personal mobility, self-care, and some domestic tasks: percentages unable to manage on their own: *GHS* 1980 and *GHS* 1985 compared with *The Elderly at Home*, 1976.

Persons aged 65 or over

Percentage unable on own to:	GHS: 1985[3]	GHS: 1980[2]	The Elderly at Home 1976[1]
walk out of doors	13	12	13 — go out of doors
get up and down stairs and steps	9	8	6 — get up and down stairs and steps
get around the house (on the level)	2	2	2 — get around the house or flat
get to the toilet	2	2	2 — get to the lavatory
get in and out of bed	2	2	2 — get in and out of bed
cut toenails	29	28	25 — cut toenails
bath, shower, wash all over	9	9	16 — bath
brush hair (females), shave (males)	2	2	2 — brush hair (females) shave (males)
wash face and hands	1	1	2 — wash
feed	1	0	1 — feed
wash paintwork	20	18	24 — wash paintwork
clean windows inside	19	17	24 — clean windows inside
sweep or clean floors	12	10	11 — sweep floors
do jobs involving climbing	31	33	43 — do jobs involving climbing
wash small amounts of clothing by hand	8	7	15 — wash clothes
open screw-top bottles or jars	10	10	10 — open screw-top bottles or jars
cook a main meal	8	7	9 — cook a main meal
use a frying pan	5	4	5 — use a frying pan
make a cup of tea	2	2	3 — make a cup of tea

From: [1] Hunt, A., *The Elderly at Home*, OPCS, HMSO, 1978, Tables 10.8.1 p. 73 and 10.11.1. p. 81
[2] OPCS, *The General Household Survey*, 1980, HMSO, 10.44. p. 214.
[3] OPCS, *The General Household Survey*, 1986 (relates to 1985 *GHS*); HMSO, 1989. Table 12.45, p. 213.

281

The Beveridge Committee in their report on social insurance and allied services concluded that there were three special problems. One of these was age and they discussed alternative proposals for pensions.

CONCLUSION

254.   There is no valid objection, either on the ground of equity or on the ground that a means test may discourage thrift, to postponing introduction of adequate contributory pensions for a substantial period of transition, during which needs are met by pensions subject to means test. As regards equity, the people who reach pensionable age during the transition period will not have paid contributions at the new rates for any substantial time. As regards thrift, only those who are now so old that they may expect to require pensions before the transition period ends can be affected at all, and of these only a small proportion can be affected substantially. The rising scale of contributory pensions will make it possible for everyone except people who are already close to pension age, by a very moderate additional provision of their own, to secure income adequate for subsistence and have no need for any means pension. There is all the difference in the world between a permanent system of pensions subject to means test and a transitional system of supplementation of rising contributory pensions, such as is suggested here. The first must be rejected; the second is not open to serious objection.

255.   There is no reason also to doubt the power of large numbers of people to go on working with advantage to the community and happiness to themselves after reaching the minimum pensionable age of 65 for men or 60 for women. The numbers of people past the pensionable age who, at each census, described themselves as still occupied rather than retired is very great. So is the number of those working as exempt persons after this age under the present schemes of health and unemployment insurance. There is no statistical evidence that industrial development is making it harder for people to continue at work later in life than it used to be; such

evidence as there is points in the opposite direction. The natural presumption from the increasing length of total life is that the length of years during which working capacity lasts will also rise, as health improves, as by freedom from want in childhood and by freedom from want and idleness in working years the physique and the courage of the citizens are maintained. A people ageing in years need not be old in spirit, and British youth will rise again.

From: Beveridge, Sir W., *Social Insurance and Allied Services* (The Beveridge Report), HMSO, 1942, p. 99.

THE GUIDING PRINCIPLES OF THE BEVERIDGE REPORT

The Beveridge Committee lay down the three guiding principles behind their recommendations for social insurance and allied services.

THREE GUIDING PRINCIPLES OF RECOMMENDATIONS

6. In proceeding from this first comprehensive survcy of social insurance to the next task – of making recommendations – three guiding principles may be laid down at the outset.

7. The first principle is that any proposals for the future, while they should use to the full the experience gathered in the past, should not be restricted by consideration of sectional interests established in the obtaining of that experience. Now, when the war is abolishing landmarks of every kind, is the opportunity for using experience in a clear field. A revolutionary moment in the world's history is the time for revolutions, not for patching.

8. The second principle is that organisation of social insurance should be treated as one part only of a comprehensive policy of social progress. Social insurance fully developed may provide income security; it is an attack upon Want. But Want is one only of five giants on the road of reconstruction and in some ways the easiest to attack. The others are Disease, Ignorance, Squalor and Idleness.

9. The third principle is that social security must be achieved by cooperation between the State and the individual. The State should offer security for service and contribution. The State in organising security should not stifle incentive, opportunity, responsibility; in establishing a national minimum, it should leave room and encouragement for voluntary action by each individual to provide more than that minimum for himself and his family.

10. The Plan for Social Security set out in this Report is built upon these principles. It uses experience but is not tied by experience. It is put forward as a limited contribution to a wider social policy, though as something that could be achieved now without waiting for the whole of that policy. It is, first and foremost, a plan of insurance – of giving in return for contributions

benefits up to subsistence level, as of right and without means test, so that individuals may build freely upon it.

From: Beveridge, Sir W., *Social Insurance and Allied Services* (The Beveridge Report), HMSO, 1942, pp. 6–7.

THE END OF THE POOR LAW

The National Assistance Act 1948 set up the NAB with a duty to assist persons in need and gave local authorities powers.

An Act to terminate the existing poor law and to provide in lieu thereof for the assistance of persons in need by the National Assistance Board and by local authorities; to make further provisions for the welfare of disabled, sick aged and other persons and for regulating homes for disabled and aged persons and charities for disabled persons; to amend the law relating to non-contributory old age pensions; to make provision as to the burial or cremation of deceased persons; and for purposes connected with the matters aforesaid.

[13th May 1948.]

PART I. INTRODUCTORY

1. The existing poor law shall cease to have effect, and shall be replaced by the provisions of Part II of this Act as to the rendering, out of moneys provided by Parliament, of assistance to persons in need, the provisions of Part III of this Act as to accommodation and other services to be provided by local authorities, and the related provisions of Part IV of this Act.

From: National Assistance Act 1948, p. 1.

ESTIMATES OF PREVALENCES OF DISABILITY

Figure 3.5   Estimates of prevalence of disability among adults by age ??
seventy category for men and women.

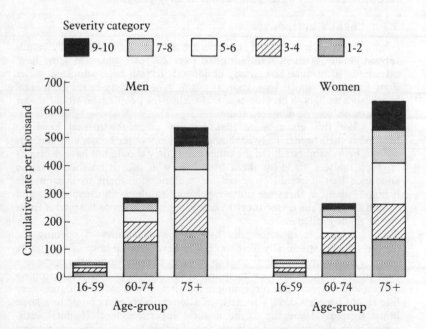

Martin, J., Meltzer, H. and Elliot, D., *The Prevalence of Disability among Adults*, OPCS surveys of disability in Great Britain, No. 1, HMSO, 1988, Fig 3.5, p. 21

Document fifteen
ELDERLY MENTALLY HANDICAPPED PEOPLE IN INSTITUTIONAL CARE

In a report of the Secretary of State for Social Services by the National Development Group for the Mentally Handicapped entitled *Helping Mentally Handicapped People in Hospital* special recommendations were made about elderly people.

6.7 ELDERLY RESIDENTS

6.7.1. Most elderly hospital residents are only mildly intellectually handicapped. Many of them were admitted over 20 years ago, and some have even lived in hospital since early childhood, having been admitted under Poor Laws and similar legislation at a time when society relied on mental handicap hospitals to provide care and shelter for people who would under no circumstances be admitted today.

6.7.2. For this group more than for any other the mental handicap hospital is their home. They have not known any other home, and may not wish to be 'rehabilitated' On the other hand, they should not have decisions on such matters made for them by others who take it on themselves to announce that it would be 'cruel' or 'unkind' for them to live outside hospital. many of them are quite capable of thinking for themselves, and should be given the opportunity to consider alternatives to hospital if these can be made available.

6.7.3. A number of authorities have followed a policy of opening old people's homes specifically for people who have lived in hospitals for many years. These homes enable friends to stay together and to use the home as a base from which to use local facilities. A few live in ordinary old people's homes, and others, while remaining in hospital, live in accommodation very like an old people's home – sometimes a converted nursing home or a large house formerly belonging to the medical superintendent. Hospital authorities have also purchased or made use of larger houses in the community for elderly mentally handicapped people.

6.7.4. Particular care must always be taken in moving any elderly person from one environment to another. The transition should be very carefully planned and should be effected very slowly and by small degrees. The resident should be able to change his mind if he decides that he would rather stay in hospital after all, and should be allowed to return to hospital if his new life in a hostel or an old people's home does not suit him. Every effort must be made to involve the resident himself in the determination of his needs and, like all residents, the elderly should be individually reviewed as part of the process of assessment and meeting of needs that we discuss in Chapter 5.

6.7.5. The BGS/RCN Report referred to above, identified four main categories of problems as regards the care of the elderly:

i. The lack of consideration of feelings and of maintenance of dignity, privacy and personal identity.

ii. Failure to maintain independence and mobility.

iii. Shortcomings related to personal hygiene and physiological needs.

iv. Lack of social, remedial and recreational stimulation.

These problems apply just as forcefully to the elderly residents of mental handicap hospitals.

From: DHSS, The National Development Group for the Mentally Handicapped, *Helping Mentally Handicapped People in Hospital*, HMSO, 1978, pp. 67–8.

Document sixteen
VIEWS ABOUT SERVICES FOR THE ELDERLY FROM THE ROYAL COMMISSION ON THE NATIONAL HEALTH SERVICE

The Royal Commission on the National Health Service felt that the health needs of the elderly were one of the major problems facing the NHS.

6.33.   Services for the elderly demonstrate very clearly the requirements for community care already discussed. Everything possible should be done to assist old people to remain independent, healthy and in their own homes. It is important to detect stress and practical problems, and to ward off breakdown, for example by regular visiting of those who are identified through GP case registers as being at risk, by providing physical aids or adapted or sheltered housing, and by assistance from home helps, chiropodists, or meals on wheels. Planned short-term admissions to residential care play an increasing part in helping the elderly remain in their own homes or with relatives. The supporting role of relatives is of great importance and their needs for relief from time to time must be met. Voluntary bodies and volunteers can often help in numerous understanding ways.[1] Where there is illness the full resources of the primary care team have often to be deployed, and a heavy load of work and responsibility falls on the district nurses and the home help services. Day centres are helpful, and day hospitals have been widely developed: their place in a comprehensive service urgently requires critical evaluation and this is being studied by the DHSS. When independence at home is no longer possible, care in a nursing home or local authority residential home may be appropriate.

6.34.   Illness in old age commonly has both physical and mental aspects. A deterioration in an old person's faculties may or may not be accompanied by disturbances of behaviour, and may or may not be due to or worsened by physical illness. Detailed assessment is often necessary and the skill of geriatricians, psychiatrists, nurses and social workers may be jointly called upon. We recommend that all professions concerned with the care of the elderly should receive more training in understanding their needs.

[1] Personal Social Services Research Unit, University of Kent, *Kent Community Care Project: an interim report*, 1979.

6.35.   Many elderly patients admitted to district general hospitals do not need the technology which that type of hospital can provide. They frequently remain in hospital long after any investigations or active treatment have been completed because they are not fit to go home and there is nowhere else for them to go. Residential homes cannot care for those who are physically very dependent and need nursing care, or whose behaviour is more than mildly disturbed.

From: *Royal Commission on the NHS, Report* (the Merrison Committee), Cmnd 7615 (1979), pp. 62–3.

A VARIETY OF HOUSING FOR ELDERLY PEOPLE RECOMMENDED IN 1944

In 1944 the Ministry of health, which was responsible for housing, published a *Housing Manual* giving guidance to local authorities on the types of provision that were needed. The section on the elderly started with some general considerations:

OLD PEOPLE

The type of accommodation required for old people will vary according to their age and disabilities. For the very old who may require a certain amount of care, the accommodation can take the form of small self-contained dwellings grouped together with a common day-room, a room for laundry work, a spare room for visitors, and quarters for a nurse or warden, as shown in Fig. 8. Consideration should be given to the possibility of providing hot water to the bathrooms from a common source and a small amount of central heating to give 'background' warmth.   [73

For able-bodied old people who can look after themselves, accommodation might be provided in self-contained dwellings, either one or two storey cottages or cottage flats or on the lower floors of blocks of flats. Where there are lifts, the flats could even be on the higher floors.   [74

All dwellings for old people should be sited within easy distance of churches and shops and in a position which will give an interesting outlook from the living room window. So far as possible the dwellings should not be segregated, as old people like to have contact with younger generations. (An interesting example of the setting of old people's dwellings among other houses is shown in Figs. 44 and 45). To assist in keeping the dwelling warm a sheltered site should be chosen.   [75

From: MOH, *Housing Manual 1944*, HMSO, p. 22.

Document eighteen
CO-ORDINATION OF SERVICES FOR OLD PEOPLE

Advice was given to local authorities in 1961 about services for old people. The need for co-operation was highlighted as is shown below. Later sections dealt with specific services and the role of voluntary organisations.

SERVICES FOR OLD PEOPLE

Co-operation between housing, local health and welfare authorities and voluntary organisations

1. The Minister of Housing and Local Government and the Minister of Health have been considering together how to improve the provisions made for the well-being of old people.
2. Housing, health and welfare authorities are concerned. So are voluntary organisations. All these must work in the closest co-operation if all the varying needs of old people are to be covered. The several services should be regarded as parts of a whole, the authorities and organisations responsible each making their contribution to the whole. This means that all concerned (including in a county borough the different committees) should make it a regular feature of their administration to meet together from time to time to review the provision made in their area, and to decide where and how it needs to be supplemented.
3. It is widely recognised today that old people want to lead an independent life in their own homes for as long as they can, and that to do so gives them the best chance of an active and contented old age. To make this possible, housing authorities must provide, in adequate numbers, a full range of small bungalows, flats and flatlets designed for old people: some in which they can be fully independent (though with neighbours at hand in case help is wanted): others in which some friendly help is available in the person of a warden: others still in which provision can be made for some communal services in addition to a warden. The changes in subsidy proposed in the Housing Bill now before Parliament should enable every housing authority, the less well-off as well as those with adequate resources,

to meet, in time, all the demands of their area. With a fully adequate range of housing designed to meet the different tastes and needs of the old, hospital and welfare accommodation can be used by those who really require it.

From: MHLG Circular 10/61; MOH Circular 12/61, *Services for Old People*, 1961, HMSO, p. 1.

GUIDANCE ON DESIGNING OLD PEOPLE'S HOUSING

A circular in 1969 gave advice to local authorities on both the principles of housing for elderly people and detailed design guidance which had to be adhered to if a subsidy was required.

APPENDIX VI

This check list is offered as a guide to the special aspects of designing for old people's dwellings.

Introduction to the check list
The mandatory requirements for accommodation specially designed for old people are set out in Appendix I to Circular 82/69 (Welsh Office Circular 84/69), and the yardstick additions in Appendix II to that Circular are based on those standards.

The purpose which underlies the design of housing for the elderly is the provision of accommodation which will enable them to maintain an independent way of life for as long as possible. With improved health services more people may be expected to remain in a home of their own for the rest of their lives. If they are to do this in comfort, they will need housing designed with the special requirements of the elderly in mind, coupled with the availability, as far as possible, of a balanced range of different types of accommodation to meet their varying needs and preferences. It has to be remembered too that most old people for whom housing is being provided will eventually be living alone and all housing for old people needs to be planned for sociability so as to avoid loneliness and isolation. This is particularly desirable where rehousing involves moving to a new area and, though the subject is outside the scope of this circular, good housing management practice can assist by keeping together groups of friends and neighbours as far as practicable.

Of the different types of housing which can be provided for the elderly, bungalows – traditionally regarded by old people themselves as the ideal form of housing – are best suited to couples who are able to maintain a greater degree of independence, who can manage rather more housework and who may want a small garden.

Two storey flats are more economical of land than bungalows, can provide a more compact layout, fit in well with family housing and can be used on infill sites. Many people over the age of 65 can still manage one flight of stairs and an upper flat may be preferred by those who dislike sleeping on the ground floor. Taller blocks with lifts can provide acceptable accommodation for old people, if suitably designed and sited, in those places where the density justifies their use.

For less active old people, often living alone, who need smaller and labour-saving accommodation, grouped flatlets as described in circular 36/67 (Welsh Office Circular 28/67) and the two publications 'Flatlets for Old People' and 'More Flatlets for Old People' are the most suitable. The tenants of these flatlets will have the services of a warden and also communal facilities such as a common-room and laundry; and possibly a guest room as well. Bathrooms may be shared for one-person flatlets (in a ratio of one bathroom to four flatlets) or private in the case of two-person flatlets but every flatlet will contain a w.c. and hand basin. Additional facilities such as a call-bell system will also be needed.

From MHLG, *Housing Standards and Costs: accommodation specially designed for old people, Circular 82/69, 1969, HMSO, p. 14.*

THE CONDITION OF THE HOME OF ELDERLY PEOPLE

The table shows by age of the head of the household, those living in dwellings which lack basic amenities, are in poor repair or are unfit to live in.

Table A 6.3 Age of head of household by households in dwellings which lacked basic amenities, were unfit or were in poor repair

thousands/% dwellings

	Amenities[1]		Fitness		Poor repair		All households
	All amenities present	Lacking basic amenities	Fit	Unfit	Under £1,000	Over £1,000	
Aged 17–39	5,952 (98.8) (33.2)	74 (1.2) (20.6)	5,778 (95.9) (32.9)	248 (4.1) (34.8)	5,271 (87.5) (33.1)	755 (12.5) (31.9)	6,026 (33.0)
Aged 40–59	6,037 (99.0) (33.7)	63 (1.0) (17.5)	5,913 (96.9) (33.7)	187 (3.1) (25.9)	5,317 (87.2) (33.4)	783 (12.8) (33.1)	6,100 (33.4)
Aged 60–74	4,193 (97.4) (23.4)	110 (2.6) (30.7)	4,136 (96.1) (23.5)	167 (3.9) (23.3)	3,753 (87.1) (23.6)	550 (12.9) (23.4)	4,303 (23.5)
Aged 75 and Over	1,735 (93.9) (9.7)	112 (6.1) (31.2)	1,731 (93.7) (9.9)	116 (6.3) (16.0)	1,572 (85.1) (9.9)	275 (14.9) (11.6)	1,847 (10.1)
All Ages	17,917 (98.0) (100)	359 (2.0) (100)	17,558 (96.1) (100)	718 (3.9) (100)	15,913 (87.1) (100)	2,363 (12.9) (100)	18,276 (100)

Sample: 11

[1] Five basic amenities – bath, sink, WC inside dwellings, wash hand basin, hot and cold water at 3 points

From: DOE, *English House Condition Survey, 1986*, HMSO, 1988, p. 104.

COMPARATIVE COSTS OF CARE

The table shows the comparative cost of Care for a person of high dependency between a hospital, very sheltered housing, sheltered housing or staying at home with an innovatory scheme.

Table 10.4 A comparison of resource costs and transfer payments for a person of high dependency[1] in hospital. Part III, very sheltered housing, sheltered housing and staying at home with an innovatory service.

1986–87	Resource costs[2]	Resource costs and retirement pension or allowance for personal expenses[3]	Resource costs and retirement pension and supplementary pension or allowance for personal expenses[3]
		£ per person per annum	
Hospital:			
Acute	22,014	22,417	22,417
Geriatric	19,525	19,928	19,928
Long-stay	18,649	19,052	19,052
Part III	7,844	8,247	8,247
Very sheltered housing:			
All	4,698	6,710	7,591
All excluding registered residential homes (RRH)	4,137	6,149	7,030
All LA	4,095	6,107	6,988
All HA	5,241	7,253	8,134
All HA excluding RRH	3,811	5,823	6,704
Registered residential homes	7,487	7,958	7,958
1 bed self-contained			
New build	4,842	6,854	7,735
Rehabilitated	3,427	5,429	6,320

Table 10.4 (Cont'd)

1986–87	Resource costs[2]	Resource costs and retirement pension or allowance for personal expenses[3]	£ per person per annum Resource costs and retirement pension and supplementary pension or allowance for personal expenses[3]
Bedsitters with shared facilities			
New build	8,414	8,885	8,885
(1 scheme)			
Rehabilitated	7,030	7,501	7,501
All (those are HC pilots)	7,616	8,087	8,087
Sheltered housing – 1 bed self-contained new-build:			
LA	4,381	6,393	7,274
HA	4,359	6,371	7,252
Innovatory schemes:			
All	3,724	5,736	6,617
Alarms	3,682	5,694	6,575
Care	3,777	5,789	6,670

[1] Leeds scale 8–12. See Appendix 7 Tables before A7.8.
[2] Separately identified in Table 10.3.
[3] See Appendix 10.1 for details.

From: Tinker, A., *An Evaluation of Very Sheltered Housing*, HMSO, 1989, Table 10.4, p. 114.

RESIDENTIAL QUALIFICATIONS AND ELDERLY
PEOPLE

Elderly people in local authority accommodation who want to move to another area may face problems because they lack a residential qualification in the latter. The Cullingworth Committee identified a number of groups of elderly people who may be debarred from council accommodation by residential rules:

297. The evidence we received suggests that there are at least six ways in which elderly people may be debarred from council houses by residential rules:

i. Elderly people who, for one reason or another, give up their houses on moving into hospital.

ii. Elderly people who, because of the nature of their employment, have been highly mobile.

iii. Those who wish to move from an isolated rural area to a less isolated location which happens to be in the district of another local authority.

iv. Those retiring from employment to which their housing was 'tied' and which is in an area with little or no council accommodation, or who again wish to settle in another area.

v. Elderly people who wish to move to be near younger relatives living in other parts of the country.

vi. Those who break their residence connection by moving to live with relatives in another area, but who for various social reasons wish to return to the area which they have left.

From: MHLG, WO, *Council Housing Purposes, Procedures and Priorities* (the Cullingworth Committee), 1969, HMSO, p. 99.

POWERS TO PROVIDE HOME HELPS AND OTHER SERVICES

Under the National Health Service Act 1946 local authorities were given powers to provide home helps and certain preventive services.

PREVENTION OF ILLNESS, CARE AND AFTER-CARE

28.–(1) A local health authority may with the approval of the Minister, and to such extent as the Minister may direct, shall make arrangements for the purpose of the prevention of illness, the care of persons suffering from illness or mental defectiveness, or the after-care of such persons, but no such arrangements shall provide for the payment of money to such persons, except in so far as they may provide for the remuneration of such persons engaged in suitable work in accordance with the arrangements.

(2) A local health authority may, with the approval of the Minister, recover from persons availing themselves of the services provided under this section such charges (if any) as the authority consider reasonable, having regard to the means of those persons.

(3) A local health authority may, with the approval of the Minister, contribute to any voluntary organisation formed for any such purpose as aforesaid.

DOMESTIC HELP

29.–(1) A local health authority may make such arrangements as the Minister may approve for providing domestic help for households where such help is required owing to the presence of any person who is ill, lying-in, an expectant mother, mentally defective, aged, or a child not over compulsory school age within the meaning of the Education Act, 1944.

(2) A local health authority may, with the approval of the Minister, recover from persons availing themselves of the domestic help so provided such charges (if any) as the authority consider reasonable, having regard to the means of those persons.

From: National Health Service Act 1946, paras 28–9.

POWERS TO PROMOTE WELFARE

Under the National Assistance Act 1948 local authorities were empowered to promote the welfare of certain disadvantaged groups. Elderly people who came into any of these categories benefited from this legislation.

WELFARE SERVICES

29.–(1) A local authority shall have power to make arrangements for promoting the welfare of persons to whom this section applies, that is to say persons who are blind, deaf or dumb, and other persons who are substantially and permanently handicapped by illness, injury, or congenital deformity or such other disabilities as may be prescribed by the Minister.

(2)   In relation to persons ordinarily resident in the area of a local authority the authority shall, to such extent as the Minister may direct, be under a duty to exercise their powers under this section.

Local authorities were also empowered to make contributions to voluntary organisations.

31.   A local authority may make contributions to the funds of any voluntary organisation whose activities consist in or include the provision of recreation or meals for old people.

From: National Assistance Act 1948, Section 29 (1), (2) and 31.

Note: Consolidating legislation relating to the provision of meals and recreation for old people was given in the Health and Social Services and Social Security Adjudications Act 1983.

A DUTY TO PROVIDE RESIDENTIAL ACCOMMODATION

The National Assistance Act 1948 laid a duty on local authorities to provide residential accommodation for needy old people.

LOCAL AUTHORITY SERVICES

Provision of accommodation

21.–(1) It shall be the duty of every local authority, subject to and in accordance with the provisions of this Part of this Act, to provide –

(*a*) residential accommodation for persons who by reason of age, infirmity or any other circumstances are in need of care and attention which is not otherwise available to them;

(*b*) temporary accommodation for persons who are in urgent need thereof, being need arising in circumstances which could not reasonably have been foreseen or in such other circumstances as the authority may in any particular case determine.

(2) In the exercise of their said duty a local authority shall have regard to the welfare of all persons for whom accommodation is provided, and in particular to the need for providing accommodation of different descriptions suited to different descriptions of such persons as are mentioned in the last foregoing subsection.

From: National Assistance Act 1948, Part III, Section 21 (1) and (2).

POWER TO PROVIDE WELFARE SERVICES FOR ELDERLY PEOPLE

The general power for a local authority to provide welfare services for elderly people, either itself or through a voluntary organisation, was given in the Health Services and Public Health Act 1968.

PROMOTION BY LOCAL AUTHORITIES OF THE WELFARE OF OLD PEOPLE

45.–(1) A local authority may with the approval of the Minister of Health, and to such extent as he may direct shall, make arrangements for promoting the welfare of old people.

(2) A local authority may recover from persons availing themselves of any service provided in pursuance of arrangements made under this section such charges (if any) as, having regard to the cost of the service, the authority may determine, whether generally or in the circumstances of any particular case.

(3) A local authority may employ as their agent for the purposes of this section any voluntary organisation having for its sole or principal object, or among its principal objects, the promotion of the welfare of old people.

From: The Health Services and Public Health Act 1968, Section 45 (1), (2) and (3).

Under the National Health Service and Community Care act 1990, Part III, para, 42 (7) for the words 'any voluntary organisation' onwards there was substituted 'any voluntary organisation or any person carrying on, professionally or by way of trade or business, activities which consist of or include the provision of services for old people, being an organisation or person appearing to the authorities to be capable fo promoting the welfare of old people'.

THE SEEBOHM COMMITTEE AND ELDERLY PEOPLE

The Committee on *Local Authority and Allied Personal Social Services* (the Seebohm Report) 1968, recommended the creation of a new social service department which would have a co-ordinated approach to people's problems. Comments were made about the need for the development of domiciliary services, as well as a comprehensive approach, for elderly people.

THE DEVELOPMENT OF THE DOMICILIARY SERVICES

309.   Although for many years it has been part of national policy to enable as many old people as possible to stay in their own homes, the development of the domiciliary services which are necessary if this is to be achieved has been slow. There are certain services of home care, such as home nursing and domestic help, which are provided by all local authorities. Neither service is specially for the old though both are used largely by them. There is also a wide variety of other help for old people, like meals on wheels, chiropody, and laundry services, which is provided by local authorities or voluntary committees or sometimes jointly, but the extent of their cover differs considerably from place to place and nowhere do they assist more than a very small proportion of the old. Furthermore it appears that individual services have been started without sufficient thought for priorities or evidence of need over the whole area to be served. This piecemeal and haphazard development is unlikely to use scarce resources to the best advantage even though some assistance may be given to a fortunate few.

310.   A unified social service department will be able to take a more comprehensive view of the development of such services, but to do so it will have to know the extent and pattern of need in its area and be aware of all the local resources likely to be available. It will have to discover from local voluntary organisations what part they can play in providing a comprehensive service to the maximum number of old people. It will have to investigate fully the contribution which relatives, neighbours and the wider community can make and how the social service department can best

enable such potential assistance to be realised. In this sense a considerable development of community care for the old may be achieved, even in the near future, by enlisting such help.

311. In particular, of course, services for old people in their own homes will not be adequately developed unless greater attention is paid to supporting their families who in turn support them. The problems of old people living alone have attracted much attention, but many of those who are most dependent live with younger relatives who often are themselves getting on in years. Just as we emphasised the need for shared responsibility between the family and the personal social services where there were problems in the social care of children (Chapter VIII) so we wish to stress it in the case of the old. If old people are to remain in the community, support and assistance must often be directed to the whole family of which they are members. This is one of the reasons which convinced us that services for the elderly should become an integral part of the social services department.

From: Home Office *et al.*, Local Authority and Allied Personal Social Services (the Seebohm Committee), HMSO, 1968, p. 96.

2. FUNDAMENTAL UNDERLYING PROBLEMS

49.   There are a number of factors causing difficulties with the introduction of community care. Some result from the greater complexity of organising care in the community and from the difficulties of managing change. These are unavoidable and are an inherent aspect of the implementation process. However, there are also difficulties which should be avoidable.

50.   One reason that is frequently advanced to explain the slow progress is a lack of finance. However, a much wider range of community based services could be provided within present levels of funding – although, as with all health and personal social services, more money can always be put to good use. Increased funding is, at best, only part of the answer to the problems described in the previous chapter. At worst, it could mask, temporarily at least, the need for some basic changes in the way that care for mentally ill, mentally handicapped, physically handicapped and elderly people is provided and paid for. The Commission has concluded that the slow and uneven progress towards community care is due to some fundamental underlying problems which need to be tackled directly:

   (i)   Although out of the total amounts of money being spent (some £6 billion a year) there should be enough to provide at least a much improved level of community-based services, the methods for distributing the available finance do not match the requirements of community care policies.

   (ii) Additional short-term bridging finance is required to fund the transition to community care.

   (iii) Social security policies are undermining any switch from residential to community care.

   (iv) A fragmented organisation structure causes delays and difficulties; and there has been a failure to adapt systems and structures to accommodate the shift in policy.

   (v)   Staffing arrangements are inadequate, with a failure to provide sufficient re-training for existing staff in hospitals and to recruit the additional staff required in the community.

From: Audit Commission, *Making a Reality of Community Care*, HMSO, 1986, p. 29.

Document twenty-nine
THE BRITISH ASSOCIATION OF SOCIAL WORKERS LAYS DOWN GUIDELINES FOR SOCIAL WORK WITH ELDERLY PEOPLE

In 1977 BASW pointed out that many agencies seemed to give work with elderly people a low priority and often workers with little experience or training were expected to undertake all, or a large proportion of, the work with this group. They suggested certain guidelines which they summarised as:

1. These guidelines have illustrated the same need for expertise in social work with the elderly as with other vulnerable groups. Those who are most vulnerable amongst the elderly are those whose identity is damaged by retirement, those who are bereaved and who suffer loss of any kind and the mentally and physically frail, many of whom will be over 75.

2. Many agencies seem to give work with the elderly a low priority and often workers with little experience or training are expected to undertake all, or a large proportion of, work with this group. The enormous contribution made by volunteers, social work assistants, relatives, neighbours and *all* others concerned with the social and emotional care of the elderly is neither denied nor minimised by emphasising those areas wyhich are seen to be most appropriately dealt with by the qualified social worker. These can be summarised as follows:

(*a*) Assessing need in deciding the help required and by whom it should be given. This should, where possible, be multidisciplinary in nature, the social worker operating as a member of a caring team.

(*b*) Providing skilled social work help with problems of relationship, problems arising from crises, loss, change or other social, emotional or medical condition. The complex nature of many problems in old age arising from medical, social or psychological sources should be continuously borne in mind.

(*c*) Providing the skill in helping to overcome psychological problems related to receiving practical, financial and advocatory help. More skill is required to enable the elderly to make the best use of the practical resources than is often appreciated.

(*d*) Providing group and community work, where the social worker has received training in appropriate skills. Group work with the elderly offers a further dimension to social work with the elderly. Both the elderly and their relatives gain mutual strength and ability to cope with their problems through group discussions.

(*e*) Understanding and accepting the degree of risk which the client is prepared to take, and balancing this with the sometimes over-anxious reaction of society. Enabling relatives and neighbours to tolerate these dilemmas.

(*f*) Enabling and supporting others in caring, such as relatives, 'good neighbours' and volunteers.

(*g*) Participating in planning and policymaking related to elderly people. This is not the exclusive terrain of the qualified social worker, though her knowledge of areas of social need will give her an important role in this process.

3. Another conclusion which must be drawn from these guidelines is that Social work courses should include more teaching on the process of ageing and work with the elderly, and more placements for students in this field.

4. Social work with elderly people is as demanding and rewarding as work with and other client group. It can succeed in making life positive and meaningful for those with whom we have been most concerned in these guidelines.

From: *Social Work Today*, 12.4.77, p. 13.

NUMBERS AND AGES OF RESIDENTS IN HOMES FOR ELDERLY PEOPLE

The table shows the number of residents in homes for elderly people in England during the period 1979–89.

Table B Total numbers of residents, by age, in homes for elderly people¹ England 1979–89

As at 31 March	All residents 65 and over				All residents 75 and over				All residents 85 and over			
	LA homes	Vol homes	Priv homes	All homes	LA homes	Vol homes	Priv homes	All homes	LA homes	Vol homes	Priv homes	All homes
1979	102,086	24,716	26,095	152,897	–	20,909	22,861	–	–	10,060	11,310	–
1980	102,890	25,449	28,854	157,193	76,078	21,626	25,220	122,924	35,938	10,761	12,467	59,166
1981	103,090	26,037	31,838	160,965	82,862	22,163	28,014	133,039	39,229	11,157	14,516	64,902
1982	103,720	26,116	35,675	165,675	84,072	22,345	31,851	138,268	40,425	11,308	16,272	68,005
1983	103,598	26,468	42,142	172,208	86,146	22,699	37,431	146,276	41,120	11,543	19,031	71,694
1984	101,996	26,005	52,675	180,676	85,580	22,442	46,955	154,977	42,025	11,662	23,685	77,372
1985	101,526	25,818	66,143	193,487	85,298	22,023	59,055	166,376	42,101	11,471	29,701	83,273
1986	101,704	25,121	77,557	204,382	85,288	21,873	69,444	176,605	41,925	11,823	35,281	89,029
1987	99,750	25,105	84,945	209,801	85,592	21,893	74,895	182,380	42,554	11,789	38,774	93,117
1988	97,380	25,633	96,161	219,175	83,927	22,293	85,061	191,281	42,938	12,241	44,857	100,036
1989	95,335	25,801	111,391	232,527	83,573	22,832	100,266	206,671	43,763	13,109	53,954	110,826

¹ Includes 248 residents whose age is not known: 17 in LA homes, 68 in voluntary homes and 163 in private homes.

From: DOH Personal Social Services, *Local Authority Statistics, Residential Accommodation for Elderly and for Younger Physically Handicapped People: All Residents in Local Authority, Voluntary and Private Homes, Year ending 31.3.89*, RA/89/2, DOH, 1989, Table B.

Document thirty-one
THE PRINCIPLES BEHIND A MOVE TO RESIDENTIAL CARE

PRINCIPLES

People who move into a residential establishment should do so by positive choice. A distinction should be made between the need for accommodation and need for services. No one should be required to change their permanent accommodation in order to receive services which could be made available to them in their own homes.

Living in a residential establishment should be a positive experience ensuring a better quality of life than the resident could enjoy in any other setting.

Local authorities should make efforts, as a matter of urgency, to meet the special needs of people from ethnic minority communities for residential and other services.

Every person who moves into a residential establishment retains their rights as a citizen. Measures need to be taken to ensure that individuals can exercise their rights. Safeguards should be applied when rights are curtailed.

People who move into a residential establishment should continue to have access to the full range of community support services.

residents should have access to leisure, educational and other facilities offered by the local community and the right to invite and receive relatives and friends as they choose.

Residential staff are the major resource and should be valued as such. The importance of their contribution needs to be recognised and enhanced.

From: Wagner Report, 1988a, *Residential Care: a positive choice*, HMSO, p. 114.

Document thirty-two
THE LAST REFUGE

In a survey of residential institutions and homes for elderly people Professor P. Townsend presented disquieting evidence about their conditions:

So far as it is possible to express in a few words the general conclusion of this book it is that communal Homes of the kind which exist in England and Wales today do not adequately meet the physical, psychological and social needs of the elderly people living in them, and that alternative services and living arrangements should quickly take their place.

and about the lack of alternative accommodation:

In investigating the physical and mental capacities of elderly residents, the events and circumstances leading to their admission and the life they follow in Homes, we reached certain important conclusions. The majority are not so handicapped by infirmity that they could not, given a small amount of support from the domiciliary social services, live in homes of their own in an ordinary community. A large number enter Homes for reasons of poverty, lack of housing, social isolation and absence of secondary sources of help among relatives and friends, and they do so unwillingly. Few of them take the initiative themselves and rarely are they offered practicable alternatives – such as housing, emergency grants and services or permanent help from the domiciliary services. Nearly all, once admitted, are expected to stay permanently, although the great majority, so it seems, would prefer not to do so.

From: Townsend, P., *The Last Refuge*, Routledge & Kegan Paul, 1964, pp. 222 and 226.

EXPENDITURE ON COMMUNITY CARE SERVICES

The table shows the gross expenditure on community care services from 1979–80 and 1987–88.

Table 1   Gross expenditure on core services for community care
All figures in millions for Great Britain

	79/80 £m	87/88 £m		79/80 £m	87/88 £m
LA domiciliary care			**LA residential care**		
Home helps	209	535	Elderly	458	914
Meals on wheels	27	59	YPH	30	44
Aids and adaptations	15	49	MH children	16	52
Day care for elderly	27	77	MH adults	44	144
for YPH, MI, MH	35	78	Mental illness	12	29
Adult training	63	167			
Social work	88	202			
LA domiciliary care	464	1,167	**LA residential care**	560	1,183
Community Health			**Income Support**		
*District nursing	109	261	For residential and nursing		
*Health visiting	7	15	home care	10	774
Chiropody	19	44			
Community health	135	320	**Income support**	10	774
Total domiciliary	599	1,487	**Total residential**	570	1,957
Total community care	1,169	3,444			

NB: Administration costs, joint finance and the community care element of some social security benefits have been excluded. In particular expenditure on Attendance Allowance and Invalid Care Allowance has risen from 205m in 1979/80 to 1,081 in 1987/88 – a real terms increase of 200%.

It has been assumed that only 45% of social work, 70% of district nursing and 8% of health visiting expenditure is appropriate to community care for these client groups. It has been also assumed that all of this is for people in non-residential settings.

* Welsh figures for 1979/80 are estimated.

From Secretaries of State for Health *et al*, 1989b, *Caring for People*, HMSO, Table 1, p. 99

FAMILY OBLIGATIONS IN THE PUBLIC DOMAIN

I have placed the emphasis so far on the personal and negotiated elements in both family support and the morality of obligation which underscores it. But it is plain that such negotiations do not take place in a social vacuum. Indeed, governments' attempts to encourage people to develop a sense of responsibility towards their relatives place these arrangements firmly in the public domain, and imply that apparently private arrangements are open to pressure – even manipulation from outside.

I have emphasized in early chapters that social and economic circumstances in general do have an important bearing upon the structures of support which are developed in families. The economic climate, as it affects individuals and their relatives, creates the conditions under which some people have need for support and others have the capacity to provide it. The demographic structure of the population at any given point in time affects the shape of individual kin groups, and therfore the range of options for giving, receiving and sharing assistance. Most dramatically at the present time, demographic change has created much larger numbers of very elderly people than ever had to be supported by previous generations, at a time when the numbers of people born in succeeding generations has shrunk.

If we take a fairly long historical perspective, we can see that people in the present are not necessarily any more or less willing to support their relatives than in the past; but the circumstances under which they have to work out these commitments themselves have changed and created new problems to be solved. External conditions of this kind do not straightforwardly determine what any of us does for our relatives, but they do form part of the materials out of which we have to create our own commitments. They affect the nature of the choices which present themselves. For example (to stay with the question of the care of elderly people), a decision about whether you should take an elderly father to live with you looks very different if you are an only child, than it would have done under the demographic conditions of early generations, when you could expect to have several siblings. It looks different again if economic circumstances have worked in your favour, so that you can afford to pay a professional nurse to look after him, by comparison with someone for whom the choice about co-residence also entails using their own labour to provide nursing care.

In this complex equation we also have to insert the action of governments who, through the law and through their policies, modify the external circumstances under which commitments to relatives are negotiated. How important a factor is this? Can governments make us do more for our kin, or even alter the morality of family obligations, to fit their own policy preferences? If government keeps up the pressure, will we find in the future that the family becomes the first, rather than the last, port of call when any of us needs assistance?

We move into the realms of speculation here, but that speculation can be informed by looking at what has happened in similar circumstances in the past. There have been several times during the last two centuries when governments have tightened the screws, to try to ensure that people relied on their families rather than on the state for financial assistance: the creation of the New Poor Law in 1834; the tightening of Poor Law regulations in the late nineteenth century; the creation of the household means test for unemployed people in the 1930s. The historical evidence suggests that on each occasion the measures were less successful than their hard-line advocates would have wished. On each occasion when government was attempting to impose a version of family responsibilities which people regarded as unreasonable, many responded by developing avoidance strategies: moving to another household, losing touch with their relatives, cheating the system. If anything it has been the state's assuming some responsibility for individuals – such as the granting of old age pensions – which has freed people to develop closer and more supportive relationships with their kin. It seems that it is not in the power of governments straightforwardly to manipulate what we do for our relatives, let alone what we believe to be proper.

Of course we cannot tell precisely what governments will try to do in the future, nor what the consequences will be. But the lesson of our past is that governments are quite capable of promoting a view of family obligations which is out of step with what most people regard as proper or reasonable, and with the commitments people have arrived at themselvesw, through the delicate processes of negotiation described above. Undoubtedly that situation creates great difficulties for some people, who feel that they are under sustained and unreasonable pressure, and eventually some will give in. But on the evidence of the past, many will not. Governments in this situation may try to ensure that their own views prevail, but their chances of success are probably partial at best. Happily, I should like to add.

From: Finch, J., *Family Obligations and Social Change*, Polity Press, 1989, pp. 242–3.

Document thirty-five
FREQUENCY OF SEEING RELATIVES OR FRIENDS

Table 12.23 Frequency of seeing relatives or friends by sex and age, persons aged 65 or over, Great Britain: 1985

Frequency of seeing relatives or friends	65–69 %	70–74 %	75–79 %	80–84 %	85 or over %	All 65 or over %
Men						
Every day or nearly	29 ⌉	31 ⌉	28 ⌉	25 ⌉	[17] ⌉	29 ⌉
2–3 times a week	31 ⎬ 84	29 ⎬ 83	27 ⎬ 80	29 ⎬	[6] ⎬	29 ⎬ 82
Once a week	24 ⌋	23 ⌋	25 ⌋	26 ⌋	[16] ⌋	24 ⌋
Less often, but seen last month	10 ⌉ 13	10 ⌉ 15	9 ⌉ 15	12 ⌉ 17	[13] ⌉	11 ⌉ 15
Not seen last month	3 ⌋	5 ⌋	6 ⌋	4 ⌋	[3] ⌋	4 ⌋
Not seen at all nowadays	2	2	4	4	[4]	3
Base = 100%	526	443	322	136	59	1486
Women						
Every day or nearly	38 ⌉	36 ⌉	36 ⌉	33 ⌉	32 ⌉	36 ⌉
2–3 times a week	21 ⎬ 77	29 ⎬ 88	27 ⎬ 85	30 ⎬ 82	25 ⎬ 78	29 ⎬ 86
Once a week	18 ⌋	23 ⌋	21 ⌋	19 ⌋	21 ⌋	21 ⌋
Less often, but seen last month	7 ⌉ 11	7 ⌉ 9	8 ⌉ 12	11 ⌉ 15	12 ⌉ 19	8 ⌉ 12
Not seen last month	4 ⌋	2 ⌋	4 ⌋	4 ⌋	7 ⌋	4 ⌋
Not seen at all nowadays	1	2	3	3	4	2
Base = 100%	595	619	496	273	196	2179

Table 12.23 (Cont'd)

Frequency of seeing relatives or friends

	Age					
	65–69 %	70–74 %	75–79 %	80–84 %	85 or over %	All 65 or over %
All elderly						
Every day or nearly	34 ⎤	34 ⎤	33 ⎤	30 ⎤	31 ⎤	33 ⎤
2–3 times a week	31 ⎬ 86	29 ⎬ 86	27 ⎬ 83	30 ⎬ 81	22 ⎬ 75	29 ⎬ 84
Once a week	21 ⎦	23 ⎦	23 ⎦	22 ⎦	23 ⎦	22 ⎦
Less often, but seen last month	9 ⎤ 13	8 ⎤ 11	8 ⎤ 13	11 ⎤ 16	14 ⎤ 20	9 ⎤ 13
Not seen last month	4 ⎦	3 ⎦	5 ⎦	4 ⎦	6 ⎦	4 ⎦
Not seen at all nowadays	2	2	3	3	4	2
Base = 100%	1121	1062	818	409	255	3665

From: OPCS, *General Household Survey, 1986* relates to 1985 data, HMSO, 1989, Table 12.23, p. 199.

SOURCES OF HELP FOR DOMESTIC TASKS

The table shows the usual source of help for those unable to carry
out tasks by themselves.

Table 12.35 Domestic tasks: usual source of help for those unable to do tasks by themselves by household type, persons aged 65 or over, Great Britain: 1985

					Domestic tasks		
Household type and usual source of help	Household shopping	Wash paintwork	Clean windows inside	Sweep or clean floors	Jobs involving climbing	Wash clothing by hand	Open screw tops
	%	%	%	%	%	%	%
Lives with husband only							
Husband	10	8	10	5	17	2	12
Non-household relative	2	2	2	0	4	1	1
Non-household friend	0	0	1	0	1	0	0
Home help	0	2	2	2	1	0	0
Paid help	0	1	2	1	1	0	0
Other		0	0	0	1		
Task not done	nil	2	0	NIL	2	1	0
Total unable to do task	13	16	16	8	27	5	14
Base = 100%	722	715	716	720	705	723	715
Lives with wife only							
Wife	7	8	7	6	11	7	4
Non-household relative	1	2	1	0	4	1	1
Non-household friend	0	0	0	nil	1	0	nil
Home help	0	1	2	0	1	0	0
Paid help	0	1	1	0	1	nil	nil
Other	0	nil	nil	nil	0	nil	nil

Table 12.35 (Cont'd)

Household type and usual source of help

						Domestic tasks	
	Household shopping	Wash paintwork	Clean windows inside	Sweep or clean floors	Jobs involving climbing	Wash clothing by hand	Open screw tops
	%	%	%	%	%	%	%
Task not done	nil	1	0	nil	2	0	0
Total unable to do task	8	12	11	8	20	9	5
Base = 100%	930	923	926	926	919	921	929
Lives alone							
Non-household relative	8	7	5	2	16	3	3
Non-household friend	4	1	1	0	4	0	2
Home help	4	8	10	8	10	1	1
Paid help	1	1	3	1	2	0	1
Other	1	1	0	0	2	0	0
Task not done	nil	5	2	0	4	1	1
Total unable to do task	16	23	22	12	37	6	7
Base = 100%	1,316	1,308	1,307	1,318	1,290	1,324	1,323
Miscellaneous							
Spouse	4	2	3	2	4	2	2
Other household member	19	20	20	14	29	11	16
Non-household relative	1	2	1	0	3	0	0
Non-household friend	1	0	nil	nil	0	nil	nil
Home help	0	0	1	1	1	0	nil

Table 12.35 (Cont'd)

Household type and usual source of help	Household shopping %	Wash paintwork %	Clear windows inside %	Sweep or clean floors %	Jobs involving climbing %	Wash clothing by hand %	Open screw tops %
Paid help	nil	0	1	0	1	nil	nil
Other	nil	nil	nil	nil	0	nil	nil
Task not done	0	1	1	nil	1	1	nil
Total unable to do task	25	26	26	18	38	14	17
Base = 100%	653	648	653	658	645	659	658
All household types							
Spouse	4	4	4	3	7	3	4
Other household member	3	4	4	3	5	2	3
Non-household relative	4	4	3	1	8	1	1
Non-household friend	2	0	1	0	2	0	1
Home help	2	4	5	4	4	0	0
Paid help	0	1	2	1	2	0	0
Other	0	0	0	0	1	0	0
Task not done	nil	3	1	0	3	1	0
Total unable to do task	15	19	19	11	31	8	10
Base = 100%	3,621	3,594	3,602	3,622	3,559	3,627	3,625

0 less than 1
From: OPCS, *General Household Survey, 1986 relates to 1985 data*, HMSO, 1989, Table 12.35, p. 207.

Document thirty-seven
THE PREVALENCE OF INFORMAL CARE

SUMMARY

1. At the request of the Department of Health and Social Security, a series of questions was included in the 1985 General Household Survey to identify people looking after a sick, handicapped or elderly person. The main aim of the questions was to provide national estimates of the number of people who were providing informal care of this kind and the numbers in different sub-groups of carers.* (Chapter 1)

2. Information was collected from a nationally representative sample of approximately 18,500 adults living in private households in Great Britain. 'Carers' were defined as people who were looking after, or providing some regular service for, a sick, handicapped or elderly person living in their own or in another household. (Chapter 2)

The prevalence of informal care

3. One adult in seven (14%) was providing informal care and one in five households (19%) contained a carer. (Sections 2.2, 2.6)

4. Four per cent of adults cared for someone living with them and 10% looked after people living elsewhere. The survey findings indicate that there are about six million carers overall in Great Britain with about 1.7 million caring for someone in the same household. (Section 2.2)

5. Three per cent of adults in Great Britain (representing about 1.4 million) devoted at least twenty hours per week to caring and 8% (about 3.7 million) carried the main responsibility for looking after someone (that is, they spent more time than anyone else on the dependant). (section 2.2)

6. Women were more likely to be carers than men but the difference was not very marked, 15% compared with 12%. However, since there are more

---

* Those providing care are referred to as 'carers' and those being cared for as 'dependants' in this report.

women than men in the total adult population of Great Britain, it is true that the number of women caring is considerably greater than that of men, 3.5 million compared with 2.5 million. (Section 2.2)

7. The small difference between the proportions of women and men caring was attributable to the higher proportion of women looking after someone outside the household (11% of women and 8% of men). Women were also more likely to carry the main responsibility for caring (10% of women and 6% of men). There were no differences, however, between the proportions of women and men caring for someone living with them (4% for both sexes) and similar proportions (4% of women and 3% of men) devoted at least twenty hours per week to caring. (Section 2.2)

8. Five per cent of adults looked after parents and 4% cared for friends and neighbours. Men and women were equally likely to care for relatives but women were more likely than men to look after non-relatives. (Section 2.2)

9. The peak age for caring was 45 to 64. One fifth of adults in this age-group were providing informal care and the difference between the proportions of men and women caring was much more marked than for adults as a whole. Twenty-four per cent of women aged 45 to 64 were carers compared with 16% of men. (Section 2.3)

10. Among all adults, there was no association between the proportion caring and marital status but, among people aged 45 to 64, single women were more likely than others to carry the heaviest burden. For example, they were twice as likely as single men or ever-married women to devote at least twenty hours per week to caring. However, single female carers are a relatively small group, representing only 11% of all female carers. (Section 2.3)

11. While single women aged 45 to 64 were more likely than their married or male counterparts to care for friends and relatives outside the immediate family, there is no evidence that the responsibility for parental care fell disproportionately on single daughters. (Section 2.3)

12. Carers were found equally among people in different social groups and in groups with different levels of educational qualification. (Section 2.4)

13. Among women, part-time workers were more likely to be carers than full-time workers. The proportion caring among men were unrelated to economic status. (Section 2.4)

14. Most households with carers looking after someone in the same household contained one carer looking after one dependant (72%), but nearly one in five (18%) contained two carers looking after the same person. (Section 2.6)

15. The majority of carers lived in families consisting of a married couple

with children (44%) or with no children (34%). One third of carers had dependent children, in most cases in addition to the person they were looking after. These percentages are similar to those for the general population. (Section 2.6)

From: Green, H, *Informal Carers*, HMSO, 1988, p. 1.

BIBLIOGRAPHY

(Please see list of abbreviations on p. xiv–xv)

ABEL-SMITH, B. and TOWNSEND, P., 1965, *The Poor and the Poorest*, G. Bell & Sons.

ABEL-SMITH, B. (1978), *The National Health Service: the first thirty years*, HMSO.

ABRAMS, M., 1975, 'The new elderly', *New Society*, 26.6.75, p. 778.

ABRAMS, M., 1978, *Beyond Three Score and Ten*, First Report, Age Concern England.

ABRAMS, M., 1980, *Beyond Three Score and Ten*, Second Report, Age Concern England.

ABRAMS, M. and O'BRIEN, J., 1981 *Political Attitudes and Ageing in Britain*, Age Concern England.

ABRAMS, P., ABRAMS, S., HUMPHREY, R. and SNAITH, R., 1986, in: Leat, D. (ed.), *Creating Care in the Neighbourhood*, Advance.

ABRAMS, P., ABRAMS, S., HUMPHREY, R. and SNAITH, R., 1989, *Neighbourhood Care and Social Policy*, HMSO.

AGATE, J. and MEACHER, M., 1969, *The Care of the Old*, Fabian Society.

AGE CONCERN ENGLAND (ACE) 1972a, *Good Neighbours*, ACE.

ACE, 1972b, *Easing the Restrictions on Ageing*, ACE.

ACE, 1973, *Voluntary Organisations and the Retired and Elderly*, ACE.

ACE, 1974, *The Attitudes of the Retired and Elderly*, ACE.

ACE, 1975, *Manifesto on the Place of the Retired and the Elderly in Modern Society*, ACE.

ACE, 1977–8, *Profiles of the Elderly*, ACE.

ACE, 1984, *Sheltered Housing for Older People*, ACE.

ACE, 1986, *The Law and Vulnerable Elderly People*, ACE.

ACE, 1989, *The Discretionary Social Fund – its impact on old people* (ACE Briefings), ACE, May.

ACE, 1990a, *Transport and Older People* (ACE Briefings), ACE, March.

ACE, 1990b, *The Impact of Technology, The Economic Equation, The Lifelong Environment, The Human Factor, Rights and Choices* (Resource Papers), ACE.

ACE and HELP THE AGED HOUSING TRUST, 1984, *Housing for Ethnic Elders*, ACE/Help the Aged Housing Trust.

ACE and NATIONAL HOUSING AND TOWN PLANNING COUNCIL, 1989, *A Buyer's Guide to Sheltered Housing*, ACE and National Housing and Town Planning Council.

ALCOCK, P., 1987, *Poverty and State Support*, Longman.

ALLEN, D., 1987, 'Performance indicators in the health service', *Social Policy and Administration* 21(1), Spring, pp. 70–84.

ALLEN, I., 1983, *Short-Stay Residential Care for the Elderly*, Policy Studies Institute.

ALLEN, I. (ed.), 1989, *Social Services Departments as Managing Agencies*, Policy Studies Institute.

ALLON-SMITH, R., 1982, 'The evolving geography of the elderly in England and Wales', in: Warnes, A. (ed.), 1982, pp. 35–52.

ANDERSON, W.F. and JUDGE, T., 1974, *Geriatric Medicine*, Academic Press.

ANDREWS, K. and BROCKLEHURST, J., 1987, *British Geriatric Medicine in the 1980s*, King's Fund.

ARBER, S., GILBERT, N. and EVANDROU, M, 1988, 'Gender, household composition and receipt of domiciliary services by the elderly disabled', *Journal of Social Policy* 17(2), April, pp. 153–76.

ARIE, T. (ed.), 1981, *Health Care of the Elderly*, Croom Helm.

ARIE, T., 1985, *Recent Advances in Psychogeriatrics*, Churchill Livingstone.

ARIE, T., 1986, 'Management of dementia: a review', *British Medical Bulletin*, **42** (1), 1986, pp. 91–6.

ARIE, T., 1988, 'Questions in the psychiatry of old age', in: Evered, D. and Whelan, J. (eds), 1988, pp. 86–105.

ARMSTRONG, J., MIDWINTER, E. and WYNNE-HARLEY, D., 1987, *Retired Leisure: four ventures in post-work activity*, CPA.

ASKHAM, J., 1989, 'The need for support', in: Warnes, A. M. (ed.), 1989, pp. 107–18.

ASKHAM, J., GLUCKSMAN, E., OWENS, P., SWIFT, C., TINKER, A. and YU, G., 1990, *A Review of Research on Falls Among Elderly People*, Department of Trade and Industry.

ASKHAM, J. and THOMPSON, C., 1990, *Dementia and Home care*, ACE.

ATKINSON, A.B., 1991, *The Development of State Pensions in the*

United Kingdom, Suntory-Toyota International Centre for Economics and Related Disciplines, London School of Economics.

ATTENBURROW, J., 1976, *Grouped Housing for the Elderly*, Department of the Environment, Building Research Establishment.

AUDIT COMMISSION, 1985, *Managing Social Services for the Elderly More Effectively*, HMSO.

AUDIT COMMISSION, 1986, *Making a Reality of Community Care*, HMSO.

AUDIT COMMISSION, 1989, *Housing the Homeless: the local authority role*, HMSO.

AUDIT INSPECTORATE, 1983, *Social Services: provision of care to the elderly*, Department of the Environment.

BAKER, S. and PARRY, M., 1983, *Housing for Sale to the Elderly*, Housing Research Foundation.

BAKER, S. and PARRY, M., 1984, *Housing for Sale to the Elderly* (Second Report), Housing Research Foundation.

BAKER, S. and PARRY, M., 1986, *Housing for Sale to the Elderly* (Third Report), Housing Research Foundation.

BALDWIN, S., PARKER, G. and WALKER, R. (eds), 1988, *Social Security and Community Care*, Avebury.

BALDWIN, S., GODFREY, C. and PROPPER, C. (eds), 1990, *Quality of Life: perspectives and policies*, Routledge.

BARKER, C., WATCHMAN, P. and ROBINSON, J., 1990, 'Social security abuse', *Social Policy and Administration*, 24(7), August, pp. 104–19.

BARKER, J., 1983, *Black and Asian Old People in Britain*, ACE.

BEBBINGTON, A., 1979, 'Changes in the provision of social services to the elderly in the community over fourteen years', *Social Policy and Administration*, 13(2), 1979, pp. 111–23.

BEBBINGTON, A. and DAVIES, B., 1982, 'Patterns of social service provision for the elderly', in: Warnes, A.M. (ed.), 1982, pp. 355–74.

BELL, C.R., 1969, *Middle Class Families*, Routledge & Kegan Paul.

BELLAIRS, C., 1968, *Old People: cash and care*, Conservative Political Centre.

BENGTSON, V. and ROBERTSON, J. (eds), 1985, *Grandparenthood*, Sage, San Francisco.

BERGMANN, K. and JACOBY, R. with collaboration from COLEMAN, P., JOLLEY, D. AND LEVIN, E., 1983, 'The limitations and possibilities of community care for the elderly demented', in: DHSS, 1983a.

BERLINER, H., 1988, 'Old but cold', *Health Service Journal*, 4.8.88, p. 885.

BEVERIDGE, W., 1942, *Social Insurance and Allied Services*, HMSO.

BEYER, G. and NIERSTRASZ, F., 1967, *Housing the Aged in Western Countries*, Elsevier.

BHALLA, A. and BLAKEMORE, K., 1981, *Elders of the Ethnic Minority Groups*, Birmingham, All Faiths for One Race.

BILLIS, D., 1989, 'The rise and rise of the voluntary sector', *Community Care*, 1.6.89, pp. 25–7.

BIRREN, J.E., 1964, *The Psychology of Ageing*, Prentice-Hall, New Jersey.

BIRREN, J.E. and SCHAIE, K.W., 1990, *Handbook of the Psychology of Ageing* (3rd edition), Van Nostrand Reinhold, New York.

BLAKEMORE, K., 1985, 'The state, the voluntary sector and new developments in provision for the aid of minority social groups', *Ageing and Society*, 5, pp. 175–90.

BLYTHE, R., 1979, *The View in Winter*, Allen Lane.

BOARD FOR SOCIAL RESPONSIBILITY, CHURCH OF ENGLAND GENERAL SYNOD, 1990, *Ageing*, Church House Publishing.

BOLDY, D., ABEL, P. and CARTER, K., 1973, *The Elderly in Grouped Dwellings – a profile*, University of Exeter.

BOND, J., BOND, S., DONALDSON, C., GREGSON, B. and ATKINSON, A., 1989, *A Summary Report of an Evaluation of Continuing-Care Accommodation for Elderly People*, Health Care Research Unit, University of Newcastle upon Tyne.

BOND, J. and COLEMAN, P. (eds), 1990, *Ageing in Society: an introduction to social gerontology*, Sage.

BOOKBINDER, D., 1987, *Housing Options for Older People*, ACE.

BOSANQUET, N., 1975, *New Deal for the Elderly*, Fabian Society.

BOSANQUET, N. and GRAY, A., 1989, *Will You Still Love Me?*, National Association of Health Authorities.

BOWL, R., 1986, 'Social work with old people', in: Phillipson, C. and Walker, A. (eds), 1986, pp. 128–45.

BOWLING, A., 1991, *Measuring Health: a review of quality of life measurement scales*, Open University Press.

BOWLING, A. and CARTWRIGHT, A., 1982, *Life after Death*, Tavistock.

BOWLING, B., 1990, *Elderly People from Ethnic Minorities: a report on four projects*, Age Concern Institute of Gerontology.

BRACEY, H.E., 1966, *In Retirement*, Routledge & Kegan Paul.

BRADSHAW, J., 1972, 'The concept of social need', *New Society*, 3.3.72, pp.640–3.

BRADSHAW, J., 1988, 'Financing private care for the elderly', in: Baldwin, S. *et al.* (eds), 1988, pp. 175–90.

BRADSHAW, J., CLIFTON, M. and KENNEDY, J., 1978, *Found Dead*, ACE.

BRADSHAW, J., GIBBS, I., LAWTON, D., HARDMAN, G. and BALDWIN, S., 1987, *Supplementary Benefit and Residential Care*, Social Policy Research Unit, University of York.

BRANDON, R., 1972, *Seventy Plus: easier living for the elderly*, British Broadcasting Corporation.

BREARLEY, P., 1975, *Social Work, Ageing and Society*, Routledge & Kegan Paul.

BRENTON, M., 1985, *The Voluntary Sector in British Social Services*, Longman.

BRIGGS, A. and OLIVER, J. (eds), 1985, *Caring: experiences of looking after disabled relatives*, Routledge & Kegan Paul.

BRITISH ASSOCIATION FOR THE ADVANCEMENT OF SCIENCE, 1976, *Old Age – today and tomorrow*, British Association for the Advancement of Science.

BRITISH COUNCIL FOR AGEING, 1976, *Research in Gerontology*, Bedford Square Press.

BRITISH GERIATRICS SOCIETY, 1990, *Abuse of Elderly People: guidelines for action for those working with elderly people*, ACE.

BROCKINGTON, F. and LEMPERT, S., 1966, *The Social Needs of the Over Eighties*, Manchester University Press.

BROMLEY, D.B., 1984, *Gerontology: social and behavioural perspectives*, Croom Helm.

BROMLEY, D.B., 1988, *Human Ageing* (3rd edition), Penguin.

BROMLEY, D.B., 1990, *Behavioural Gerontology: central issues in the psychology of ageing*, Wiley.

BUCKLE, J., 1971, *Work and Housing of Impaired Persons in Great Britain*, HMSO.

BULL, J. and POOLE, L., 1989, *Not Rich Not Poor*, Shelter Housing Advice Centre/Anchor Housing Trust.

BULMER, M., 1987, *The Social Basis of Community Care*, Allen & Unwin.

BULMER, M., LEWIS, J. and PIACHAUD, D. (eds), 1989, *The Goals of Social Policy*, Unwin Hyman.

BULUSU, L. and ALDERSON, M., 1984, 'Suicides 1950–82', *Population Trends*, 35, pp. 11–17.

BURY, M. and HOLME, A., 1991, *Life after Ninety*, Routledge.

BURY, M. and MACNICOL, J. (eds), 1990, *Aspects of Ageing*, Royal Holloway and Bedford New College, Egham, Surrey.

BUTLER, A. (ed.), 1985, *Ageing: recent advances and creative responses*, Croom Helm.

BUTLER, A., OLDMAN, C. and GREVE, J., 1983, *Sheltered Housing for the Elderly: policy, practice and the consumer*, Allen & Unwin.

BUTLER, A. and TINKER, A., 1983, *Housing Alternatives for the Elderly*, Centre for Applied Social Studies, Occasional Paper No. 10, University of Leeds.

BYTHEWAY, W. and JAMES, L., 1978, *The Allocation of Sheltered Housing*, Medical Sociology Research Centre, University College of Swansea.

BYTHEWAY, W. and JOHNSON, J. (ed), 1990, *Welfare and the Ageing Experience*, Avebury.

CAMBRIDGE, P. and KNAPP, M. (eds), 1988, *Demonstrating Successful Care in the Community*, Personal Social Services Research Unit, University of Kent.

CAMPBELL, S., 1990, 'Contracting with the voluntary sector: results of a recent Association of County Councils survey', in: Morton, J. (ed.), 1990a, pp.3–7.

CARTER, J., 1981, *Day Services for Adults: somewhere to go*, Allen & Unwin.

CARTWRIGHT, A. and HENDERSON, G., 1986, *More Trouble with Feet*, HMSO.

CARTWRIGHT, A., HOCKEY, L. and ANDERSON, J., 1973, *Life Before Death*, Routledge & Kegan Paul.

CENTRAL OFFICE OF INFORMATION, 1977, *Care of the Elderly in Britain*, Central Office of Information.

CENTRAL STATISTICAL OFFICE (CSO), 1976, *Social Trends 7*, HMSO.

CSO, 1979, *Social Trends 9*, HMSO.

CSO, 1980, *Social Trends 11*, HMSO.

CSO, 1983, *Social Trends 13*, HMSO.

CSO, 1987, *Social Trends 17*, HMSO.

CSO, 1989, *Social Trends 19*, HMSO.

CSO, 1990, *Social Trends 20*, HMSO.

CSO, 1991, *Social Trends 21*, HMSO.

CENTRE FOR POLICY ON AGEING (CPA), 1982, *Out of Sight – Out of Mind*, CPA.

CPA, 1984, *Home Life: a code of practice for residential care*, CPA.

CPA, 1990, *Community Life: a code of practice for community care*, CPA.

CHALLIS, D. and DAVIES, B., 1986, *Case Management in Community Care*, Gower.

CHALLIS, D. and FERLIE, E., 1988, 'The myth of general practice: specialization in social work', *Journal of Social Policy*, **17**(1), January, pp. 1–22.

CHANCELLOR OF THE EXCHEQUER, 1954, *Report of the Committee on the Economic and Financial Problems of the Provision for Old Age* (Phillips Report), HMSO.

CHANT, J., 1986, *Health and Social Services: collaboration or conflict?*, Policy Studies Institute.

CHARLES, S. and WEBB, A., 1986, *The Economic Approach to Social Policy*, Wheatsheaf.

CHARLESWORTH, A., WILKIN, D. and DURIE, A., 1984, *A Comparison of Men and Women Caring for Dependent Elderly People*, Equal Opportunities Commission, Manchester.

CHEESEMAN, D., LANSLEY, J. and WILSON, J., 1972, *Neighbourhood Care and Old People*, National Council for Social Service.

CLAPHAM, D. and MUNRO, M. with MACDONALD, J. and ROBERTS, M., 1988, *A Comparison of Sheltered and Amenity Housing for Older People*, Centre for Housing Research, University of Glasgow.

CLAPHAM, D. and MUNRO, M., 1990, 'Ambiguities and contradictions in the provision of sheltered housing for older people', *Journal of Social Policy*, **19**(1), January, pp. 27–46.

CLARKE, J., 1987, 'Ageing in Europe: introductory remarks', in: Noin, D. and Warnes, A. (eds), 'Elderly people and ageing', *Espace, Populations Sociétés* No. 1, pp. 23–8.

CLARKE, M. and STEWART, J., 1990, 'The future of local government: issues for discussion', *Public Administration*, **68**(2), Summer, pp. 249–58.

CLEGG, J., 1971, *Dictionary of Social Services*, Bedford Square Press.

CLOUGH, R., 1981, *Old Age Homes*, Allen & Unwin.

COLE, D. and UTTING, J., 1962, *The Economic Circumstances of Old People*, Codicote Press.

COLEMAN, A., 1983, *Preparation for Retirement in England and Wales*, Centre for Health and Retirement Education.

COLEMAN, P., 1986, *Ageing and Reminiscence Processes: social and clinical implications*, Wiley.

COLLINS, K., 1989, 'Hypothermia and seasonal mortality in the elderly', *Care of the Elderly*, **1**(6), pp. 257–9.

COMFORT, A., 1965, *The Process of Ageing*, Weidenfeld & Nicolson.

COMFORT, A., 1977, *A Good Age*, Mitchell Beazley.

CONSUMERS ASSOCIATION, 1969, *Arrangements for Old Age*, The Consumers Association.

CONSUMERS ASSOCIATION, 1977, *Where to Live After Retirement*, The Consumers Association.

CONSUMERS ASSOCIATION, 1986, 'Sounding the alarm', *Which?*, July, pp. 318–21.

COX, B.D., BLAXTER, M., BUCKLE, A., FENNER, H., GOLDING, J., GORE,

M., HUPPERT, F., HICKSON, J., ROTH, M., STARK, J., WADSWORTH, M. and WHICHELOW, M., 1987, *The Health and Lifestyle Survey*, The Health Promotion Research Trust.

CULLINGWORTH, B., 1960, *Housing Needs and Planning Policy*, Routledge & Kegan Paul.

CUMBERLEGE REPORT, 1986, *Neighbourhood Nursing – A Focus for Care*, Report of the Community Nursing Review, HMSO.

CUNNINGHAM-BURLEY, S., 1986, 'Becoming a grandparent', *Ageing and Society*, 6(4), pp. 453–70.

DANISH MEDICAL BULLETIN, 1985–9, *Gerontology Special Supplement Series between 1985–89 on Alzheimer's Disease, Primary Care, Hearing Problems, Prevention of Falls, Long-Term Care, Social Isolation, Multidisciplinary Health Assessment and Urinary Incontinence*, University of Michigan.

DANT, T., CARLEY, M., GEARING, B. and JOHNSON, M., 1989, *Co-ordinating Care*, Final Report of the Care for Elderly People at Home Project, Gloucester, Open University/Policy Studies Institute.

DAVIES, B., BARTON, A., MCMILLAN, I. and WILLIAMSON, V., 1971, *Variations in Services for the Aged*, G. Bell.

DAVIES, B. and CHALLIS, D., 1986, *Matching Resources to Needs in Community Care*, Gower.

DAVIES, C. and RITCHIE, J., 1988, *Tipping the Balance: a study of non-take-up of benefits in an inner city area*, HMSO.

DAVIES, L., 1981, *Three Score Years . . . and Then?*, Heinemann Medical Books.

DAWSON, A. and EVANS, G., 1987, 'Pensioners' incomes and expenditure 1970–85', *Employment Gazette*, May, pp. 243–52.

DAY, P. and KLEIN, R., 1987, 'The business of welfare', *New Society*, 19.6.87, pp. 11–13.

DE BEAUVOIR, S., 1972, *Old Age*, Penguin.

DEPARTMENT OF THE ENVIRONMENT (DOE) and WELSH OFFICE (WO), 1973a, *Widening the Choice: the next steps in housing*, HMSO.

DOE and WO, 1973b, *Better Homes: the next priorities*, HMSO.

DOE, 1976, *Housing for Old People: a consultation paper*, DOE/DHSS/WO.

DOE, 1977, *Housing Policy: a consultative document*, HMSO.

DOE, 1978, *Organising a Comprehensive Housing Service*, DOE.

DOE, 1983, *English House Condition Survey 1981*, HMSO.

DOE, 1985, *Home Improvement: a new approach*, HMSO.

DOE, 1987, *Housing: the government's proposals*, HMSO.

DOE, 1988, *English House Condition Survey 1986*, HMSO.

DOE, 1989, *The Government's Review of the Homelessness Legislation*, DOE.

DOE/DHSS/WO, 1984, *Housing Services for Disabled People*, DOE/DHSS/WO.

DOE HOUSING SERVICES ADVISORY GROUP, 1977, *The Assessment of Housing Requirements*, DOE.

DOE HOUSING SERVICES ADVISORY GROUP, 1978, *Allocation of Council Housing*, DOE.

DEPARTMENT OF HEALTH (DOH), 1989a, *Personal Social Services, Local Authority Statistics, Residential Accommodation for Elderly and for Younger Physically Handicapped People: local authority supported residents*, Year ending 31.3.89, RA/89/1, DOH.

DOH, 1989b, *Personal Social Services, Local Authority Statistics, Residential Accommodation for Elderly and for Younger Physically Handicapped People: all residents in local authority voluntary and private homes*, Year ending 31.3.89, RA/89/2, DOH.

DOH, 1989c, *A Strategy for Nursing*, DOH.

DOH, 1990a, *Community Care in the Next Decade and Beyond: policy guidance*, HMSO.

DOH, 1990b, *On the State of the Public Health for the Year 1989*, HMSO.

DOH, 1991, Economic Advisers' Office, *Economic Issues*, Paper presented at DOH Meeting on the Health of Elderly People 28.2.91, DOH Economic Advisers' Office (unpublished).

DOH SOCIAL SERVICES INSPECTORATE (SSI), 1989, *Homes are for Living In*, HMSO.

DOH SSI, 1990, *Caring for Quality: guidance of standards for residential homes for elderly people*, HMSO.

DOH STANDING MEDICAL ADVISORY COMMITTEE, 1990, *The Quality of Medical Care*, HMSO.

DEPARTMENT OF HEALTH AND SOCIAL SECURITY (DHSS), 1971, *Better Services for the Mentally Handicapped*, HMSO.

DHSS, 1972, *A Nutrition Survey of the Elderly*, HMSO.

DHSS, 1973, *Report of the Committee on Abuse of Social Security Benefits* (Fisher Report), HMSO.

DHSS, 1975, *Better Services for the Mentally Ill*, HMSO.

DHSS, 1976a, *The Elderly and the Personal Social Services*, DHSS.

DHSS, 1976b, *Sharing Resources for Health in England*, HMSO.

DHSS, 1976c, *Prevention and Health: everybody's business*, HMSO.

DHSS, 1976d, *A Lifestyle for the Elderly*, DHSS.

DHSS, 1976e, *Priorities for Health and Personal Social Services in England. A consultative document*, HMSO.

DHSS, 1977, *Priorities in the Health and Social Services. The way forward*, HMSO.

DHSS, 1978a, *A Happier Old Age. A discussion document*, HMSO.

DHSS, 1978b, *Collaboration in Community Care. A discussion document*, HMSO.

DHSS, 1979, *Nutrition and Health in Old Age*, HMSO.

DHSS, 1981a, *Care in Action*, HMSO.

DHSS, 1981b, *Report of a Study on Community Care*, DHSS.

DHSS, 1981c, *Care in the Community*, DHSS.

DHSS, 1981d, *Growing Older*, HMSO.

DHSS, 1981e, *The Report of a Study on the Acute Hospital Sector*, HMSO.

DHSS, 1981f, *The Respective Roles of the General Acute and Geriatric Sectors in the Care of the Elderly Hospital Patient*, DHSS.

DHSS, 1982a, *Ageing in the United Kingdom*, DHSS.

DHSS, 1982b, *Public Expenditure on the Social Services. Reply by the Government to the Second Report from the Select Committee on Social Services, Sessions 1981–82*, HMSO.

DHSS, 1982c, *A Good Home: a consultative document on the registration system for accommodation registered under the Residential Homes Act 1980*, DHSS/WO.

DHSS, 1983a, *Elderly People in the Community: their service needs*, HMSO.

DHSS, 1983b, *Explanatory Notes on Care in the Community*, DHSS.

DHSS, 1983c, *Health Services Costings Returns year ended 31.3.82*, NHS, HMSO.

DHSS, 1985, *Progress in Partnership. Report of the Working Group on Joint Planning*, DHSS.

DHSS, 1986, *Hospital In-Patient Enquiry 1984 Summary Tables*, OPCS Series MB4, No. 24, HMSO.

DHSS, 1988, *Resourcing the National Health Services: short term issues*, DHSS.

DHSS JOINT CENTRAL AND LOCAL GOVERNMENT WORKING PARTY, 1985, *Supplementary Benefit and Residential Care*, DHSS.

DHSS JOINT CENTRAL AND LOCAL GOVERNMENT WORKING PARTY, 1987, *Public Support for Residential Care* (Firth Report), DHSS.

DHSS SOCIAL SERVICES INSPECTORATE (SSI), 1985, *Assessment Procedures for Elderly People Referred for Local Authority Residential Care*, DHSS.

DHSS SSI, 1987, *From Home Help to Home Care: an analysis of policy, resourcing and service management*, DHSS.

DHSS SSI, 1988a, *Managing Policy Change in Home Help Services*, DHSS.

DHSS SSI, 1988b, *Conference on Services for Black Elders*, DHSS.

DHSS SOCIAL WORK SERVICE DEVELOPMENT GROUP, 1983, *Supporting the Informal Carers*, DHSS.

DHSS SOCIAL WORK SERVICE DEVELOPMENT GROUP, 1984, *Supporting the Informal Carers: 'Fifty Styles of Caring'*, DHSS.

DEPARTMENT OF TRADE AND INDUSTRY CONSUMER SAFETY UNIT, 1990, *Home and Leisure Accident Research*, Twelfth Annual Report Home Accident Surveillance System 1988 Data, DTI.

DEX, S. and PHILLIPSON, C., 1986, 'Social policy and the older worker', in: Phillipson, C. and Walker, A. (eds), 1986, pp. 45–60.

DI GREGORIO, S. (ed.), 1987, *Social Gerontology: new directions*, Croom Helm.

DONALDSON, C., ATKINSON, A., BOND, J. and WRIGHT, K., 1988, 'QALYS and long-term care for elderly people in the UK: scales for assessment of quality of life', *Age and Ageing*, 17(6), pp. 379–87.

DONALDSON, L., 1986, 'Health and social status of elderly Asians: a community survey', *British Medical Journal* 293, 25.10.86, pp. 1079–81.

DRAKE, M., O'BRIEN, M. and BIEBUYCK, T., 1981, *Single and Homeless*, HMSO.

DRURY, E., 1990, *Social Developments Affecting Elderly People in the European Commission Member States*, Eurolink Age, Mitcham, Surrey.

DUNCAN, S., DOWNEY, P. and FINCH, H., 1983, *A Home of their Own*, DOE.

DUNN, D., 1987, *Food, Glorious Food: a review of meals services for older people*, Centre for Policy on Ageing.

ELDER, G., 1977, *The Alienated*, Writers and Readers Publishing Cooperative.

ELFORD, J. (ed.), 1987, *Medical Ethics and Elderly People*, Churchill Livingstone.

EQUAL OPPORTUNITIES COMMISSION, 1980, *The Experience of Caring for Elderly Handicapped Dependents*, Equal Opportunities Commission.

EQUAL OPPORTUNITIES COMMISSION, 1982, *Caring for the Elderly and Handicapped: community care policies and women's lives*, Equal Opportunities Commission.

ERMISCH, J., 1990, *Fewer Babies, Longer Lives*, Joseph Rowntree Foundation.

EUROLINK AGE, 1990, *Age and Disability: a challenge for Europe*, Eurolink Age.

EVANDROU, M., 1987, *The Use of Domiciliary Services by the Elderly: a survey*, Suntory-Toyota International Centre for Economics and Related Disciplines, London School of Economics.

EVANDROU, M., 1990, *Challenging the Invisibility of Carers: mapping informal care nationally*, Suntory-Toyota International Centre for Economics and Related Disciplines, London School of Economics.

EVANDROU, M., ARBER, S., DALE, A. and GILBERT, N., 1986, 'Who cares for the elderly? Family care provision and receipt of statutory services', in: Phillipson, C., Bernard, M. and Strang, P. (eds), 1986, pp. 150–66.

EVANDROU, M. and VICTOR, C., 1988, *Differentiation in Later Life: social class and housing tenure cleavages*, Suntory-Toyota International Centre for Economics and Related Disciplines, London School of Economics.

EVANS, A. and DUNCAN, S., 1988, *Responding to Homelessness: local authority policy and practice*, HMSO.

EVANS, J. GRIMLEY, 1981, 'Institutional care', in: Arie, T. (ed.), 1981, pp. 176–93.

EVANS, J. GRIMLEY, 1988, 'Ageing in disease', in: Evered, D. and Whelan, J. (eds), 1988, pp. 38–57.

EVERED, D. and WHELAN, J., 1988, *Research and the Ageing Population*, Wiley.

EYDEN, J., 1971, *The Welfare Society*, Bedford Square Press.

FALKINGHAM, J. and GORDON, C., 1988, *Fifty Years On: the income and household composition of the elderly in Britain*, Suntory-Toyota International Centre for Economics and Related Disciplines, London School of Economics.

FALKINGHAM, J. and VICTOR, C., 1991, *The Myth of the Woopie?: incomes, the elderly and targetting welfare*, Suntory-Toyota International Centre for Economics and Related Disciplines, London School of Economics.

FEATHERSTONE, M. and HEPWORTH, M., 1990, 'Images of ageing', in: Bond, J. and Coleman, P. (eds), 1990, pp. 250–75.

FENNELL, G., 1986, *Anchor's Older People: what do they think?*, Anchor Housing Association.

FENNELL, G., 1987, *A Place of My Own*, Bield Housing Association.

FENNELL, G., PHILLIPSON, C. and EVERS, H., 1988, *The Sociology of Old Age*, Open University Press.

FERLIE, E., CHALLIS, D. and DAVIES, B., 1989, *Efficiency – improving innovation in social care of the elderly*, Gower.

FIEGEHEN, G., 1986, 'Income after retirement', Central Statistical Office *Social Trends*, **16**, HMSO. pp. 13–18.

FINCH, J., 1989, *Family Obligations and Social Change*, Polity Press.

FINCH, J. and GROVES, D., 1980, 'Community care and the family: a case for equal opportunities?', *Journal of Social Policy*, **9**(4), pp. 487–514.

FINCH, J. and GROVES, D. (eds), 1983, *A Labour of Love: women, work and caring*, Routledge & Kegan Paul.

FLEISS, A., 1985, *Home Ownership Alternatives for the Elderly*, HMSO.

FLETCHER, R., 1966, *The Family and Marriage in Britain*, Penguin.

FOGARTY, M., 1987, *Meeting the Needs of the Elderly*, The European Foundation for the Improvement of Living and Working Conditions, Dublin, Ireland.

FORDER, A., 1974, *Concepts in Social Administration*, Routledge & Kegan Paul.

FORUM ON THE RIGHTS OF ELDERLY PEOPLE TO EDUCATION (FREE), 1983, *Manifesto*, FREE.

FOSTER, P., 1983, *Access to Welfare*, Macmillan.

FREER, C., 1988, 'Old myths: frequent misconceptions about the elderly', in: Wells, N. and Freer, C. (eds), 1988, pp. 3–16.

FREER, C. and WILLIAMS, I., 1988, 'The role of the general practitioner and the primary health care team', in: Wells, N. and Freer, C. (eds), 1988, pp. 143–54.

FROGGATT, A., 1990, *Family Work with Elderly People*, Macmillan.

GEORGE, S. and EBRAHIM, S. (eds), 1991, *Health Care for Older Women*, Oxford University Press.

GEORGE, V. and WILDING, P., 1984, *The Impact of Social Policy*, Routledge & Kegan Paul.

GENERAL HOUSEHOLD SURVEYS – see OPCS.

GIBSON, C.C., 1990, 'Widowhood: patterns, problems and choices', in: Bury and MacNicol, 1990, pp. 82–103.

GILLEARD, C., 1984, *Living with Dementia*, Croom Helm.

GILMORE, A. and GILMORE, S. (eds), 1988, *A Safer Death*, Plenum Press, New York.

GLENDENNING, F. (ed.), 1985, *Educational Gerontology: international perspectives*, Croom Helm.

GLENNERSTER, H., 1983, *The Future of the Welfare State*, Gower.

GLENNERSTER, H., 1985, *Paying for Welfare*, Blackwell.

GLENNERSTER, H., FALKINGHAM, J. and EVANDROU, M., 1990, 'How much do we care?', *Social Policy and Administration*, **24**(2), August, pp. 93–103.

GOLDBERG, E., 1970, *Helping the Aged: a field experiment in social work*, Allen & Unwin.

GOLDBERG, E. and CONNELLY, N., 1982, *The Effectiveness of Social Care for the Elderly*, Heinemann.

GOLDSMITH, S., 1974, *Mobility Housing*, DOE, Housing Development Directorate.

GOLDSMITH, S., 1975, *Wheelchair Housing*, DOE, Housing Development Directorate.

GOODMAN, A., 1976, *Charity Law and Voluntary Organisations*, Bedford Square Press.

GOUGH, I., 1979, *The Political Economy of the Welfare State*, Macmillan.

GRAY, J.A M., 1987, 'Preventive care for elderly people', *Practitioner*, **231**, June, pp. 829–30.

GRAY, M., JOHNSON, M., SEAGRAVE, J. and DUNNE, M. 1977, *A Policy for Warmth*, Fabian Society.

GREEN, H., 1988, *Informal Carers*, HMSO.

GREENGROSS, S., 1990, 'A force for change', in: McEwen (ed.), 1990, pp. 8–11.

GREENGROSS, W. and GREENGROSS, S., 1989, *Living, Loving and Ageing*, ACE.

GRIFFIN, J. and DEAN, C., 1975, *Housing for the Elderly: the size of grouped schemes*, HMSO.

GRIFFITHS, A., GRIMES, R. and ROBERTS, G., 1990, *The Law and Elderly People*, Routledge.

GRIFFITHS REPORT, 1983, *NHS Management Inquiry*, HMSO.

GRIFFITHS, R., 1988, *Community Care: agenda for action*, A Report to the Secretary of State for Social Services, HMSO.

GRUNDY, E., 1983, 'Demography and old age', *Journal of the American Geriatrics Society*, **31**, pp. 799–802.

GRUNDY, E., 1987, 'Retirement migration and its consequences in England and Wales', *Ageing and Society*, **7**, pp. 57–82.

GRUNDY, E., 1989, 'Longitudinal perspectives on the living arrangements of the elderly', in: Jefferys, M. (ed.), 1989, pp. 128–47.

GRUNDY, E., 1991a, 'Women and ageing: demographic aspects', in: George, S. and Ebrahim, S. (eds), 1991.

GRUNDY, E., 1991b, 'Age-related change in later life', in: Hobcraft, J. and Murphy, M. (eds), *Population Research in Britain*, Supplement to Population Studies 45 (in press), 1991.

GRUNDY, E. and ARIE, T., 1982, 'Falling rates of provision of residential care for the elderly', *British Medical Journal*, **284**, pp. 799–802.

HADLEY, R., WEBB, A. and FARRELL, C., 1975, *Accross the Generations: old people and young volunteers*, Allen & Unwin.

HAFFENDEN, S., 1991, *Getting it Right for Carers*, HMSO.

HALL, M., 1988, 'Geriatric medicine today', in: Wells, N. and Freer, C. (eds), 1988, pp. 65–86.

HAM, C., 1991, *The New National Health Service*, Radcliffe Medical Press, Oxford.

HARDIE, M., 1978, *Understanding Ageing*, Hodder & Stoughton.

HARDING, T., 1990, 'Opportunities and pitfalls: a voluntary sector view of the legislation', in: Morton, J. (ed.), 1990a, pp. 27–31.

HARPENDEN, S., 1991, *Getting it Right for Carers*, DOH Social Services Inspectorate.

HARRIS, A., 1968, *Social Welfare for the Elderly*, HMSO.

HARRIS, A., 1971, *Handicapped and Impaired in Great Britain*, HMSO.

HARRIS, C., 1969, *The Family*, Allen & Unwin.

HARRIS, D., 1990, *Sociology of Aging*, Harper & Row, New York.

HARROP, A., 1990, *The Employment Position of Older Women in Europe*, Age Concern Institute of Gerontology.

HARROP, A. and GRUNDY, E., 1991, 'Geographic variations in moves into institutions among the elderly in England and Wales', *Urban Studies*, **28**, pp. 65–86.

HART, D. and CHALMERS, K., 1990, *The Housing Needs of Elderly People in Scotland*, Central Research Unit, Scottish Office.

HASKEY, J., 1989, 'Families and households of the ethnic minority and white populations of Great Britain', *Population Trends* 57, Autumn 1977, pp. 8–19.

HATCH, S. and MOCROFT, I., 1977, 'Factors affecting the location of voluntary organisation branches', *Policy and Politics*, **6**(2), pp. 163–72.

HATCH, S., 1978, *Voluntary Work*, The Volunteer Centre.

HEALTH ADVISORY SERVICE, 1982, *The Rising Tide: developing services for mental illness in old age*, National Health Service, Health Advisory Service.

HEDLEY, R. and NORMAN, A., 1982, *Home Help: key issues in service provision*, Centre for Policy on Ageing.

HENDRICKS, J. and HENDRICKS, D., 1986, *Aging in the Mass Society – myths and realities*, Little, Brown, Boston and Toronto.

HENWOOD, M., 1990, *Community Care and Elderly People*, Family Policy Studies Centre.

HENWOOD, M. and WICKS, M., 1984, *The Forgotten Army: family care and elderly people*, Family Policy Studies Centre.

HICKS, C., 1988, *Who Cares: looking after people at home*, Virago.

HIGGINS, J., 1989, 'Defining community care', *Social Policy and Administration*, 23(1), May, pp. 3–16.

HILL, M., 1976, *The State, Administration and the Individual*, Fontana.

HILL, M. and BRAMLEY, G., 1986, *Analysing Social Policy*, Blackwell.

HILLMAN, M. and WHALLEY, A., 1979, *Walking is Transport*, Policy Studies Institute.

HILLS, D., 1991, *Carer Support in the Community*, DOH Social Services Inspectorate.

HINTON, C., 1991, *Using your Home as Capital*, ACE.

HINTON, J., 1972, *Dying*, Penguin.

HOBMAN, D. (ed.), 1981, *The Impact of Ageing*, Croom Helm.

HOBMAN, D., 1989, *Coming of Age: a positive guide to growing older*, Hamlyn.

HODKINSON, H., 1975, *An Outline of Geriatrics*, Academic Press.

HOLE, W. and POUNTNEY, M., 1971, *Trends in Population, Housing and Occupancy Rates 1861–1961*, HMSO.

HOLME, A. and MAIZELS, J., 1978, *Social Workers and Volunteers*, British Association of Social Workers.

HOME OFFICE, DEPARTMENT OF EDUCATION AND SCIENCE, MINISTRY OF HOUSING AND LOCAL GOVERNMENT AND MINISTRY OF HEALTH, 1968, *Report of the Committee on Local Authority and Allied Personal Social Services* (Seebohm Report), HMSO.

HOOKER, S. 1976, *Caring for Elderly People*, Routledge & Kegan Paul.

HOUSE BUILDERS FEDERATION, 1990, *Guidance Note on Management and Services*, House Builders Federation.

HOUSE BUILDERS FEDERATION and NATIONAL HOUSING AND TOWN PLANNING COUNCIL, 1988, *Sheltered Housing for Sale*, An Advice Note, HBF and NHTPC.

HOUSE OF COMMONS, 1980, *Report from the Social Services Committee. The Government's White Papers on Public Expenditure: the Social Services*, vol. 1, HMSO.

HOUSE OF COMMONS, 1981. *Third Report from the Social Services Committee, Public Expenditure on the Social Services*, HMSO.

HOUSE OF COMMONS, 1982, *Second Report from the Social Services Committee, Session 1981–82. 1982 White Paper: Public Expenditure on the Social Services*, vol. 1, HMSO.

HOUSE OF COMMONS, 1985, *Social Services Committee, Second Report*

Session 1984–85. Community Care: with special reference to adult mentally ill and mentally handicapped people, vol. 1, HMSO.

HOUSE OF COMMONS, 1989, *Employment Committee, Second Report. The Employment Patterns of the Over-50s*, vol. 1, HMSO.

HOUSE OF COMMONS, 1990a, *Social Services Committee, Fifth Report. Community Care: carers*, HMSO.

HOUSE OF COMMONS, 1990b, *Social Services Committee, Eleventh Report. Community Care: services for people with a mental handicap and people with a mental illness*, HMSO.

HUGHES, B., 1990, 'Quality of life', in: Peace, S. (ed.), 1990, pp. 46–58.

HUNT, A., 1970, *The Home Help Service in England and Wales*, HMSO.

HUNT, A., 1978, *The Elderly at Home*, Office of Population Censuses and Surveys, Social Survey Division, HMSO. 1978.

HUNTER, D., BURLEY, L., HEADLAND, L. and KILLEEN, J. (eds), 1987, *Dementia: developing innovative services in the community*, Scottish Action on Dementia.

ISAACS, B. and EVERS, H., 1984, *Innovations in the Care of the Elderly*, Croom Helm.

ISAACS, B., LIVINGSTONE, M. and NEVILLE, Y., 1972, *Survival of the Unfittest*, Routledge & Kegan Paul.

JACKSON, B., 1968, *Working Class Community*, Routledge & Kegan Paul.

JAMIESON, A. AND ILLSLEY, R. (eds), 1990, *Contrasting European Policies for the Care of Older People*, Avebury.

JEFFERYS, M., 1965, *An Anatomy of Social Welfare Services*, Michael Joseph.

JEFFERYS, M. (ed.), 1989, *Growing Old in the Twentieth Century*, Routledge.

JEFFERYS, M. and THANE, P., 1989, 'An ageing society and ageing people', in: Jefferys, M. (ed.), 1989, pp. 1–20.

JERROME, D. (ed.), 1983, *Ageing in Modern Society*, Croom Helm.

JERROME, D., 1990, Intimate relationships', in: Bond, J. and Coleman, P. (eds), 1990, pp. 181–208.

JOHNSON, M., 1972, 'Self-perception of need among the elderly', *Sociological Review*, **20**(4), 1972, pp. 521–31.

JOHNSON, M., 1990, 'Dependency and interdependency', in: Bond and Coleman (eds), 1990, pp. 209–28.

JOHNSON, M. with DI GREGORIO, S. and HARRISON, B., 1981, *Ageing, Needs and Nutrition*, Policy Studies Institute.

JOHNSON, P., CONRAD, C. and THOMSON, D. (eds), 1989, *Workers versus Pensioners: intergenerational justice in an ageing world*, Manchester University Press.

JOHNSON, P. and FALKINGHAM, J., 1988, 'Intergenerational transfers and public expenditure on the elderly in modern Britain', *Ageing and Society*, **8**(2), pp. 1129–46.

JOLLY, J., CREIGH, S. and MINGAY, A., 1980, *Age as a Factor in Employment*, Department of Employment.

JONES, C., 1985, *Patterns of Social Policy*, Tavistock.

JONES, R., 1984, *The Registered Homes Act 1984*, Sweet & Maxwell.

JONES, S. (ed.), 1976, *The Liberation of the Elders*, Beth Foundation Publications and Department of Adult Education, University of Keele.

JOSHI, H. (ed.), 1989, *The Changing Population of Britain*, Blackwell.

JOWELL, R., WITHERSPOON, S. and BROOK, L., 1988, *British Social Attitudes: the 5th report*, Gower.

JUDGE, K. and SINCLAIR, I. (eds), 1986, *Residential Care for Elderly People*, HMSO.

KAFETZ, K., 1987, 'Hypothermia and elderly people', *Practitioner* **231**, 1987, pp. 864–7.

KALACHE, A., WARNES, A. and HUNTER, D., 1988, *Promoting Health Among Elderly People*, King's Fund.

KARN, V., 1977, *Retiring to the Seaside*, Routledge & Kegan Paul.

KEDDIE, K., 1978, *Action with the Elderly*, Pergamon.

KELLAHER, L. 1986, 'Determinants of quality of life in residential settings for old people', in: Judge, K. and Sinclair, I. (eds), 1986, pp. 127–38.

KELLAHER, L., PEACE, S., WEAVER, T. and WILLCOCKS, D., 1988, *Coming to Terms with the Private Sector: regulatory practice for residential care homes and elderly people*, Report 1, Polytechnic of North London.

KENNEDY, I. (Chairman), 1988, *The Living Will: a working party report*, Age Concern Institute of Gerontology and Centre of Medical Law and Ethics, King's College, University of London, Edward Arnold.

KETTLE, D. and HART, L., 1973, *Health of the Elderly Project: an experiment in the voluntary visiting of old people*, King Edward Hospital Fund and Young Volunteer Force Foundation.

KING EDWARD'S HOSPITAL FUND and NATIONAL ASSOCIATION OF HEALTH AUTHORITIES, 1987, *Care of the Dying: a guide for health authorities*, King Edward's Hospital Fund.

KLEIN, R., 1975, *Inflation and Priorities*, Centre for Studies in Social Policy.

KLEIN, R. and O'HIGGINS, M., 1985, *The Future of Welfare*, Blackwell.

KNAPP, M., 1981, Cost information and residential care of the elderly', *Ageing and Society*, **1**(2), July, pp. 199–228.

KNAPP, M., 1984, *The Economics of Social Care*, Macmillan.

KROLL, U., 1988, *Growing Older*, Collins.

KÜBLER-ROSS, E., 1970, *Death and Dying*, Tavistock.

LACZKO, F., 1990, 'New poverty and the old poor: pensioners' incomes in the European Community', *Ageing and Society*, **10**(3), September, pp. 261–78.

LACZKO, F. and PHILLIPSON, C., 1990, 'Defending the right to work: age discrimination in employment', in: McEwen (ed.), 1990, pp. 84–96.

LASLETT, P., 1980, *The Education of the Elderly in Britain*, Unpublished.

LASLETT, P., 1989, *A Fresh Map of Life: the emergence of the third age*, Weidenfeld & Nicolson.

LAW, C.M. and WARNES, A.M., 1982, 'The destination decision in retirement migration', in: Warnes, A.M. (ed.), 1982, pp. 53–82.

LEAT, D., 1979, *Limited Liability?*, The Volunteer Centre.

LEAT, D., 1990a 'Care and the voluntary sector', in: Sinclair *et al.* (eds), 1990, pp. 227–90.

LEAT, D., 1990b, *For Love and Money*, Joseph Rowntree Foundation.

LEAT, D. and DARVILL, G., 1977, *Voluntary Visiting of the Elderly*, The Volunteer Centre.

LEAT, D. and GAY, P., 1987, *Paying for Care*, Policy Studies Institute.

LEATHARD, A., 1990, *Health Care Provision: past, present and future*, Chapman & Hall.

LEATHER, P. and MACKINTOSH, S., 1990, *Monitoring Assisted Agency Services. Part 1: Home Improvement Agencies – An Evaluation of Performance*, HMSO.

LEATHER, P. and WHEELER, R., 1988, *Making Use of Home Equity in Old Age*, Building Societies Association.

LEE, P. and RABAN, C., 1988, *Welfare Theory and Social Policy*, Sage, San Francisco.

LE GROS CLARK, F., 1966, *Work, Age and Leisure*, Michael Joseph.

LEVIN, E., 1983, 'The elderly and their informal carers', DHSS, HMSO, 1983a.

LEVIN, E., SINCLAIR, I. and GORBACH, P., 1989, *Families, Services and Confusion in Old Age*, Gower.

LEWIS, J. and MEREDITH, B., 1988, *Daughters who Care*, Routledge.

LIVESLEY, B., 1982, 'Silent epidemic', *Health Services*, **24**, p. 14.

MCCREADIE, C., 1991, *Elder Abuse: an exploratory study*, Age Concern Institute of Gerontology.

MCDERMENT, L. and GREENGROSS, S., 1985, *Social Care for Elderly People: an international perspective*, Social Care Association.

MCEWEN, E. (ed.), 1990, *Age: the unrecognised discrimination*, ACE.

MCMANUS, L., 1985, *Hypothermia: the facts*, ACE.

MACE, N. and RABINS, P., 1985, *The 36 Hour Day*, Edward Arnold in conjunction with ACE.

MACK, J. and LANSLEY, S., 1985, *Poor Britain*, Allen & Unwin.

MACKINTOSH, S., MEANS, R. and LEATHER, P., 1990, *Housing in Later Life*, School for Advanced Urban Studies, University of Bristol.

MACLENNAN, D., GIBB, K. and MORE, A., 1990, *Paying for Britain's Housing*, National Federation of Housing Associations.

MACLENNAN, W., 1986, 'Subnutrition in the elderly', *British Medical Journal*, **293**, 8.11.86, pp. 1189–90.

MARKET AND OPINION RESEARCH INTERNATIONAL (MORI), 1990, *Voluntary Activity: a survey of public attitudes*, The Volunteer Centre, UK.

MARSHALL, M., 1990, *Social Work with Old People*, Macmillan.

MARTIN, B., 1990, 'The cultural construction of ageing: or how long can the summer wine really last?' in: Bury, M. and MacNicol, J. (eds), 1990, pp. 53–81.

MARTIN, J. and ROBERTS, J., 1984, *Women and Employment: a lifetime perspective*, HMSO.

MARTIN, J., MELTZER, H. and ELLIOT, D.M., 1988, *The Prevalence of Disability Among Adults*, OPCS surveys of disability in Great Britain, Report 1, HMSO.

MARTIN, J. and WHITE, A., 1988, *The Financial Circumstances of Disabled Adults Living in Private Households*, OPCS surveys of disability in Great Britain, Report 2, HMSO.

MARTIN, J., WHITE, A. and MELTZER, H., 1989, *Disabled Adults: services, transport and employment*, OPCS surveys of disability in Great Britain, Report 4, HMSO.

MEACHER, M., 1972, *Taken for a Ride*, Longmans.

MEANS, R., 1990, 'Allocating council housing to older people', *Social Policy and Administration*, **24**(1), April, pp.52–64.

MELLOR, H., 1987, *Work in Later Life: a plea for flexible retirement*, Employment Institute.

MIDWINTER, E., 1982, *Age is Opportunity: education and older people*, Centre for Policy on Ageing.

MIDWINTER, E., 1985, *The Wage of Retirement: the case for a new pensions policy*, Centre for Policy on Ageing.

MIDWINTER, E., 1987, *Redefining Old Age: a review of CPA's recent contributions to social policy*, Centre for Policy on Ageing.

MIDWINTER, E., 1990, *Creating Chances: arts by older people*, Centre for Policy on Ageing.

MIDWINTER, E. and TESTER, S., 1987, *Polls Apart?: older voters and the 1987 general election*, Centre for Policy on Ageing.

MINISTER OF HEALTH (MOH), 1956, *Report of the Committee of Enquiry into the Cost of the National Health Service* (Guillebaud Report), HMSO.

MOH, 1957, *Survey of Services Available to the Chronic Sick and Elderly 1954–55*, Summary report prepared by Boucher, C.A., HMSO.

MOH, 1962, *Hospital Plan*, HMSO.

MOH, 1963, *Health and Welfare: the development of community care*, HMSO.

MOH, 1965, *Care of the Elderly in Hospitals and Residential Homes*, MOH.

MOH, 1966, *Health and Welfare: the development of community care*, HMSO.

MINISTRY OF HEALTH and DEPARTMENT OF HEALTH FOR SCOTLAND, 1959, *Report of the Working Party on Social Workers in Local Authority Health and Welfare Services* (Younghusband Report), HMSO.

MINISTRY OF HOUSING, 1958, *Flatlets for Old People*, HMSO.

MINISTRY OF HOUSING, 1960, *More Flatlets for Old People*, HMSO.

MINISTRY OF HOUSING AND LOCAL GOVERNMENT (MHLG), 1962a, *Some Aspects of Designing for Old People*, HMSO.

MHLG, 1962b, *Grouped Flatlets for Old People*, HMSO.

MHLG, 1963, *Housing*, HMSO.

MHLG, 1965, *The Housing Programme 1965 to 1970*, HMSO.

MHLG, 1966, *Old People's Flatlets in Stevenage*, HMSO.

MHLG, 1967, *Management of Local Government* (Maud Report), vol. 1, Report of the Committee, HMSO.

MHLG, 1969, *Council Housing Purposes, Procedures and Priorities* (Cullingworth Report), HMSO.

MINISTRY OF PENSIONS AND NATIONAL INSURANCE, 1954, *Reasons Given for Retiring or Continuing at Work*, HMSO.

MINISTRY OF PENSIONS AND NATIONAL INSURANCE, 1966, *Financial and Other Circumstances of Retirement Pensioners*, HMSO.

MORLEY, D., 1974, *Day Care and Leisure Provision for the Elderly*, ACE.

MORONEY, R., 1976, *The Family and the State*, Longmans.

MORRIS, M., 1969, *Voluntary Work in the Welfare State*, Routledge & Kegan Paul.

MORTON, J., 1982, *Ferndale: a caring repair service for elderly home owners*, Shelter/Help the Aged, September.

MORTON, J. (ed.), 1989a, *Enabling Elderly People with Dementia to Live in the Community*, Age Concern Institute of Gerontology.

MORTON, J. (ed.), 1989b, *Achieving Change in Home Care Services*, Age Concern Institute of Gerontology.

MORTON, J. (ed.), 1989c, *New Approaches to Day Care for Elderly People*, Age Concern Institute of Gerontology.

MORTON, J. (ed.), 1990a, *Packages of Care for Elderly People: how can the voluntary sector contribute?*, Age Concern Institute of Gerontology.

MORTON, J. (ed.), 1990b, *Packages of Care for Elderly People: how can the private sector contribute?*, Age Concern Institute of Gerontology.

MORTON, J. (ed.), 1991, *Very Sheltered Housing*, Age Concern Institute of Gerontology.

MURPHY, E. (ed.), 1986a, *Affective Disorders in the Elderly*, Churchill Livingstone.

MURPHY, E., 1986b, 'Social factors in late life depression', in: Murphy, E. (ed.), 1986a.

MURRAY, G., 1968, *Voluntary Organisations and Social Welfare*, Oliver & Boyd.

NATIONAL ASSISTANCE BOARD, 1966, *Homeless Single Persons*, HMSO.

NATIONAL ASSOCIATION OF HEALTH AUTHORITIES (NAHA), 1987, *Care of the Dying: a guide for health authorities*, King Edward's Hospital Fund and NAHA.

NATIONAL ASSOCIATION OF HEALTH AUTHORITIES, 1988, *Actions Not Words: a strategy to improve health services for black and minority ethnic groups*, NAHA, Birmingham.

NATIONAL AUDIT OFFICE, 1987, *Community Care Developments*, HMSO.

NATIONAL AUDIT OFFICE, 1991, *The Social Fund*, HMSO.

NATIONAL CONSUMER COUNCIL, 1990, *Consulting Consumers in the NHS: a guideline study*, NCC.

NATIONAL COUNCIL OF SOCIAL SERVICE, 1954, *Living Longer*, NCSS.

NATIONAL COUNCIL OF SOCIAL SERVICE, 1967, *Caring for People: staffing residential homes* (Williams Report), Allen & Unwin.

NATIONAL COUNCIL OF SOCIAL SERVICE and NATIONAL INSTITUTE FOR SOCIAL WORK TRAINING, 1969, *The Voluntary Worker in the Social Services* (Aves Report), Bedford Square Press and Allen & Unwin.

NATIONAL ECONOMIC DEVELOPMENT OFFICE, 1989, *Defusing the Demographic Time Bomb*, NEDO.

NATIONAL FEDERATION OF HOUSING ASSOCIATIONS, 1985, *Report of the Inquiry into British Housing: chaired by HRH The Duke of Edinburgh*, NFHA.

NATIONAL FEDERATION OF HOUSING ASSOCIATIONS/MIND, 1987, *Housing: the foundation of community care*, NFHA.

NATIONAL FEDERATION OF HOUSING ASSOCIATIONS and SPECIAL NEEDS HOUSING ADVISORY SERVICE, 1987, *A Guide to the Registered Homes Act*, NFHA.

NATIONAL HOUSE BUILDING COUNCIL (NHBC), 1990, *The NHBC Sheltered Housing Code of Practice*, NHBC, April.

NATIONAL INSTITUTE FOR SOCIAL WORK, 1982, *Social Workers: their role and tasks* (Barclay Report), Bedford Square Press.

NEILL, J., SINCLAIR, I., GORBACH, P. and WILLIAMS, J., 1988, *A Need for Care? Elderly applicants for local authority homes*, Avebury.

NEUBERGER, J., 1987, *Caring for Dying People of Different Faiths*, Austen Cornish.

NINER, P., 1989, *Housing Needs in the 1990s. An interim assessment*, National Housing Forum.

NISSEL, M. and BONNERJEA, L., 1982, *Family Care of the Handicapped Elderly: who pays?*, PSI.

NORMAN, A., 1977, *Transport and the Elderly*, National Corporation for the Care of Old People (NCCOP).

NORMAN, A., 1980, *Rights and Risk*, National Corporation for the Care of Old People.

NORMAN, A., 1985, *Triple Jeopardy: growing old in a second homeland*, Centre for Policy on Ageing.

NORMAN, A., 1987, *Severe Dementia: the provision of longstay care*, Centre for Policy on Ageing.

NORMAN, A., 1988, *Rights and Risk: a discussion document on civil liberty in old age*, Centre for Policy on Ageing.

NORTON, C., 1989, 'Continence: a real case for team work', *Social Work Today*, 24.8.89, pp. 23–5.

NORTON, D., 1987, *Education and Older People*, Centre for Policy on Ageing.

NUFFIELD FOUNDATION, 1986, *The Nuffield Inquiry into Pharmacy*, Nuffield Foundation.

OFFICE OF POPULATION CENSUSES AND SURVEYS (OPCS), 1982, *General Household Survey 1980*, HMSO.

OPCS, 1983, *General Household Survey 1981*, HMSO.

OPCS, 1987, *General Household Survey 1985*, HMSO.

OPCS, 1989, *General Household Survey 1986*, HMSO (including a chapter on *GHS* 1985).

OPCS, 1990, *General Household Survey 1988*, OPCS.

OLDMAN, C., 1990, *Moving in Old Age: new directions in housing policies*, HMSO.

OPPENHEIM, C., 1990, *Poverty: the facts*, Child Poverty Action Group.

ORIEL, W., '1981, 'Ageing as a political force', in: Hobman, D. (ed.), 1981, pp. 33–52.

OSBORN, A., 1988, *Developing Local Services and Actions for Dementia Sufferers and their Carers*, Age Concern Scotland.

PACIONE, M. (ed.), 1987, *Social Geography: progress and prospect*, Croom Helm.

PAGE, D. and MUIR, T., 1971, *New Housing for the Elderly*, Bedford Square Press.

PAHL, J., 1988, *Day Services for Elderly People in the Medway Health District*, Health Services Research Unit, University of Kent at Canterbury.

PARKER, G., 1985, *With Due Care and Attention: a review of research on informal care*, Family Policy Studies Centre.

PARKER, R., 1981, 'Tending and social policy', in: Goldberg, E. and Hatch, S. (eds), *A New Look at the Personal Social Services*, Policy Studies Institute, pp. 17–32.

PARKER, R., 1990, 'The role of the private sector in the care of the elderly', in: Morton, J. (ed.), 1990b, pp. 3–9.

PARKES, C., 1975, *Bereavement: studies of grief in adult life*, Penguin.

PATHY, M. (ed.), 1985, *Principles and Practice of Geriatric Medicine*, John Wiley.

PEACE, S. (ed.), 1990, *Researching Social Gerontology*, Sage.

PEACE, S., KELLAHER, L. and WILLCOCKS, D., 1982, *A Balanced Life. A consumer study of residential life in one hundred local authority old people's homes*, Research Report No. 14, Survey Research Unit, School of Applied Social Studies and Sociology, Polytechnic of North London.

PEAKER, C., 1986, *The Crisis in Residential Care*, National Council for Voluntary Organisations.

PEAKER, C., 1988, *Who Pays? Who cares?*, National Council for Voluntary Organisations.

PHILLIPSON, C., 1982, *Capitalism and the Construction of Old Age*, Macmillan.

PHILLIPSON, C., (ed.), 1983, *New Directions in Pre-Retirement Education*, Beth Johnson Foundation.

PHILLIPSON, C., BERNARD M. and STRANG, P. (eds), 1986, *Dependency and Interdependency in Old Age*, Croom Helm.

PHILLIPSON, C. and WALKER, A. (eds), 1986, *Ageing and Social Policy: A critical assessment*, Gower.

PILCH, M., 1974, *The Retirement Book*, Hamish Hamilton.

PINCUS, L., 1974, *Death and the Family*, Faber & Faber.

PINKER, R., 1971, *Social Theory and Social Policy*, Heinemann.

PINKER, R., 1979, *The Idea of Welfare*, Heinemann.

PLANK, D., 1977, *Caring for the Elderly. A report of a study of various means of caring for dependent elderly people in eight London boroughs*, Greater London Council Research Memorandum, GLC.

POWELL, W.W. (ed.), 1987, *The Non-Profit Sector: a research handbook*, Yale University Press, New Haven.

POWER, M., 1981, *Volunteer Support for Very Elderly People Living in Residential Homes*, Report to Department of Health and Social Security.

POWER, M., 1986, 'Volunteer support to residential homes', in: Judge, K. and Sinclair, I. (eds), 1986, pp. 151–8.

PRUNER, M., 1974, *To the Good Long Life*, Universe Books, New York.

QURESHI, H. and WALKER, A., 1989, *The Caring Relationship*, Macmillan.

RANDOLPH, W. and LEVISON, D., 1988, *A Profile of New Tenancies*, NFHA.

RAPHAEL, B., 1984, *The Anatomy of Bereavement*, Hutchinson.

RAPOPORT, R., RAPOPORT, R. and FOGARTY, M., 1982, *Families in Britain*, Routledge & Kegan Paul.

RATTEE, A., 1977, *A Study on Boarding Out of the Elderly*, Brunel University.

RAUTA, I., 1986, *Who Would Prefer Separate Accommodation?*, HMSO.

REDFERN, S., 1989, 'Key issues in nursing elderly people', in: Warnes, A. (ed.), 1989, pp. 146–60.

RESEARCH INSTITUTE FOR CONSUMER AFFAIRS (RICA), 1986, *Dispersed Alarms. A guide for organisations installing systems*, RICA, July.

RIDDELL, P., 1985, *The Thatcher Government*, Blackwell.

RIGGS, L. and MELTON, L., 'Osteoporosis and age-related fracture syndromes', in: Evered, D. and Whelan, J. (eds), 1988, pp. 129–42.

ROBB, B., 1967, *Sans Everything*, Nelson.

ROBERTS, N., 1970, *Our Future Selves: care of the elderly*, Allen & Unwin.

ROSSER, C. and HARRIS, C., 1965, *Family and Social Change*, Routledge & Kegan Paul.

ROTH, M. and WISCHIK, C., 1985, 'The heterogeneity of Alzheimer's disease and its implications for scientific investigations of the disorder', in: Arie (ed.), 1985, pp. 71–92.

ROWLINGS, C., 1981, *Social Work with Elderly People*, Allen & Unwin.

ROWNTREE, B. SEEBOHM, 1947, *Old People. Report of a Survey Committee on the Problems of Ageing and the Care of Old People*, The Nuffield Foundation, Oxford University Press.

ROYAL COLLEGE OF PHYSICIANS and THE ROYAL COLLEGE OF PSYCHIATRISTS (Joint Report), 1989, *Care of Elderly People with Mental Illness: specialist services and medical training*, The Royal College of Physicians of London and the Royal College of Psychiatrists, February.

ROYAL COMMISSION ON THE NATIONAL HEALTH SERVICE, 1979, *Report (Merrison Committee)*, HMSO, July.

SALAMON, L., 1987, 'Partners in public service: the scope and theory of government-non profit relations', in: Powell (ed.), 1987.

SALVAGE, A., 1989, 'Cold homes, cold comfort', *Primary Health Care* 7(10), pp.10–13.

SALVAGE, A., 1991, *Elderly People in Cold Conditions: a bibliography*, Age Concern Institute of Gerontology.

SAUNDERS, C., 1978, *The Management of Terminal Disease*, Edward Arnold.

SCRUTTON, S., 1988, 'How diet can improve the health of older people', *Social Work Today* 21.7.88, pp.16–17.

SCRUTTON, S., 1989, *Counselling Older People – A creative response to ageing*, Edward Arnold.

SECRETARIES OF STATE FOR THE ENVIRONMENT, SCOTLAND AND WALES, 1986, *The Local Government Councillor*, HMSO.

SECRETARIES OF STATE FOR HEALTH, FOR WALES, NORTHERN IRELAND AND SCOTLAND, 1989a, *Working for Patients*, HMSO.

SECRETARIES OF STATE FOR HEALTH, SOCIAL SECURITY, WALES AND SCOTLAND, 1989b, *Caring for People: community care in the next decade and beyond*, HMSO.

SECRETARY OF STATE FOR HEALTH, 1991, *The Health of the Nation: a consultative document for health in England*, HMSO.

SECRETARIES OF STATE FOR SOCIAL SERVICES, FOR WALES, NORTHERN IRELAND AND SCOTLAND, 1986, *Primary Health Care: an agenda for discussion*, HMSO.

SECRETARIES OF STATE FOR SOCIAL SERVICES, FOR WALES, NORTHERN

IRELAND AND SCOTLAND, 1987, *Promoting Better Health: the Government's programme for improving primary health care*, HMSO, 1987.

SECRETARY OF STATE FOR SOCIAL SERVICES, 1985a, *Reform of Social Security*, vol. 1, HMSO.

SECRETARY OF STATE FOR SOCIAL SERVICES, 1985b, *Reform of Social Security: programme for action*, HMSO.

SHANAS, E., TOWNSEND, P., WEDDERBURN, D., HENNING, F., MILHOF, P. and STEHOUWER, J., 1968, *Old People in Three Industrial Societies*, Routledge & Kegan Paul.

SHELDON, J., 1948, *The Social Medicine of Old Age*, Nuffield Foundation.,

SHENFIELD, B., 1957, *Social Policies for Old Age*, Routledge & Kegan Paul.

SHENFIELD, B. with ALLEN, I., 1972, *The Organisation of Voluntary Services*, Political and Economic Planning.

SIMMONS, L., 1962, 'Ageing in primitive society', *Law and Contemporary Problems*, Winter, p. 42.

SINCLAIR, I., 1988, 'The client reviews: elderly', in: *Wagner Report. The Research Reviewed*, HMSO, pp. 241–92.

SINCLAIR, I., CROSBIE, D., O'CONNOR, P., STANFORTH, L. and VICKERY, A., 1989, *Bridging Two Worlds: social work and the elderly living alone*, Avebury.

SINCLAIR, I., PARKER, R., LEAT, D. and WILLIAMS, J. (eds), 1990, *The Kaleidoscope of Care: a review of research on welfare provision for elderly people*, National Institute for Social Work, HMSO.

SINCLAIR, I. and WILLIAMS, J., 1990, 'Allocation: the roles of general practitioners, social workers, hospitals and health visitors', in: Sinclair, I. *et al.* (eds), 1990, pp.139–58.

SINCLAIR, I. and WILLIAMS, J., 1990, 'Elderly People: coping and quality of life', in: Sinclair, I. *et al.* (eds), 1990, pp.67–86.

SIXSMITH, A., 1988, *The Meaning and Experience of 'Home' in Later Life*, Paper to the British Society of Gerontology, Annual Conference, Swansea.

SMITH, K., 1986, *I'm Not Complaining*, Kensington and Chelsea Staying Put for the Elderly Ltd in association with Shelter Housing Advice Centre.

SOCIAL AND COMMUNITY PLANNING RESEARCH, 1990, *On Volunteering: a qualitative research study of images, motivations and experiences*, The Volunteer Centre, UK.

SOCIAL SECURITY ADVISORY COMMITTEE, 1982, *First Report 1981*, HMSO.

SOCIAL SECURITY ADVISORY COMMITTEE, 1988, *Sixth Report 1988*, HMSO.

SOCIAL SECURITY CONSORTIUM, 1986, *Of Little Benefit: a critical guide to the Social Security Act 1986*, Social Security Consortium.

STACEY, M., 1969, *Comparability in Social Research*, Heinemann.

STANDING CONFERENCE OF ETHNIC MINORITY CITIZENS, 1986, *Ethnic Minority Senior Citizens – the question of policy*, Standing Conference of Ethnic Minority Citizens.

STATHAM, R., KORCZAK, J. and MONAGHAN, P., 1988, *House Adaptations for People with Physical Disabilities: a guidance manual for practitioners*, HMSO.

STEVENSON, O., 1989, *Age and Vulnerability*, Edward Arnold.

STEVENSON, O. and PARSLOE, P. (eds), 1978, *Social Service Teams: the practitioner's view*, HMSO.

STEWART, M., 1974, *Social Rehabilitation of the Elderly*, ACE.

STILWELL, B., 1986, 'Nurses as co-practitioners: threat or promise?', *Practitioner* 230, June, pp.501–2.

STOTT, M., 1981, *Ageing for Beginners*, Blackwell.

STRAKA, G., 1990, 'Training older workers for and in the years after 2000', *Journal of Educational Gerontology*, 5(2), pp. 68–78.

SWIFT, C., 1987, 'Nutrition in the elderly', *Chemistry and Industry*, 2.3.87, pp. 146–8.

TAIT, E., 1983, *Report of the Findings of a Questionnaire Conducted Among Local Authorities in England of Adult Boarding Out Schemes*, London Borough of Brent.

TARPEY, M.-R., 1990, 'Service provision to elderly people from black and minority ethnic groups', *Generations* 14, Autumn, 1–6.

TAYLOR, H., 1983, *The Hospice Movement in Britain: its role and its future*, Centre for Policy on Ageing.

TAYLOR, R., FORD, G. and BARBER, H., 1983, *The Elderly at Risk*, ACE.

TAYLOR, R. and BUCKLEY, E., 1987, *Preventive Care of the Elderly: a review of current developments*, Royal College of General Practitioners.

TAYLOR, J. and TAYLOR, D., 1989, *Mental Health in the 1990s: from custody to care?*, Office of Health Economics.

TESTER, S., 1989, *Caring By Day: a study of day care services for older people*, Centre for Policy on Ageing.

TESTER, S. and MEREDITH, B., 1987, *Ill-informed? A study of information and support for elderly people in the inner city*, Policy Studies Institute.

THANE, P., 1982, *The Foundations of the Welfare State*, Longman.

THIENHAUS, O., CONTER, E. and BOSMAN, B., 1986, 'Sexuality and ageing', *Ageing and Society*, **6**(1), March, pp. 39–54.

THOMAS, A., 1981, *Agency Services: their role in house improvement*, Centre for Urban and Regional Studies, University of Birmingham.

THOMAS, T., PLYMAT, K., BLANNIN, J. and MEADE, T., 1980, 'Prevalence of urinary incontinence', *British Medical Journal*, **281**, pp. 1243–5.

THOMASON, C., 1990, 'The voluntary sector contribution: examples from the "Care in the Community" programmes', in: Morton, J. (ed.), 1990a, pp.8–16.

THOMPSON, P., ITZIN, C. and ABENDSTERN, M., 1990, *I Don't Feel Old: the experience of later life*, Oxford University Press.

THOMSON, D., 1986, 'The overpaid elderly?', *New Society*, 7.3.86, pp. 408–9.

THOMSON, D., 1989, 'The welfare state and generation conflict: winners and losers', in: Johnson *et al.* (eds), 1989, pp. 33–56.

THORNTON, P., 1989, *Creating a Break*, ACE.

THORNTON, P. and MOORE, J., 1980, *The Placement of Elderly People in Private Households*, Department of Social Policy Research Monograph, University of Leeds.

TINKER, A., 1976, *Housing the Elderly: how successful are granny annexes?*, Department of the Environment, Housing Development Directorate (reprinted HMSO, 1980).

TINKER, A., 1980a, *The Elderly in Modern Society*, Longman.

TINKER, A., 1980b, *Housing the Elderly Near Relatives: moving and other options*, HMSO.

TINKER, A., 1983, 'Improving the quality of life and promoting independence of elderly people', in: DHSS, 1983a; pp.47–68.

TINKER, A., 1984, *Staying at Home: helping elderly people*, HMSO.

TINKER, A., 1989a, *The Telecommunications Needs of Disabled and Elderly People*, Office of Telecommunications.

TINKER, A., 1989b, *An Evaluation of Very Sheltered Housing*, HMSO.

TINKER, A., 1990a, *Why the Sudden Interest in Ageing?*, Inaugural Lecture, 13.11.89, King's College London.

TINKER, A., 1990b, 'Private domiciliary care', in: Morton (ed.), 1990b, pp.16–22.

TITMUSS, R., 1968, *Commitment to Welfare*, Allen & Unwin.

TITMUSS, R., 1970, *The Gift Relationship*, Allen & Unwin.

TOBIN, G., 1987, 'Incontinence in the elderly', *Practitioner*, **231**, June, pp.843–7.

TOMPKINS, P., 1989, *Flexibility and Fairness*, Lane, Clark & Peacock, 1989.

TOWNSEND, P., 1957, *The Family Life of Old People*, Routledge and Kegan Paul

TOWNSEND, P., 1964, *The Last Refuge*, Routledge & Kegan Paul.

TOWNSEND, P., 1979, *Poverty in the United Kingdom*, Penguin.

TOWNSEND, P., 1981, 'The structured dependency of the elderly: creation of social policy in the twentieth century', *Ageing and Society* 1(1), March, pp.5–28.

TOWNSEND, P., 1986, Ageism and social policy, in Phillipson and Walker A. (eds) pp. 15–44.

TOWNSEND, P. and DAVIDSON, N., 1982, *Inequalities in Health*, Penguin.

TOWNSEND, P. and WEDDERBURN, D., 1965, *The Aged in the Welfare State*, G. Bell & Sons.

TUNSTALL, J., 1966, *Old and Alone*, Routledge & Kegan Paul, 1966.

TWIGG, J., ATKIN, K. and PERRING, C., 1990, *Carers and Services: a review of research*, HMSO.

TWIGGER, R., 1989, *The Pension and Pensioners' Incomes*, House of Commons Library Research Division, Research Note No.485, 7.12.89.

UNGERSON, C., 1987, *Policy is Personal: sex, gender and informal care*, Tavistock.

UNITED NATIONS, 1975, *The Ageing: trends and policies*, Centre for Studies in Social Policy, New York.

VICTOR, C., 1987, *Old Age in Modern Society*, Croom Helm, 1987.

VICTOR, C., 1990, 'A survey of the delayed discharge of elderly people from hospitals in an inner city health district', in: Bytheway, W. and Johnson, J. (eds), 1990, pp. 69–80.

VICTOR, C. and VETTER, N., 1986, 'Poverty, disability and use of services by the elderly', *Social Science and Medicine* 22(10), pp.1087–91.

VOLUNTEER CENTRE, 1990, *Guidelines for Relations between Volunteers and Paid Workers in the Health and Personal Social Services*, The Volunteer Centre.

WADE, B., SAWYER, L. and BELL, J., 1983, *Dependency with Dignity: different care provisions for the elderly*, Bedford Square Press.

WAGER, R., 1972, *Care of the Elderly: an exercise in cost benefit analysis*, Institute of Municipal Treasurers and Accountants.

WAGNER REPORT, 1988a, *Residential Care: a positive choice*, HMSO.

WAGNER REPORT, 1988b, *Residential Care: the research reviewed*, HMSO.

WAGSTAFF, P. and COAKLEY, D., 1988, *Physiotherapy and the Elderly Patient*, Croom Helm.

WALKER, A. (ed.), 1982, *Community Care: the family, the state and social policy*, Blackwell.

WALKER, A., 1990a, 'Poverty and inequality in old age', in: Bond, J. and Coleman, P. (eds), 1990, pp. 229–49.

WALKER, A., 1990b, 'The benefits of old age?', in: McEwen (ed.), 1990, pp.58–70.

WALKER, K., 1952, *Commentary on Age*, Jonathan Cape.

WALLIS, J., 1975, *Thinking about Retirement*, Pergamon Press.

WARNES, A. (ed.), 1982, *Geographical Perspectives on the Elderly*, John Wiley.

WARNES, A., 1987, 'Geographical locations and social relationships among the elderly', in: Pacione, M. (ed.), 1987, pp.253–93.

WARNES, A., (ed.) 1989, *Human Ageing and Later Life*, Edward Arnold.

WARNES, A., 1990, 'Geographical questions in gerontology: needed directions for research', *Progress in Human Geography*, **14**(1), pp.24–56.

WATSON, M. and ALBROW, M., 1973, *The Needs of Old People in Glamorgan*, Department of Sociology, University College Cardiff.

WEALE, R., 1989, 'Eyes and age', in: Warnes, A. (ed.), 1989, pp.38–46.

WEBB, A. and WISTOW, G., 1987, *Social Work, Social Care and Social Planning: the personal social services since Seebohm*, Longman.

WELLS, N. and FREER, C., 1988, *The Ageing Population: burden or challenge?*, Macmillan.

WENGER, C., 1984, *The Supportive Network: coping with old age*, Allen & Unwin.

WENGER, C., 1990, 'Elderly carers: the need for appropriate intervention', *Ageing and Society*, **10**(2), pp.197–220.

WESTLAND, P., 1986, 'Joint planning – the last chance?', in: Chant, J. (ed.), 1986, pp.63–9.

WESTON, T. and ASHWORTH, P., 1963, *Old People in Britain*, Bow Group.

WHEELER, R., 1985, *Don't Move: we've got you covered*, Institute of Housing.

WHITEHEAD, C., 1989, *Housing Finance in the UK in the 1980s*, Suntory-Toyota International Centre for Economics and Related Disciplines, London School of Economics.

WICKS, M., 1978, *Old and Cold*, Heinemann.

WILDING, P., 1982, *Professional Power and Social Welfare*, Routledge & Kegan Paul.

WILKIN, D. and THOMPSON, C., 1989, *Users Guide to Dependency Measures for Elderly People*, Joint Unit for Social Services Research, University of Sheffield.

WILLCOCKS, D., 1986, 'Residential care', in: Phillipson, C. and Walker, A. (eds), 1986, pp. 146–62.

WILLCOCKS, D., PEACE, S. and KELLAHER, L., 1986, *Private Lives in Public Places*, Tavistock.

WILLIAMS, F., 1989, *Social Policy: a critical introduction*, Blackwell.

WILLIAMS, G., 1990, *The Experience of Housing in Retirement*, Gower.

WILLIAMS, I., 1979, *The Care of the Elderly in the Community*, Croom Helm.

WILLIAMS, J., 1990, 'Elders from black and ethnic minority communities', in: Sinclair *et al.* (eds), 1990, pp.107–36.

WILLMOTT, P., 1963, *The Evolution of a Community*, Routledge & Kegan Paul.

WILLMOTT, P., 1986, *Social Networks, Informal Care and Public Policy*, Policy Studies Institute.

WILLMOTT, P. and YOUNG, M., 1960, *Family and Class in a London Suburb*, Routledge & Kegan Paul.

WIRZ, H., 1982, *Sheltered Housing in Scotland – a research report*, Scottish Office.

WISTOW, G. and WEBB, A., 1983, 'Public expenditure and policy implementation: the case of community care', *Public Administration*, **61**(1), pp.21–44.

WOLFENDEN, L., 1978, *The Future of Voluntary Organisations* (The Wolfenden Committee), Croom Helm.

WRIGHT, F., 1986, *Left to Care Alone*, Gower.

WRIGHT, F., (forthcoming) 1991 Multi-purpose homes.

WRIGHT, F. and RANDALL, F., 1970, *Basic Sociology*, Macdonald & Evans.

WRIGHT, K., 1982, 'The economics of community care', in: Walker, A. (ed.), 1982, pp.161–78.

WRIGHT, K., CAIRNS, J. and SNELL, M., 1981, *Costing Care*, Joint Unit for Social Services Research, University of Sheffield, 1981.

YOUNG, M. and WILLMOTT, P., 1957, *Family and Kinship in East London*, Penguin.

YOUNG, P. , 1988, *The Provision of Care in Supported Lodgings and Unregistered Homes*, HMSO.

INDEX